MEN AND M

Men and Menswear
Sartorial Consumption in Britain 1880–1939

University of Wolverhampton, UK

LONDON AND NEW YORK

First published 2007 by Ashgate Publishing

2 Park Square, Milton Park, Abingdon, Oxon OX14 4RN
711 Third Avenue, New York, NY 10017, USA

Routledge is an imprint of the Taylor & Francis Group, an informa business

First issued in peperback 2016

British Library Cataloguing in Publication Data
Ugolini, Laura, 1980–
  Men and menswear : sartorial consumption in Britain,
  1880–1939. – (The history of retailing and consumption)
  1. Men's clothing – Great Britain – History – 20th century
  2. Men's clothing – Great Britain – History – 19th century
  3. Male consumers – Great Britain – History – 20th century
  4. Male consumers – Great Britain – History – 19th century
  5. Clothing and dress – Social aspects – Great Britain – History – 20th century
  6. Clothing and dress – Social aspects – Great Britain – History – 19th century I. Title
  305.3'2'0941

Library of Congress Cataloging-in-Publication Data
Ugolini, Laura, 1980–
  Men and menswear : sartorial consumption in Britain 1880–1939 / by Laura Ugolini.
    p. cm. – (History of retailing and consumption)
  Includes bibliographical references and index.
  ISBN 978-0-7546-0384-9 (alk. paper)
  1. Men's clothing industry–Great Britain–History.
  2. Masculinity–Great Britain–History. I. Title.

  HD9940.G82U46 2007
  381'.456870810941–dc22

                                                              2006033062

  ISBN 13: 978-0-7546-0384-9 (hbk)
  ISBN 13: 978-1-138-25641-5 (pbk)

Contents

General Editor's Preface

The History of Retailing and Consumption

It is increasingly recognised that retail systems and changes in the patterns of consumption play crucial roles in the development and societal structure of economies. Such recognition has led to renewed interest in the changing nature of retail distribution and the rise of consumer society from a wide range of academic disciplines. The aim of this multidisciplinary series is to provide a forum of publications that explore the history of retailing and consumption.

Gareth Shaw, University of Exeter, UK

List of Figures

Acknowledgments

Many years ago a friend showed me what we agreed had to be one of the best acknowledgments sections we had ever come across. There were very few thanks. The author had, to put it mildly, not enjoyed his time at a particular university, memorably describing his colleagues as 'sinister'. Clearly, here was a model 'Acknowledgments' that I should aspire to. Unfortunately, my colleagues at the University of Wolverhampton have proved to be helpful and distinctly un-sinister. A number of them are even retailing historians, from whose own expertise and willingness to support yet another CHORD event I have benefited greatly. For this, special thanks are due to Margaret Ponsonby and Malcom Wanklyn. Nancy Cox and Karin Dannehl have made me feel welcome and shared an office with me for longer than I like to think about. But particular thanks are due to John Benson, not only for reading and commenting on various chapters of this book, but also for his kindness and support over the years. He has indeed taught me all I know about retailing history.

I would also like to thank the various scholars I have met over the years at CHORD and other conferences, where I have had the opportunity to discuss my research with an audience that never scoffed at the idea that menswear might be a serious topic of historical investigation – or at least was too polite to do so in my presence. Thank you particularly to Paul Cornish and Matthew Hilton for reading chapters of this book and for their helpful comments. Gareth Shaw has read the whole manuscript and also made very useful comments: thank you. An especially warm thank you is due to Christopher Breward and Katrina Honeyman, both for reading chapters of this book, and for their generous help and kindness since the early stages of my research.

On the subject of generosity, I should also like to express my gratitude to the British Academy and the Pasold Research Fund for the grants I received while undertaking the research for this book.

Last but not least: the people who never were too polite to have a good laugh at menswear. Special thanks to: Carol Adams, mamma and first-class student; Philip de Jersey, who heroically proof-read the whole manuscript and muttered something about conspicuous consumption (I am very grateful for the first and have ignored the second); Sarah Henning, who is still not convinced that I'm not writing the Big Bumper Book of Men's Trousers; and Lisa Ugolini, and Maurizio and Giacomo Perli, snappy dressers all.

Introduction

Men and Menswear, 1880–1939

Not long before the outbreak of the First World War, 'M.R.', a seventeen-year-old Birmingham boy 'who seemed fitted for skilled work but had succeeded in getting into unskilled', described how he spent a fairly typical Saturday afternoon. After dinner, he read the *Birmingham Weekly Post* until about 2.30 pm, then 'rote [*sic*] to London for a list of banjo music'. Having finished his letter, he 'went out to buy a cap and tie'. By the time he returned home, it was time to get ready for the evening, which he spent at a local music hall.[1]

This is not exactly the stuff that makes for a thrilling history book. On the Saturday in question, 'M.R.' did not have a 'life-changing experience'. Neither did he witness nor commit an act that would 'change the course of history', to use two well-worn clichés. This was a normal Saturday afternoon, filled with mundane consumer activities: reading a newspaper, sending off for a catalogue, buying a couple of small items of clothing, enjoying an evening at a music hall. Nonetheless, the fact that these were unremarkable, routine events, does not mean that they were either unimportant or meaningless. Indeed, thrilling or not, these are the sort of 'ordinary' consumer activities to which this book is devoted.

'Routine' consumption could of course involve the acquisition, exchange or use of a variety of goods and services, sometimes all at the same time: a packet of cigarettes, a pint of beer, a bet on the horses, or for the more comfortably-off, a glass of wine, a newspaper, a cigar.[2] However, the aim of this book is to explore the consumer practices associated with one particular commodity: clothing. Or, to be more accurate, British men's clothing in the half-century before the outbreak of the Second World War. My intention is to focus on three particular points in this commodity's 'life': use, sale and purchase. That said, this book is not primarily concerned with the goods *per se*. It does not describe in any detail the actual garments worn or sold by men and boys in this period, and neither does it attempt to chart changes in clothing style or form. Rather, the purpose of this book is to explore men's relationships with clothes, and the motivations and influences that lay behind male consumer behaviour. In a sense, therefore, this book is more about men than menswear, and more about 'M.R.' than about his cap and tie, as it seeks to find out what the use, sale and acquisition of clothes reveal about men's lives and identities in this period.

---

[1]   A. Freeman, *Boy Life and Labour: The Manufacture of Inefficiency* (P.S. King and Son, London, 1914), p. 113.

[2]   Paul Glennie and Nigel Thrift have pointed out that the consumption of individual commodities is not generally self-contained and sealed off from other activities. P.D. Glennie and N.J. Thrift, 'Modern consumption: theorising commodities *and* consumers', *Environment and Planning D: Society and Space*, vol. 11, no. 5 (1993), pp. 603–6.

The commodity: clothing

In 2001 Jukka Gronow and Alan Warde included clothes consumption among those aspects of consumption to which social scientists – they suggested – had hitherto devoted a misleadingly large amount of attention. 'The sociology of consumption', they suggested, 'has concentrated unduly on the more spectacular and visual aspects of contemporary consumer behaviour, thereby constructing an unbalanced and partial account.'[3] They have a point. The consumption of dress, and especially the most visually arresting forms of 'fashionable' dress, has certainly received more attention than the consumption of seemingly mundane but widely used commodities such as – to name the first that come to mind – hair-brushes, pens or watches.

Nevertheless, there *are* reasons why clothes are a useful lens through which to view consumption in general, and male consumer practices in particular, especially during the period covered by this book. First, and most obviously, the use of clothing was universal. Not only was nakedness 'wholly inappropriate in almost all social situations',[4] but everybody would have experienced clothes consumption in some form, even if only the routine wearing of the same garments day after day. At the same time, the nature of the items worn, the ways in which they were sold and acquired could differ widely: clothes spanned the spectrum between miserable necessity and extravagant luxury. But perhaps more important than their ubiquity and variety, was the fact that clothes were perceived by contemporaries to be commodities whose consumption possessed a 'special' meaning, even if there was no consensus about what that meaning was.[5]

Then, as now, the questions of why people wore particular clothes, and perhaps most notably, what influence constantly changing fashions had on individuals' sartorial choices, were a source of endless – even if not always wholly serious – speculation. Among sociologists, psychologists and other thinkers, contemporary Western dress, and 'fashionable' dress in particular, was variously theorised as, for example, providing a conspicuously visible way of indicating wealth, status and worth, as enabling the elite to differentiate itself from the rest of the population, constantly evolving new styles as others sought to emulate it, or as reflecting changing notions of 'modesty' and enhancing sexual attractiveness.[6] Alongside these 'serious' discussions, contemporary dress was also widely described, discussed and indeed joked about in novels, songs, cartoons and the press (including the menswear

---

[3]   J. Gronow and A. Warde, 'Introduction', in J. Gronow and A. Warde (eds), *Ordinary Consumption* (Routledge, London, 2001), pp. 3–4.

[4]   J. Entwistle, *The Fashioned Body: Fashion, Dress and Modern Social Theory* (Polity Press, Cambridge, 2000), p. 6.

[5]   An interesting comparison is provided, for example, by the 'special' meanings attached to tobacco and to smoking. See M. Hilton, *Smoking in British Popular Culture 1800–2000: Perfect Pleasures* (Manchester University Press, Manchester, 2000).

[6]   T. Veblen, *The Theory of the Leisure Class* (Dover Publications, New York, 1994; first published 1899), especially chapter vii; G. Simmel, 'Fashion', *International Quarterly*, vol. 10, no. 1 (1904), pp. 130–55; J.C. Flügel, *The Psychology of Clothes* (The Hogarth Press, London, 1930). For early theories on dress, see also M. Carter, *Fashion Classics: From Carlyle to Barthes* (Berg, Oxford, 2003); K.K.P. Johnson, S.J. Torntore and J.B. Eicher (eds), *Fashion Foundations: Early Writings on Fashion and Dress* (Berg, Oxford, 2003).

trade press), as well as in subsequent autobiographical writings and reminiscences. These discussions and personal reflections provide vital insights into attitudes towards the sale, purchase and use of dress, generally reflecting those contemporary 'common-sense' views that are frequently hidden from the historical record. Indeed, they are the main foundations on which this book is built.[7]

One further aspect of clothing makes it a particularly useful commodity through which to examine male consumer practices: the fact that dress, and 'fashionable' dress in particular, was overwhelmingly associated with women and femininity, even though in practice, as Christopher Breward's pioneering work has been particularly important in showing, men wore, bought and sold clothes just as enthusiastically.[8] This paradox has given rise to a variety of discourses and theories, which have sought to portray British men as hidden, reluctant or even non-consumers of fashionable dress, at least until the emergence of the so-called 'new man' of the 1980s. The late eighteenth century, J.C. Flügel suggested in 1930, saw the beginning of a 'sudden great reduction of male sartorial decorativeness ... Man abandoned his claim to be considered beautiful. He henceforth aimed at being only useful.'[9] Without wishing to simply rehearse the arguments already ably put forward by Breward about the limitations of the notion of a 'great masculine renunciation',[10] it is one of the aims of this book to explore the nature of men's (and to a lesser extent boys') 'encounters' and relationships with this deeply gendered commodity.[11] How did men negotiate the purchase, consumption and sale of a commodity (or set of commodities) overwhelmingly associated with femininity and its largely negative attributes? The relationship between masculinity, 'manliness' and consumption is thus a central theme of this book. However, alongside gender, it is also an aim of this book to explore the relationship between consumption and identities more generally, taking into account issues such as class, age and ethnicity, and investigating the ways in which men constructed identities for themselves as users, buyers and sellers of clothes.

Of course, this is easier said than done. In practice, disentangling the different strands that made up men's identities, and identifying which were the most important

---

[7]   As Christopher Breward explains: 'it is incumbent upon the fashion historian to pursue ... alternative maps and self-realisations if connections between clothing, consumption and gender identities are to be made ... popular novels, music hall dramatisations, store promotions and *cartes de visite*'. C. Breward, *The Hidden Consumer: Masculinities, Fashion and City Life 1860–1914* (Manchester University Press, Manchester, 1999), pp. 19–20.

[8]   Breward, *The Hidden Consumer*. See also T. Edwards, *Men in the Mirror: Men's Fashion, Masculinity and Consumer Society* (Cassell, London, 1997). For the association of dress with femininity, see E. Tseëlon, *The Masque of Femininity* (Sage, London, 1995). For an ethnographic perspective, see R. Barnes and J.B. Eicher (eds), *Dress and Gender: Making and Meaning in Cultural Contexts* (Berg, Oxford, 1992).

[9]   Flügel, *The Psychology of Clothes*, p. 111.

[10]   Breward, *The Hidden Consumer*, chapter 2.

[11]   It can rightly be argued that all commodities are imbued with particular gendered connotations. What seems to set clothing apart, however, is the extent to which discourses and representations differed from actual practice. The relationship between consumption and gender is explored, for example, in V. de Grazia with E. Furlough (eds), *The Sex of Things: Gender and Consumption in Historical Perspective* (University of California Press, Berkeley, 1996).

in influencing consumer behaviour at different times, is far from an easy task. All too often, consumers' (and to a lesser extent sellers') identities seem to fragment into a myriad of component parts, making generalisation seem impossible. The youthful Siegfried Sassoon's trip to London to try his new (and first London-bought) hunting clothes, described in his semi-fictional autobiography, *Memoirs of a Fox-Hunting Man*, provides a useful example of the complexities of even an apparently straightforward shopping trip. A few years before the outbreak of the First World War, Sassoon travelled up to London from his rural home to try on the garments he had ordered from an illustrious West End tailoring firm. This seems to point to the future poet's identity as a member of the upper classes, engaged in shopping practices perfectly suited to his status. However, the autobiography recounts this episode in order to illustrate Sassoon's uncertain status and identity at this time. The preliminary visit to this and other shops had left him rather nervous: 'the individuals who patrolled the interiors of those eminent establishments had received me with such lofty condescension that I had begun by feeling an intruder'. He was afraid that the cut and style of his clothes had marked him as a provincial nonentity. 'Emerging from Charing Cross I felt my personality somehow diluted. At Baldock Wood station there had been no doubt that I was going up to town in my best dark blue suit, and London had been respectfully arranged at the other end of the line. But in Trafalgar Square my gentlemanly uniqueness had diminished to something almost nonetitive [*sic*]'. So, should the Sassoon who went shopping for hunting clothes be seen as a young gentleman and a member of the rural gentry, or as an inexperienced, immature provincial nobody, left without an older male relative to advise him on consumer matters?[12]

It is tempting to approach this question from a different standpoint. Working on the reasonable assumption that identities were constructed in the very act of consumption, it then becomes more important to discover the identity thus created, rather than the messier business of trying to work out the factors that led to particular consumer practices. At least in part through his purchases, thus, Siegfried Sassoon was seeking to become a 'fox-hunting man': simple! The problem with this approach, however, is that it presupposes that individuals were free to create their own identities by making particular sartorial choices, and that all choices were viewed as equally valid and acceptable. Consequently, it does not take into account the influence of hierarchies and of both material and cultural limitations on consumer 'freedom'.[13] Indeed, even putting aside for the moment issues of disposable income and availability of supply, it only requires the most cursory examination of contemporary discourses on dress to reveal that there existed more or less explicit rules and codes about what should be worn by different people at different times and in different places. This does not simply mean that contemporary (whether Victorian, Edwardian, or inter-war) society was especially 'formal' or rule-bound. Rather, it suggests a link between clothes consumption and the organisation of power and authority within contemporary society, and promises to provide insights into the ways in which these operated in

---

[12] S. Sassoon, *Memoirs of a Fox-Hunting Man* (Faber and Faber, London, 1989; first published 1928), pp. 114–15.

[13] Discussed, for example, in M. Featherstone, *Consumer Culture and Postmodernism* (Sage Publications, London, 1991), pp. 86–7.

practice, as well as into how compliance was enforced.[14] Thus, one of the aims of this book is to discover the pressures that were brought to bear on men's consumer decisions, as well as on the ways in which individuals negotiated their way through the more or less explicit 'rules' that governed dress.

The sale, purchase and consumption of clothes are thus approached in this book primarily as social activities, rather than as having exclusively to do with the individual 'self'. Indeed, the self-fashioning consumer (or retailer) who created a distinctive identity for himself out of sartorial and other consumer acts features little in this book, while the consumer who managed to do so with impunity, appears hardly at all. Clothes consumption, it will be argued, served to forge and reinforce identities, but these were primarily social and collective identities, not unique, individual ones. It is clearly impossible to weigh the relative importance of class, age, gender or other factors in the consumer acts of all men and boys. However, in a context where consumer decisions were influenced by social and cultural, as well as economic pressures, it is certainly possible to investigate the nature of such pressures, and the ways in which they influenced the consumption of menswear: this is what this book sets out to do.

Use, sale and purchase

In their contributions to the 1986 collection of essays on *The Social Life of Things*, Arjun Appadurai and Igor Kopytoff suggested that adopting a 'biographical' approach to the study of 'things' can provide valuable insights into the nature of the circulation of commodities within different societies. They argued that there does not exist a fundamental distinction between 'commodities' that are suitable for exchange, and goods that cannot and should not enter the market. Rather, most (if not all) 'things' move in and out of the 'commodity state', and have the potential to become commodities in the course of their 'social lives',[15] their connotations changing as they move from hand to hand and from context to context. A tie for sale in a shop at the turn of the century, for example, was a commodity among many others, ready to be exchanged for cash, either immediately or through a variety of credit arrangements. The tie might be hidden away in a box, or it might be displayed in a window, its selling points shown off to potential customers. It could then become the object of negotiations between buyer and seller, its 'value' being evaluated, and

---

[14] See the detailed description of late-Victorian and Edwardian middle-class men's sartorial codes in W. Macqueen-Pope, *Twenty Shillings in the Pound* (Hutchinson, London, n.d. [c. 1949]), chapter xi. The relationship between male dress and power is explored in D. Kuchta, *The Three-Piece Suit and Modern Masculinity: England, 1550–1850* (University of California Press, Berkeley, 2002). See also M. Barnard, *Fashion as Communication* (Routledge, London, 1996), pp. 39–40; Entwistle, *The Fashioned Body*, p. 9.
[15] A. Appadurai, 'Introduction: commodities and the politics of value'; I. Kopytoff, 'The cultural biography of things: commoditization as process': both in A. Appadurai (ed.), *The Social Life of Things: Commodities in Cultural Perspective* (Cambridge University Press, Cambridge, 1992; first published 1986), pp. 3–63 and 64–91. See also the notion of 'systems of provision' developed in B. Fine and E. Leopold, *The World of Consumption* (Routledge, London, 1993).

hopefully agreed on by all the parties involved. The negotiation safely over, the tie could acquire new characteristics, including as a treasured possession, a mark of wealth, status and good taste (or the very opposite), or a gift for a third party.

Using the notion of commodities' 'social life' as a departure point, this book aims to explore men's relationships with clothes as the latter moved through three stages in their 'social lives': the moment when they were worn, when they were sold, and when they were acquired. This does not mean that other stages in menswear's life-cycle are entirely absent from this book. The disposal of clothes, for example, will crop up again and again, as discarded garments were often sold or handed down, patched and adapted for other, generally younger, wearers. But most notably, perhaps, in a context where even on the eve of the Second World War the manufacturing and retailing processes had not yet become entirely separate, it would be impossible to examine the consumption and especially the sale of garments without at least some reference to production and craft work.

That said, manufacturing takes a back seat in this book, the focus being primarily on consumption, retailing and shopping, with a section devoted to each. Indeed, the original plan was to arrange these three sections so that they followed the chronological order of the commodity's life-cycle: having previously been manufactured, the commodity was offered for sale, then purchased, and subsequently used. The hitch, however, turned out to be that men's attitudes towards the sale and purchase of menswear cannot really be fully understood without first having some insight into attitudes towards use: as this book will suggest, both tailors' and other menswear retailers' supposed lack of manliness, as well as the often difficult negotiations between buyers and sellers in the menswear shop, need to be seen in the wider context of male attitudes towards the use of clothes. For this reason, the book opens with a section dealing with consumption, and with the factors that – it is suggested – influenced male sartorial practices and decisions. The first two chapters concentrate on continuities, and on those pressures and influences that remained as relevant in 1939 as they had been in 1880. Chapter 3 then turns to sartorial practices in the context of the First World War, while the final chapter of Part I focuses on, and questions the extent and nature of changes in clothing consumption in the two decades following the 1918 Armistice.

This investigation does not take place in a vacuum. Indeed, reflecting the increasing attention being paid by historians to issues of consumption, the relationship between men, masculinities and consumer cultures has recently become the focus of a small, but growing, body of scholarship.[16] However, the 1980s, and especially the

---

[16]   See, for example, P. Jobling, *Man Appeal: Advertising, Modernism and Menswear* (Berg, Oxford, 2005); K. Honeyman, 'Style monotony and the business of fashion: the marketing of menswear in inter-war England', *Textile History*, vol. 34, no. 2 (2003), pp. 171–91; L. Ugolini, 'Men, masculinities, and menswear advertising c.1890–1914', in J. Benson and L. Ugolini (eds), *A Nation of Shopkeepers: Five Centuries of British Retailing* (I.B. Tauris, London, 2003), pp. 80–104; K. Honeyman, 'Following suit: men, masculinity and gendered practices in the clothing trade in Leeds, England, 1890–1940', *Gender & History*, vol. 14, no. 3 (2002), pp. 426–46; C. Breward (ed.), Special issue on masculinities, *Fashion Theory*, vol. 4, issue 4 (2000); N. Stevenson, P. Jackson and K. Brooks, 'Ambivalence in men's lifestyle magazines', in P. Jackson, M. Lowe, D. Miller and F. Mort (eds), *Commercial Cultures: Economies, Practices, Spaces* (Berg, Oxford, 2000), pp. 189–212; J. Greenfield, S. O'Connell and

phenomenon of the 'new man', have been researched much more extensively than other historical periods and topics, while 'commercial epistemologies',[17] journalistic prescriptions and cultural representations and images, have all received a good deal more attention than men's everyday practices and experiences.[18] Quite apart from the influence on histories of consumption of semiotics and especially of what can generically be termed post-structuralism (particularly the work of Michel Foucault), there are also very good methodological reasons for the privileging of texts over practices.[19] Indeed, if there exists a book, manuscript or oral history recording by A. Man, *How My Contemporaries and I Felt About Clothes Consumption, 1880–1939*, I certainly have not come across it. The evidence for men's experiences of sartorial consumption, let alone feelings, desires and expectations is extremely patchy, and sometimes frustratingly difficult to find. However, it *does* exists, tucked away in autobiographies, oral history recordings and other contemporary writings. Once found, what clearly emerges from these sources is the fact that dress was an interesting and sometimes controversial (but never taboo) topic, about which men from the whole range of social backgrounds had something to say, whether it was to look back in bemusement at the folly of their youth, to lament contemporary manners and modes, or simply to relate an anecdote that readers might find amusing. Opinionated, prejudiced, occasionally very funny and sometimes depressing, angry

---

C. Read, 'Gender, consumer culture and the middle-class male, 1918–39', in A. Kidd and D. Nicholls (eds), *Gender, Civic Culture and Consumerism: Middle-Class Identity in Britain, 1800–1940* (Manchester University Press, Manchester, 1999), pp. 183–97; S. Nixon, 'Advertising executives as modern men: masculinity and the UK advertising industry in the 1980s', in M. Nava, A. Blake, I. MacRury and B. Richards (eds), *Buy this Book: Studies in Advertising and Consumption* (Routledge, London, 1997), pp. 103–19; S. Nixon, *Hard Looks: Masculinities, Spectatorship and Contemporary Consumption* (Routledge, London, 2003; first published 1996); J. Harvey, *Men in Black* (Reaktion Books, London, 1995); K. Breazeale, 'In spite of women: *Esquire* magazine and the construction of the male consumer', *Signs*, vol. 20, no. 1 (1994), pp. 1–22; J. Craik, *The Face of Fashion: Cultural Studies in Fashion* (Routledge, London, 1994); F. Mort and P. Thompson, 'Retailing, commercial culture and masculinity in 1950s Britain: the case for Montague Burton, tailor of taste', *History Workshop Journal*, issue 38 (1994), pp. 106–27.

[17]   I have borrowed the terms 'commercial epistemologies' from 'Commercial epistemologies: advertising, marketing and retailing since the 1950s', the title of part 2 of F. Mort, *Cultures of Consumption: Masculinities and Social Space in Late-Twentieth Century Britain* (Routledge, London, 1996).

[18]   Works that do consider consumers' experiences include L. Ugolini, 'Ready-to-wear or made-to-measure? Consumer choice in the British menswear trade, 1900–1939', *Textile History*, vol. 34, no. 2 (2003), pp. 192–213; M.C. Finn, 'Men's things: masculine possessions in the consumer revolution', *Social History*, vol. 25, no. 2 (2000), pp. 133–55; Hilton, *Smoking in British Popular Culture*, especially chapters 5 and 7; L. Ugolini, 'Clothes and the modern man in 1930s Oxford', *Fashion Theory*, vol. 4, issue 4 (2000), pp. 427–46; I. Zweiniger-Bargielowska, *Austerity in Britain: Rationing, Controls, and Consumption, 1939–1955* (Oxford University Press, Oxford, 2000), especially chapter 2; D. Wight, *Workers not Wasters. Masculine Respectability, Consumption and Unemployment in Central Scotland: A Community Study* (Edinburgh University Press, Edinburgh, 1993).

[19]   For an excellent discussion of the various theoretical approaches to the study of dress and adornment, see Entwistle, *The Fashioned Body*, especially chapter 1.

or detached, these personal accounts of clothes consumption are, in brief, enormously valuable. They may be short on detail about what was actually worn, and inevitably, individual accounts generally only present a partial and often idiosyncratic picture of sartorial practices, but collectively, they (hopefully) provide this book with unique insights into experiences and attitudes, and a useful counterpoint to commercial images, prescriptive texts and 'serious' writings on dress.

Following this consideration of attitudes towards the consumption of clothes, Part II in a sense moves back a stage in the commodity's life-cycle. Focusing on the moment when the garment was put on the market, the chapters in this section explore men's experiences of selling menswear. In a way this is a more straightforward task than trying to gain an insight into attitudes towards consumption, for although the autobiographical material originating from tailors and other retailers is not abundant, there do exist alternative sources of information about their opinions and feelings. Among these, the most useful has proved to be the tailoring trade press. Periodicals such as *The Tailor and Cutter*, *Men's Wear* and *The Outfitter*, along with a variety of other magazines and technical publications, aimed to provide readers in the trade with guidance on technical matters (particularly relating to garment cutting) and on the latest (especially 'West End') styles, as well as advice on all aspects of conducting a tailoring business, including buying supplies, organising the workshop, dealing with workers, and implementing the most up-to-date methods of shop display, advertising and salesmanship. Information was also carried about administrative and legal matters, trade organisations, meetings and charitable activities, as well as other educational, social and (to a far lesser extent) political initiatives. And, of course, plenty of space was devoted to advertisements by wholesalers, manufacturers and (increasingly) firms that offered to relieve retailers of part or all of the garment-making process, and by shop-fitting, advertising and display specialists.

Usefully, these publications sought their readership primarily among the men who are the main focus of this section of the book: those who were chiefly involved in the selling, rather than the production side of the business, the small (and not so small) businessmen, managers, salesmen and cutters whose central function was in the 'front' shop, selling goods and interacting with customers.[20] It is these men's roles as sellers of clothes and 'fashion' to a specifically male clientele, and their attempts to create positive identities for themselves as men and as businessmen, in the face of both old

---

[20]   The partial exception were cutters, who, as the job title suggests, also had a manufacturing role: taking the customer's measures and cutting the cloth accordingly. Male retail employment remains an under-researched area. But see, for example, G. Crossick (ed.), *The Artisan and the European Town, 1500–1900* (Scolar Press, Aldershot, 1997), pp. 1–40; G. Crossick and H.-G. Haupt, *The Petite Bourgeoisie in Europe, 1780–1914* (Routledge, London, 1995); C.P. Hosgood, 'The "pigmies of commerce" and the working-class community: small shopkeepers in England, 1870–1914', *Journal of Social History*, vol. 22, no. 3 (1989), pp. 439–60; J. Benson, *The Penny Capitalists: A Study of Nineteenth-Century Working Class Entrepreneurs* (Gill and Macmillan, Goldenbridge, 1983), chapter 10; M.J. Winstanley, *The Shopkeeper's World 1830–1914* (Manchester University Press, Manchester, 1983).

prejudices and new challenges to established trade practices, which will be explored in this section of the book.[21]

However, here too there are difficulties, due at least in part to the nature of the menswear trade in this period, and particularly to its sheer diversity. Outlets selling clothes included market stalls offering a variety of fusty second-hand garments, no-frills shops specialising in cheap ready-to-wear items, well-appointed hosiers or outfitters selling underwear, shirts, and other small garments such as collars and ties, and bespoke tailoring shops, where made-to-measure outfits – most notably, suits – could be obtained. There were also enormous differences even between businesses nominally selling the same goods, reflected in the wide range of prices, location and services offered. Taking the example of bespoke suits, these could be sold in venues ranging from a village one-man shop, to a high-class outlet situated in the most prestigious areas of London's West End. They could also be obtained by mail order, or in shops where no one had any craft knowledge of tailoring, and from where the order would be sent off to be executed by a separate firm. Especially in the inter-war years, they could also be purchased from a branch shop of one of the rapidly expanding number of multiple businesses. These examples, while by no means exhausting all the possibilities, give an indication of the difficulties of trying to make generalisations about opinions and identities within a trade that was much more diverse in this period than it is at the beginning of the twenty-first century.

Rather than attempt to generalise, therefore, this book focuses principally on retailers based in fixed outlets, and particularly (although by no means exclusively) those who sold garments made to measure. Of course, these retailers were not necessarily 'typical' of the menswear trade as a whole, although as Table I.1 shows, they represented by far its largest section: between 1881 and 1911, tailors comprised just under 30 per cent of the whole male workforce engaged in making *and* selling clothes in England and Wales. Furthermore, bespoke tailors catered for a wide range of the population, with the exception of the very poorest, even though the goods they sold were not necessarily 'typical'. By the 1880s, the overwhelming

---

[21] For an interesting parallel, see Frank Mort's exploration of what he terms 'the forms of knowledge generated by ... consumer professionals' in the 1980s. Mort, *Cultures of Consumption*, p. 1, and especially part 1. Retailers' and shop assistants' ambiguous social standing, and their attempts to create more positive identities for themselves have been considered, for example, in R. Coopey, S. O'Connell and D. Porter, *Mail Order Retailing in Britain: A Business and Social History* (Oxford University Press, Oxford, 2005), especially chapter 4; A. Taylor, *Working Class Credit and Community Since 1918* (Palgrave Macmillan, Basingstoke, 2002), especially chapter 3; M.C. Finn, 'Scotch drapers and the politics of modernity: gender, class and national identity in the Victorian tally trade', in M. Daunton and M. Hilton (eds), *The Politics of Consumption: Material Culture and Citizenship in Europe and America* (Berg, Oxford, 2001), pp. 89–107; C.P. Hosgood, '"Mercantile monasteries": shops, shop assistants and shop life in late-Victorian and Edwardian Britain', *Journal of British Studies*, vol. 38, no. 3 (1999), pp. 322–52; M. Hilton, 'Retailing history as economic and cultural history: strategies of survival by specialist tobacconists in the mass market', *Business History*, vol. 40, no. 4 (1998), pp. 115–37; G.R. Rubin, 'From packmen, tallymen and "perambulating scotchmen" to Credit Drapers' Associations, c. 1840–1914', *Business History*, vol. 28, no. 2 (1986), pp. 206–25.

majority of male consumers bought most of their clothing ready-made, while the made-to-measure trade relied mostly on suits and, to a lesser extent, overcoats. In addition, ready-to-wear suits were certainly available, although despite the efforts of firms like Austin Reed, they never really took off beyond the cheaper end of the market before the Second World War. Despite these reservations, an argument can nevertheless certainly be made for the centrality, both numerically and culturally, of 'tailors' to the menswear trade, as well as for the continued importance of the made-to-measure suit to the male wardrobe and to male fashions.

However, tailors' real usefulness in this book is primarily as a case study of the relationship between commercial activity, masculinity and identity, in a context where both the practice of retailing and the commodities they sold had deeply ambivalent cultural and gendered connotations. Thus, the second section of the book will question how tailors sought to create positive identities for themselves and for their trade out of what were – as will be seen – some exceptionally unpromising circumstances. Bespoke tailors also provide a valuable study of responses to crisis, firstly as they and other menswear retailers sought to adapt to wartime conditions during the First World War, and secondly as new forms of retailing – some of them destined to become highly successful – constantly emerged, leading to sometimes bitter battles for market share. Chapter 4, then, focuses on responses from within the trade to well-established negative characterisations of tailors, tailoring and shopkeeping in general, as well as to the new challenges to emerge in the pre-1914 period, epitomised by the competition of the so-called 'brass and glass' shops. Chapter 5 goes on to consider menswear retailers' responses to the cultural climate and trading conditions of the First World War, while Chapter 6 examines the competing claims of independents and multiples in the inter-war years, as they sought to convince customers of the superiority of the products and service, and the overall shopping experience each could offer.

Table I.1   Men 'working and dealing in dress', England and Wales, 1881–1911 *Source*: **Census reports, 1881, 1891, 1901, 1911.**[22]

	Total	**Tailors**	**Tailors as percentage of total**	**Next largest category (excl. boots and shoes) as percentage of total**
1881	365,000	108,000	29.6 %	5 % (hosiery manufacture)
1891	408,000	119,000	29.2 %	4.4 % (hosiery manufacture)
1901	415,000	120,000	29 %	4.3 % (clothiers, outfitters / dealers)
1911	439,000	122,000	27.8 %	14.6 % (dealers)

---

[22]   Changes in the ways occupations were classified (particularly the separation of manufacturing from retailing) makes it impossible to directly compare employment in the 'dress' trades in the pre- and post-First World War censuses. It should also be noted that between 1881 and 1911 many of the occupational categories included under the general heading of 'working and dealing in dress' also changed. For example, the category of 'clothiers, outfitters / dealers' only appeared in 1901.

Following this discussion of men's roles as consumers and as retailers of menswear, the book's third and final section is then devoted to the moment when the two finally got to meet: the shopping process. If little empirical research has yet been undertaken by historians on men's experiences of consumption or retailing, this is even more so in the case of the acquisition of commodities. Again, this is hardly surprising, given the scattered nature of the evidence, as well as the lack of market research surveys or similar material for the pre-Second World War period. It should also be added that the belief that men – quite simply – did not shop has not exactly encouraged research either. As Breward pointed out in 1999, 'the role of men within a burgeoning culture of city shops and fashionable spaces [in the nineteenth century] has not yet been studied in its own right, presumably because the majority of males are assumed to have been absent from this sphere of activity'.[23]

As recent research, including this book, is beginning to acknowledge, there is actually plenty of evidence that British men were fully engaged within contemporary consumer culture, and that shopping for clothes and other commodities was more than a marginal or minority activity, relegated to effeminate or 'unmanly' men, even before the rise of the so-called 'new man' in the 1980s. That said, despite the lack of empirical research, there nonetheless seems to be an overwhelming agreement within the literature on consumption that when men did shop, they did so differently from women: they bought different commodities, generally from different shops, and their choices were influenced by different motivations.[24] Tempting as it is to try and disprove this (partly, it has to be admitted, out of sheer contrariness), in fact the issue of gender differences (or similarities) in shopping practices is not a major concern of this book. This is partly because of the often overlooked fact that, although we do know a great deal about contemporary perceptions and representations of women shoppers, we actually still know relatively little about their practices and experiences in this period.[25] It is also partly because once we turn away from the representations of shopping in the contemporary media (which are indeed full of contrasting

---

[23] Breward, *The Hidden Consumer*, pp. 1–2. An exception is, for example, F. Anderson, 'Fashioning the gentleman: a study of Henry Poole and Co., Savile Row tailors 1861–1900', *Fashion Theory*, vol. 4, issue 4 (2000), pp. 405–26.

[24] See, for example, J. Benson, *Affluence and Authority: A Social History of Twentieth-Century Britain* (Hodder Arnold, London, 2005), p. 17; T. Edwards, *Contradictions of Consumption: Concepts, Practices and Politics in Consumer Society* (Open University Press, Buckingham, 2000), p. 136; Craik, *The Face of Fashion*, p. 72.

[25] For studies of shopping practices in later periods, which show that (unsurprisingly) they were a good deal less straightforward than stereotypical representations, see, for example, P. Lyon, A. Colquhoun and D. Kinney, 'UK food shopping in the 1950s: the social context of customer loyalty', *International Journal of Consumer Studies*, vol. 28, no. 1 (2004), pp. 28–39; N. Gregson and L. Crewe, *Second-Hand Cultures* (Berg, Oxford, 2003); A. Clarke, '"Mother swapping": the trafficking of nearly new children's wear', in Jackson, Lowe, Miller and Mort (eds), *Commercial Cultures*, pp. 85–100; N. Gregson, K. Brooks and L. Crewe, 'Narratives of consumption and the body in the space of the charity / shop', in Jackson, Lowe, Miller and Mort (eds), *Commercial Cultures*, pp. 101–21; D. Miller, *A Theory of Shopping* (Polity Press, Cambridge, 1998); D. Miller, P. Jackson, N. Thrift, B. Holbrook and L. Rowlands, *Shopping, Place and Identity* (Routledge, London, 1998); P. Falk and C. Campbell (eds), *The Shopping Experience* (Sage, London, 1997);

images of enthusiastic female shoppers and their opposites, the disinterested male ones), the need – or desire – to differentiate their shopping activities from those of women does not actually feature with any prominence in men's personal narratives of consumption.[26] Although of course women (especially as mothers and siblings) were not entirely absent, it seems to have been other men – either in the guise of fellow consumers or of retailers of menswear – who were of central importance in influencing male shopping practices. The former were particularly important in influencing, and indeed even shaping, the process of making shopping choices, which will be considered in Chapter 8. Perhaps unsurprisingly, the relationship with the latter was central to the actual shopping experience, which will be the subject of Chapter 9, the book's final chapter.

As with Parts I and II of the book, exploring these issues is not as straightforward as it may seem at first glance. Indeed, if there are problems with the nature of the evidence about male consumer and commercial activities, these are multiplied tenfold in the case of purchasing practices. There exists, of course, a wealth of advertising material produced by manufacturers and retailers, which sought to inform, guide and influence male shoppers. However, this cannot provide direct insights into consumers' experiences, desires or expectations. Much more useful are personal narratives, autobiographical writings and reminiscences. Indeed, these regularly deal with shopping, although, as one might expect, one-off, exceptional purchases were a good deal more likely to be recorded than mundane, day-to-day provisioning, while accounts are by their very nature highly individual and fragmentary, providing snapshots of purchasing activities at particular times in the narrator's life, rather than a coherent narrative of shopping.

Nevertheless, it remains the case that shopping frequently appears in autobiographical accounts, alongside other recurrent themes, such as family life and work experiences, as men tried to make sense of their past, and to place their life experiences in a larger historical context. Recounting the ways in which they had acquired various garments at different points in their lives provided a key way of recalling and placing into a wider context personal experiences and relationships. To return for a moment to Sassoon, his description of the London shopping trip was not only intended to entertain the reader by describing an activity – a visit to a high-class tailoring shop – that he or she may have been unfamiliar with. It was also intended to provide the reader with a revealing perspective through which to view an apprehensive and unsophisticated young man before his life was irrevocably

N. Gregson and L. Crewe, 'Performance and possession: rethinking the act of purchase in the light of the car boot sale', *Journal of Material Culture*, vol. 2, no. 2 (1997), pp. 241–63.

[26]   Of course, this may have been because these differences were so much taken for granted. Representations of gender differences in shopping are explored, for example, in C.P. Hosgood, '"Doing the shops" at Christmas: women, men and the department store in England, c. 1880–1914', in G. Crossick and S. Jaumain (eds), *Cathedrals of Consumption: The European Department Store, 1850–1939* (Ashgate, Aldershot, 1999), pp. 97–115. See also E.D. Rappaport, *Shopping for Pleasure: Women in the Making of London's West End* (Princeton University Press, Princeton, 2000), pp. 128, 171–2, 203–6; P. Glennie and N. Thrift, 'Consumption, shopping and gender', in N. Wrigley and M. Lowe (eds), *Retailing, Consumption and Capital: Towards the New Retail Geography* (Longman, Harlow, 1996), pp. 221–37.

changed by the experience of combat during the First World War. Indeed, as this book seeks to show, acquiring clothes and shopping may often have been a routine and even boring activity, but it was not an insignificant or somehow meaningless part of men's lives.

The late-Victorian menswear trade

By the 1880s, the clothing trade had already undergone half a century of considerable change, a trend that was to continue to the outbreak of the Second World War and, of course, beyond. Technical innovations, particularly the invention of the sewing machine, had revolutionised the manufacture of clothes. As Andrew Godley has shown, although sewing machines had been available since the 1850s and 1860s, it was the 1890s that witnessed the most rapid growth of labour productivity in the clothing trades before 1950, reflecting the fact that the 1880s and 1890s had seen a rapid increase in the use of technically much improved machines.[27] However, the reorganisation of the production process had been an equally important factor in the process of change, with the subdivision of tasks previously undertaken by one operative making possible the employment of cheaper, unskilled labour. The 1830s have been identified as a key period of change (especially in London), although the seeds had seemingly already been sown by the system of army and navy contracting developed during the Napoleonic wars, which had created a sharp rise in the demand for cheap, ready-to-wear military clothing. According to Barbara Taylor, during the 1830s 'the transformative agents were usually not steam-powered machines and factory masters but profiteering merchant investors and sub-contracting systems which undercut the craft strength of the skilled man and introduced thousands of unskilled workers – particularly women workers – into his trade'.[28] This analysis begs further questions about the causes, nature, timing and extent of these developments, all of which are outside the scope of this book. However, it certainly was the case that by the 1880s the clothing trade was already on its way to becoming a mass production industry, although not based in large-scale, steam-driven and mechanised units of production. By then, sewing machines had almost entirely replaced hand sewing, but garment production remained a labour intensive process, whereby the work was often minutely subdivided into a series of repetitive tasks: throughout the period, large-scale, mechanised factories and small, sometimes tiny units of

---

[27] A. Godley, 'Singer in Britain: the diffusion of sewing machine technology and its impact on the clothing industry in the United Kingdom, 1860–1950', *Textile History*, vol. 27, no. 1 (1996), pp. 59–76; A. Godley, 'The development of the UK clothing industry, 1850–1950: output and productivity growth', *Business History*, vol. 37, no. 4 (1995), pp. 46–63. Other technical innovations included the band knife, developed by the Leeds firm of Barran. This made it possible to simultaneously cut through several layers of cloth. K. Honeyman, *Well Suited: A History of the Leeds Clothing Industry 1850–1990* (Pasold Research Fund and Oxford University Press, Oxford, 2000), pp. 21–2.

[28] B. Taylor, *Eve and the New Jerusalem: Socialism and Feminism in the Nineteenth Century* (Virago, London, 1991; first published 1983), p. 101.

production remained inter-dependent. Both, however, shared a reliance on cheap, frequently female or foreign (especially Jewish) labour.[29]

By the 1880s, it was thus increasingly rare for all aspects of the production of clothes to take place under the same roof, or to be undertaken by the same firm. Particularly as far as urban retailers were concerned, the shop and the workshop were increasingly becoming separate entities, with outwork, whether in large or small workshops, or in the worker's own home, fast becoming the norm. Arrangements could be complex, with production usually taking place in far less glamorous or prestigious areas than the shop.[30] In the late 1880s, for example, the ten-year-old A.E. Coppard started working as a presser in an East End workshop, where half a dozen women were employed making 'men's trousers at 1 and ninepence a time for the various smart tailoring establishments of the city' of London. This small business, owned by a Jewish master called Alabaster, had its

> most cherished house ... in Cheapside; there the whole suit was designed and cut out to measures of the particular customer, but the trousers part, cloth trimmings, buttons and so on, would be ... fashioned by Mr. Alabaster of Whitechapel, the waistcoat somewhere in Spitalfields, and – Allah knows where the coat graduated, it might be from Wapping, certainly not Cheapside.[31]

Furthermore, quite apart from the stalls, barrows or packs from which garments could also be sold, the nature of the retail outlets that dealt with menswear varied enormously, as did individual firms' marketing strategies. Some shops crammed windows and entrances with garments, and prominently displayed prices, while

---

[29] Honeyman, *Well Suited*. Eighteenth- and nineteenth-century developments in the manufacture and supply of clothes are explored in B. Harris (ed.), *Famine and Fashion: Needlewomen in the Nineteenth Century* (Ashgate, Aldershot, 2005); J. Styles, 'Product innovation in early modern London', *Past & Present*, vol. 168 (2000), pp. 124–69; A. Godley (ed.), Special issue on the history of the ready-made clothing industry, *Textile History*, vol. 28, no. 1 (1997); B. Lemire, *Dress, Culture and Commerce: The English Clothing Trade Before the Factory, 1660–1800* (Macmillan, Basingstoke, 1997); A.J. Kershen, *Uniting the Tailors: Trade Unionism Amongst the Tailors of London and Leeds, 1870–1939* (Frank Cass, Ilford, 1995); P. Sharpe, '"Cheapness and economy": manufacturing and retailing ready-made clothing in London and Essex 1830–50', *Textile History*, vol. 26, no. 2 (1995), pp. 203–13; J. Styles, 'Clothing the North: The supply of non-elite clothing in the eighteenth-century North of England', *Textile History*, vol. 25, no. 2 (1994), pp. 139–66; S. Chapman, 'The innovating entrepreneurs in the British ready-made clothing industry', *Textile History*, vol. 24, no. 1 (1993), pp. 5–25; S. Levitt, 'Cheap mass produced men's clothing in the nineteenth and early twentieth centuries', *Textile History*, vol. 22, no. 2 (1991), pp. 179–92; J.A. Schmiechen, *Sweated Industries and Sweated Labor: The London Clothing Trades, 1860–1914* (Croom Helm, London, 1984); M. Stewart and L. Hunter, *The Needle is Threaded: The History of an Industry* (Heinemann and Newman Neame, London, 1964).

[30] Not, of course, that shops were always located in glamorous or prestigious areas.

[31] A.E. Coppard, *It's Me, O Lord!* (Methuen, London, 1957), pp. 22, 46. See also A. Hartog, *Born to Sing* (Dennis Dobson, London, 1978), p. 41. Hartog began working for a tailor in London's East End in 1937. He points out that 'we were working at all hours on rubbish and selling it at fancy prices', but 'we didn't make mass-produced rubbish'.

other – generally higher-class – shops either avoided displays entirely, or simply placed a few rolls of cloth in the window (where a window even existed). Some firms were enthusiastic advertisers, regularly placing notices in local and occasionally even national newspapers or sending circulars out to potential customers. Others operated chiefly through connections, and saw advertising as unnecessary or even harmful to their reputation. Some shops were small, dingy and unappealing, while others were well-lit, well-appointed with good-quality fixtures, and elegantly laid out. The majority of businesses, no doubt, operated somewhere between these extremes, their window displays, advertising strategies and interiors never appearing in the pages of the trade press, either as examples of the 'best', most up-to-date and successful retail methods, or as examples of the 'worst', most reprehensible trade practices, a warning to other retailers.[32]

What the majority of menswear shops – or perhaps more specifically urban shops – had in common, however, was the fact that with the exception of the cutter, customers were unlikely to have anything to do with the actual makers of their clothes, or to witness garments being manufactured. Even firms that continued to combine production and retailing (of which the inter-war multiples were a notable example), generally located production and distribution in separate spaces. The sale of menswear may have continued to be replete with the symbols and language of craft work, but by the 1880s, the customer who went to 'his' tailor would have been fairly certain to enter a shop, not a workshop.

He does not seem to have cared. After all, the advantages to the consumer of sub-division, sub-contracting and mass production were considerable: they provided him with the opportunity of buying new clothes of reasonable quality at an affordable price. Even, for a little extra expense, made to his individual measures! On the eve of the First World War, a working-class customer could buy a decent, although perhaps not terribly sturdy, made-to-measure suit for less than thirty shillings. A solidly middle-class tailor-made suit could be purchased for around £2 2s.[33] Despite the often highly misleading reassurances provided by retailers in their advertising material, some individuals may have worried about the exploitation of clothing workers that they must have suspected lay behind very cheap garments, particularly

---

[32]   The various categories of retailer selling menswear are considered in Breward, *The Hidden Consumer*, chapter 4, although the differences between the types of shop are perhaps slightly overstated. See also J. Benson and G. Shaw (eds), *The Evolution of Retail Systems, c. 1800–1914* (Leicester University Press, Leicester, 1992); D. Alexander, *Retailing in England During the Industrial Revolution* (The Athlone Press, London, 1970), especially pp. 136–42; J.B. Jefferys, *Retail Trading in Britain, 1850–1950* (Cambridge University Press, 1954), especially pp. 295–321.

[33]   A.L. Bowley, *Prices and Wages in the United Kingdom, 1914–1920* (The Clarendon Press, Oxford, 1921), p. 64. Macqueen-Pope, *Twenty Shillings in the Pound*, p. 223. Most historians agree that demand-side factors (the growth of demand for good-quality clothing among a better-off population) had a fundamental impact on the clothing trade, fuelling changes to the production process that eventually resulted in lower prices. Supply-side factors, on the other hand, have received little attention, but cheaper textile materials must surely also have had an impact on lower clothing prices. See, for example, D.T. Jenkins and K.G. Pointing, *The British Wool Trade Industry 1770–1914* (Heinemann Educational Books and The Pasold Research Fund, London, 1982), p. 47. More research is needed into the relationship between the textile and the clothing trades.

during the well-publicised anti-sweating agitation at the turn of the century.[34] That said, I have found little evidence of wide-spread concern about the conditions under which garments were manufactured. Clothes consumption, this book argues, was a 'social' activity, influenced by an awareness of 'others'. In choosing what to wear, where to buy it and how to sell it, men were very well aware that they did not exist in a vacuum, or that sartorial decisions were seen by the people around them with a sort of benign indifference. However, the 'others' whose opinions mattered were rarely the female or foreign 'hands' who made the garments, generally tucked away out of sight in factories, workshops or their own homes. Much more important were the fellow men with whom consumers came into contact in their day-to-day existence, as they moved between home, work, street, pub, club, school, and so on. It was they who could make life miserable for the man or boy who did not conform with the 'norm': as far as the average consumer was concerned, menswear was, indeed, overwhelmingly men's business.

---

[34]   Ugolini, 'Men, masculinities, and menswear advertising', pp. 90–91.

PART I
Consuming Menswear

Chapter 1

Identities, 1880–1939

Writing in 1930, J. Lewis May described his dismay at finding out that his wife had exchanged his beloved twenty-five-year-old Norfolk coat for a pot plant. What to her had simply been a 'shabby, fusty old thing', to him had been the repository of all sorts of precious memories of his past life.[1] Clothes, both old and new, could possess powerful but hidden meanings, which an outside observer might easily be unaware of. Their look and feel could also be the source of private pleasure, without the need for an 'audience', admiring or otherwise. In the late 1930s, a young engineering worker described a typical weekday for Mass Observation. After work, he changed from his stained overalls into his best suit, and went out to meet his girlfriend. He described his pleasure at being outdoors on a warm summer evening, after 'the oily, fumy, sweaty atmosphere of the shops ... I felt alive, I was clean and cool, clean vest, shirt and best suit, polished shoes and cool breeze through my hair as I walked quickly along'.[2]

More commonly, however, contemporaries saw clothes not as possessing deeply personal or secret meanings, but as having the more public role of broadcasting information about the wearer's singular personality and character. In 1941, reminiscing about the country village where he was born and brought up, C.H. Middleton suggested that the 'countrymen' of the pre-First World War era had frequently adopted idiosyncratic clothing styles, especially in the matter of hats, thereby expressing their unique individualities and preferences. The village schoolmaster, for example, had always been known to wear a remarkable 'square-topped bowler, which would have looked ridiculous on anybody else, but he would have looked ridiculous without it, because everybody had become accustomed to it'.[3] Apart from revealing individual tastes, clothes were also occasionally described by contemporaries as providing the outward, and not always conscious, expression of a man's 'real' self. Immediately after the First World War, the poet Siegfried Sassoon settled in Oxford, where, dressed in corduroy trousers and a bright red tie,

---

[1] J.L. May, *The Path Through the Wood* (Geoffrey Bles, London, 1930), pp. 142–5. See also G. Thomas, *A Tenement in Soho: Or Two Flights Up* (Jonathan Cape, London, 1931), p. 27. Under certain circumstances clothes could literally acquire the status of 'inalienable possessions', becoming inextricably bound with the owner's sense of self, and making them very difficult to get rid of. A. Wiener, *Inalienable Possessions: The Paradox of Keeping-While-Giving* (University of California Press, Berkeley, 1992).

[2] C. Madge and T. Harrison, *Britain by Mass-Observation* (Penguin Books, Harmondsworth, 1939), p. 214.

[3] C.H. Middleton, *Village Memories: A Collection of Short Stories and Reminiscences of Village Life* (Cassell, London, 1941), pp. 71–2.

he 'went about exploiting my Labour Movement personality and my reputation as an anti-war poet'. Occasionally, however, he would revert to riding breeches and a 'loud' check cap, a style of dress that 'caused me to be more my authentic self than I realised. For the fox-hunting man was irrepressible.'[4]

It is unsurprising, then, to find that clothes were regularly used as a means of judging people's 'worth', despite the fact that it was well known that judgements made on the basis of an individual's dress and looks could lead to misleading assumptions not only about his financial status,[5] but also about his character and moral qualities (Figure 1.1). In the case of Dudley Carew's great-uncle, a successful stockbroker, his 'faultless' attire never entirely seemed to fit him, being undermined by his air of 'indefinable raciness', and by the 'hint ... of decadence, of orgies, of chorus-girls drinking champagne out of their slippers'.[6]

QUOTATIONS ON 'CHANGE.

On 'Change.   At home.

Figure 1.1   'Quotations on 'change'. Appearances could be deceptive. *Judy*, 5 August 1903. Courtesy of the Bodleian Library, University of Oxford, N.2706 d.12.

---

[4]   S. Sassoon, *Siegfried's Journey 1916–1920* (Faber and Faber, London, 1945), p. 135. The relationship between exterior appearance and the interior 'self' is discussed by R. Sennett, *The Fall of Public Man* (Cambridge University Press, Cambridge, 1974), pp. 20, 146, 153–69. See also E. Wilson, *Adorned in Dreams: Fashion and Modernity* (Virago, London, 1985), pp. 136–7, 155.

[5]   *Comic Cuts*, 10 March 1900; J. Paton, *Proletarian Pilgrimage: An Autobiography* (George Routledge and Sons, London, 1935), p. 89.

[6]   D. Carew, *The House is Gone: A Personal Retrospective* (Robert Hale, London, 1949), p. 28.

Roughly half a century later, the 'mystery' lodger living with the McRobbies in a Glasgow slum in the 1930s, with his expensive-looking suits, well-tailored overcoat and polished shoes, may have 'looked the image of a distinguished businessman', but actually made a seedy living by selling pornographic photographs.[7] Nonetheless, despite cautionary tales such as these, as Joanne Finkelstein points out, 'the essential idea ... that the image and appearance of the individual is somehow representative of character and sensibility' remains a powerful, if generally tacit, one.[8] 'Not even the wisest of us' wrote Hugh Stutfield in 1909, 'can wholly get rid of the idea that the clay which lies hid under purple and fine linen is of finer quality than that which is covered by fustian or corduroy'.[9]

That said, it does not follow that clothing choices were either exclusively, or arguably even predominantly, a matter of satisfying and expressing one's own preferences or individuality, so that these could be 'communicated' to others. Indeed, very few men would have dared or wished to adopt the idiosyncratic clothing styles presumably necessary to reflect their unique self. After all, as Joanne Entwistle observes: 'The individual and very personal act of getting dressed is an act of preparing the body for the social world, making it appropriate, acceptable, indeed respectable and possibly even desirable also'.[10] Clothes, this book will argue, acquired meaning and significance most powerfully when placed in a social context, where they could be seen, sometimes touched, and generally assessed by others. For most boys and men in the six decades before the outbreak of the Second World War, the choice (to the extent that a choice was available) of clothes they wore was primarily influenced by the pressure – and indeed often the desire – to fit into a particular 'group' of people, and into a particular mould of masculinity.[11] In a sense, the clothing choices of individuals were mediated through what Pierre Bourdieu has termed their *habitus*: 'the unconscious dispositions, the classificatory schemes, taken-for-granted preferences which are evident in the individual's sense of the appropriateness and validity of his taste for cultural goods and practices'.[12]

---

[7] A. McRobbie, *A Privileged Boyhood* (Richard Stenleke Publishing, Ochiltree, 1996), pp. 183–4. See also the playwright John Osborne's description of his father in J.O. Osborne, *A Better Class of Person: An Autobiography. Vol. I: 1929–1956* (Faber and Faber, London, 1981), p. 14. The unreliability of dress as a carrier of meaning is emphasised in C. Campbell, 'When the meaning is not a message: a critique of the consumption as communication thesis', in M. Nava, A. Blake, I. MacRury and B. Richards (eds), *Buy This Book: Studies in Advertising and Consumption* (Routledge, London, 1997), pp. 103–19.

[8] J. Finkelstein, *The Fashioned Self* (Polity Press, Cambridge, 1991), p. 11.

[9] H.E.M. Stutfield, *The Sovrainty of Society* (T. Fisher Unwin, London, 1909), pp. 168–9.

[10] J. Entwistle, *The Fashioned Body: Dress and Modern Social Theory* (Polity Press, Cambridge, 2000), p. 7. The ways in which a sense of self can be constructed from bodily and consumer practices that – paradoxically – are deeply conformist to prevailing norms, are explored in Finkelstein, *The Fashioned Self*.

[11] Or, more rarely, by a wish to reject them.

[12] Although useful for its emphasis on the social and 'situated' character of modern consumption, Pierre Bourdieu's notion of *habitus* is almost entirely a class-based one. See P. Bourdieu, *Distinction: A Social Critique of the Judgement of Taste* (Routledge, London, 1992; first published 1979). Also P. Bourdieu, 'Structures, *habitus* and practices',

However, clothes did not simply reflect membership of a group and adherence to a particular model of masculinity; they also contributed to constituting and reinforcing both.[13]

In some cases, the relationship between certain garments and a particular male group was obvious: soldiers' and policemen's uniforms, clergymen's vestments, or the items issued to workhouse inmates, were all intended to enable the accurate identification of the wearer.[14] In other cases, the elements of clothing associated with a particular group were more fluid and less easy to pin down with any degree of precision. Nevertheless, even where there were no institutional rules governing the clothes worn by men and boys belonging to the same workplace, school, club or neighbourhood, conventions and expectations about an 'appropriate' appearance could operate equally powerfully, and could be enforced with some strictness, most often by ridicule, but sometimes even by violence. Sartorial choice – it will be argued – while by no means non-existent, was hedged in by often unspoken notions of what was acceptable in a particular context.

In a way, therefore, most men's clothing choices may be described as 'conformist'. However, such conformity was generally local and contingent in nature. Not only were male identities complex and diverse, but very few men were members of one single group throughout their lives, or even throughout their days. Conventions changed with the different stages of the male life-course, from childhood to old age, or even in the course of a single day, as men moved between workplace, home, pub, club, and so on. This means that there did not exist at any one time a single sartorial standard against which all men were judged. Rather, reflecting, and indeed reinforcing, the complexities of men's identities and their membership to a multiplicity of 'groups', there existed a variety of male sartorial models that influenced choices about what to wear. Central to such models, it is argued here, were issues of gender, ethnicity, class, age and location in time and space. It is to these that the rest of this chapter will now turn, considering the influence of each (as far as it is possible, of course, to disentangle one from the others) on men's sartorial decisions.

---

in *The Polity Reader in Social Theory* (Polity Press, Cambridge, 1994), pp. 95–110. The quotation is from M. Featherstone, *Consumer Culture and Postmodernity* (Sage Publications, London, 1991), p. 90. For a useful cross-cultural perspective on clothing (and adornment) as the mark of a collective identity, see A. Gell, 'Newcomers to the world of goods: consumption among the Muria Gonds', in A. Appadurai (ed.), *The Social Life of Things: Commodities in Cultural Perspective* (Cambridge University Press, Cambridge, 1992; first published 1986), pp. 110–38, especially pp. 119–23. But for a critique of this approach, see C. Campbell, 'The sociology of consumption', in D. Miller (ed.), *Acknowledging Consumption: A Review of New Studies* (Routledge, London, 1995), pp. 96–126, especially pp. 111–17.

[13]   M. Barnard, *Fashion as Communication* (Routledge, London, 1996), p. 37.

[14]   However, as Tammy Proctor has pertinently observed in relation to Scouts and Guides, 'the ambiguity of clothing seems less obvious with a uniformed movement, whose members are presumably dressed alike, but the fact of uniformity meant that any deviations in style, colour or function are highlighted even more'. T.M. Proctor, 'Scouts, Guides, and the fashioning of empire, 1919–39', in W. Parkins (ed.), *Fashioning the Body Politic: Dress, Gender, Citizenship* (Berg, Oxford, 2002), pp. 125–44, especially p. 131.

Gender and masculinity

Perhaps most fundamentally, male dress served to signal that a man belonged to the most comprehensive group of all: that of men. Indeed, clothing played a central role in asserting and reinforcing the boundary between men and women, between masculinity and femininity. As Robert Connell has observed of contemporary gender distinctions in Western dress and adornment: 'They are part of a continuing effort to sustain the social definition of gender, an effort that is necessary precisely because the biological logic, and the inert practice that responds to it, cannot sustain the gender categories.'[15] At least until the First World War, trousers represented an unambiguous signal of masculine identity. But perhaps more significantly, except in the context of theatrical masquerades, it would have been unthinkable for men to wear feminine long skirts: transvestism was associated with sexual transgression, or with the carnivalesque and riotous atmosphere of 'the world turned upside down'.[16] Wearing items associated with femininity could taint the wearer with effeminacy and unmanliness. Male corset-wearing, for example, was deeply suspect. One apparently scandalised commentator reported in 1889 that Prince Victor Albert was guilty of wearing such a garment, and expressed the hope that action would be taken 'to prevent such effeminate habits from spreading among our young men … The Lord preserve the nation from a generation of male corset wearers.'[17] The association of particular garments with masculinity or femininity provided a ready source for the caricaturist's pen. In the popular press, men such as William Booth, the founder of the Salvation Army, whose manliness was seen as open to question, were portrayed as wearing 'feminised' garments, while 'unwomanly' women, such as Victorian and Edwardian feminists and suffrage activists, were portrayed as

---

[15] R.W. Connell, *Gender and Power: Society, the Person and Sexual Politics* (Polity Press, Cambridge, 1987), p. 81. The relationship between dress and gender has attracted the attention of scholars from a variety of disciplines, including history, sociology, social psychology, anthropology and design. See, for example, Entwistle, *The Fashioned Body*, p. 21; C. Breward, *The Hidden Consumer: Masculinities, Fashion and City Life 1860–1914* (Manchester University Press, Manchester, 1999); T. Edwards, *Men in the Mirror: Men's Fashion, Masculinity and Consumer Society* (Cassell, London, 1997), pp. 14–15; E. Tseëlon, *The Masque of Femininity* (Sage Publications, London, 1995), especially pp. 14–18; R. Barnes and J.B. Eicher (eds), *Dress and Gender: Making and Meaning in Cultural Contexts* (Berg, Oxford, 1992); F. Davis, *Fashion, Culture and Identity* (The University of Chicago Press, Chicago, 1992), chapter 3; C. Brush Kidwell and V. Steele (eds), *Men and Women: Dressing the Part* (Smithsonian Institution Press, Washington, 1989).

[16] S.R. Grayzel, 'Nostalgia, gender and the countryside: placing the "Land Girl" in First World War Britain', *Rural History*, vol. 10, no. 2 (1999), pp. 155–70; A. McLaren, *The Trials of Masculinity: Policing Sexual Boundaries 1870–1930* (The University of Chicago Press, Chicago, 1997), chapter 9; M. Garber, *Vested Interests: Cross-Dressing and Cultural Anxiety* (Routledge, New York, 1992). For women and trousers, see Wilson, *Adorned in Dreams*, pp. 162–9.

[17] *Modern Society*, June 1889, quoted in Breward, *The Hidden Consumer*, p. 71. See also, for example, *The Weekly Record of Fashion*, 25 October 1882, for a scathing criticism of 'Men in stays'.

trouser-wearing viragos. Inter-war dress reformers, furthermore, were gleefully portrayed as advocating and wearing feminised garments.[18]

In practice, this meant that very few adult men would have wished or dared to dress in 'feminine' clothes. The insults and violence meted out to Quentin Crisp, and described in his famous autobiography *The Naked Civil Servant*, showed the dangers faced by a man who chose to openly express his homosexual identity by wearing idiosyncratically effeminate clothes.[19] At least until the First World War, and possibly beyond, it remained the common practice across classes to dress both boys and girls under the ages of four or five in petticoats, reflecting their common identity as 'infants'. After that age, however, it was considered necessary to assert the different genders through dress and, while girls continued to be dressed in skirts, boys were 'breeched'. Herbert Palmer wore petticoats until he was three or four, at which age he began to feel self-conscious about them, having become aware that 'most other little boys wore knicker-bockers'. For Palmer, his desire to wear different clothes to those of his sisters reflected a 'natural', biological difference between the sexes: 'certain physical differences in my sisters demanded frocks, while mine demanded something more manly'.[20] Financial necessity might on occasion prove to be a more pressing concern than gender differentiation. Stan Dickens always wore cast-offs on school-days. He did not mind this 'if they were my brother's cast-offs but sometimes they were those of my sisters'. Even decades after the event, he clearly remembered 'the shame and indignity I experienced in wearing them'.[21]

Ethnicity and Britishness

If that of 'men' was the most capacious of sartorial groups, that of 'British' men was almost as important, although perhaps less easy to define by reference to specific garments. The sartorial image of the 'British man' was complicated by the power of the well-known image of the impeccably tailored and debonair 'English gentleman', an image made up of specific class and ethnic elements, which actually excluded the

---

[18]   P.J. Walker, "'I live but not yet I for Christ liveth in me": men and masculinity in the Salvation Army, 1865–90', in M. Roper and J. Tosh (eds), *Manful Assertions: Masculinities in Britain Since 1800* (Routledge, London, 1991), pp. 92–112; *The Sartorial Gazette*, April 1932. See also J. Bourke, 'The great male renunciation: men's dress reform in inter-war Britain', *Journal of Design History*, vol. 9, no. 1 (1996), pp. 23–33, especially p. 30. For women wearing male garments, see W. Parkins, "'The epidemic of purple, white and green": fashion and the suffragette movement', in Parkins (ed.), *Fashioning the Body Politic*, pp. 97–124; K. Luck, 'Trouble in Eden, trouble with Eve: women, trousers and utopian socialism in nineteenth-century America', in J. Ash and E. Wilson (eds), *Chic Thrills: A Fashion Reader* (Pandora Press, London, 1992), pp. 200–212; A. Ribeiro, 'Utopian dress', in Ash and Wilson (eds), *Chic Thrills*, p. 230.

[19]   Q. Crisp, *The Naked Civil Servant* (Jonathan Cape, London, 1968).

[20]   H.E. Palmer, *The Mistletoe Child: An Autobiography of Childhood* (J.M. Dent and Sons, London, 1935), pp. 24–5.

[21]   S. Dickens, *Bending the Twig* (Arthur H. Stockwell, Ilfracombe, 1975), p. 18. See also P. Horn, *The Victorian Country Child* (Sutton Publishing, Stroud, 1997; first published 1974), p. 26.

majority of British or indeed English citizens.[22] In his autobiography, the well-to-do American H.C. Chatfield-Taylor recollected his youthful attempts to 'disguise my outlandish origin' during a stay in London in the 1880s. His description makes clear that it was not simply the acquisition of the persona of an Englishman that he wished to achieve, but rather the more specific one of a 'gentleman'. Wearing grey gloves and a white gardenia in the button-hole of his frock coat, he strolled down London's New Bond Street:

> From time to time I glance sideways at a reflection of my self in a window in order to make sure that a 'topper' is jammed on a transatlantic head at just the angle to make the wearer pass for the heir to an earldom, or at least a baronetcy.[23]

Elitist images of 'English' sartorial elegance continued to be meaningful in the inter-war period. In Michael Arlen's best-selling 1924 novel, *The Green Hat*, one of the central characters, an alcoholic young man, 'had a grey suit. It was thin as paper, but still defiantly retained a little of that casual elegance which not even Gerald could wholly divorce from the combination of a good tailor and a lean Englishman.'[24]

However, alternative sartorial images of 'Britishness' did exist. The kilts and tartans of Highland dress (as well as other aspects of Highland history and landscape) enjoyed a certain glamour – at least outside Scotland – in the closing years of Victoria's reign. At the age of fourteen, L.E.O. Charlton, the son of an English gentry family, developed a fascination with Highland chiefs, which then led to an obsession with all 'things Highland'. This obsession eventually 'outgrew all bounds and reached ... the height of demanding from his mother that he should be dressed in a kilt'. His mother did not reject the request out-of-hand, but, understandably, given its obvious incongruity, 'nothing happened to make the dream come true'.[25]

By the end of the nineteenth century, it was common to hear complaints that 'traditional' local dress styles had largely disappeared.[26] This does not mean, however, that local distinctiveness had entirely ceased to exist: throughout the

---

[22]   Breward, *The Hidden Consumer*, pp. 54–75. This point was made also by K. Silex, *John Bull at Home* (George G. Harrap, London, 1931), p. 157.

[23]   H.C. Chatfield-Taylor, *Cities of Many Men: A Wanderer's Memories of London, Paris, New York and Chicago During Half a Century* (Stanley Paul, London, 1925), p. 22.

[24]   M. Arlen, *The Green Hat: A Romance for a Few People* (The Boydell Press, Woodbridge, 1983; first published 1924), p. 41. See also H. Amies, *The Englishman's Suit* (Quartet Books, London, 1994).

[25]   L.E.O. Charlton, *Charlton* (Faber and Faber, London, 1931), p. 28. For the kilt as an 'invented tradition', see R. Nicholson, 'From Ramsay's *Flora MacDonald* to Raeburn's *Mac Nab*: the use of tartan as a symbol of identity', *Textile History*, vol. 36, no. 2 (2005), pp. 146–67; M. Chapman, '"Freezing the frame": dress and ethnicity in Brittany and Gaelic Scotland', in J.B. Eicher (ed.), *Dress and Ethnicity: Change Across Space and Time* (Berg, Oxford, 1995), pp. 7–28. Also N. Maclean, *The Former Days* (Hodder and Stoughton, London, 1945), p. 81. See also *Judy*, 7 August 1895, for a cartoon ridiculing the English tourist in the Highlands, who dressed 'in what he thinks is the national costume'.

[26]   Carole Shammas suggests that as early as the sixteenth century, 'few regional differences in *English* dress remained' (my emphasis). C. Shammas, *The Pre-Industrial Consumer in England and America* (Clarendon Press, Oxford, 1990), p. 27.

period, considerable diversity remained within the category of British men's dress, with local peculiarities often connected to occupation. As G.W. Nellist pointed out, 'A man from the [Yorkshire] Wolds could usually be recognised by his dress, and was looked down upon, and supposed to be a bit dumb.'[27] Distinctive garments continued to be worn. In the Norfolk village of Heathley, agricultural labourers' working clothes were composed of a 'sleeved waistcoat', corduroy trousers and 'stout' boots. To these were added leggings when the weather required it (locally known as 'buskins'), and a hat with a 'broadish' brim called a 'chummy'.[28] In a late-nineteenth-century Staffordshire mining village, on the other hand, colliers wore 'corduroy bell-bottomed trousers, melton cloth jacket and waistcoat, coloured scarf knotted round the throat', while in the inter-war village of North Wootton, in Norfolk, most farm labourers 'wore corduroy trousers with a strap below the knee, called yorks. They all wore good jackets with a large inside pocket'.[29] In Craigneuk, it was the heavy nailed boots, 'which, in keeping with the tradition of the district, would be brightly polished', that set the steel furnacemen apart from other workers.[30] Most spectacularly, perhaps, just before the outbreak of the First World War, A.S. Jasper's soon-to-be brother-in-law (a 'rough diamond', involved in petty crime) arrived at his wedding sporting the type of outfit worn at the time by all the local Hoxton 'boys':

> Bulldog-toe shoes, peg-top trousers, a silk sash round his stomach, white shirt, no collar, a large silk scarf tied in a double-knot around his neck, with the ends tucked in his braces, a long coat with turnback cuffs and pearl buttons and a flat cap like a pancake.[31]

There clearly did not exist a single sartorial definition of the 'British man'. However, this category did acquire further meaning when it served to distinguish the British from non-British 'others'. Certain garments marked out the wearer as a foreigner: in Joseph Conrad's novel *The Secret Agent*, first published in serial form in 1906, simply donning a 'short jacket' and 'low, round hat' served to transform 'the Assistant Commissioner' into 'one ... of the queer foreign fish that can be seen of an evening ... flitting around [Charing Cross's] ... dark corners'.[32] Willy Goldman's father was one such 'queer foreign fish'. A Russian immigrant, his way of dressing

[27]   G.W. Nellist, *The Yorkshire Wolds of Yesteryear* (The Author, Driffield, n.d. [c. 1982]), p. 31. See also D. de Marly, *Working Dress: A History of Occupational Clothing* (B.T. Batsford, London, 1986), chapters 5 and 6.

[28]   M. Home, *Autumn Fields* (Methuen, London, 1944), p. 63.

[29]   E. James, *Unforgettable Countryfolk: Midlands Reminiscences* (Cornish Brothers, Birmingham, n.d. [c. 1948]), p. 53; Norfolk Federation of Women's Institutes, *Norfolk Within Living Memory* (Countryside Books and Norfolk Federation of Women's Institutes, Newbury, 1995), p. 19.

[30]   P. McGeown, *Heat the Furnace Seven Times More* (Hutchinson, London, 1967), p. 23.

[31]   A.S. Jasper, *A Hoxton Childhood* (Barrie and Rockliff: The Cresset Press, London, 1969), p. 27. See also, for the distinctive – and regionally-based – dress of horsemen and keelmen, G.E. Evans, *The Horse in the Furrow* (Faber and Faber, London, 1960), pp. 72–84; H. Fletcher, *A Life on the Humber: Keeling to Shipbuilding* (Faber and Faber, London, 1975), pp. 55–6. The relationship between dress and geographical space is explored in C. Breward, *Fashioning London: Clothing and the Modern Metropolis* (Berg, Oxford, 2004).

[32]   J. Conrad, *The Secret Agent: A Simple Tale* (Penguin Books, London, 1990; first published in book form 1907), p. 151.

both embarrassed and infuriated his son. Trousers and cap 'were the sole articles of dress you could get him to replenish. He only wore a shirt and waistcoat as a gesture to society'. According to Goldman, as the family plunged ever deeper into poverty, 'his curious apparel was no longer a symbol of fun for me, but of barbarism'.[33]

Goldman senior's clothing marked him out as foreign, and as one of the 'others'. 'Others' could include white men of different nationalities, such as the supposedly brash Americans,[34] but a further degree of 'otherness' was to be found among the empire's indigenous subjects: these could adopt the clothes and purchasing habits of Britons only at the risk of being made the objects of crudely racist ridicule and hostility.[35] Significantly, the contrary was not necessarily always true. As Graham Dawson's study of Lawrence of Arabia has shown, the adoption of Arab dress on Lawrence's part during the First World War was represented in contemporary narratives not as a simple – and problematic – 'going native'. Rather, it symbolised Lawrence's adoption of the positive qualities of Arab masculinity, while maintaining his essentiallly superior 'Britishness'.[36] Nevertheless, it was widely believed that the colonial experience would inevitably leave its tell-tale and regrettable signs on a British body, demeanour and apparel, ranging 'from the boils, mosquito bites and the altered composition of the fibres and tissues of the body, to the [Anglo-Indian] colonist's characteristic clothing and confident demeanour'.[37]

---

[33]   W. Goldman, *East End my Cradle* (Faber and Faber, London, 1940), pp. 192, 196. At the opposite end of the social spectrum, see the experiences of the Dutch G.J. Renier, *He Came to England: A Self-portrait* (Peter Davies, London, 1933), p. 141.

[34]   Breward, *The Hidden Consumer*, pp. 44–5. See also *Punch*, 8 October 1913; H.G. Wells, *Mr. Britling Sees it Through* (Cassell, London, 1917; first published 1916), pp. 5, 8–9. According to the editor of *The Gentleman's Magazine of Fashion*, writing in 1882, 'very few Americans are neatly dressed'. *The Gentleman's Magazine of Fashion*, September 1882.

[35]   *Comic Cuts*, 12 October 1912. See also E.M. Collingham, *Imperial Bodies: The Physical Experience of the Raj, c. 1800–1947* (Polity Press, Cambridge, 2001), p. 186 and H. Callaway, 'Dressing for dinner in the bush: rituals of self-definition and British imperial authority', in Barnes and Eicher (eds), *Dress and Gender*, pp. 239–40, for Anglo-Indian hostility towards anglicised Indians, and M. Boscagli, *Eye on the Flesh: Fashions of Masculinity in the Early Twentieth Century* (Westview Press, Oxford, 1996), pp. 178–86, for the case of Peter Lobengula, self-proclaimed son of the King of Matabeleland.

[36]   G. Dawson, *Soldier Heroes: British Adventure, Empire and the Imagining of Masculinities* (Routledge, London, 1994), especially pp. 166–92. For a fictional example of British men adopting 'native' dress, see H. Rider Haggard, *King Solomon's Mines* (Oxford University Press, Oxford, 1991; first published 1885), pp. 199–201.

[37]   Collingham, *Imperial Bodies*, p. 2. Also pp. 159–65. See also E. Buettner, 'From somebodies to nobodies: Britons returning home from India', in M. Daunton and B. Rieger (eds), *Meanings of Modernity: Britain from the Late Victorian Era to World War II* (Berg, Oxford, 2001), pp. 221–40.

Class, status and respectability

Gender and ethnicity both played fundamental parts in influencing the nature of the clothes worn by British men: class also played a central part alongside these.[38] That said, the extent to which clothes were useful in accurately determining individuals' social status should not be exaggerated. In a London suburb at the turn of the century, for example, doctors could easily be recognised because they were the only men in top hats and black coats to be seen in the neighbourhood during weekdays. When it came to distinguishing *between* doctors, however, it was felt better to 'grade' them according to whether they owned a carriage, and, if they did, how many horses they used. 'Clothes did not indicate ability or success, or anything else, for the doctors dressed alike.'[39] Some commentators openly acknowledged that for them, the information concerning status apparently conveyed by clothes was incomprehensible. According to a 'bankrupt bookseller', 'If "clothes oft do proclaim the man" to some, they leave me in darkness'.[40]

However, there is little doubt that class was strongly reflected in dress throughout the period considered in this book, and, conversely, that clothes served to reinforce class identities. When Jack London decided to immerse himself in the 'abyss' of London's East End in 1903, a change of clothes proved sufficient to effect his transformation from well-to-do American writer to a member of 'the English lower classes': his 'soft, grey travelling suit' was replaced by second-hand clothes that had belonged to 'other and unimaginable men', including 'a pair of stout though well-worn trousers, a frayed jacket with one remaining button … and a very dirty cloth cap'. In his new garments, London became a member of the working class: 'My frayed and out-at-elbows jacket was the badge and advertisement of my class, which was their class.' Although he did not state this explicitly, it was not only the nature of the clothes that marked them as working-class garments (the cap instead of a hat, or corduroy instead of wool), but also – and perhaps especially – their dilapidated condition: old, in need of repair, smelly and dirty. Indeed, the whole of the East End was likened by him to a 'vast and malodorous sea'.[41]

Almost thirty years later, George Orwell graphically described not only the sights, but also the smells associated with the destitution of workhouse casual wards. The bathroom presented a 'disgusting sight':

> All the indecent secrets of our underwear were exposed; the grime, the rents and patches … the layers … of fragmentary garments, some of them mere collections of holes, held

---

[38]   C. Horwood, *Keeping Up Appearances: Fashion and Class Between the Wars* (Sutton Publishing, Thrupp, 2005).

[39]   R. Carton, *The Gentle Adventure: A Victorian Prelude* (J.M. Dent, London, 1933), p. 41.

[40]   Anon., *The Private Papers of a Bankrupt Bookseller* (Oliver and Boyd, Edinburgh, 1931), p. 47. See also P. O'Mara, *The Autobiography of a Liverpool Slummy* (The Bluecoat Press, Liverpool, n.d. [c. 1934]), p. 39.

[41]   J. London, *The People of the Abyss* (Isbister, London, 1903), pp. 20–24.

together by dirt. The room became a a press of steaming nudity, the sweaty odours of the tramps competing with the sickly, sub-faecal stench native to the spike.[42]

The opportunity to change one's clothes, as well as to have them regularly cleaned and properly cared for, provided the basis for important social distinctions, and continued to do so throughout the period. In the 1930s, the embarrassed and miserable twenty-one-year-old Peter Donnelly was acutely aware, on his first day's work as a shop assistant, of his down-at-heel appearance: 'the knees of my trousers were baggy; the elbows of my jacket were shiny'.[43] Although only the very poor would not have had access to a 'Sunday best' (even if regularly pawned), it was the sign of relative comfort to be able to change from one set of working clothes into another if the first was soiled or wet. In the years immediately preceding the First World War, it was rare for agricultural labourers to be able to afford the luxury of a change of clothes. Be they wet, blood-stained, or covered with mud or dust, 'he must wear them until he goes to bed, and must put them on again as he finds them in the morning'.[44] As a Lincolnshire labourer told George Ewart Evans, referring to the same period: '"I was earning about one and six a day", and I had one spare suit and one spare pair of boots – that was when I was in bed'.[45]

Christopher Breward has examined the stereotypes of class against which 'real' men confronted themselves and defined their identities, and 'the several ways in which consumers were encouraged to imagine, identify and interpret a range of social models'.[46] Indeed, in the course of their lives, men had to negotiate their place within a broad class framework: in some cases this was a straightforward process, in others it was anything but. Neal Harman's father's case belonged to the latter category. Having been born into an 'old and proud family' that had fallen on hard times, he had been forced to go into 'business' (this term being considered less degrading than that of 'trade'), and opened an antique shop on London's Bond Street. He had been 'cast penniless upon the world in an age when, by society, commerce was despised', and had negotiated this loss of caste by developing a unique personal style. He wore grey-striped black trousers, black double-breasted waistcoat and coat ('short and square cut, very large in the lapels'),

---

[42] G. Orwell, 'The spike', *Adelphy*, April 1931, reproduced in G. Orwell, *The Collected Essays, Journalism and Letters of George Orwell, vol. I. An Age Like This 1920–1940*, ed. S. Orwell and I Angus (Penguin Books, Harmondsworth, 1970; first published in this edition 1968), pp. 59–60.

[43] P. Donnelly, *The Yellow Rock* (Eyre and Spottiswoode, London, 1950), p. 97.

[44] G. Bourne, *Change in the Village* (Gerald Duckworth, London, 1912), p. 16. For the lack of clothing and footwear associated with extreme poverty, see, for example, National Social Policy and Social Change Archive, Albert Sloman Library, University of Essex (NSPSC Archive), The Edwardians: Family Life and Work Experience Before 1918, oral history collection (The Edwardians), QD1/FLWE/90, interview transcript, Mr Arthur Turner, engineer.

[45] Evans, *The Horse in the Furrow*, p. 73. See also R. Roberts, *The Classic Slum: Salford Life in the First Quarter of the Century* (Penguin, Harmondsworth, 1974; first published 1971), p. 38. Carole Turbin emphasises the symbolic role of cleanliness in C. Turbin, 'Collars and consumers: changing images of American manliness and business', in P. Scranton (ed.), *Beauty and Business: Commerce, Gender and Culture in Modern America* (Routledge, New York, 2001), pp. 87–108, especially pp. 88–90.

[46] Breward, *The Hidden Consumer*, p. 57.

'straight and stiff' collar, 'surrounded by a black stock and a fine pearl pin'.[47] At the other end of the social spectrum, A.S. Jasper's father attempted to depart from his usual ragged style of dress and adopt a supposedly more genteel image on the occasion of his daughter's wedding, just before the First World War. His attire included not only brown boots, striped trousers, a bobtail coat green with age and a flat cap, but also collar and tie, items which he had never worn before in his life: 'eventually [his daughters] got it on for him after a lot of swearing and blinding'. The result pleased him: 'What was good enough for the gentry was good enough for him, he insisted.'[48]

Differences in dress within classes were in some ways just as important as those between them. This was as true of working-class people as of other sections of the population, despite the fact that, as the protagonist of William Cameron's 1938 novel *Common People*, put it: 'they talk about the working class as if we was all alike. You know – everybody wearing scarves round their necks, an' corduroy trousers.'[49] Certain garments served to mark the boundary between the 'respectable' and the 'non-respectable' or 'rough', within a community. For example, the 'sad, dark, coarse, respectable trousers' that 'could be seen hanging like bunches of bananas under the gas brackets and naphtha flares in every quarter of London', for sale at 6s 6d a pair, were worn by 'Shopmen and clerks ... for everyday work', while 'church going artisans wore them for Sunday'.[50] The exact meaning of 'respectability' was elusive, involving 'aspirations and concerns both about self-respect and about self-presentation', and definitions of rough and respectable behaviours were elastic. In certain circumstances and in certain communities, activities such as drinking and frequenting pubs were acceptable, and did not involve a loss of caste and self-respect, while doing so in others. Generally, however, as Anna Davin has observed, respectability 'required display', and some garments – most notably collar and tie and Sunday suit – seem to have played an important role in signalling a man's position in society, and his adherence to a particular code of conduct that did not challenge the established order. It is significant that in a mid-Victorian court case in Bolton, the police prosecuting both players and spectators in one of the town's 'street games', felt it important to mention whether the defendant was wearing a jacket or a collar when he was arrested.[51] Fred Kitchen's Methodist parents were among those who embraced such an image of respectability, and managed to maintain it even on a

───────────

[47]   N. Harman, *Loose End* (Arthur Barker, London, 1937), pp. 10–11; 21.

[48]   Jasper, *A Hoxton Childhood*, p. 26.

[49]   W. Cameron, *Common People* (Victor Gollancz, London, 1938), pp. 30–31. The social gradations within the working class are explored, for example, in J. Benson, *The Working Class in Britain, 1850–1939* (I.B. Tauris, London, 2003; first published 1989); J. Bourke, *Working Class Cultures in Britain, 1890–1960: Gender, Class and Ethnicity* (Routledge, London 1999; first published 1994); R. McKibbin, *The Ideologies of Class: Social Relations in Britain 1880–1950* (Clarendon Press, Oxford, 1994; first published 1991).

[50]   G. Kersh, *The Thousand Deaths of Mr Small* (Heinemann, London, 1951), p. 86. Thank you to Philip de Jersey for this reference.

[51]   A. Davin, *Growing Up Poor: Home, School and Street in London, 1870–1914* (Rivers Oram Press, London, 1996), pp. 70–71, 78; P. Bailey, '"Will the real Bill Banks please stand up?" Towards a role analysis of mid-Victorian working-class respectability', *Journal of Social History*, vol. 12, no. 3 (1979), p. 343. See also R. Samuel, *East End Underworld: Chapters in*

tiny weekly wage of 17 shillings, which his father earned as a cowman. The results could be seen on their dignified weekly walk to the church: in his father's walking stick and 'well-brushed black coat with two large buttons shining in the rear', in his mother's black bonnet and his own pork-pie hat.[52]

That said, items such as collars and ties were more than the outward symbol of masculine worth and probity: they were also inextricably linked to men's status within the workplace. Working- or lower-middle-class men who wore collars and ties for work, as well as on Sundays, were not necessarily always viewed with admiration, especially if their poverty was obvious: impoverished clerks and shop assistants were often viewed with a mixture of pity and contempt. Nevertheless, there *was* a tendency to associate these garments with a higher and more desirable status. Upon getting work as a commercial traveller for Abel Heywood and Sons in the decade before the outbreak of the First World War, Rowland Kenney began to feel that finally, after a succession of dead-end labouring jobs, he 'had really got a foot firmly planted in the camp of the collared and tied'.[53] In the very different context of the steelworks of Craigneuk, near Glasgow, the furnacemen's foreman could be recognised by his blue gutty collar: 'It was his badge of office, the one thing ... that separated him from the swine; otherwise he was as nondescript as the rest of us.'[54]

In general, collars and ties or clean, tidy clothes, were visible signs that a man did not have to undertake manual work. In the Orkney island of Wyre, the shop owner was the only man who shaved and put on a collar every day, 'and this set him apart from other men as a sort of priest smelling perpetually of the clean odours of tea, tobacco, and paraffin oil'.[55] The jealously guarded nature of the gradations of status associated with – and reinforced by – particular clothes, are highlighted by an unpleasant incident involving Cliff Hills, the son of an Essex farm worker. When he was fifteen, during the First World War, his mother somehow managed to buy him a new suit, his first one ever. This prompted a scandalised response from the local baker, one of the village's 'important' men: 'Ee ... I see you've got a new suit on. It looks like a new suit to me. Good gracious me ... some of you people are going to be as well dressed as we are.'[56]

---

the Life of Arthur Harding (Routledge and Kegan Paul, London, 1981), p. 73, for references to a respectable 'collar-and-tie man'.

[52] F. Kitchen, *Brother to the Ox: The Autobiography of a Farm Labourer* (Penguin, Harmondsworth, 1983; first published 1940), p. 9.

[53] R. Kenney, *Westering: An Autobiography of Rowland Kenney* (J.M. Dent and Sons, London, 1939), p. 100. The availability of 'decent' clothes also influenced the types of jobs boys and men could obtain. See C.E.B. Russell, *Manchester Boys: Sketches of Manchester Lads at Work and Play* (Neil Richardson, Manchester, 1984; first published 1905), p. 6.

[54] McGeown, *Heat the Furnace*, p. 69; also pp. 56–7. See also V.W. Garratt, *A Man in the Street* (J.M. Dent and Sons, London, 1939), pp. 79–80; J. Bullock, *Bowers Row: Recollections of a Mining Village* (EP Publishing, Wakefield, 1976), p. 47.

[55] E. Muir, *The Story and the Fable: An Autobiography* (George G. Harrap, London, 1940), p. 68. See also J. Ashley, *Journey into Silence* (The Bodley Head, London, 1973), p. 38.

[56] Quoted in T. Thompson, *Edwardian Childhoods* (Routledge and Kegan Paul, London, 1981), p. 52. For the hazards of being seen as too well-dressed and 'stuck-up', see Davin, *Growing Up Poor*, p. 78. See also Chapter 2 below.

Age and life-course

Alongside gender, ethnicity and class, age was also central to male sartorial identities. And conversely, dress played an important role in marking the different stages in a man's life-course. To varying extents, clothing styles appropriate specifically for children and men of different ages existed throughout the period. In particular, the distinction between children's and adults' clothes was widely recognised, and boys frequently wore items such as sailor suits, knickerbockers and Norfolk suits, at least among the more comfortably off sections of the population (Figure 1.2).

More generally, it was widely accepted that a new set of clothes could play a central role in marking significant turning points in boys' and men's lives. This was particularly the case in the process of 'growing up' from childhood into adulthood: 'the great symbols of initiation into the brotherhood of men are the first watch, the first pair of long trousers, and the first cigarette'.[57] As mentioned above, the first moment of change was usually 'breeching', the shift from petticoats to short trousers, which at least until the early twentieth century often marked the passage from infancy to boyhood at the ages of four or five.[58] This was not always a pleasant shift. W.H. Lax had been delighted to abandon the petticoats that had caused him 'the most acute misery', and Sam Shaw's breeching made him 'feel quite a man',[59] but for F.T. Bullen, an orphan living with his dressmaker aunt, breeching meant abandoning his 'much-loved and comfortable petticoats' for a pair of 'tubes' obtained by modifying an old pair of his grandfather's trousers. 'My little legs felt as forlorn and distant in them as if they had no connection with me.'[60] Although this was the ritual most frequently mentioned in autobiographies and reminiscences, breeching was not the only sartorial rite of passage in a man's life. Indeed, it often was only the first in a series of steps towards the achievement of adulthood, steps that were characteristic of the inter-war as much as of the pre-First World War period. On the eve of the outbreak of the Second World War, for example, the fourteen-year-old Alexander McRobbie became an Army Cadet. Before then, he had often been the victim of his father's violence, but 'wearing a khaki uniform somehow transformed me, and from a lad who cowered under vicious blows from my father I suddenly became a man … I drew my bayonet and snarled "come and get me!"': his father backed down.[61]

The sartorial rites of passage of most boys were rather less dramatic. As the child of an upper-middle-class family living in Newcastle-upon-Tyne towards the end of the nineteenth century, Martin Armstrong eventually discarded his sailor suit, replaced by a more 'grown-up' Norfolk coat, cap and knickerbockers of brown tweed. Even in adulthood, he clearly recalled the momentous nature of such a change, which apparently

---

[57]   E.E. Wood, *Is this Theosophy?* (Rider, London, 1936), p. 34.

[58]   J. Tosh, *A Man's Place: Masculinity and the Middle-Class Home in Victorian England* (Yale University Press, New Haven, 1999), pp. 103–4.

[59]   W.H. Lax, *Lax his Book: The Autobiography of Lax of Poplar* (The Epworth Press, London, 1937), p. 34; S. Shaw, *Guttersnipe* (Sampson Low, Marston, London, 1946), p. 8.

[60]   F.T. Bullen, *Recollections* (Seeley, Service, London, 1915), pp. 28–9. For breeching, see also Davin, *Growing Up Poor*, p. 18; C.H. Rolph, *London Particulars* (Oxford University Press, Oxford, 1980), pp. 26–7.

[61]   McRobbie, *A Privileged Boyhood*, p. 153.

had affected not only his appearance, but also his 'manner, speech and thought'. Such sartorial shifts acquired meaning most powerfully when they were witnessed by the wearer's peer group. Resplendent in his new clothes, Armstrong felt as if 'I towered head and shoulders above my [younger] friend as I strode by his side with a slightly condescending smile on my face'. A few years later, the acquisition of a new set of clothes on his eleventh birthday was not quite such an unalloyed pleasure. His parents had bought him a silver watch and chain, and a new suit to go with them: not a Norfolk suit, 'but an open coat and waistcoat, like a grown up person'. The problem was not the suit in

FATHER AND SON.
(*The effects of cycling.*)

Figure 1.2 **'Father and son. The effects of cycling.' Adults dressed as boys and vice versa. *Judy*, 29 January 1896. Courtesy of the Bodleian Library, University of Oxford, N.2706 d.12.**

itself, but rather the fact that the audience of his new sartorial display had changed into a potentially more critical one. He had by then begun to attend a day-school, 'and the prospect of facing a crowd of friends, acquaintances and enemies in my new rig-out' was a source of 'misgiving rather than pride. It was a very different matter from swaggering in front of a single friend'.[62]

The role of clothes in marking stages in a man's life was as significant among the poor as it was among the well-off, among rural as well as urban inhabitants. Except perhaps among the very poorest sections of the population, reaching the age of six or seven seems to have been a further important landmark in most boys' lives, and one that was marked by some form of sartorial change, even if the clothes

---

[62] M. Armstrong, *Victorian Peep-Show* (Michael Joseph, London, 1938), pp. 128–9.

received were frequently only second-hand ones. The symbolic value of this change was not lost on its recipients. Writing of his childhood in the village of Bungay in Suffolk, George Baldry remembered that at the age of about five a suit had been made for him out of old corduroys of his father's, 'and a rare man I thought myself when I had it on'.[63] The shift from childhood to the adult world of full-time waged work was also a fundamental one in the life-course of most men, and one that was often symbolically marked by a change of clothes.[64] V.W. Garratt was very much aware of the momentous significance of such a change. He left school at the age of thirteen, thus putting an end to the 'first epoch' of his life, a transition marked by 'the shedding of knickerbockers in favour of long trousers'. Unlike many other young boys, he did not do so lightly: 'for apart from the terrors I had of what other boys would say, the prospects of stepping over the boundary of boyhood into adolescence was like parting from a dear friend for all time'.[65] Decades later, in 1936, the fourteen-year-old Jack Ashley experienced a similar sense of ambivalence on starting work as a labourer in an asbestos factory, clad in his first long trousers and grown-up leather clogs, complete with metal reinforcements. He was conscious 'that this was the beginning of a new era in my life, with new relationships and new responsibilities'.[66] However, the new sense of adulthood could easily be undermined by the contrast between the 'grown-up' clothes and a youngster's physical limitations. The twelve-year-old Bob Copper set off on his first day of flint-picking with a new 'feeling of self-importance', but he 'soon found that the new leather spats encasing my spindly legs kept twisting round until the swelling curve designed to accommodate the calves bulged out in the front of my shins ... This played havoc with the illusion of being a grown-up working man' (Figure 1.3).[67]

By their late teens, however, at least some young men were able to experience the pleasure of wearing grown-up clothes on a newly grown-up body. In the inter-war period, Alex Granger was earning 30 shillings a week delivering groceries, and had managed to acquire a 'best suit', as well as two extra shirts and ties. His pleasure in these goods lay not only in their ownership, but especially in the way they interacted with his newly acquired good looks and sense of identity:

---

[63]   G. Baldry, *The Rabbit Skin Cap* (The Boydell Press, Woodbridge, 1984; first published 1939). Baldry is rather vague about dates, but these events seem to refer to the 1870s, so somewhat earlier than the period covered by this study. See also Horn, *The Victorian Country Child*, p. 26.

[64]   In some cases, financial constraints meant that money to buy clothes had to be earned first. Goldman, *East End my Cradle*, p. 76. But note also the case of the fifteen-year-old Leslie Halward, who in 1921 was still at school, but 'wore long trousers, considering myself a man'. L. Halward, *Let Me Tell You* (Michael Joseph, London, 1938), p. 82.

[65]   Garratt, *A Man in the Street*, p. 72. See also J. Jones, *Unfinished Journey* (Hamish Hamilton, London, 1937), p. 67; M.G. Llewelyn, *Sand in the Glass* (John Murray, London, 1943), p. 41.

[66]   Ashley, *Journey into Silence*, p. 37. See also R. Johnston and A. McIvor, 'Dangerous work, hard men and broken bodies: masculinity in the Clydeside heavy industries, c. 1930–1970s', *Labour History Review*, vol. 62, no. 2 (2004), pp. 135–41, especially p. 142, for young men's pride in being 'put on their own can', and being responsible for their own clothes purchasing.

[67]   B. Copper, *Early to Rise: A Sussex Boyhood* (Heinemann, London, 1976), p. 124.

I had grown tall and filled out a lot and had wavy hair and the knack of keeping myself tidy. There was always a knife edge to my trousers, my boots were polished and I tried to be somebody, not just the son of a horrible man – as everyone called my Dad.[68]

A new-found sexual attractiveness may have been implied here, and yet it is notable that women featured little in personal narratives of clothing, especially as potential or actual sexual partners (rather than, most notably, as mothers). The approval of other men was apparently more important than that of women. As Jerry White points out, writing of Islington between the wars, 'taking care to dress well did not necessarily demonstrate concern with sexual attractiveness, even though it clearly related to masculine self-esteem'.[69] Of course, it is possible that for a man to acknowledge that he chose to wear a particular outfit in order to attract women's admiration would have smacked too much of admitting to a behaviour that was strongly associated with femininity.[70] Nevertheless, it is difficult to believe that the desire to be sexually attractive had no influence at all on clothing choices. Evidence for this, although admittedly scarce, is not entirely lacking. When Fred Kitchen began 'courting', he started 'wearing stiff collars on Sunday', while when J.H. Sparkes first turned his 'attention to "girls"', he slowly began to save up, so that his sister could buy him 'a suit, shoes, socks, collar, shirt and tie, so I was made up' and ready to join the local Monkey Parade.[71] Shortly before the outbreak of the First World War, William Holt (then working as a weaver in Todmorden) and his best friend both became interested in the same girl. As a result, he 'began to "dress up". For the first time in my life I became really concerned about my appearance.' Both a sense of rivalry and a desire to look attractive were evident as the two friends prepared for an evening out. Wearing a new suit, Holt 'brushed [his] … hair, arranged [his] … tie with great care, and with great contempt watched [his] … rival prepare himself'.[72] The look of the body encased by the clothes was obviously not unimportant either, when sexual admiration was being sought. M.G. Llewelyn's headmaster would generally make sure he was wearing his check breeches when 'walking out' with his sweetheart: 'He evidently believed in showing a good leg.'[73]

---

[68] A. Granger, *Life's a Gamble* (New Horizon, Bognor Regis, 1983), p. 23. From the opposite perspective, see also the description of tramps' 'bad' clothes concealing their 'far worse' bodies in G. Orwell, *Down and Out in Paris and London* (Penguin Books, London, n.d.; first published 1933), pp. 148–9. See also the discussion of men's bodies in R.W. Connell, *Masculinities* (Polity Press, Cambridge, 1995), chapter 2.

[69] J. White, *The Worst Street in North London: Campbell Bunk, Islington, Between the Wars* (Routledge and Kegan Paul, London, 1986), p. 170. The desire to appear sexually attractive to other men was not mentioned in any of the memoirs and reminiscences I have consulted.

[70] V. Steele, 'Clothing and sexuality', in Brush Kidwell and Steele (eds), *Men and Women*, pp. 60–63. Wilson, *Adorned in Dreams*, pp. 91–116, considers the relationship between 'fashion and eroticism', but only in relation to women.

[71] Kitchen, *Brother to the Ox*, p. 163; J.H. Sparkes, *The Life and Times of a Grimsby Street Urchin* (Arthur H. Stockwell, Ilfracombe, 1981), p. 12. See also G.A.W. Tomlinson, *Coal-Miner* (Hutchinson, London, n.d. [c. 1937]), pp. 77–8.

[72] W. Holt, *I Haven't Unpacked: An Autobiography* (George G. Harrap, London, 1939), p. 51.

[73] Llewelyn, *Sand in the Glass*, p. 111.

Figure 1.3   **'Clothes make the man.' Older men's bodies could let them down.** *Tit-Bits*, **5 April 1924. Courtesy of the Bodleian Library, University of Oxford, N.2706 c.6.**

Time and fashion

Clothes served to place individuals within a context marked by specific connotations of gender, ethnicity, class and age. They also served to place them within a particular time frame. Indeed, if 'fashionable' dress is understood as 'dress that embodies the latest aesthetic … dress defined at a given moment as desirable, beautiful, popular', then it is clear that fashion – however local and specific to a particular section of the population – also played a part in influencing men's dress.[74] Very few men explicitly stated that they aimed to achieve a 'fashionable' appearance, even fewer than admitted to a desire to look sexually attractive, and probably at least partly for similar reasons: as is well known, fashion was associated with the superficiality, frivolity and hedonistic heedlessness of femininity. Clothes consumption was not incompatible with a positive masculine identity, but an obsession with fashion arguably was.

However, although the very nature of autobiographies – which generally provide snapshots of dress at particular moments in the author's life – make it difficult to quantify the importance of stylistic change, there are indications that a quick turnover of styles, beyond the relatively slow pace of change in male dress identified

---

[74]   Entwistle, *The Fashioned Body*, p. 1. Entwistle points out that 'to understand dress in everyday life requires acknowledging a wide range of social factors that frame individual clothing decisions, of which fashion is important, but by no means the only factor'. Ibid., p. 55; see also pp. 44–52.

by historians over the period, was an important sartorial element for many men, especially among the more affluent sections of society. W. Macqueen Pope pointed out that in the course of the two decades before the outbreak of the First World War:

> A [middle-class] man's fashions in suits and collars changed considerably. Coats were worn long or short. They had vents at the back or they had not. They had long rolling collars, moderate rolls, or the lapels were cut high and almost level with the collarbones. Waistcoats could be cut low, or so high that there was hardly any opening at all for the display of the shirt. Sleeves were short or long.[75]

At the other end of the social scale, there were plenty of cases where poverty made notions of fashionability largely irrelevant. According to Mary Lakeman, the daughter of a Cornish fisherman, 'Fashion was an almost irrelevant factor during the bad time of our early youth, and played no part at all in the clothing of our older brothers and sisters in the first decade of the century. Thrift and ingenuity combined were scarcely enough to keep us all warm and clean, and what was as important, respectable.'[76] Many boys and men had no say at all in the clothes they had to wear. When their garments reflected their membership – voluntary or otherwise – of a particular institution, for example, the same style of clothes was often worn for years on end, leaving little room for individual choice, fashionable or otherwise. Francis Anthony spent a dreary childhood in an orphanage: as they grew up, he and the other boys 'had no separate identity. We were ciphers ... we all dressed alike ... grey knickerbockers, grey flannel shirts, dark blue coat, black woollen stockings and heavy ankle boots robbed all but the most outstanding boys of all character.'[77]

Between these two ends of the spectrum, the majority of men and boys arguably wore clothes that had perhaps been chosen without explicit reference to a 'fashionable' aesthetic, but which nonetheless in varied ways 'belonged' to a particular moment in time. In this context, it may not have been that important to wear garments that were distinctively 'fashionable', but it was certainly not desirable to wear others that were definitely 'old-fashioned'. Thus, in the Yorkshire Wolds – and indeed elsewhere in the country – the first decades of the twentieth century saw the 'old-fashioned' Sunday outfit of breeches and leather or cloth leggings being replaced by a more up-to-date 'smart trouser suit' made of serge.[78] The more old-fashioned garments, especially when worn by men who had not yet reached old age, were the object of more or less open derision. Writing in 1933, Arthur Beckett expressed his disapproval of the disappearance from the Sussex countryside of the smock frock, except among some of the older farm hands. It was, he believed, 'Fashion [that] declared that the former looked better in a cheap cloth suit than in a picturesque round frock but in

---

[75]   W. Macqueen-Pope, *Twenty Shillings in the Pound* (Hutchinson, London, n.d. [c. 1949]), p. 180. See also Edwards, *Men in the Mirror*, p. 15.

[76]   M. Lakeman, *Early Tide: A Mevagissey Childhood* (Dyllanson Truran, Redruth, 1983; first published 1978), pp. 158–9.

[77]   F. Anthony, *A Man's a Man* (Duckworth, London, 1932), pp. 9–10. For workhouse clothes, see W. Greenwood, *There Was a Time* (Jonathan Cape, London, 1967), p. 22; Shaw, *Guttersnipe*, p. 28.

[78]   Nellist, *The Yorkshire Wolds of Yesteryear*, p. 31

that matter Fashion lied'. Beckett himself made a point of wearing a frock when working in the house or the garden, and occasionally when walking in the village. The latter, however, was a nerve-racking experience, as the villagers were obviously scornful of a middle-class man 'who might, if he liked, always wear a cloth coat', but chose instead to favour 'a garment that was worn by their grandfathers ... When I am wearing the round frock in the village I am as self-conscious as a school girl in her creaking Sunday shoes.'[79]

Public and private dress

In his autobiography, L.E.O. Charlton recalled that one of the greatest pleasures to be found while training to become an army officer at Sandhurst had been the thrill of wearing the uniform. Sundays were 'red-letter days', because they brought 'church parade in scarlet tunic and helmet burnished bright'. Best of all was the fact that for the small group of Catholic cadets, who had to march to a church in town, such splendour had an audience. The civilians, Charlton hoped, 'would notice their smartness and admire their air of detachment as of a select body set apart from the general run of humanity for the sole purpose of defending with their lives their King and Country'.[80] The glamour of the uniform would have been dulled without spectators: there clearly was a difference between 'public' and 'private' clothes.

However, the distinction between private and public sartorial consumption was not always a straightforward one. J.J. Bell, evoking his childhood in the 1880s in a middle-class Glasgow suburb, vividly described the sartorial changes made by his father, a moderately prosperous manufacturer, in the course of the working day, as he moved between public and private spheres. On his way to his office in the factory he would wear a grey lounge suit, a dark light-weight overcoat, a bowler hat, a scarf tied with a rather dashing cameo of the head of Minerva, 'and, since he is not elderly, he carries a light stick of cherry-wood, with a narrow silver band'. Upon arrival in his private office, he could get rid of his shirt cuffs, and exchange his smart jacket with an old one, 'on the left sleeve of which he can so conveniently wipe his pen'. However, if by any chance he had to leave the office in the course of the day, for example to go to the bank, then the cuffs and a more presentable coat would have to come back on. Significantly, the conventions concerning the 'correct' dress for different milieus were not suddenly suspended on returning

---

[79]   A. Beckett, *Adventures of a Quiet Man* (Lambridges, Hove, 1933), pp. 259–60. See also R. Worth, 'Rural working-class dress, 1850–1900: a peculiarly English tradition?', in C. Breward, B. Conekin and C. Cox (eds), *The Englishness of English Dress* (Berg, Oxford, 2002), pp. 97–112. Also note, for example, Gordon Comstock's shame at his father's 'dismally shabby and hopelessly out of date' appearance. G. Orwell, *Keep the Aspidistra Flying* (Penguin Books, London, 1989; first published 1936), pp. 44–5. See also the comic song performed by Harry Bedford: R.P. Weston, F.J. Barnes and H. Bedford (authors and composers), *It's Bound to Come in Fashion By and By* (Francis, Day and Hunter, London, 1910).

[80]   Charlton, *Charlton*, pp. 46–7.

home. In the case of Bell senior, the return to the domestic arena meant 'A wash, an easy old jacket, but still the cuffs, and he is prepared for a quiet evening'.[81]

Not all men changed their clothes during the course of the day, while others changed them much more dramatically and frequently than Bell senior.[82] However, the notion that it was desirable to wear different clothing in public and in private was widely accepted. The domestic sphere of the home was often seen as the place where more 'relaxed' and 'comfortable' clothes could be worn, which for the most part seems to have meant warm, soft and loose-fitting items.[83] For Bob Copper's father, an agricultural labourer, for example, the end of the working day was marked by the simple but significant ritual of sitting in his favourite chair, taking off his heavy working boots and replacing them with comfortable slippers.[84]

However, there did not always exist a simple demarcation between the 'private' sphere of the home, where more relaxed styles could be worn, and 'public' spaces such as the workplace, where clothes had to be more formal. Firstly, the home was by no means always a place where shabby and 'comfortable' clothing could acceptably be worn. The 'best clothes' worn by the 'respectable' on Sundays and on other special occasions were a case in point. Many boys and men put them on 'gingerly, resigning ourselves to their unyielding hold'.[85] Rhys Davies, for example, could well remember 'the fanged childhood shirts of Welsh flannel, fresh-washed for Sunday, and tough as our theology' (Figure 1.4).[86] Secondly, as the case of Bell senior shows, the 'office' could allow a certain amount of 'relaxation'. Older garments that could stand the wear and tear of office life could be worn, at least by the boss, if not by employees.[87] Even for the boss, however, the ambiguous nature of the office's 'privacy' could lead to problems: when in 1895 the Countess of Warwick first went to visit Robert Blatchford, the editor of the socialist newspaper *The Clarion*, in his office, she found him wearing a 'garment ... which was something between a dressing gown and a lounge coat, [and] was most undignified'. Ruefully, Blatchford described the 'garment' she was referring to: 'a pilot jacket of the best Russian cloth, very warm and soft and comfortable, and I was really rather proud of it'.[88]

---

[81]   J.J. Bell, *I Remember* (The Porpoise Press, Edinburgh, 1932), pp. 29–37.

[82]   Lord Goring's practice of changing five times a day in Oscar Wilde's play *An Ideal Husband* may have been a comic exaggeration, but reflected actual aristocratic practices. O. Wilde, *An Ideal Husband* (1895), quoted in K. Thomas (ed.), *The Oxford Book of Work* (Oxford University Press, Oxford, 1999), pp. 45–6.

[83]   Judging from the humorous popular press, another arena where more 'relaxed' styles were worn was the seaside. See, for example, *Fun*, 21 July 1896.

[84]   Copper, *Early to Rise*, pp. 10–11. For later examples, see R. McKibbin, *Classes and Cultures: England 1918–1951* (Oxford University Press, Oxford, 2000; first published 1998), pp. 166, 168.

[85]   Carton, *The Gentle Adventure*, p. 168.

[86]   R. Davies, *Print of a Hare's Foot: An Autobiographical Beginning* (Seren, Bridgend, 1998; first published 1969), p. 175.

[87]   See also D.H. Lawrence, *Sons and Lovers* (1913), quoted in Thomas (ed.), *The Oxford Book of Work*, p. 236.

[88]   R. Blatchford, *My 80 Years* (Cassell, London, 1931), pp. 210, 212.

The distinction between 'work' and 'leisure', and between the spaces devoted to each, were clearly sartorially important ones. In the years leading up to the First World War, for example, the sixth earl of Spencer, 'a handsome, elegant man famous for his exceptionally high collars … made no concession to heat or holiday clothing, continuing to wear his usual rough black suit', but his unyielding attitude was rather unusual.[89] In the case of Franklin Lushington's father, a barrister in London's Inner Temple, for example, leisure meant the opportunity to wear 'baggy, loose-fitting, old clothes' and 'tramp the still and silent downs, his gun under his arm and his dog by his side'.[90] At the other end of the social scale, the distinction between work and leisure was still valid, but often operated in the opposite way. Among the ironworkers of turn-of-the-century Middlesbrough, for example, it made sense to wear old and shabby clothes to work, since the nature of the iron works meant that all garments were in any case quickly ruined. However, the very man who in the morning left for work 'clad almost in rags', wearing 'a greasy, torn old coat with holes in it, [and] patched trousers, frayed at the edge', would in the evening get changed and 'turn himself out like an entirely respectable citizen'.[91] In the case of John Blake's father, it was a suit, newly redeemed from the pawnshop, which served to 'keep up appearances when he visited the pub for the weekend session with his mates', while A.L. Roswe's father, a small shopkeeper in the Cornish village of Tregonissey, would always dress up in his favourite outfit of 'pepper-and-salt jacket and waistcoat, dark grey breeches and shining black leggings' for his Friday evening trip to the market.[92] Even in the inter-war period, supposedly characterised by a 'relaxation' of male clothing codes, particularly of leisure wear, it was only 'the more unconventional' among a largely working-class crowd, who on a hot July day went as far as to walk around not only with their waistcoats unfastened, but also with 'their jackets on their arms'.[93] As Ifan Edwards pointed out, 'at the end of the week … you felt like as complete and clean a change as was possible after a week of fierce slogging and dirt and working clothes. You could then join the crowds with a joyous feeling of having well earned the right to look a bit smart.'[94]

---

[89]   Norfolk Federation of Women's Institutes, *Norfolk Within Living Memory*, p. 102. See also Breward, *The Hidden Consumer*, pp. 196–201.

[90]   F. Lushington, *Portrait of a Young Man* (Faber and Faber, London, n.d. [c. 1940]), pp. 19–20. But see also, for example, the formal tail coat and top hat worn by H.G. Wells for Sunday walks with his cousin in the 1880s. H.G. Wells, *Experiment in Autobiography: Discoveries and Conclusions of a Very Ordinary Brain (since 1866)* (Faber and Faber, London, 1984; first published 1934), pp. 284–6.

[91]   Lady Bell, *At the Works: A Study of a Manufacturing Town* (Virago, London, 1985; first published 1907), p. 71. See also F. Willis, *Peace and Dripping Toast* (Phoenix House, London, 1950), p. 150.

[92]   J. Blake, *Memories of Old Poplar* (Stepney Books Publications, London, 1977), p. 11; A.L. Rowse, *A Cornish Childhood: Autobiography of a Cornishman* (Jonathan Cape, London, 1974; first published 1942), p. 12. See also W. Woodruff, *The Road to Nab End: A Lancashire Childhood* (Eland, London, 2000; first published 1993), p. 241.

[93]   P. Allingham, *Cheapjack* (William Heinemann, London, 1934), p. 17.

[94]   I. Edwards, *No Gold on my Shovel* (The Porcupine Press, London, 1947), p. 89.

Figure 1.4　'When a minute seems an hour.' Relaxing at home? *Tit-Bits*, 3 May 1930.
Courtesy of the Bodleian Library, University of Oxford, N.2706 c.6.

Indeed, perceptions of what constituted private and public spaces, and of what was suitable wear in either context were no less complex among the poor than among the affluent. According to a study of family budgets carried out for the Economic Club in the 1890s, for example, a jobbing plumber with three dependent children and in irregular employment, sought – like many other respectable working men and women – to hide his poverty: when 'outdoors' he wore an overcoat, 'which is warm and conceals the deficiency of other clothing'. But both when at home *and* when at work, 'the overcoat is removed, and reveals him in shirt sleeves'.[95] In the Lancashire and Cheshire coalfields, the working conditions demanded an extremely 'relaxed' clothing style, despite the job's 'public' nature. When temperatures were high, clothes were peeled off and some men even worked naked, since 'there were no women, they were all men'. Nonetheless, there were limits: in certain collieries, 'if you were a Christian you wore a pair of drawers'.[96]

---

[95]　*Family Budgets: Being the Income and Expenses of Twenty-Eight British Households 1891–1894* (P.S. King and Son, London, 1896), p. 21.

[96]　K. Howarth, *Dark Days: Memories and Reminiscences of the Lancashire and Cheshire Coalmining Industry up to Nationalisation* (n.k., Manchester, 1978), p. 10. See also Willis, *Peace and Dripping Toast*, p. 150

Male groups and hierarchies of dress

The interplay of gender, ethnicity, class, age and location in time and place, all played a part in influencing male dress in the half-century before the outbreak of the Second World War. It is likely, however, that, if asked, most men would not have singled out such large and relatively abstract themes as having a primary influence on their sartorial decisions. Rather, they would have mentioned the impact of more local and contingent factors, and most notably the – mostly masculine – peer groups with which they came into everyday contact, including friends, colleagues, neighbours and relatives.

In some cases, individuals' clothes were explicitly chosen and worn as a visual badge of membership to a well-defined, often locally-based, tightly-knit – and generally relatively short-lived – group. Occasionally, an explicitly political agenda lay behind the choice of garments. In the early 1930s, for example, Joe Jacobs was promoted to head presser of the tailoring workshop where he was employed. 'This meant a big jump in my income and I could be quite "extravagant".' He could now indulge his love of good clothes, his penchant for smart, tailor-made suits making him stand out from many of his fellow Communist Party members. 'Many of the young Communists were fond of dressing in an outlandish way. Khaki or Red shirts were common. Also they liked to wear sandals. Even some boys who could afford it, didn't go in for tailor-made suits.'[97] Rather different was the case of groups such as the 'Peaky Blinders', a gang of 'roughs' based in Edwardian Birmingham, who distinguished themselves by wearing peaked caps and bell-bottomed trousers, while 'a line of vivid brass buttons down the front gave added distinction'.[98] Most men and youths would of course not have worn (nor wished to wear) such a distinctive 'uniform'. However, in seeking to structure and maintain their identities as members of a masculine collectivity at least partly through their clothes, groups such as youthful Communist Party members or Peaky Blinders differed in extent, but not in essence from the perhaps less spectacularly attired mass of their contemporaries.[99]

---

[97]   J. Jacobs, *Out of the Ghetto: My Youth in the East End. Communism and Fascism 1913–1939* (Janet Simon, London, 1978), pp. 79–80. See also, for example, 'the standard outfit for artists in the thirties', described in P. Johnson, *The Vanished Landscape: A 1930s Childhood in the Potteries* (Weidenfeld and Nicolson, London, 2004), p. 125.

[98]   Garratt, *A Man in the Street*, pp. 65–6. For the 'scuttlers', Manchester-based Edwardian gangs, see Russell, *Manchester Boys*, p. 16. See also S. Humphries, *Hooligans or Rebels? An Oral History of Working-Class Childhood and Youth 1889–1939* (Basil Blackwell, Oxford, 1981), chapter 7. Comparable post-Second World War rebellious 'sub-cultural' groups, such as Punks, Mods or Teddy boys, with their distinctive clothing styles and mostly youthful membership, have attracted a good deal more scholarly attention than their earlier counterparts. G. Pearson, *Hooligan: A History of Respectable Fears* (Macmillan, London, 1983), p. 22. See, for example, Breward, *Fashioning London*, chapter 5; D. Hebdige, *Subculture: The Meaning of Style* (Routledge, London, 2003; first published 1979); C. Breward, 'Style and subversion: postwar poses and the neo-Edwardian suit in mid-twentieth-century Britain', *Gender & History*, vol. 14, no. 3 (2002), pp. 560–83; P. Hodgkinson, *Goth: Identity, Style and Subculture* (Berg, Oxford, 2002); P.E. Willis, *Profane Culture* (Routledge and Kegan Paul, London, 1978).

[99]   For a convincing critique of the supposed dichotomy between 'mainstream' and 'alternative' cultures, see S. Thornton, *Club Cultures: Music, Media and Subcultural Capital* (Polity Press, Cambridge, 1995), especially pp. 87–115.

As boys and men moved between different spaces – home, school, neighbourhood, workplace, club, pub, and so on – so their clothes reflected their membership of a peer group within each context.[100] This does not of course mean that all the men who, for example, worked in the same office, frequented the same pub, or perhaps hung around the same street corner, at roughly the same time, would have dressed identically. Rather, it is suggested here that there existed more or less well-defined and well-known 'local' boundaries of sartorial acceptability, beyond which individuals could stray only at the risk of being made the objects of ridicule, or on occasion even violence.

That said, the importance of local 'styles', and the fact that there did not exist a single, 'hegemonic', sartorial model followed by all British men, is not to suggest that all clothes enjoyed the same status, or were seen as equally desirable, even if worn in the 'correct' context. Some clothes were more enhancing to self-worth than others. It was not simply that certain materials, colours, trimmings or accessories were more expensive or obviously better quality than others. Certain garments, particularly those associated with images of manliness and of desirable male life-styles, enjoyed positive connotations, and an allure that other items did not. However, this does not mean that it is possible to state categorically which items were desirable, and which were not.[101] This ambiguity is well illustrated, for example, by clerks' and shop assistants' black coats. These garments, with their associations of servility, enjoyed at best a very ambiguous reputation, as will be seen further in Chapter 5. With hindsight, A.V. Christie congratulated himself on having begun his working life as a railwayman, rather than entering the drapery business, where 'wearing a choker collar, a black tail-coat and striped trousers, I would … [have been] obliged to satisfy … the whims of ladies'.[102] In other cases, however, even the garb of clerks could acquire desirable, almost glamorous, connotations. As a child growing up in the mining community of Newtown, in South Wales, Joseph Keating's dearest wish had been to join 'the big miners and their boys, stained by dust and toil'. After a few years working down the pit, however, he began to envy the men who were able to go to work in clean clothes: 'I thought that if I could be allowed to earn my living, free from the inconvenience of dust-black clothes I should be content'.[103] According to James Mahoney, in the pre-First World War period, 'The white collar worker was looked upon as something

---

[100] The relationship between dress and 'social space' is considered in Entwistle, *The Fashioned Body*, pp. 34–5. For the relationship between individuality and group identities, see also pp. 115–18.

[101] The shifting and unstable association of certain items of clothing with powerful and authoritative identities are explored in very different historical contexts by D. Kuchta, *The Three-Piece Suit and Modern Masculinity: England, 1550–1850* (University of California Press, Berkeley, 2002); S. White, '"Wearing 3 or 4 handkerchiefs around his collar and elsewhere about him": slaves' constructions of masculinity and ethnicity in French Colonial New Orleans', *Gender & History*, vol. 15, no. 3 (2003), pp. 528–49; G. McCracken, *Culture and Consumption: New Approaches to the Symbolic Character of Consumer Goods and Activities* (Indiana University Press, Bloomington, 1990; first published 1988), chapter 6.

[102] A.V. Christie, *Brass Tacks and a Fiddle* (The Author, Kilmarnock, 1944; first published 1943), p. 21. See also Russell, *Manchester Boys*, p. 13.

[103] J. Keating, *My Struggle for Life* (Simpkin, Marshall, Hamilton, Kent, London, 1916), pp. 53, 87. See also Garratt, *A Man in the Street*, p. 75.

higher than the factory or the dock worker'. He may not have been better paid, but his advantage was that 'he went out to work as smart as he possibly [could]'.[104]

Soldiers' uniforms were also not universally admired before the Boer and especially the First World War, and neither were soldiers themselves. According to Neville Cardus, born illegitimate in a working-class Manchester family, turn-of-the-century soldiers, swaggering around in their round caps, short jackets and 'tremendously long trousers', were perceived as 'common fellows who ... swore and winked at girls and carried canes with which they could severely smite themselves on the thighs'. It was a sign of their low status that, even though his aunt Beatrice had forsaken her parents' 'respectable' life-style, she would never have considered going out with a soldier.[105] Army officers' uniforms, on the other hand, particularly those of certain illustrious regiments, were generally acknowledged to enjoy a unique glamour.[106] A very young Bruce Bairnsfather, for example, later to become a well-known comic illustrator, was so dazzled by the Seaforth Highlanders, marching to church in full-dress uniform, that he decided to join the army. It had been 'a magnificently stirring sight, with band playing, kilts swinging, and all the rest of the complicated but alluring adjuncts peculiar to a highlander's make-up'. All these accoutrements did not suggest to him images of violence, war or hardship. Rather, the army represented 'travel, romance ... adventure'. He could hardly wait to don the much desired uniform: 'How I could swell around in front of my friends and relations'.[107]

Conclusion

This chapter has argued that in the half-century between 1880 and 1939, most men did not choose their clothes primarily in order to express their unique individuality or to externalise their inner selves. Rather, they sought to chart a course through the social environments within which they spent their days and their lives. Reflecting the ways in which identities were – and are – constructed and reinforced, primarily

---

[104] NSPSC Archive, The Edwardians, QD1/FLWE/70, interview transcript, Mr James Mahoney, warehouseman. See also the ambivalent image of shop assistants – as both 'raffish' and 'subservient' – in R. Hoggart, *A Local Habitation: Life and Times 1918–1940* (Chatto and Windus, London, 1988), p. 16. Also C.P. Hosgood, '"Mercantile monasteries": shops, shop assistants and shop life in late-Victorian and Edwardian Britain', *Journal of British Studies*, vol. 38, no. 3 (1999), pp. 322–52.

[105] N. Cardus, *Autobiography* (Collins, London, 1947), p. 21. For a useful comparison with French uniforms, see A. Matthews David, 'Decorated men: fashioning the French soldier, 1852–1914', *Fashion Theory*, vol. 7, issue 1 (2003), pp. 3–38.

[106] But for the prejudice against officers in 'a mere line regiment', or in 'the cavalry organization known derisively as "The Merchant Tailors' Own"', see Chatfield-Taylor, *Cities of Many Men*, p. 24.

[107] B. Bairnsfather, *Wide Canvas: An Autobiography* (John Lang, London, 1939), pp. 27–8. The glamour of Highland regiments is discussed in J.W.M. Hinchberger, *Images of the Army: The Military in British Art, 1815–1914* (Manchester University Press, Manchester, 1988), pp. 106–9. See also M. Paris, *Warrior Nation: Images of War in British Popular Culture, 1850–2000* (Reaktion Books, London, 2000), although the author does not deal directly with uniforms.

by reference to 'others', sartorial identities showed both who the individual was and who he was not, where he belonged and where he did not: codes relating to gender, ethnicity, class, age, location in time and space, all played a part in creating and sustaining collective, rather than individual, male sartorial identities. At the same time, just as not all male identities were equal and equally powerful, neither were all sartorial identities equally desirable and aspired to. Clothes consumption was not somehow immune from hierarchies or unequal power relations, although it is difficult, if not impossible, to provide a straightforward classification of least and most admired garments. Furthermore, not only did there exist enough uncertainties and grey areas in clothing codes for mistakes and misunderstandings to occur, but perhaps most importantly, it was not always possible for an individual to make sure that his clothes 'fitted in'. What could – and all too often did – go wrong, and what happened to those who strayed from the fold, will be the subject of the next chapter.

Chapter 2

Non-conformity, 1880–1939

In his 1935 autobiography, Jack Hilton, born in 1900 to a poor family in a 'smoky industrial town', described with characteristic bitterness the often unspoken pressures towards conformity that had characterised his childhood. At school, 'cellulose collars (washable) and blackened clogs were the veneered hall-mark, and just as indispensable to our education, as are now the pinstripe, spats and horn-rims, to our present-day black-cloth imbeciles. One never dared to go to school otherwise'.[1] Most boys, youths and men accepted unquestioningly and matter-of-factly the necessity of adhering to a style 'suitable' to the particular context in which they found themselves. It was when individuals broke the sartorial 'rules', and wore inappropriate garments, whether they were the wrong colour or shape, or presented the wrong details, or perhaps were too new or too old, too pristine or too ragged, too dirty or too clean, that the power of dress codes became all too clear. Ridicule and occasionally even violence were then used to enforce conformity, or perhaps more accurately, to punish difference.[2]

It is the aim of this chapter to explore non-conformity further, and question the reasons that could lie at the basis of individuals' sartorial faux pas. It begins by taking a closer look at the ways in which pressure to conform operated, with teasing and ridicule from one's own peer group emerging as the most important elements in ensuring compliance. Whilst not wishing to underestimate the importance of conscious and sometimes politically-motivated rebellions against established dress codes, this chapter nonetheless focuses on some of the reasons for what might be termed 'unwilling', or perhaps more accurately non-political, non-conformity: financial pressures, a rejection of the role of family bread-winner and the powerlessness of childhood being – it is argued – particularly significant. The chapter then concludes by considering further the unstable boundary between an acceptable and an unacceptable appearance, focusing on the highly revealing moment when a proper and manly attention to dress was seen to go wrong, and turn into unacceptable, weak-chinned and morally dubious 'dandyism'.

---

[1]   J. Hilton, *Caliban Shrieks* (Cobden-Sanderson, London, 1935), p. 5.

[2]   See also J. Barraclough Paoletti, 'Ridicule and role models as factors in American men's fashion change, 1880–1910', *Costume*, vol. 19 (1985), pp. 121–34. Deviance from accepted codes of masculine dress, and, by extension, from acceptable masculine norms, could on occasion have even more serious consequences. For a later period, see S. Cosgrove, 'The zoot suit and style warfare', in A. McRobbie (ed.), *Zoot Suits and Second-Hand Dresses: An Anthology of Fashion and Music* (Macmillan, Basingstoke, 1989), pp. 3–22.

Enforcing conformity

Throughout the period covered by this book, it was uncommon for men to openly and purposely flout sartorial conventions. In 1904 Neville Cardus found employment as a clerk in a Manchester marine insurance agency. There he became very friendly with a boy named Seddon, who was a great believer in physical culture and in the health-giving properties of fresh air. According to Cardus he was, in fact, a 'crank'. 'I did not share all his views but I went so far as to discard a hat.' As a result, 'we were as nudists of the period, and wherever we walked people turned round and looked at us'.[3] As a young shop assistant at the turn of the century, Ernest Egerton Wood whiled away tedious hours fantasising about creating a dress style of his own:

> There would be long stockings, supported from a light corset, which would ... give my back comfortable support through the long hours of waiting ... some soft kind of tennis shirt – emphatically no collar, no front, no cuffs, no hard hat ... no waistcoat, but a simple coat ... light shoes ... with perhaps a 2-inch heel to add a little to my height.

Unsurprisingly, he never wore such an outfit: 'The demands of a ridiculous and cruel orthodoxy in dress, associated with caste ideas, have always been inexorable.'[4]

Ridicule was frequently directed at the clothing styles not only of particular individuals, but also of whole groups of men. Thomas Crosland's tirade against 'suburbans' in 1905 was a good example. According to Crosland, the 'male suburban', with his 'unscrupulous respectability', could be recognised anywhere:

> Regard his well-brushed silk hat, his frock-coat with the pins in the edge of the lapel (they are always there) and the short sleeves, the trousers that are forever about to have a fringe on them, the cuffs with paper protectors and a pocket-handkerchief stuffed up one of them, the 'gamp' and its valuable case, the cheap ring, the boisterous watch-chain ...

This was not a sign that 'the suburban' had no interest in his appearance, or that he lacked the wherewithal to afford better garments, added Crosland. Indeed, 'He believes himself to be the glass of fashion and the mould of form. If he were otherwise, he thinks he might die.'[5]

Nevertheless, despite such tirades against whole groups of men, the evidence of autobiographies suggests that rather than such 'general' taunts, it was ridicule and pressure from *within* one's own peer group, which had a much more direct and immediate impact on individuals and their sartorial choices.[6] Basing his opinion on

---

[3]   N. Cardus, *Autobiography* (Collins, London, 1947), p. 43.

[4]   E.E. Wood, *Is this Theosophy?* (Rider, London, 1936), pp. 56–7.

[5]   T.W.H. Crosland, *The Suburbans* (John Lang, London, 1905), p. 38. For the literary elite's more general contempt towards 'suburbans' and 'clerks', see J. Carey, *The Intellectuals and the Masses: Pride and Prejudice Among the Literary Intelligentsia 1880–1939* (Faber and Faber, London, 1992), chapter 3.

[6]   See also A.J. Hammerton, 'The English weakness? Gender, satire and "moral manliness" in the lower middle-class, 1870–1920', in A. Kidd and D. Nicholls (eds), *Gender, Civic Culture and Consumerism: Middle-Class Identity in Britain, 1800–1940* (Manchester University Press, Manchester, 1999), pp. 164–82.

the experience of working in a gas meter manufactory, for example, V.W. Garratt came to the conclusion that individuality could not flourish in a factory: 'To be oneself courageously and unashamedly in matters of dress, talk and action, meant running the gauntlet of ridicule and tribal opposition.' It was a good deal easier to conform, or as Garratt put it disparagingly, 'to fall into the rut and become moulded to mediocrity'.[7] B.L. Coombes was also a man who appreciated good clothes. Indeed, not long before the outbreak of the First World War he left his native Herefordshire, where his parents were tenant farmers, because he wanted 'good clothes, money to spend ... fresh places and faces, and – well, many things'. Having found work as a miner in South Wales, however, he discovered that he had to exercise restraint in his choice of clothes, at least while at work, because teasing would inevitably follow if they were thought to be 'too good'. Generally, anything beyond the narrow confines of moleskin trousers, 'cloth cap, old scarf, worn jacket and waistcoat, old stockings, flannel shirt, singlet and pants' would have counted as 'too good'.[8]

Some men were brave enough to defy conventions. One of these was Francey 'Milord', the telling nickname of one of the 'gaffers' in the Craigneuk steelworks: 'his linen stood out in a district of cloth caps and mufflers ... it took a brave man to wear a bowler hat in Craigneuk, but Francey did'.[9] Willy Goldman's sartorial non-conformity, on the other hand, in a sense took a shape opposite to that of Francey: he refused to wear anything other than a tweed jacket and flannel trousers. This proved a handicap when seeking lodgings within the Jewish community. Had he looked like a '"low-life" ... [with] a precocious too-big-for-your-boots manner, and a natty taste in hosiery', that would have explained 'the phenomenon of a Jewish youth on his own', but his slightly shabby appearance, not fitting into the popular conception of a ne'er-do-well, was the perfect way 'of creating suspicion in Jewish hearts'.[10]

Ridicule and pressure to conform were not confined to working-class communities. In his autobiography, Alexander Pearson described how in the late 1880s two young men articled with his father, a country solicitor, had one day arrived in the office wearing their riding kits. These included 'sporting' check coats, smart breeches and 'resplendent' waistcoats. One of the local 'characters' was therefore moved to ask when the circus was arriving in town, since the 'flashy young fellows' looked 'like the ring-master and the ... animal tamer'.[11] More seriously, almost thirty years later, the rector Edward Synnott gave grave offence to his parishioners in the Sussex village of Rusper, by wearing the garb of a farmer (farming being one of his passions),

[7]   V.W. Garratt, *A Man in the Street* (J.M. Dent and Sons, London, 1939), p. 80.

[8]   B.L. Coombes, *These Poor Hands: The Autobiography of a Miner Working in South Wales* (Victor Gollancz, London, 1939), pp. 8, 31. On the importance of 'fitting in', see also K. Howarth, *Dark Days: Memories and Reminiscences of the Lancashire and Cheshire Coalmining Industry up to Nationalisation* (n.k., Manchester, 1978), p. 10; J. Gormley, *Battered Cherub* (Hamish Hamilton, London, 1982), p. 3; R. McKibbin, *Classes and Cultures: England 1918–1951* (Oxford University Press, Oxford, 2000; first published 1998), pp. 131–2.

[9]   P. McGeown, *Heat the Furnace Seven Times More* (Hutchinson, London, 1967), p. 56. See also 'the gentleman collier' described in R. Davies, *Print of a Hare's Foot: An Autobiographical Beginning* (Seren, Bridgend, 1998; first published 1969), p. 73.

[10]   W. Goldman, *East End my Cradle* (Faber and Faber, London, 1940), p. 262.

[11]   A. Pearson, *The Doings of a Country Solicitor* (The Author, Kendal, 1947), p. 25.

rather than 'the melancholy black uniform standardised for clergymen'.[12] Pressure to conform could be just as strong among children as it was among adults. According to Franklin Lushington, 'the first object of every public schoolboy is to become exactly like every other public schoolboy'.[13] Of course, not all boys (or indeed men) found 'fitting in' either difficult or uncomfortable. Lord Latymer, for instance, described his time at public school in the late 1880s and early 1890s as mostly happy. After all, 'Not having been born a rebel ... it never worried me that I might not wear brown boots, or a stick-up collar, or a bow tie; that my flannel trousers were grey, and not white'.[14]

Understandably, individuals were more likely to remember – and record – instances when inappropriate clothes had led to embarrassment and ridicule, rather than when they had passed unremarked.[15] Indeed, the penalties suffered by those who for various reasons did not 'fit in', could be devastating. In 1887 Ernest Barker, the son of a farmer, won a scholarship to a Manchester grammar school. Barker's move to the new school meant that he had to learn new codes of conduct and dress, stop speaking in dialect, wear a collar and a tie, and shoes instead of clogs. However, his parents' poverty meant that, even when he had mastered the 'rules', he could never entirely adhere to them. On one occasion, his mother adapted for him an old pair of trousers that had once belonged to his grandfather. 'They were farmer's trousers, of a sort one never sees nowadays – and seldom saw even then; and they involved me in jeers and ridicule'. Looking back at these incidents from the vantage point of adulthood, Barker was apologetic about devoting space in his autobiography to such 'foolish little things'. However, he was clearly right in pointing out that 'they counted in their day'.[16] In Barker's case, the inappropriate clothes were clearly part of a whole package that did not 'fit in' the grammar school. Similarly, as the narrator in Anthony Powell's novel *A Question of Upbringing* put it of an old school fellow, whose slightly unconventional overcoat had acquired a certain notoriety within the school: 'As a matter of fact the overcoat was only remarkable in itself as a vehicle for the comment it aroused, inasmuch that an element in Widmerpool himself had proved indigestible to the community.'[17]

Among boys, just as among many adults, to be seen as dressing 'too well' could be just as disastrous as not dressing well enough. In the 1930s, Alexander McRobbie may have worn the uniform of his '"snob" school' 'with pride' and without trepidation, despite being the only boy in his slummy Glasgow neighbourhood to do so, but

---

[12] E.F. Synnott, *Five Years' Hell in a Country Parish* (Stanley Paul, London, 1920), p. 72. Synnott's concession to his calling was to wear his clerical collar at all times, 'so that all ... should have no doubt about my profession', p. 73.

[13] Something that Lushington himself found difficult to achieve. F. Lushington, *Portrait of a Young Man* (Faber and Faber, London, n.d. [c. 1940]), p. 76.

[14] Lord Latymer, *Chances and Changes* (William Blackwood and Sons, Edinburgh, 1931), p. 10. But see also pp. 38–9.

[15] They were also much more likely to record instances when they were teased, rather than when they themselves teased others.

[16] E. Barker, *Father of the Man: Memories of Cheshire, Lancashire and Oxford, 1874–1898* (The National Council of Social Service, London, m.d., [c. 1948]), p. 24. See also L. Golding, *The World I Knew* (Hutchinson, London, n.d. [c. 1940]), p. 10.

[17] A. Powell, *A Question of Upbringing* (Mandarin, London, 1991; first published 1951), p. 5.

his insouciance seems to have been the exception, rather than the rule.[18] Around thirty years earlier, V.W. Garratt and his brother had become choir boys. This meant wearing their best suits, starched linen collars and mortarboard hats, which marked them as belonging to a 'Grand Order of Respectability'. They were met with howls of derision from the other boys in their working-class Birmingham neighbourhood, and with calls of 'Garrity the howlers', 'look at the starchies' and 'twoppence for yer splice, Garrity!'[19] Retribution was likely to follow from small, as well as from more thorough deviations from the accepted style. While studying at Eton in the immediate post-First World War period, Henry Green had taken to wearing 'a greatcoat which was longer than it might have been'. Even for this relatively mild rebellion, 'for some time ... [he] was not allowed to forget'.[20] Ultimately, among boys as among adults, it arguably was difference itself, rather than specific garments, the way of wearing them or their condition, that was the real object of condemnation. After all, if dress served both to signal and to reinforce collective male identities, sartorial non-conformity could imply their rejection: many, if not most, men clearly found this threatening and impossible to tolerate.

There were a variety of reasons why an individual could fail to 'fit in', and perform the 'face work' needed to be perceived by others as 'normal'.[21] Scholars have to date devoted most attention to conscious attempts – by a minority of men and women – to challenge and subvert dominant styles, in order to pursue more or less coherent and explicit political or cultural agendas.[22] However, less attention has been paid to the motives for 'unwilling', or perhaps more accurately, 'apolitical' non-conformity. The kind of non-conformity practised by individuals like the youthful G.R. Lamb. When the ten-year-old Lamb, the son of a hard-pressed working-class widow, won a grammar-school scholarship in the inter-war period, this meant a constant struggle to find the money for the necessary pieces of kit. On one particularly memorable

---

[18]   A. McRobbie, *A Privileged Boyhood* (Richard Stenleke Publishing, Ochiltree, 1996), p. 11. See also Chapter 1 above.

[19]   Garratt, *A Man in the Street*, pp. 35–6. See also J. Springhall, 'Building character in the British boy: the attempt to extend Christian manliness to working-class adolescents, 1880 to 1914', in J.A. Mangan and J. Walvin (eds), *Manliness and Morality: Middle-Class Masculinity in Britain and America, 1800–1940* (Manchester University Press, Manchester, 1987), p. 60, for jeers directed at the uniforms of organisations such as the Boys' Brigade.

[20]   H. Green, *Pack My Bag: A Self-Portrait* (The Hogarth Press, London, 1992; first published 1940), p. 68.

[21]   E. Goffman, *The Presentation of Self in Everyday Life* (1971), quoted in J. Entwistle, *The Fashioned Body: Fashion, Dress and Modern Social Theory* (Polity Press, Cambridge, 2000), p. 11.

[22]   See, for example, C. Breward, *Fashioning London: Clothing and the Modern Metropolis* (Berg, Oxford, 2004), chapters 1 and 5; D. Hebdige, *Subculture: The Meaning of Style* (Routledge, London, 2003; first published 1979); P. Hodgkinson, *Goth: Identity, Style and Subculture* (Berg, Oxford, 2002); W. Parkins (ed.), *Fashioning the Body Politic: Dress, Gender, Citizenship* (Berg, Oxford, 2002); D. Muggleton, *Inside Subculture: The Postmodern Meaning of Style* (Berg, Oxford, 2000); J. Bourke, 'The great male renunciation: men's dress reform in inter-war Britain', *Journal of Design History*, vol. 9, no. 1 (1996), pp. 23–33; B. Burman, 'Better and brighter clothes: the Men's Dress Reform Party, 1929–1940', *Journal of Design History*, vol. 8, no. 4 (1995), pp. 275–90; Cosgrove, 'The zoot suit and style warfare'; E. Wilson, *Adorned in Dreams: Fashion and Modernity* (Virago, London, 1985), pp. 179–227.

occasion, he had asked his mother for a pair of football shorts. She convinced him that a cut-down bathing costume would serve just as well, and – wrongly, as it turned out – that nobody would be able to tell the difference. According to Lamb, her refusal to buy the 'proper' garment 'may have been because my mother did not realise the gravity of the matter', but even he had to admit that it was 'more probably because the five or six shillings were more than she could afford that week'.[23]

Incomes, expenditure and affordability

G.R. Lamb's mother was undoubtedly not alone in having her family's sartorial options curtailed by financial necessity. Indeed, although this book has up to this point stressed the social and cultural pressures on men's sartorial decisions, there is no doubt that economic factors, and most notably income and availability of supply, also played a fundamental role in determining men's choice of clothes and methods of acquiring them. Having said this, it is almost impossible to make generalisations about how much, or what proportion of their (or their family's) income men spent on clothes in this period. There were simply too many variables, alongside those of price and income, including the expectations associated with individuals' status and occupation, the dressmaking abilities of family members (most often the mother or wife), the extent of other responsibilities and drains on income, particularly family responsibilities, the ability and opportunity to secure 'bargains', and so on.[24]

B. Seebohm Rowntree calculated in 1901 that 26 shillings was the very lowest sum a man could spend on clothes every year, where 'the clothing should be adequate to keep the man in health, and should not be so shabby as to injure his chances of obtaining respectable employment'. Unsurprisingly, in reality the annual expenditure on clothes of individual working-class interviewees varied considerably, ranging from a man who claimed an expenditure of only 22 shillings a year, to a man who spent the, by comparison, princely sum of 37s 3d.[25] The amounts spent may have differed, but the purchases were broadly similar: one change of outerwear and a few shirts and socks per year. For a skilled man in regular employment, earning an annual wage of around £100, an expenditure of 26s a year on clothes was neither

[23] Once on the football pitch, one of the other boys asked Lamb whether his shorts were part of a bathing costume. No one laughed, or in any way teased him, but Lamb 'felt deeply the difference between thick, wide, blue shorts and narrow, thin, black bathing trunks, and this to me was all the difference between the average fee-paying pupil at the grammar school and the boys like me, the scholarship boys'. G.R. Lamb, *Roman Road* (Sheed and Ward, London, 1950), pp. 24–5.

[24] A. Morrison, 'Family budgets no. 1: a workman's budget', *The Cornhill Magazine*, April 1901, p. 454. It is also worth noting that when contemporary social investigators provided information concerning budgets, they tended to give details of families' expenditure and income, rather than those of individuals.

[25] B.S. Rowntree, *Poverty: A Study of Town Life* (Macmillan, London, 1903; first published 1901), pp. 107–8, 393–4. The former included a pair of boots and repairs for 7s, 4 pairs of socks for 2s, a second-hand coat, vest (waistcoat) and trousers for 8s, 2 shirts for 4s and a cap and scarf for 1s; the latter included boots and repairs for 11s, 4 pairs of socks for 3s, a second-hand coat and vest for 5s 6d, one pair of trousers and repairs for 7s 6d, an overcoat for 15s spread over three years, 3 shirts at 4s, a cap and scarf at 1s 3d.

unreasonable nor unattainable. However, much could disrupt a family's purchasing strategies: unemployment, illness, or a variety of competing demands on the family budget. For the majority of working men who earned a good deal less than £100 a year, expenditure on clothes could rarely have reached 26s: for the 27 per cent of the population that in 1901 lived in poverty, either 'primary' or 'secondary', even such modest expenditure was wholly unthinkable.[26]

According to the social investigator and philanthropist Mrs Bosanquet, expenditure on dress was the most elastic item in working-class family budgets: it could expand if finances permitted, and contract if circumstances became more straitened, with boots being the most onerous item. In the case of the very poorest, she believed that 'a few pence during the year for each member of the family will probably suffice to keep them covered, at more than that they scarcely aim'.[27] More polemically, the economist L.G. Chiozza Money stated that in 1905 roughly half of the population was forced to live on such slender and insecure incomes that, once food, rent, fuel and light had all been paid for, only 'a few odd shillings' were left over for all other expenditure, including clothes and footwear.[28]

Clothes purchase could prove problematic also outside the ranks of the poor. According to George Orwell, a seemingly decent income of £400 a year meant that 'theoretically you knew how to wear your clothes and how to order dinner, although in practice you could never afford to go to a decent tailor or a decent restaurant'.[29] Furthermore, it was widely acknowledged that certain occupations that paid a good deal less than £400 a year, nevertheless required an unreasonably high expenditure on dress: clerical and shop work being two obvious examples. In his (her?) contribution to *The Cornhill Magazine*'s 1901 study of family budgets, G.S. Layard stressed that, in those occupations which involved contact with the public, 'employees, whether they be salesmen in shops or clerks in banks or offices, must be habited in what may be called a decent professional garb', or risk losing their position. Relatively cheap clothing was certainly available. Although evening clothes bought from the best Savile Row tailors would have cost up to 11 guineas, made-to-measure lounge suits could be purchased at the turn of the century for around 30s, and indeed for as little as 20s, while the average price of a made-to-measure lounge suit considered suitable for a middle-class customer seems to have been £2 2s, ranging between 35s and 44s 6d. Nevertheless, 'the average "lower-middle" breadwinner is forced into an extravagance in the matter of clothes out of all proportion to his income'. According to Layard, lower-middle-class men earning between £150 and £200 per year would

---

[26] Terms coined by Rowntree, *Poverty*. Discussed in R. Floud, 'Britain, 1860–1914: a survey', in R. Floud and D. McCloskey (eds), *The Economic History of Britain since 1700. Vol. 2: 1860–1939* (Cambridge University Press, Cambridge, second edition 1994; first published 1981), p. 11. In 1906, it was estimated that average adult male earnings (taking into account overtime and short time) were 27s a week, or c. £70 a year. J. Stevenson, *British Society 1914–45* (Penguin, Harmondsworth, 1990; first published 1984), p. 38. The expenditure figures for the inter-war period are discussed in Chapter 4.

[27] Mrs B. Bosanquet, *Rich and Poor* (Macmillan, London, 1896), p. 85.

[28] L.G. Chiozza Money, *Riches and Poverty* (Methuen, London, 1905), p. 141. See also J. Burnett, *A History of the Cost of Living* (Penguin Books, Harmodsworth, 1969), pp. 278–9.

[29] Quoted in Stevenson, *British Society 1914–45*, pp. 32–3.

have to spend approximately £6 on clothes.[30] A higher income, it was estimated, did not necessarily correspond to an equal increase in the proportion spent on clothes: of a comfortable yearly income of £800, £40 would be spent on the man's clothes; of £1800, £200 would serve for both husband and wife; and of £10000, 'Both the man and the woman would require £450 for clothes, private expenses, and subscriptions'.[31] Perhaps less obvious, but no less real, was the heavy expense incurred by workers engaged in heavy industrial occupations, such as those employed in the Warrington ironworks. This was partly because the nature of the work meant that clothes and boots had to be replaced fairly frequently, and partly because it was considered healthier to wear items such as flannel shirts, rather than the cheaper cotton ones.[32]

Turning for a moment from the bewildering array of individual circumstances to the general picture provided by national statistics, it is clear that the trend from the Victorian to the inter-war period was one of increased expenditure on clothing and other consumer goods on the part of a growing population,[33] which in the long run benefited from rising real incomes and smaller families.[34] It has been estimated that at constant (1900) prices, consumers' expenditure more than doubled between 1870 and 1913, further increasing by a fourth between 1913 and 1939 (at constant 1938 prices).[35] In the

---

[30]   G.S. Layard, 'Family budgets no. 2: a lower-middle-class budget', *The Cornhill Magazine*, May 1901, pp. 660–61, 666. This represented between 4 and 3 per cent of the budget. £13 was the sum spent on clothes for the wife and two children. For prices, see J. Camplin, *The Rise of the Plutocrats: Wealth and Power in Edwardian England* (Constable, London, 1978), quoted in C. Breward, *The Hidden Consumer: Masculinities, Fashion and City Life 1860–1914* (Manchester University Press, Manchester, 1999), p. 60; L. Ugolini, 'Men, masculinities and menswear advertising, c. 1890–1914', in J. Benson and L. Ugolini (eds), *A Nation of Shopkeepers: Five Centuries of British Retailing* (I.B. Tauris, London, 2003), pp. 80–104; W. Macqueen-Pope, *Twenty Shillings in the Pound* (Hutchinson, London, n.d. [c. 1949]), p. 184.

[31]   G. Colmore, 'Family budgets no. 3: eight hundred a year', *The Cornhill Magazine*, June 1901, p. 796; Mrs Earle, 'Family budgets no. 4: eighteen hundred a year', *The Cornhill Magazine*, July 1901, p. 51; Lady Agnew, 'Family budgets no. 5: ten thousand a year', *The Cornhill Magazine*, August 1901, p. 190. The average spent on the paterfamilias' clothes ranged between 4.5 and 5.5 per cent in all budgets of £800 a year and over.

[32]   A.L. Bowley and A.R. Burnett-Hurst, *Livelihood and Poverty* (G. Bell, London, 1915), p. 119. See also Lady Bell, *At the Works: A Study of a Manufacturing Town* (Virago, London, 1985; first published 1907), pp. 71–2. For the relationship between income and expenditure on clothes, see also Breward, *The Hidden Consumer*, pp. 81–6.

[33]   The population of Britain grew from just over 23 million in 1861 to almost 41 million in 1911, then much more slowly to over 46 million in 1939. D. Baines, 'Population, migration and regional development, 1870–1939', in Floud and McCloskey (eds), *The Economic History of Britain*, p. 30.

[34]   J. Benson, *Affluence and Authority: A Social History of Twentieth-Century Britain* (Hodder Arnold, London, 2005), chapters 1 and 2; J. Benson, *The Rise of Consumer Society in Britain 1880–1980* (Longman, Harlow, 1994), chapter 1; Floud, 'Britain, 1860–1914: a survey', pp. 1–28; Stevenson, *British Society 1914–45*, chapter 1.

[35]   C.H. Feinstein, *National Income, Expenditure and Output of the United Kingdom 1855–1965* (Cambridge University Press, Cambridge, 1972) pp. T14–16. See also C. Lee, 'The service industries', in Floud and McCloskey (eds), *The Economic History of Britain*, p. 126. The two world wars were the exceptions to this picture of steadily increasing consumer expenditure: pre-First World War expenditure levels were not restored until 1927.

shorter term, however, the picture presented by statistics of Edwardian consumption does not seem quite so rosy. John Stevenson points out that in the 1890s the prices of consumer goods had begun to increase after almost fifty years of decline, so that by 1914 real wages were lower than at the turn of the century, having fallen by as much as 6 per cent between 1900 and 1912.[36] As far as clothing was concerned, Figure 2.1 shows that expenditure in the UK increased steadily between 1900 and 1919, despite dips between 1913–14 and 1915–16. By 1919, expenditure had more than quadrupled from its 1900 level (from £127m to £597m).

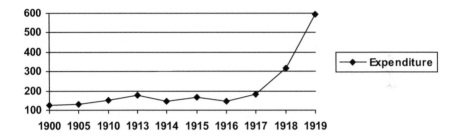

Figure 2.1   Total   UK   expenditure   on   clothing,   1900–1919   (in   £m).
Source: **A.R. Prest with A.A. Adams, *Consumers' Expenditure in the United Kingdom, 1900–1919* (Cambridge University Press, Cambridge, 1954), p. 123.**

However, while apparently impressive, these figures are in reality misleading, as they do not take into account price inflation. As Figure 2.2 indicates, the price of clothing grew steadily between 1900 and 1915 (with a dip between 1913 and 1914), peaking sharply between 1915 and 1919. It is not surprising, then, to find that the quantity of clothes sold grew slowly and uncertainly before the war, and actually fell after 1915, only beginning to recover after the end of hostilities.[37] According to A.R. Prest, 'It does appear that consumption … [of clothing] failed to show any expansion in the early years of the century. Even the rise between 1900 and 1913 was little more than sufficient to compensate for the increased population.'[38]

Of course, it is not easy to relate such general trends to individuals' varied experiences of clothes consumption. However, some conclusions can be drawn. Firstly, in the thirty-odd years before the outbreak of the First World War (changes during and after the war will be considered in greater detail in the next two chapters), a significant minority of the population could ill afford the purchase of even a bare minimum of clothing, although very cheap clothes (especially second-hand ones) were available, particularly for consumers with access to urban markets.

---

[36]   Stevenson, *British Society 1914–45*, pp. 37–8.

[37]   Clothes consumption during the war will be considered further in Chapter 3.

[38]   A.R. Prest with A.A. Adams, *Consumers' Expenditure in the United Kingdom, 1900–1919* (Cambridge University Press, Cambridge, 1954), p. 9.

Secondly, this period was also characterised by a staggering inequality in incomes and wealth, whereby around 5 per cent of the population enjoyed almost 50 per cent of the national income.[39] Among this small minority of very rich people could be found the small, but highly visible, section of the male population who could

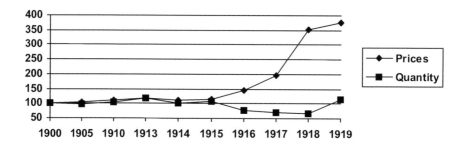

Figure 2.2   UK price increases and quantity index: clothing 1900–1919 (1900=100).
Source: **A.R. Prest with A.A. Adams, *Consumers' Expenditure in the United Kingdom, 1900–1919* (Cambridge University Press, Cambridge, 1954), p. 123.**

afford to patronise the best – and most expensive – tailors in London's West End, and construct for themselves an identity as 'English gentlemen'.

Between the two extremes of the very poor and the very rich, there was the majority of the population, who, when all went well, could afford regular purchases of outfitting items and footwear, as well as the occasional splash-out on a new suit and overcoat, perhaps once or twice a year. However, there was little sign of a sartorial consumer boom in the first two decades of the century: more money was spent as prices rose, but increases in the quantity of clothes purchased barely matched the population growth. Furthermore, as far as individuals were concerned, when illness, death or unemployment struck, or when there were too many mouths to feed on wages or salaries that were simply too small to cope with all the demands made upon them, then it was time to tighten the belt. Perhaps the purchase of a new spring suit would have to be postponed, or new patches added to underwear, or, indeed, an old pair of swimming trunks would have to be cut down to try and provide Lamb junior with a much desired pair of football shorts.

Family responsibilities and bread-winning

It has been suggested in the preceding section that it is impossible to generalise about the amount of money paid by British men for clothes, or to provide reliable

---

[39]   Stevenson observes that 'In 1914 under 4 per cent of those who died in Britain accounted for nearly 90 per cent of the entire capital value bequeathed'. Stevenson, *British Society 1914–45*, p. 30.

figures detailing the annual expenditure of the 'typical' consumer. Nonetheless, there clearly did exist more or less explicit understandings about the appropriate amounts that men could spend on their appearance, without being tainted by suggestions of selfish extravagance. Such understandings were closely linked to age, or perhaps more accurately, to life-cycle stage. Indeed, throughout the period being considered in this book, young unmarried wage-earners enjoyed a greater leeway in their sartorial expenditure than their fathers and other married men. According to Jim Bullock, in the mining village of Bowers Row it was 'the bachelors' who on Sundays 'dressed particularly smartly, some of them wearing spats over their shoes as well as velvet waistcoats adorned with a watch chain'.[40] Similarly, among the middle classes, 'youth was allowed to have its fling. The young man's clothes were more jaunty and more amenable to fashion. He could ... wear brown suits, and he did. He could have striped suits and checked suits, and he did.'[41]

Especially in families living on limited budgets, any sartorial and other extravagances on the part of the father were perceived as a reprehensible deflecting of resources away from the family onto individual consumption. In the case of John Blake's father, selfish expenditure on dress and drink were inextricably linked.[42] For a paterfamilias to dress too well implied a reprehensible rejection of the role of husband and family provider. In the Glasgow tenement where Molly Weir grew up in the inter-war years, 'there was even a dandy ... who donned yellow chamois gloves when he went out courting another woman, not his wife'. He was, according to his mother-in-law, '"a rotter. He's lived on the steps o' the jile a' his life."'[43]

Such reckless expenditure tended to attract particular opprobrium when undertaken by poor working-class men, but was not unique to them: V.S. Pritchett's mother, for example, viewed with bitterness the elegant and expensive suits owned by her husband, 'the impressive Managing Director ... knowing she couldn't get a penny out of him' for their children's clothes.[44] In Guy Thorne's sensational novel *When it Was Dark: The Story of a Great Conspiracy*, a 1903 best-seller, the debauched side of one of the characters' nature was demonstrated not only by the fact that he

---

[40]   J. Bullock, *Bowers Row: Recollections of a Mining Village* (EP Publishing, Wakefield, 1976), pp. 19–20.

[41]   Macqueen-Pope, *Twenty Shillings in the Pound*, p. 179.

[42]   J. Blake, *Memories of Old Poplar* (Stepney Books Publications, London, 1977), p. 11. Expenditure on drink or gambling was considered by contemporaries as a much more common source of 'wrongful' masculine consumption than dress. E. Ross, *Love and Toil: Motherhood in Outcast London, 1870–1918* (Oxford University Press, Oxford, 1993), especially chapters 2 and 3; Garratt, *A Man in the Street*, p. 7; V. de Vesselitsky, *Expenditure and Waste: A Study in War-Time* (Ratan Tata Foundation, London, 1917), p. 45. The same was true of the inter-war period. See, for example, Goldman, *East End my Cradle*, p. 6; A. Granger, *Life's a Gamble* (New Horizon, Bognor Regis, 1983), p. 1; A. Hughes, 'Representation and counter-representation of domestic violence on Clydeside between the two world wars', *Labour History Review*, vol. 62, no. 2 (2004), pp. 169–84; S. Humphries and P. Gordon, *A Labour of Love: The Experience of Parenthood in Britain 1900–1950* (Sidgwick and Jackson, London, 1993), p. 99.

[43]   M. Weir, *Shoes Were for Sunday* (Hutchinson, London, 1970), p. 17.

[44]   V.S. Pritchett, *A Cab at the Door* (1968), quoted in J. Watt (ed.), *The Penguin Book of Twentieth-Century Fashion Writing* (Penguin Books, London, 2000; first published 1999), p. 5.

possessed 'A huge wardrobe, full of clothes neatly folded and put away, [which] suggested a man about town, a dandy with many sartorial interests', but also by the fact that this extravagance was not matched by any comparable expenditure on his family. He gave no money to his wife, and treated their home as a hotel, further clear proof of his despicable nature.[45] This was of course a fictional exaggeration, but the impact an improvident and selfish father could have on the well-being of his family was well-known. It was vividly illustrated by a song, popular in the vicinity of the Sussex village of Rottingdean, entitled 'Corduroy': 'My father was fond of lush and emptied many a butt / And for to get a suit of togs we had to stinge our guts / Oftimes my mother and I dine off a savaloy / to save up the "browns" to buy me a suit of corduroy.' On the other hand, when the father was a 'carefully respectable' bread-winner, like C.H. Rolph's policeman father, a non-smoker and teetotaller, 'his children could have shoes on their feet, adequate if makeshift clothes on their bodies, an occasional haircut, and reasonably distended bellies', even on the slender wage of 28 shillings a week.[46]

The association of an interest in clothes with youth, rather than with married, middle-aged or older men, seems to have been born out of a complex relationship with financial and cultural constraints on the expenditure of men with dependent families. It is not therefore surprising that autobiographies of the period often tended to distance the – now older – author from his younger self, who could acceptably acknowledge an interest in clothes: '… when I was young and particular, I was inclined to be rather dressy'.[47] Or, as the writer and broadcaster J.B. Priestley put it, his sixteen-year-old self was 'going through a dandy phase, trying to be dressy – in a floppy-tie and pegtop trousers style – on tuppence'.[48] However, disapproval of attention to appearance on the part of married or middle-aged men should not be exaggerated. According to Alexander Paterson, the 'personal vanity' that was at the

---

[45]   G. Thorne, *When it Was Dark: The Story of a Great Conspiracy* (Greening, London, 1904; first published 1903), pp. 58–60.

[46]   B. Copper, *Early to Rise: A Sussex Boyhood* (Heinemann, London, 1976), p. 222; C.H. Rolph, *London Particulars* (Oxford University Press, Oxford, 1980), pp. 11–12. For the male bread-winner ideal, see also B. Turner, *About Myself 1863–1930* (Humphrey Toulmin at the Cayme Press, London, 1930), p. 67; P. Ayers, 'The making of men: masculinities in interwar Liverpool', in M. Walsh (ed.), *Working Out Gender: Perspectives from Labour History* (Ashgate, Aldershot, 1999), pp. 66–83, especially pp. 71–5; A. Davies, *Leisure, Gender and Poverty: Working-Class Culture in Salford and Manchester 1900–1939* (Open University Press, Buckingham, 1992), pp. 31–54. What from one perspective was seen as selfish self-indulgence, from another was seen as the assertion of rightful male authority. According to Edward Wifen, born in Colchester in 1897, in his youth 'the general idea and even now is that if a man hands everything over to his wife and she gives him some back is that he's not much of a man'. National Social Policy and Social Change Archive, Albert Sloman Library, University of Essex (NSPSC Archive), The Edwardians: Family Life and Work Experience Before 1918, oral history collection (The Edwardians), QD1/FLWE/9, interview transcript, Mr Edward William Wifen, mineral water bottler, Colchester.

[47]   Pearson, *The Doings of a Country Solicitor*, p. 78.

[48]   J.B. Priestley, *Margin Released: A Writer's Reminiscences and Reflections* (Heinemann, London, 1962), p. 20.

basis of the 'passion for new clothes that are very obviously new, and that are also tight, smart, and uncomfortable', 'may be curbed forcibly by low wages and high prices, but never dies'.[49] Others agreed, whilst adopting a less censorious tone. The dockers who in pre-World War One Salford frequented the Britannia Inn at the week-end, for example, made a point of dressing up 'by adding a 6½ d dicky in front of their old shirt'. This was perceived within the local community not as a useless waste of scarce resources, but as an important signal of 'respectability', and a resolute attempt at 'keeping up appearances' in the face of grinding poverty.[50] Indeed, the clothes of even the most responsible and provident of paterfamilias were not always entirely plain and functional. Stan Dickens's large family may have been poor and frugal, 'deprived of luxuries and sometimes of necessities', but his father's appearance was not devoid of small extra ornaments, such as the 'medallions and ... gold sovereign suspended from a large watch chain suspended across [his] ... waistcoat'.[51] While the hostility of men like John Blake towards their fathers' spending habits is clear, others adopted a different attitude. Alfred Green, for example, remembered how in the 1920s his much-loved father would always manage to look 'well turned out', even during spells of unemployment. Tellingly, Green was at pains to emphasise that neither this well-dressed appearance, nor his father's enjoyment of an occasional 'flutter' on the horses, was at the family's expense: 'I never remember his having a new suit or coat', and the amount of money he spent on himself 'was the barest amount possible to meet his needs'.[52]

Where financial circumstances permitted (or employment required it), expenditure on clothes and interest in sartorial matters on the part of the paterfamilias seems to have been taken for granted. Jack Smithers' father, the well-known publisher Leonard Smithers, 'dressed well, and insisted on all in his house doing the same'.[53] Richard Wollheim's father, a successful theatrical impresario, was for his son a great source of sartorial information, if not of much in the way of a 'moral education'. By watching him getting dressed in the morning, the younger Wollheim

> learnt how to choose a shirt ... how to hold up my socks with garters ... how to use the forefinger of the right hand to make a dimple in the knot of my tie ... how to fold a handkerchief, and to dab it with eau de cologne before putting it into my breast pocket, and, above all, I learnt that it was only through the meticulous attention to such rituals that a man could hope to make his body tolerable to the world.[54]

In such cases, it was a slovenly appearance that was seen as reprehensible. A very

[49]   A. Paterson, *Across the Bridges or Life by the South London River-Side* (Edward Arnold, London, 1911), pp. 37–8.

[50]   Davies, *Leisure, Gender and Poverty*, p. 35. See also Copper, *Early to Rise*, p. 112.

[51]   S. Dickens, *Bending the Twig* (Arthur H. Stockwell, Ilfracombe, 1975), p. 19.

[52]   A. Green, *Growing Up in Attercliffe: Honey with a Ladle, Vinegar with a Teaspoon* (New City, Sheffield, 1981), pp. 54–6.

[53]   J. Smithers, *The Early Life and Vicissitudes of Jack Smithers: An Autobiography* (Martin Secker, London, 1939), pp. 15–16.

[54]   R. Wollheim, *Germs: A Memoir of Childhood* (Black Swan, London, 2005; first published 2004), p. 24.

young Laurence Hanson was embarrassed to note, when having lunch in London with his father, a successful builder and surveyor, that most of the men sitting at other tables were wearing silk hats and elegant long black coats. Hanson 'wondered almost in panic whether they were allowed to sit in company with these gloriously apparelled people'. His father, meantime, oblivious to his scruffy appearance and his son's discomfort, 'sat up in his grey tweed jacket and breeches entirely unconcerned, issuing orders right and left'.[55] Edward Blishen's father's and uncles' 'immaculacy' in dress, furthermore, was not only a visible reflection of the Blishens' 'ability to rub two ha'pennies together', and 'their riposte to the world of the slums – but also curious evidence of their notion of manliness, which depended on the curl of the brim of a bowler hat, the set of a suit'.[56] While Edward Blishen turned against his father's punctiliousness, other youngsters were keen to follow in their fathers' footsteps, and used them as their sartorial models. George Cook grew up in Homerton in the 1930s and 1940s, where he was friendly with a nearby family. The eldest son, 'like his Dad was a bit of a "dandy"'.[57]

Childhood and consumer autonomy

Some middle-aged men with families to support may have defied sartorial conventions as part of a wider rejection of their roles as bread-winners, choosing instead to spend their earnings on goods and services for personal consumption. Children's non-conformity to accepted codes, on the other hand, seems to have been a more passive one. Indeed, the most notable characteristic of boys' clothing in this period was the almost complete parental – usually maternal – authority (and responsibility) in the matter of apparel. Remembering the awful experience of being made to wear a clean shirt made of 'loathsome' and prickly Welsh flannel, ('considered a safeguard against bronchitis, whooping cough and croup') every Sunday morning, Rhys Davies tellingly characterised it as 'the victory of authority against my howling protests ... Maturing age can at least bestow liberty. To be very young is not to be free. The worst period lies between, roughly, the ages of five and twelve.'[58]

Parental – especially maternal – ignorance and lack of understanding of what was acceptable wear among young contemporaries was often mentioned in autobiographical accounts. According to B.G.A. Cannell, the son of a doctor, it was such ignorance that led to his being dressed every Sunday in a King Charles black velvet suit. This, together with his long golden hair, meant that 'I suffered greatly

---

[55]   L. Hanson, *Shining Morning Face: The Childhood of Lance* (George Allen and Unwin, London, 1948), p. 59.

[56]   E. Blishen, *Sorry Dad* (Allison and Busby, London, 1984; first published 1978), pp. 44, 101. Blishen was referring to the 1920s. See also McRobbie, *A Privileged Boyhood*, p. 48.

[57]   G.A. Cook, *A Hackney Memory Chest* (Centerprise Trust, London, 1983), p. 25.

[58]   Davies, *Print of a Hare's Foot*, pp. 16–17. See also H. Cunningham, *Children and Childhood in Western Society since 1500* (Longman, Harlow, 1995), pp. 180–85; NSPSC Archive, The Edwardians, QD1/FLWE/11, interview transcript, Mr Norris Thompson, manger/owner of family shop.

at school from the other boys'.[59] James Barke, who grew up on an estate in central Scotland before and during the First World War, was teased by two older boys about the kilt his mother forced him to wear: 'Their chant, in unison, "kiltie, kiltie, cold baum" ... was by no means the most offensive.'[60] C.H. Middleton wondered 'whether fond mothers ... realize [*sic*] the misery they inflict by trying to make their sons look a little superior to the common herd'.[61]

It may have been the case that the priorities of at least some mothers were different, and indeed to some extent at odds, with those of their sons. Louis Heren's mother 'had firm ideas on how I should be dressed ... [which] set me apart from my ragged schoolmates' in inter-war East London. While he 'resented' his 'neatness', to his widowed mother this represented the outward symbol of her ability to earn a living and decently support her family.[62] The approval of friends and acquaintances may have been more important to many women than that of their sons. When C.H. Middleton's mother bought black 'billycock' hats for him and his brother, rather than the caps all the other boys were wearing, her choice was endorsed by her 'cronies', who 'declared that we looked "awfully nice" in them; quite little gentlemen ... compared with the other village boys'.[63]

It is possible that children's lack of control over clothes was representative of their more general powerlessness vis-à-vis adults. It was certainly the case that children rarely chose the clothes they wore, middle-class children generally having little more say in the matter than their working-class counterparts. John Tosh has observed that the last decades of the nineteenth century were characterised – as far as middle-class boys were concerned – by a 'prolonging of material dependence on adults', as entry into the professions increasingly required schooling at least until 18 or 19.[64] This powerlessness was brought home particularly painfully to the writer Laurence Housman, when as a schoolboy he was publicly told by an unpleasant

---

[59] B.G.A. Cannell, *From Monk to Busman: An Autobiography* (Skeffington, London, 1935), pp. 16–17. Cannell was born in 1876.

[60] J. Barke, *The Green Hills Far Away: A Chapter in Autobiography* (Collins, London, 1940), p. 74.

[61] C.H. Middleton, *Village Memories: A Collection of Short Stories and Reminiscences of Village Life* (Cassell, London, 1941), p. 75. See also L. Kerr, *The Eager Years: An Autobiography* (Collins, London, 1940), p. 13, where it was his sister who bought him a distinctive green sports coat.

[62] L. Heren, *Growing Up Poor in London* (Phoenix, London, 2001; first published 1973), pp. 54–5.

[63] Middleton, *Village Memories*, p. 75. See also R.L. Lee, *The Town that Died!* (R.L. Lee, London, 1930), pp. 124–5; C. Hosgood, 'Mrs Pooter's purchase: lower middle-class consumerism and the sales, 1870–1914', in Kidd and Nicholls (eds), *Gender, Civic Culture and Consumerism*, pp. 146–63. However, Daniel Miller rightly cautions against reducing women's purchasing practices to a 'selfish' weighing up of costs and benefits. Drawing upon an ethnographic investigation carried out in the 1990s in North London, he suggests that 'shopping is primarily an act of love, that in its daily conscientiousness becomes one of the primary means by which relations of love and care are constituted in practice'. D. Miller, *A Theory of Shopping* (Polity Press, Cambridge, 1998), p. 18.

[64] J. Tosh, *A Man's Place: Masculinity and the Middle-Class Home in Victorian England* (Yale University Press, New Haven, 1999), p. 150.

headmaster that he should come to school better dressed, as though he was 'responsible for the clothes with which parental carelessness had provided him', and stupidly presuming that 'a boy of eleven had the ordering of his own clothes'.[65]

The timing of the achievement of sartorial independence varied enormously between individuals. The sixteen-year-old Michael Hope, the son of a prosperous manufacturer, received an allowance from his parents, which enabled him to buy his own clothes while still at boarding school.[66] However, the experiences of Ernald James seem to have been more typical. At eighteen, after many family sacrifices, he passed his teaching exams and qualified as Uncertified Assistant Master. As a 'reward' his parents allowed him to buy a new pair of boots, and 'to go to the shop personally and unaccompanied and make my own choice'. Not only was this a 'tremendous concession', but it was also one of those 'apparently small things of life [which] leave an ineffaceable impression'.[67] Lord Latymer considered that for many public school-educated boys, university provided the first real opportunity to exercise one's own sartorial choices and express one's individuality 'after so many years of self-curtailment'.[68] The Duke of Windsor also remarked that, as Prince of Wales (and future King Edward VIII), it was only when he went to Oxford that he obtained 'some degree of social and sartorial freedom'.[69]

Entry into the world of waged work, the assumption of a male 'adult' identity and the acquisition of control over one's consumption choices were closely interwoven. According to Alexander Paterson, the average Edwardian working-class boy entered the workplace at fourteen. From this point onwards, not only was he allowed to spend his holidays as he wished and stay out until 10 or 11 o'clock in the evening, but also to a large extent buy his own clothes.[70] However, this assessment seems rather over-optimistic: teenage wage-earners, often not yet earning a 'man's' wage, frequently remained dependent on their parents – generally their mother – for the purchase of clothing, at least a few years into their working lives.[71] During the First World War, the fourteen-year-old Mr Keble left school to become a telegraph boy in Colchester. Of his meagre starting salary, he handed 4 shillings over to his mother, which only left him with 1 shilling a week to 'go towards a bit of clothing'.[72] Even teenagers from relatively

---

[65]   L. Houseman, *The Unexpected Years* (Jonathan Cape, London, 1937), pp. 85–6. See also N. Nicholson, *Wednesday Early Closing* (Faber and Faber, London, 1975), pp. 155–6.

[66]   NSPSC Archive, The Edwardians, QD1/FLWE/MUC/2019, interview transcript, Mr Michael Hope, director of family business, Birmingham.

[67]   E. James, *Unforgettable Countryfolk: Midlands Reminiscences* (Cornish Brothers, Birmingham, n.d. [c. 1948]), p. 48.

[68]   Lord Latymer, *Chances and Changes*, p. 39.

[69]   Duke of Windsor, *A Family Album* (Cassell, London, 1960), p. 44.

[70]   Paterson, *Across the Bridges*, pp. 125–6. For contemporary concerns about young men's financial independence, see H. Hendrick, *Images of Youth: Age, Class and the Male Youth Problem, 1880–1920* (Clarendon Press, Oxford, 1990), pp. 119–54.

[71]   M. Loane, *An Englishman's Castle* (Edward Arnold, London, 1909), p. 183; C.E.B. Russell, *Manchester Boys: Sketches of Manchester Lads at Work and Play* (Neil Richardson, Manchester, 1984; first published 1905), p. 7.

[72]   NSPSC Archive, The Edwardians, QD1/FLWE/1, interview transcript, Mr Keble, postman, Colchester.

well-off backgrounds could struggle to manage. While at Sandhurst, the upper-class L.E.O. Charlton had tried to 'cut a dash' in London's night spots, but had found it hard going on a 'meagre' allowance of 30s a week.[73] Sartorial independence – however limited – was connected to entry into the workplace also for many middle-class school-leavers. In his semi-autobiographical novel *How Dear is Life*, Henry Williamson had the young hero, a novice insurance clerk, spend his first pay cheque on small, but far from insignificant purchases: a tenpenny ha'penny safety razor, a fourpenny ha'penny shaving brush, a twopenny stick of shaving soap, a one-and-threepenny nickel silver watch chain, and most important of all, 'a cork-lined silk hat for 12s 6d'.[74]

As shown in Chapter 1, the ways in which shifts in apparel reflected the process of 'growing up' is the sartorial change most often recorded in personal reminiscences, and consequently is the easiest one for the historian to trace. However, the continued role of clothing in marking stages in men's lives in adulthood and beyond should not therefore be ignored. When Neville Cardus's grandmother died, his grandfather marked the event by putting on black clothes, closing 'his *Sporting Chronicle Handicap Book* for ever' and refusing to 'take off his coat even at meal-times', while on a more cheerful note, Ernst Ambrose's wedding in 1909 was marked by his momentous purchase of a top hat.[75] Significantly, each sartorial rite of passage was characterised by a different degree of autonomy and choice. Indeed, if entry into the world of waged work marked the beginning of control over clothing purchases, exit may on the contrary (at least among the poor) have signified its loss. 'Mr N', in receipt in the early 1930s of a small old age pension and outdoor relief, mentioned to the interviewer for the *New Survey of London Life and Labour* that 'his nephews were very good to him and gave him all their old clothes to wear out and sometimes gave him new things'.[76]

From manly consumer to dandy

In his reminiscences of a childhood spent in a middle-class home in 1880s Glasgow, J.J. Bell observed that men had in those days been 'dreadfully afraid of looking "funny"', a description that could also accurately characterise men's (and boys') attitudes towards appearance and dress throughout the period considered in this book.[77] However, apart from the most flagrant examples of inappropriate clothing, it was not always easy to see where the exact boundary between looking well-dressed and looking 'funny' was. Judgements about what to wear had to be made on the basis

---

[73] L.E.O. Charlton, *Charlton* (Faber and Faber, London, 1931), p. 54.

[74] H. Williamson, *How Dear is Life* (Macdonald, London, 1984; first published 1954), p. 34.

[75] Cardus, *Autobiography*, p. 15; E. Ambrose, *Melford Memories: Recollections of 94 Years* (Long Melford Historical and Archaeological Society, Long Melford, n.d. [c. 1972]), p. 113. In the 1930s, a cousin's wedding was the occasion for the purchase of John Gillett's first grown-up suit. J.W. Gillett, *Once Upon Hard Times: Life in the Village of Higher Cloughford* (Rowtenstall Civic Society, Rowtenstall, 1981), p. 37.

[76] H. Llewellyn Smith (ed.), *The New Survey of London Life and Labour* (P.S. King and Son, London, 1931), vol. III, Appendix VI, p. 461.

[77] J.J. Bell, *I Remember* (The Porpoise Press, Edinburgh, 1932), p. 102.

of knowledge and experience, and compromises had to be negotiated by men whose pockets were rarely limitless. Decisions had to be reached taking into account both social context and individual circumstances. It seems clear, then, that in order not to stand out as odd, and thereby attract unwelcome attention and ridicule, men would have had to devote at least *some* attention to their dress. What is less clear, however, is at what point such attention would begin to seem excessive. When, in other words, did it become tainted with connotations of 'dandyism'?

By the end of the nineteenth century, the image of the dandy was no longer associated with the historically specific, Brummell-like figure of the Regency period, but had become 'generalised'.[78] Despite the impact on understandings of masculinity and appropriate sartorial behaviour often attributed to Oscar Wilde's trial in 1895,[79] the terminology of dandysim continued to be used to describe a wide range of sartorial practices considered more or less aberrant, but which were not necessarily linked to homosexuality. Upon starting work on a Welsh farm, one of the local people Sam Shaw became acquainted with was a man dressed in 'striped trousers, black coat, brown shoes, billycock hat and a very prominent white waistcoat', whom he described as 'a brainless local Beau Brummell', who could not read or write.[80] Although by no means unvarying, late Victorian and Edwardian journalistic representations tended to portray the 'dandy' – or 'masher', 'toff', 'nut', and so forth – as an overwhelmingly youthful individual whose 'meticulous and obsessive preoccupation' with dress 'marked him off from the common herd', although such a preoccupation was frequently matched by only a small income. The result was a figure ripe for ridicule, whose clothes ranged from the pathetic to the grotesque, but whose style nevertheless attracted women's admiration.[81]

Indeed, the dandy of popular representation, however effete, vain, lazy and ineffectual, was strongly associated with heterosexuality and with attractiveness to women[82] (Figure 2.3). The 'mashah' of a popular 1891 music hall song, was 'a tailor-made young fellah … the latest style in town', who despite still living with

[78]   Entwistle, *The Fashioned Body*, pp. 126–30. See also C. Breward, 'The dandy laid bare: embodying practices and fashion for men', in S. Bruzzi and P. Church Gibson (eds), *Fashion Cultures: Theories, Explorations and Analysis* (Routledge, London, 2000), pp. 221–38.

[79]   A. Sinfield, *The Wilde Century: Effeminacy, Oscar Wilde and the Queer Moment* (Cassell, London, 1994); E. Cohen, *Talk on the Wilde Side: Towards a Genealogy of a Discourse on Male Sexualities* (Routledge, London, 1993).

[80]   S. Shaw, *Guttersnipe* (Sampson Low, Marston, London, 1946), pp. 88–9.

[81]   P. Bailey, 'Champagne Charlie and the music-hall swell song', in P. Bailey, *Popular Culture and Performance in the Victorian City* (Cambridge University Press, Cambridge, 1998), pp. 101–27. See also J.R. Walkowitz, *City of Dreadful Delight: Narratives of Sexual Danger in Late Victorian London* (Virago, London, 1992), pp. 43–4.

[82]   *Tit-Bits*, Summer Annual, 1925. See also Breward, *The Hidden Consumer*, pp. 170–85, 246–9; S. Bruzzi, *Undressing Cinema: Clothing and Identity in the Movies* (Routledge, London, 1997), pp. 72–5; M. Boscagli, *Eye on the Flesh: Fashions of Masculinity in the Early Twentieth Century* (Westview Press, Oxford, 1996), pp. 30–33. For inter-war representations of the 'lounge lizard' see, for example, *Punch*, 9 March 1927. But see also R. Roberts, *The Classic Slum: Salford Life in the First Quarter of the Century* (Penguin Books, Harmondsworth, 1974; first published 1971), pp. 54–5, for dandyism's association with being a 'nancy'.

his 'mamma', was everywhere met with a chorus of approval from 'the girls': 'Aint he nice? Aint he sweet? Quite the latest style! What a face, full of grace, would kill You at half a mile!'[83] In J.B. Priestley's best-selling 1929 novel *The Good Companions*, Leonard Oakroyd and his friend Albert were depicted as 'the last of a long line, the last of the Macaronis, the Dandies, the Swells, the Mashers, the Knuts'. Although they did not know it, 'with them and their like was perishing, miserably and obscurely, an old tradition ... their old home, the West End, knows these figures no longer; their canes and yellow gloves, their pearl-buttoned fawn overcoats, their brilliantine and scents and bouquets, their music-hall promenade ... their ladies ... all have gone ... on their last tide of champagne.' However, 'the tradition of dandyism and ladykilling' persisted in towns like 'Bruddersford', where lads like Leonard and Albert 'lived for dress and girls, above all – not having the opportunities of a Brummell – for girls'.[84]

Unsurprisingly, it is not easy to determine the extent to which the figure of the dandy to emerge from popular culture actually corresponded to reality. There has been a tendency on the part of historians to view dandyism, whether that of the middle- and upper-class aesthete, or that of the working-class swell, as something apart from the clothing style of the majority of men.[85] References to individuals (mostly youths) who invested time, money and energy in developing a consciously dandified identity, with a wardrobe to match, are not difficult to find. In his last year at Eton in the 1920s, Cyril Connolly 'succumbed to aestheticism'. He took to wearing a panama hat and a black dinner-jacket instead of a blazer, read *Marius the Epicurean* and *Á Rebours*, as well as the works of poets such as Baudelaire, Verlaine and Mallarmé, 'and smouldered with the "hard gem-like flame". I believed in living for "gold moments" [and] in "anything for a sensation"'.[86] Although he belonged to a very different social milieu, Joseph Keating sought to adopt a similarly explicit dandified persona. In his autobiography, he recalled how as a youth, working as a miner in the South Wales coal-fields, clothes had become important to him: 'I was careful about the cut of my coat, the hang of my trousers, the shape of my bowler hat,

---

[83] H. Dacre (author and composer), *The Mashah up to Datah!* (Francis, Day and Hunter, London, n.d. [c. 1891]), n.p. See also, for example, P. Tarling (author) and K. Lyle (composer), *My Word, I'll Have Your Socks!* (Francis, Day and Hunter, London, n.d. [c. 1909]). For the 'swell' songs of the 1860s and 1870s, see Bailey, 'Champagne Charlie'. For the 'masher' songs of the 1890s, see Breward, *The Hidden Consumer*, pp. 232–6.

[84] J.B. Priestley, *The Good Companions* (Heinemann, London, 1974; first published 1929), p. 16.

[85] S. Fillin-Yeh (ed.), *Dandies: Fashion and Finesse in Art and Culture* (New York University Press, New York, 2001); R.K. Garelick, *Rising Star: Dandyism, Gender and Performance in the Fin de Siècle* (Princeton University Press, Princeton, 1998); E. Moers, *The Dandy: Brummel to Beerbohm* (Secker and Warburg, London, 1960). But see also Bailey, 'Champagne Charlie', pp. 108–10.

[86] C. Connolly, *Enemies of Promise* (André Deutsch, London, 1988; first published 1938), pp. 262–3.

and the smartness of my collar'. Eventually, he continued, 'My dandyism reached a point where it offended people with no understanding'.[87]

Figure 2.3   'The masher candidate of the future'. The dandy as a ladies' man. *Fun*, 11 July 1883. Courtesy of the Bodleian Library, University of Oxford, N.2706 d.13.

---

[87]   J. Keating, *My Struggle for Life* (Simpkin, Marshall, Hamilton, Kent, London, 1916), pp. 111–12.

However, despite these and other examples, rather than as a fixed identity, a specific dress style or set of clothes, 'dandyism' was more often described in personal reminiscences as a 'phase', which unsurprisingly, given the constraints on middle-aged (let alone elderly) men's expenditure, was mostly associated with youth and bachelordom. Indeed, many men 'dressed up' for specific occasions, young bachelors being most likely to describe this process by using the language of 'dandysim'. Manchester lads would '"toff themselves up" [with] ... clothes of a more fashionable cut and quality' for Saturday nights out,[88] while in his autobiography, W.F. Fish recalled how as a young shop assistant in the 1880s, he had spent a summer holiday with friends in Worthing. He had managed to save enough to be able to buy 'a somewhat gaudy-looking ... blazer, with cap to match, and a pair of cheap ... white shoes with brown strappings', which he had proudly worn when 'out "mashing"'.[89] Working-class teenagers in inter-war East London 'dressed up' at the week-end 'to go to a dance or the cinema, or just walk up West'. 'They wore white shirts and bright striped ties and could look very smart. In Winter they wore white silk scarves under their back padded overcoats which were often left unbuttoned to reveal the richness of their scarves and neckties.'[90]

In Joseph Keating's case, his carefully constructed appearance meant that he was frequently the butt of jokes, and on at least one occasion physically attacked: while out walking on Pontypridd common with his brother, 'my clothes and walking stick brought jeers from some hilarious young men', who chased them and attempted to beat them up.[91] Nevertheless, this was by no means the universal response to smartly dressed young men. Admiration, envy, and the desire to emulate them were just as frequently recorded. Not long before the outbreak of the First World War, the teenage Patrick McGeown, having been to his first dance, discovered that he 'needed' a blue serge suit, a black silk tie and a white silk shirt. 'A Hughie Clark garb, in fact: he was the dressiest young fellow in the "Neuk", and I longed to be like him'.[92] In the inter-war period Robert Morgan, who like Keating grew up in a South Wales mining village, would spend Saturday evenings at a dance-hall. After careful preparations, he and his friend Ron would set out, 'Dressed in our best suits, white semi-stiff collars and white shirts, and shoes polished like mirrors'. Far from feeling awkward and self-conscious, 'we felt like princes as we took our place in the queue'.[93]

At the more comfortably-off end of the social scale, it was Mr Norris Thompson's mother who 'disapproved of being in the fashion ... what she wore was good, but it certainly wasn't tasteful, and it was old-fashioned', while 'my father was the

---

[88] Russell, *Manchester Boys*, pp. 7, 30. See also G.R. Sims, *How the Poor Live and Horrible London* (Chatto and Windus, London, 1889), pp. 81–2, for a not entirely sympathetic portrait of 'the mashers of the East'.

[89] W.F. Fish, *The Autobiography of a Counter-Jumper* (Lutterworths, London, 1929), p. 92. Unfortunately, Fish's cheap shoes came apart after being drenched in sea water, and his cap was blown out to sea.

[90] L. Heren, *Growing Up Poor in London* (Phoenix, London, 2001; first published 1973), pp. 49–50.

[91] Keating, *My Struggle for Life*, pp. 111–12.

[92] McGeown, *Heat the Furnace*, p. 67. See also Middleton, *Village Memories*, pp. 72–3.

[93] R. Morgan, *My Lamp Still Burns* (Gomer Press, Llandysul, 1981), p. 126.

opposite, he was always spic and span. Well got up.' It was his mother who was teased unmercifully by the youthful Mr Thompson for her lack of taste, rather than his father for his nattiness.[94] As a medical student in London at the end of the nineteenth century, H.H. Bashford had shared lodgings in Camden Town with two friends. One of these, Roger Bolton, was an 'extremely careful' dresser: 'no more impressively acute-angled trousers can have descended Miss Pilchard's step', although perhaps the nicest touch was the 'invisible' tube of water connected to the flower in his button-hole.[95] There is no indication that because of his care with clothes, Bolton was viewed by fellow-students as an outsider, or indeed as 'unmanly'. In a similar way, although in the very different environment of the Northamptonshire village of Byfield, the smart dress of the currant buyer who visited the village in the summer was clearly considered worthy of note, but in an admiring, rather than condemnatory way. When the hot weather forced him to take off his jacket, collar and tie, roll up his sleeves and unbutton his waistcoat before he loaded the heavy containers of fruit, 'most people felt that this was a pity, for he was a dressy man, and his get up much admired; but they had to admit that it was sweaty work ... lugging all those currants about'.[96] Most contemporaries did not automatically associate a 'dressy' man with homosexuality. Paul Vaughan's headmaster delighted in wearing suits that 'our fathers and uncles, in their conventional clerical greys and dark blues, would never have dreamed of wearing', but it did not occur to anyone in 1930s suburban New Malden that he might be homosexual.[97]

Despite journalistic or music-hall caricatures, there was no convenient dividing line between the manly, healthy and athletic youth and the 'dressy spindle-shanks who "knows a thing or two"', thus leaving the way open for sartorial faux pas and the awful possibility of 'looking funny'.[98] A 'dandified' appearance could be made up of a mixture of the sartorially acceptable and the unacceptable, the manly and the unmanly. This confusion was well illustrated by an anecdote included in Willy Goldman's reminiscences of his childhood in the East End of London. For a brief period, one of his neighbours had achieved local fame as a boxer, despite being only sixteen years old. As a result, for the first time in his life he had been able to afford a new suit, which, however, sent viewers some very mixed messages. On the one hand, the young boxer's manliness could not be doubted, given his sporting prowess. But on the other, not only was the suit of 'a peculiar mauve hue, and very, very natty',

---

[94]   NSPSC Archive, The Edwardians, QD1/FLWE/11, interview transcript, Mr Norris Thompson, manger/owner of family shop.

[95]   H.H. Bashford, *Lodgings for Twelve* (Constable, London, 1935), p. 81.

[96]   R. Hillyer, *Country Boy* (Hodder and Stoughton, London, 1966), pp. 66–7.

[97]   P. Vaughan, *Something in Linoleum: A Thirties Education* (Sinclair Stevenson, London, 1995; first published 1994), pp. 119–20; 133–4. As Matt Houlbrook has pointed out, 'there was never a singular and self-evident style that set queans wholly apart from the crowd'. M. Houlbrook, *Queer London: Perils and Pleasures in the Sexual Metropolis, 1918–1957* (University of Chicago Press, Chicago, 2005), pp. 144–9, especially p. 147. Thank you to Chris Breward for drawing my attention to this book.

[98]   Paterson, *Across the Bridges*, pp. 173–4. Miles Ogborn makes a similar point with reference to eighteenth-century Macaronis. M. Ogborn, *Spaces of Modernity: London's Geographies 1680–1780* (The Guildford Press, New York, 1998), p. 134.

but 'You had the feeling that the tailor had originally intended it for a female garment ... Archie emphasised this effect by the incorporation of a graceful sway into his walk'. The result was that 'He looked quite a number of things conspicuously unpugilistic'.[99]

Conclusion

Clothing played an important part in defining, sustaining and reinforcing men's identities throughout the half-century before the outbreak of the Second World War, and indeed arguably beyond. Just as men's identities were multi-faceted and shifting, so there did not exist one single male sartorial 'model' to which all men aspired or adhered: not only gender, but also class, age, ethnicity, location in time and place, all influenced what men wore at any one time. However, the fact that identities were diverse, does not mean that all were considered equal. Just as some men enjoyed greater power and status, so certain sartorial styles were generally (although by no means universally) considered to be more desirable. Financial factors, furthermore, were crucial in opening up more than a narrow range of sartorial choices, while issues such as family responsibilities or the powerlessness of youth, served to limit consumer 'freedom'. At various stages of a man's life, or even in the course of a single day, sartorial decisions were overwhelmingly made with the local context, past experience, and peer group 'rules' very much in mind. However, this does not mean that interest and pleasure in clothes were always considered unacceptable. Among the young and among unmarried men with no family responsibilities, in particular, they were often viewed with indulgence, as long as they remained within the boundaries of what was commonly known to be acceptable at a particular time, and within a specific locality. Knowledge was essential, and regularly put to use: the working-class boys hanging around on the streets of South London, for example, would have known when they could wear 'something a little brighter than working clothes' without too much fear of ridicule, and when they could even experiment a little, perhaps with 'a new tie of green and red and gold, or a straw hat with a brown ribbon, or a scarf pin, or a white silk scarf'.[100] In some cases, the admiration (real or imagined) of friends, family, or acquaintances proved a source of great pleasure. But in others, where for whatever reason the garments worn did not 'fit in', the result often was one of considerable distress, echoes of which still resonate even at a distance of more than half a century. Peter Kibblewhite was one of the respondents interviewed for an ambitious 'Family life and work experience before 1918' oral history project. He was born in 1901 and grew up in Sussex in a comfortable middle-class home. He had no memory of being breeched, but vividly remembered:

---

[99] Goldman, *East End my Cradle*, p. 102.

[100] Paterson, *Across the Bridges*, p. 143. See also C. Breward, 'Masculine pleasures: metropolitan identities and the commercial sites of dandyism, 1790–1840', *The London Journal*, vol. 28, no. 1 (2003), pp. 60–72.

being very embarrassed by a certain pair of shorts that my grandmother made for me and thought were very beautiful. And I thought were terribly cissy … I remember walking down – to the beach in these terrible … blue shorts and feeling, oh … terrible, terrible … you've no – no idea … how embarrassed I was … it was so unimportant looking back on it … I don't suppose anybody noticed them … But I was so – ashamed of those awful blue shorts.[101]

---

[101] NSPSC Archive, The Edwardians, QD1/FLWE/MUC/2014, interview transcript, Peter Kibblewhite, electrical engineer, London.

Chapter 3

Menswear and War, 1914–1918

In August 1916 it was announced that Captain B.H. Radford, a balloon observer with the Royal Flying Corps, had become one of the latest casualties of the by then two-year-old war. Captain Radford was better-known to contemporaries as Basil Hallam, a popular singer and actor whose most successful 'turn' had been his appearance as 'Gilbert, the Filbert' in *The Passing Show*, performed in London's Palace Theatre in 1914 and 1915[1] (Figure 3.1). Gilbert the Filbert was the personification of what was described in contemporary slang as a 'nut' or 'knut', a young, carefree, smartly dressed man-about-town who had been treated with cautious indulgence in pre-war days, but who no longer – it was believed – had a place in wartime Britain. Arguably better than anyone else, Hallam had represented on stage 'the young strugglers who probably hadn't a shilling to bless themselves with, got up to kill in morning coat, vest slip, grey trousers, spats, lemon gloves, rolled umbrella, and top hat', strolling on the streets of London 'with the aplomb of a male member of the Gaiety chorus'.[2] Even in uniform, Basil Hallam had maintained – at least in public – his stage persona as a 'nut'. Charles Carrington recalled seeing him perform at a camp concert in France, 'wearing clothes which made me sick with envy'. His khaki uniform was

> of so exquisite a cut and a colour-scheme so delicately varied from the official drab, that his clothes, somehow, did not resemble mine. He wore ... dove-coloured hunting breeches, yellow 'chammy' gloves, puttees that were almost lemon-coloured and a floppy cap arranged over one ear. Good colonels strove to prevent the likes of me from imitating the likes of him.[3]

Hallam's untimely death was viewed by contemporaries as symbolic of the wartime disappearance of this model of carefree young manhood. According to *The Tatler*, Hallam had in Gilbert the Filbert 'successfully created a type which went out when war came in'.[4] The nut, in other words, had shed his smart (if not always expensive) suit, abandoned his pre-war consumption and leisure practices and responded to the call of duty by enlisting in the armed forces and donning a uniform.[5] The verses by Private G. Newman Stewart, of the London Welsh Battalion, described the transformation brought about by the war on the 'k-nut':

---

[1]   *The Bystander*, 30 August 1916. See also ibid., 26 May 1915.

[2]   F. Willis, *101 Jubilee Road: A Book of London's Yesterdays* (Phoenix House, London, 1948), p. 39.

[3]   C. Carrington, *Soldier from the Wars Returning* (Gregg Revivals and King's College London, Aldershot, 1991; first published 1965), p. 155. Many thanks to Paul Cornish for the reference.

[4]   *The Tatler*, 30 August 1916.

[5]   *The Bystander*, 25 November 1914.

Alas! Poor Gilbert—We Knew Him Well

A FILBERT OF INFINITE JEST, OF MOST EXCELLENT FANCY

Photograph   *Foulsham and Banfield*

" *Where be your gibes now ; your gambols, your songs ? Your flashes of merriment, that were wont to set the Palace in a roar ?* "

IN MEMORIAM

Basil Hallam, erstwhile " Gilbert the Filbert," now one of the fallen heroes of the fight, in which " Filberts " have covered themselves with glory

Figure 3.1   **'Alas! Poor Gilbert' Basil Hallam as Gilbert the Filbert.** *The Bystander*, **30 August 1916. Courtesy of the Bodleian Library, University of Oxford, N.2705 d.161.**

You would know him in the old days by his smooth and well-oiled locks,
By his many-coloured ties and his many-coloured socks,
By his walk and by his talk, by the figure he would cut,
Quite a masher and a dasher was the man we call the 'K-nut'
…

Now he's fighting, and he's striking such a blow in Britain's cause
That has stopped our smiles and sniggers, that has made the nation pause.
And if he be spared to come back to his ordinary rut,
There's a cheer and a 'God bless you!' for the man we call the 'K-nut'.[6]

The image of the 'nut' in khaki was emblematic of the wartime shift in understandings of what constituted acceptable male consumer, sartorial and leisure practices, a shift that has yet to receive thorough investigation. Although a number of studies have explored the quantitative impact – through wages, prices, shortages and government controls – of the First World War on British civilian consumers,[7] we still know all too little about the relationship between consumer cultures and conflict, and about either civilian or combatant consumers' expectations, desires and aspirations in periods of war.[8] It is these issues that will be explored in this chapter, focusing particularly on attitudes towards the consumption of civilian menswear.

The symbolic role of military uniforms in the process of transforming civilians into combatants is well-known.[9] As the writer and broadcaster J.B. Priestley explained, he

---

6 *The Woolwich Herald*, 22 January 1915.

7 J.M. Winter, *The Great War and the British People* (Palgrave Macmillan, Basingstoke, 2003; first published 1985); P. Dewey, *War and Progress: Britain, 1914–1945* (Longman, London, 1997), chapter 2; J.M. Bourne, *Britain and the Great War 1914–1918* (Edward Arnold, London, 1989), chapter 8; P. Dewey, 'The new warfare and economic mobilisation', in J. Turner (ed.), *Britain and the First World War* (Unwin Hyman, London, 1988), pp. 70–84; P. Simkins, *Kitchener's Army: The Raising of the New Armies, 1914–16* (Manchester University Press, Manchester, 1988), especially chapters 10 and 11; K. Burk (ed.), *War and the State: The Transformation of British Government, 1914–1919* (George Allen and Unwin, London, 1982). Little attention has yet been paid to combatants' roles as consumers. But see J. Winter, 'Popular culture in wartime Britain', in A. Roshwald and R. Stites (eds), *European Culture in the Great War: The Arts, Entertainment and Propaganda, 1914–1918* (Cambridge University Press, Cambridge, 1999), pp. 330–48.

8 The politicisation of consumption during the war is examined in M. Hilton, *Consumerism in Twentieth-Century Britain: The Search for a Historical Movement* (Cambridge University Press, Cambridge, 2003), chapter 2; F. Trentmann, 'Bread, milk and democracy: consumption and citizenship in Britain, c. 1903–51', in M. Daunton and M. Hilton (eds), *The Politics of Consumption: Material Culture and Citizenship in Europe and America* (Berg, Oxford, 2001), pp. 129–63; J. Winter and J.-L. Robert (eds), *Capital Cities at War: Paris, London, Berlin 1914–1919* (Cambridge University Press, Cambridge, 1999; first published 1997), especially part 5; S. Pedersen, *Family Dependence and the Origins of the Welfare State: Britain and France, 1914–1945* (Cambridge University Press, Cambridge, 1993); B. Waites, *A Class Society at War: England 1914–1918* (Berg, Leamington Spa, 1987). See also I. Zweiniger-Bargielowska, *Austerity in Britain: Rationing, Controls and Consumption 1939–1955* (Oxford University Press, Oxford, 2000); B.J. Davis, *Home Fires Burning: Food, Politics, and Everyday Life in World War I Berlin* (The University of North Carolina Press, Chapel Hill, 2000).

9 J. Bourke, *Dismembering the Male: Men's Bodies, Britain and the Great War* (Reaktion Books, London, 1996), pp. 128–31; Bourne, *Britain and the Great War*, pp. 214–24.

and his fellow recruits did not 'feel' like true soldiers, and indeed 'hardly wanted to go out', until they were able to put aside the uniforms of blue cloth donated by the post office (khaki being in short supply in the first months of the war) and 'excited as girls … put on real khaki uniforms'.[10] But if uniforms 'made' combatants, what did civilian clothes in wartime 'make' of the three-quarters of the male population who did not join the armed forces?[11] In a context where combatants (particularly, but not exclusively, volunteers) were perceived as the summit of rectitude and moral manliness, and where all were expected to contribute to the national effort by making both emotional and material sacrifices, what did 'mufti' stand for?[12] In October 1915 a *News of the World* editorial was fairly typical of the contemporary press in emphasising that the time had come for those who had up to then 'tarried behind' to 'choose between the king's uniform and the livery of shame'.[13] This chapter will first of all question whether, and to what extent, this emotionally loaded language actually translated into a real and widespread revulsion towards civilian menswear, and into a sense of shame for wearing civilian clothes. Did any models of acceptable and 'manly' civilian sartorial consumption continue to exist throughout the war years, or did all men come to wear civilian clothes with dread, like F.E. Noakes, who feared being thought a 'slacker' because of his civilian dress, a great deal more than he feared 'the unknown hardships of the Army'?[14] After examining the images of civilian men endorsed by press and propaganda, the chapter will tackle the rather trickier task of assessing whether such attitudes were reflected and endorsed by 'public opinion' more generally. It will suggest

---

[10]   J.B. Priestley, *Margin Released: A Writer's Reminiscences and Reflections* (Heinemann, London, 1962), p. 91. See also A. Hamilton Gibbs, *The Grey Wave* (Hutchinson and Gibbs, London, 1920), pp. 13–14. A more ambivalent portrayal of the agonies involved in wearing a uniform for the first time can be found in H. Williamson, *How Dear is Life* (Macdonald, London, 1984; first published 1954), pp. 140–41.

[11]   Almost five million men entered the armed forces in the course of the conflict, 22 per cent of the total male population. Roughly two-thirds of these men were volunteers. Bourke, *Dismembering the Male*, p. 15. J. Stevenson, *British Society 1914–45* (Penguin, Harmondsworth, 1990; first published 1984), pp. 46–7.

[12]   On the relationship between masculinity and conscription, see I.R. Bet-El, 'Men and soldiers: British conscripts, concepts of masculinity, and the Great War', in B. Melman (ed.), *Borderlines: Genders and Identities in War and Peace, 1870–1930* (Routledge, London, 1998), pp. 73–94. On recruitment more in general, see Winter, *The Great War*, pp. 25–48; A. Gregory, 'Lost generations: the impact of military casualties on Paris, London and Berlin', in Winter and Robert (eds), *Capital Cities at War*, pp. 57–103. On masculinity, combat and the First World War, see, for example, S.M. Cullen, 'Gender and the Great War: British Combatants, Masculinity and Perceptions of Women, 1918–1939', unpublished DPhil, University of Oxford (1998); Bourke, *Dismembering the Male*; G. Dawson, *Soldier Heroes: British Adventure, Empire and the Imagining of Masculinities* (Routledge, London, 1994), especially pp. 166–92.

[13]   *News of the World*, 24 October 1915.

[14]   F.E. Noakes, *The Distant Drum: A Personal History of a Guardsman in the Great War* (The Author, Tunbridge Wells, n.d. [c. 1953]), p. 3. For women's clothes in the First World War, see, for example, C. Buckley, '"De-humanised females and Amazonians": British wartime fashion and its representation in *Home Chat*, 1914–1918', *Gender & History*, vol. 14, no. 3 (2002), pp. 516–36; S.R. Grayzel, 'Nostalgia, gender and the countryside: placing the "Land Girl" in First World War Britain', *Rural History*, vol. 10, no. 2 (1999), pp. 155–70.

that, rather than a blanket condemnation of all civilian dress, particular opprobrium was directed at the look that seemed to suggest a leisured and affluent lifestyle, as well as an infuriating lack of commitment to the war effort. Individuals who looked as if they were shirking their patriotic duty and doing well out of the conflict, making a profit while others suffered, acquired an unenviable reputation as wartime *bêtes noires*. In the highly charged atmosphere of wartime Britain, as the tally of casualties mounted with horrifying rapidity, consumers' sartorial behaviour was influenced not only by the material constraints of the wartime economy, but also by a desire not to *look* like a shirker or a profiteer.

Civvies and shirking

It would be reasonable to expect that one of the outcomes of the war would be the simplification of the distinctions between male sartorial styles, with the conflict bringing about the replacement of the pre-1914 multi-layered and often subtle differences between the consumer practices of different groups of men, with a clear-cut division between manly combatants in uniform and unmanly – or anyway less manly – civilian men. In his scathing criticism of the representation of soldiers and of the war in the contemporary press; first published in 1916, R.H. Tawney suggested that this simple division was indeed receiving widespread endorsement. He condemned not only the 'horrible suggestion that war is somehow ... ennobling', and an activity in which a man 'finds a fullness of self-expression impossible in peace' but also that 'when clothed in khaki and carrying rifles, these lads are more truly "men" than they were when working in offices or factories'.[15]

In practice, however, the distinction was never quite this stark. Even in the first year of the war, when the country's patriotic fervour was at its highest pitch, there still was a general awareness that while uniformed combatants were undoubtedly manly heroes, civilian men – even those of military age – were not necessarily the opposite. Civilian clothes, it was acknowledged, did not always necessarily indicate cowardice or 'shirking'. Indeed, images of the 'shirker' in most sections of the press and in recruiting posters overwhelmingly portrayed him not as a generic civilian man, but as a very specific 'type' of civilian: the 'nut' who, unlike Basil Hallam's Gilbert the Filbert, had *not* left his dandified ways behind him, enlisted and become 'a man'.[16] On the contrary, he continued to follow his usual sartorial, leisure, sporting and amorous pursuits, careless of the national emergency. It was often only when his erstwhile lady admirers turned their backs on him – quite rightly, it was

---

[15]   R.H. Tawney, *The Attack and Other Papers* (Spokesman, Nottingham, 1981; first published in this edition 1953), p. 26. See also M. Paris, *Warrior Nation: Images of War in British Popular Culture, 1850–2000* (Reaktion Books, London, 2000), chapter 4. According to Robert Graves and Alan Hodge, in 1918 there existed 'two distinct Britains': the 'Fighting Forces' and the 'Rest'. R. Graves and A. Hodge, *The Long Weekend: A Social History of Great Britain 1918–1939* (Abacus, London, 1995; first published 1940), p. 14.

[16]   For the recruiting call: 'I will be a man and enlist to-day', see, for example, *The Sketch*, 19 August 1914; *The Banbury Guardian and General Advertiser*, 31 December 1914; *Tit-Bits*, 2 January 1915.

agreed – and his leisure activities were curtailed, that the journalistic nut was finally driven to enlist[17] (Figure 3.2). The lack of access to consumer goods was often portrayed in the patriotic press as the last drop for 'the stay at home at the back'. Writing to a friend serving at the Front in 1915, for example, the fictional shirker complained that 'All my socks are wearing out, and I simply daren't go and ask for some new ones … I shall be landed with some rotten shoddy things at about 15s a pair … you chaps at the Front will have to … send us back some of those socks and gramophones and things you've collared. Otherwise we shall have to come out and fetch 'em.'[18]

According to *Punch*, by 1915 many of the 'knuts' had been 'commandeered and nobly transmogrified' into soldiers, sailors and airmen. Nevertheless, 'We have not been wholly purged of levity and selfishness. Football news has not receded into its true perspective; shirkers are more preoccupied with the defeat or victory of "Lambs" or "Wolves" … than with the stubborn defence, the infinite discomfort and the heavy losses of their brothers in Flanders.'[19] In contemporary propaganda, the smart lounge suit and elegant accoutrements of the shirker were the outward symbols of his selfishness and unpatriotism. He was the type of young man who, after the introduction of conscription in 1916, was happy to see his middle-aged father forced to march off to war, while himself remaining safe in a comfortable reserved occupation.[20]

Chapter 2 suggested that the young nut had been an acceptable figure in pre-war days: as an unmarried, young wage earner, it was assumed that he had few responsibilities towards others, and his self-indulgence could be tolerated and

---

[17]   *John Bull*, 5 September 1914; Christmas Number 1914; *News of the World*, 23 May 1915. Also the postcard 'He She and It' reproduced in P. Parker, *The Old Lie: The Great War and the Public School Ethos* (Constable, London, 1987), n.p.; Department of Art, Imperial War Museum (IWM Art), Parliamentary Recruiting Committee Posters (PRC Posters), PRC 112, PST / 4899,'Are YOU in this?', n.d., pre-1916. For the *Punch* view of the chinless nut as shirker (and vice versa) in the first months of the war, see *Punch*, 16 September 1914; 14 October 1914; 28 October 1914; 2 December 1914; 16 December 1914; 19 May 1915; 9 June 1915. By contrast, the man eager to enlist was portrayed as firm-jawed and plainly dressed. *Punch*, 28 October 1914; 25 November 1914. See also *The Sketch*, 9 September 1914; 9 December 1914; 28 July 1915; 17 November 1915; *The Tatler*, 23 September 1914; 8 November 1916; *Illustrated Chips*, 17 July 1915; *The Bystander*, 9 September 1914; 23 December 1914; But see also the notable absence of the nut as shirker in *Tit-Bits*, a magazine that was presumably predominantly directed at a readership composed of these very same 'nuts'. On British wartime propaganda, see M.L. Sanders and P.M. Taylor, *British Propaganda During the First World War, 1914–18* (Macmillan, Basingstoke, 1982); N. Reeves, 'Film propaganda and its audience: the example of Britain's official films during the First World War', *Journal of Contemporary History*, vol. 18, no. 3 (1983), pp. 463–94; A. Goldfarb Marquis, 'Words as weapons: propaganda in Britain and Germany during the First World War', *Journal of Contemporary History*, vol. 13, no. 3 (1978), pp. 467–98. Although very much predominant, the nut was not the only journalistic image of the shirker. See also, for example, the shabbily dressed 'habitual loafer'. *The Sketch*, 21 April 1915. For perceptions of malingering as a form of shirking, see Bourke, *Dismembering the Male*, pp. 78–89.

[18]   *The Bystander*, 27 January 1915.

[19]   *Mr. Punch's History of the Great War* (Cassell, London, 1919), pp. 22–3. See also C. Veitch, 'Play up! Play up! And win the war! Football, the nation and the First World War 1914–15', *Journal of Contemporary History*, vol. 20, no. 3 (1985), pp. 363–78, especially p. 370. See also IWM Art, First World War Posters, PST / 0970, 'Men of Millwall …', n.d.; *The Bystander*, 9 September 1914.

[20]   *The Tatler*, 8 November 1916.

even expected. In wartime, this was emphatically no longer the case: as the posters published by the Parliamentary Recruiting Committee indicated, he now had responsibilities towards his country, towards 'our brave soldiers at the Front', towards 'King and Empire', and perhaps most tellingly, towards his 'pals' already 'out there'.[21] The fun-loving consumption practices that had been tolerated, if not actually commended, before the summer of 1914, now provoked widespread anger and disdain. It could only be a truly incorrigible shirker who responded to patriotic calls to arms by buying superfluous commodities, such as flags or khaki spats.[22] A man, in other words, like the fictional Albert Spottle, who did his bit for the war effort by keeping cheerful and carrying on with his life as normal: 'I go out as usual, dress just as carefully – spats, fancy waistcoat, buttonhole, etc. – One night it's the Imperial and another it's the Cinema … I spend my money freely', most notably by buying flags with which to decorate his motorbike. The flags of course fooled nobody: these shallow symbols of patriotism were contradicted by the much clearer signs of shirking: the spats, waistcoat and buttonhole, as well as the trips to music halls and cinemas.[23]

By focusing so strongly on the 'nut' as 'shirker', the press, and semi-official and official propaganda bodies,[24] were able to step back from portraying all men of military age in mufti as 'shirkers', and more generally, all civilian menswear as symbolic of unmanly cowardice and unpatriotism, thus also tainting older men and young boys not yet of military age, as well as men who had been rejected as unfit for military service. However, beyond the confines of press and propaganda, what the opinion was among the public at large, both civilian and combatant, and the extent to which this changed in the course of the conflict, is of course much more difficult to assess. As many historians have observed, there is a good deal of evidence to suggest that, especially in the first year of the war, young (and not so young) men not in uniform – either strangers seen in public places, or acquaintances – aroused a good deal of hostile comment and ridicule.[25] According to James Barke, at the outbreak

---

[21] IWM Art, PRC Posters, PRC 9, PST / 5077, 'In her hour of need your country calls for you', n.d.; PRC 6, PST / 5108, 'Offer your services now. Our brave soldiers at the front need your help', n.d.; PRC 10, PST / 5106, 'Fight for King and Empire', n.d.; PRC 27, PST / 1576 'Why are you still here when your pals are out there?', n.d. See also PRC 38, PST / 5094 'Think! … Won't you do your bit? We shall win but YOU must help', n.d.

[22] *Punch*, 30 September 1914; 7 October 1914. But see, for example, *Tit-Bits*'s much greater tolerance towards the popularity in December 1914 – including, presumably, among its readers – of Union Jack handkerchiefs and 'socks on which little flags take the place of the usual "clock"'. *Tit-Bits*, 26 December 1914. See also *Illustrated Chips*, 20 January 1917.

[23] *Punch*, 18 November 1914. See also *The Sketch*, 25 August 1915. This type of iconography was not always uncontroversial. Luton straw hat manufacturers, for example, took exception to a poster depicting a straw boater and a khaki cap, with the caption: 'Which ought you to wear'? In response to the outcry, other types of hat were added to the poster. *The Outfitter*, 12 June 1915.

[24] A National War Aims Committee, responsible for co-ordinating home-front propaganda on behalf of the government, was established only in mid-1917. Bourne, *Britain and the Great War*, p. 203.

[25] The question of the relationship between the hostile commentator and the recipient is one that needs further analysis: was hostility directed primarily at strangers, acquaintances, or

of war a wave of patriotic and anti-German feeling swept through the Scottish estate where he lived. Soon 'every young man eligible for military service was subjected to the closest conversational scrutiny, the pros and cons of his unwillingness to join the colours was exhaustively and often acrimoniously debated. White feathers began to be delivered to unregenerate shirkers.' It was only as the lists of dead, wounded or missing became common knowledge, that white feathers lost their 'glamour'.[26]

Such patriotic fervour notwithstanding, the extent to which civilian dress was associated with cowardice and provoked hostile comment, even in the early months of the war, should not be exaggerated. Firstly, the consensus that men of military age should enlist was not universally shared. In the Essex village of Great Leighs, for example, there was a good deal of resentment about the pressures put on

HE WENT.

Gilbert : " Wheah y'off
to, Gertrude ? "
Gertrude : " Gathering
k'nuts in May for the
Army. Coming ? "

**Figure 3.2   Gilbert: the nut as shirker. *Illustrated Chips*, 12 June 1915. Courtesy
of the Bodleian Library, University of Oxford, N.2706 b.4.**

agricultural labourers to enlist, most notably by the local landowners.[27] Furthermore,

---

loved ones? As Nicoletta Gullace has shown, propaganda called upon women to encourage 'their' men to enlist, but in practice white feathers were generally handed out to strangers and acquaintances. N.F. Gullace, 'White feathers and wounded men: female patriotism and the memory of the Great War', *Journal of British Studies*, vol. 36, no. 2 (1997), pp. 178–206.

[26]   J. Barke, *The Green Hills Far Away: A Chapter in Autobiography* (Collins, London, 1940), p. 234. But note that Barke was only nine years old when war broke out. See also S. Casson, *Steady Drummer* (G. Bell and Sons, London, 1935), p. 30.

[27]   A. Clark, *Echoes of the Great War: The Diary of the Reverend Andrew Clark 1914–1919* (Oxford University Press, Oxford, 1988), pp. 58–9. See also N. Mansfield, *English Farmworkers and Local Patriotism, 1900–1930* (Ashgate, Aldershot, 2001), especially chapter 4.

even conspicuously 'civilian' clothes did not necessarily provoke any comment. When the convalescing officer Julian Tyndale-Biscoe went to see the parents of one of his fellow gunners in Millwall, London, in 1916, he was 'struck by the courtesy of the dockers. Without exception every one of whom I asked the way, dressed up as I was in my town suit, was most obliging and did his best to put me on the right way'. Tyndale-Biscoe clearly wished to convey the locals' courtesy towards a middle-class stranger. Equally clear, nonetheless, is their lack of hostility towards a young man in elegant 'mufti', whose injuries were not immediately apparent.[28]

Among combatants, the heartiest contempt seems to have been reserved not for civilian 'shirkers', but for uniformed non-combatants, whose uniform was perceived as a dishonest sham and a 'disguise'. According to Charles Carrington, the 'Men in uniform back at the base were expected to be a little ashamed of themselves and to make excuses'.[29] John Gibbons believed that men in the armed forces felt no dislike for civilians, even those who had somehow managed to evade conscription. 'The people that we did hate were the gentlemen ... who were really civilians in khaki ... men who would go on running their ordinary businesses, and ... somehow get into uniform as well.'[30] On the contrary, the accoutrements of civilian life could arouse an affectionate response. While waiting for a boat to take him on leave back to Britain, Wyn Griffith enjoyed his time walking through the streets of Boulogne, 'finding a pleasure in its noise and bustle, in its shops, and in the rubbings of shoulders with people who went home for dinner and who wore slippers of an evening'.[31] Writing in the *Daily Mirror* in 1917, Hamilton Hunter's description of visits to 'the office' while on leave expressed bemusement, rather than hostility. 'We roll in and look with magnanimous toleration on our old cronies who for some legitimate reason or other have not donned the uniform of honour and sacrifice.' The sense of distance from old friends was clear, but the tone remained affectionate: 'The comrades of a tamer life still carry on with their starched collars and their cuffs protected with sheets of the firm's white notepaper. Featherweight boots too!'[32]

More generally, as the historian Nicoletta Gullace has shown, the motives that led individuals – and especially, it seems, women – to approach strangers and attempt to shame them into enlisting, most notably by handing out white feathers, are still not well understood. As Gullace demonstrates, these actions were perceived by at least some contemporaries, and most notably by combatants and ex-combatants, as based on women's inability to 'see' beyond appearances (civilian clothes) to the 'real' man underneath, relying simply 'on that external emblem of courage – the military

---

[28]   J. Tyndale-Biscoe, *Gunner Subaltern: Letters Written by a Young Man to his Father During the Great War* (Leo Cooper, London, 1971), p. 105.

[29]   Carrington, *Soldier from the Wars Returning*, p. 15. See also C.E. Montague, *Disenchantment* (Chatto and Windus, London, 1922), p. 26; *The Sketch*, 26 January 1916.

[30]   J. Gibbons, *Roll on, Next War! The Common Man's Guide to Army Life* (Frederick Muller, London, 1935), p. 107. Although see also many 'literary' combatants' deep hostility towards civilians – especially women – and civilian life, examined in Cullen, 'Gender and the Great War', pp. 177–81; 216; 229.

[31]   W. Griffith, *Up to Mametz* (Severn House, London, 1981; first published 1931), p. 100. See also the otherwise deeply bitter Hamilton Gibbs, *The Grey Wave*, pp. 14; 26; 37.

[32]   Reprinted in *Men's Wear*, 12 May 1917.

uniform'. Often, in narratives hostile to such women, the 'real' man underneath the mufti turned out to be a wounded or disabled ex-combatant.[33] Indiscriminate verbal assaults on men in civilian dress may very well have taken place. Indeed, in the first year of the war they may even have been common. In February 1915 an exasperated leading article in the popular journal *John Bull* suggested that special badges should be issued by the War Office to all men rejected for enlistment. 'These would protect these patriotic and disappointed fellows from the cruel insults to which they are so often subjected.'[34] However, two issues should be noted here. Firstly, the enforcement of sartorial standards through ridicule and verbal abuse were hardly a new phenomenon. The significant change during the war was that the abusers were overwhelmingly perceived to be (and it would seem, actually were) female. By definition, thus, they were not members of the victim's masculine peer group, but 'outsiders' without knowledge of the group's 'rules', something that may have contributed to the hostility they frequently aroused.

Secondly, it is open to question whether such abuse was always entirely indiscriminate: were *all* men not in uniform fair game? Taking into account the strong association in press and propaganda material between shirking, the 'nut' and the 'loafer', it is at least open to question whether popular hostility was really directed generically at all men dressed in civilian clothes, or whether it was pinpointed more precisely at those men whose appearance and location gave them the look of young, carefree men of leisure. In one of the well-known versions of the white feather story, for example, the 'gallant young officer' who was awarded a Victoria Cross in the morning and offered a white feather in the afternoon, had been wearing 'mufti' when approached by the 'girls' who 'jeeringly handed him a white feather'. He had also been sitting in Hyde Park, during working hours, relaxing with a cigarette.[35] Indeed, it was a significant feature of many of the white feather anecdotes not only that they took place in public places, including on public transport (in itself hardly surprising, as these incidents generally involved encounters between strangers), but also that these public places were either associated with leisure pursuits, or that men's very presence in day-time hours could reasonably be interpreted as 'loafing'. Stuart Cloete was handed a white feather 'by a patriotic lady' while recovering from an injury incurred during the battle of the Somme. This may simply have been prompted by his appearance as a young and apparently fit young man in mufti, but it may also have been significant that Cloete had decided to spend his convalescence 'drifting about', being part of the urban 'crowd', 'eat[ing] things off barrows and spit[ting] on the pavement'.[36] At least one observer was shocked by the sight, early in 1916, of

---

[33]   Gullace, 'White feathers and wounded men', especially pp. 199–202. See also A. Woollacott, '"Khaki fever" and its control: gender, class, age and sexual morality on the British home front in the First World War', *Journal of Contemporary History*, vol. 29, no. 2 (1994), pp. 325–47.

[34]   *John Bull*, 6 February 1915. See also *The Bystander*, 10 November 1915; *John Bull*, 13 November 1915.

[35]   Gullace, 'White feathers and wounded men', p. 200.

[36]   S. Cloete, *A Victorian Son: An Autobiography 1897–1922* (Collins, London, 1972), p. 255. See also B. Tinker, *The Man who Stayed at Home* (Mills and Boon, London, 1915), a play based on the misunderstandings arising out of the assumption that an elegant appearance and leisured life-style must necessarily equate with shirking.

'crowds of men of 25 or so', not only because they were very clearly not in khaki, but especially because they sat 'all day in cafes in London, sipping coffee, smoking cigarettes and playing dominoes'[37] (Figure 3.3). It was only reasonable to assume that these men were shirkers: real-life Albert Spottles.

Menswear in wartime

Many contemporaries observed that by the summer of 1915, Hyde Park on a Sunday was characterised by the almost complete disappearance 'of one of its most familiar and engaging features – well-dressed young men, tall and good-looking, wearing their silk hats well back from their foreheads'.[38] Two years later, the only young men to be seen in London parks on Sundays were either in khaki or wounded. As Hallie Eustace Miles sadly reflected: 'It was like a new and tragic world ... I only seemed to see the ghosts of the past gay days'.[39] Any remaining nuts who had not enlisted, and who had somehow escaped conscription, would have known better than to appear in their smart pre-war-style attire, tactlessly signalling to all their lack of involvement in the national emergency. A contributor to the trade journal *The Outfitter* considered that by 1915 the general absence of 'knuttism' could be explained not only by the fact 'that so many of the "specie" are at the front', but also because 'those remaining behind, aware that the "knut's" code of honour demands his presence in the firing line, feel that a display of "dress talent" is a little unseemly in the circumstances'.[40]

Clothes that suggested a leisured and carefree existence may have been frowned upon. However, civilian menswear that in some way indicated a man's participation in the war effort was a different matter. Press and recruiting propaganda certainly went to some lengths to distance images of lazy, cowardly shirkers from men such as munitions workers, busy producing war material (and refusing to go on strike). As one Parliamentary Recruiting Committee poster put it, showing a soldier and a (male) munitions worker shaking hands: 'We're both needed to serve the Guns! Fill up the ranks! Pile up the Munitions!'[41] (Figure 3.4). Older civilian men determined to do their bit by investing money in the war debt were also portrayed in a positive light[42] (Figure 3.5).

---

[37]   Clark, *Echoes of the Great War*, p. 105.

[38]   M. MacDonagh, *In London During the Great War: The Diary of a Journalist* (Eyre and Spottiswoode, London, 1935), pp. 54–5. See also *Punch*, 16 June 1915; *The Bystander*, 1 March 1916; 28 June 1916; T. Burke, *Out and About: A Note-Book of London in War-Time* (George Allen and Unwin, London, 1919).

[39]   H.E. Miles, *Untold Tales of War-Time London: A Personal Diary* (Cecil Palmer, London, 1930), p. 129. For the absence of the 'nut' from another of his traditional haunts, the seaside resort, see, for example, *The Bystander*, 21 July 1915.

[40]   *The Outfitter*, 24 April 1915.

[41]   IWM Art, PRC Posters, PRC 85c, PST / 5112, 'We're both needed to serve the Guns!', n.d. See also *Punch*, 22 September 1915; *News of the World*, 4 July 1915; 30 July 1916; *The Tatler*, 12 July 1916 (reproduced from *The Evening News*); 26 July 1916 (reproduced from *The People*); 2 August 1916 (reproduced from *Reynolds Newspaper*).

[42]   J. Darracott and B. Loftus, *First World War Posters* (Imperial War Museum, London, n.d. [c. 1972]), p. 13; IWM Art, First World War Posters, PST / 4896, 'Back them up. Invest in the War Loan', n.d.; *News of the World*, 5 May 1918.

Figure 3.3   'Far from the trench's madding strife': loafing the days away. *The Bystander*, 19 September 1917. Courtesy of the Bodleian Library, University of Oxford, N.2705 d.161.

Many contemporaries also chose to emphasise the contribution to the war effort made by these civilian men. Queenie Hare, who in 1915 volunteered to act as a 'lady recruiting sergeant', reported of her experiences in London's Wood Green, that she had met 'very few real "shirkers"', despite clearly being on the look-out for them: 'All the fit young men I spoke to had genuine excuses for not being in khaki, and many ... were engaged in industries at home which provided equipment for the Army or Navy.' They were part of 'The industrial Army doing useful work at home'.[43] Michael MacDonagh would have agreed with these sentiments. A few months earlier, he had been impressed by a visit to the Royal Arsenal in Woolwich: 'The man of importance now is the man who makes things, and particularly things which are called engines of war'.[44] Or as the Conservative and Unionist paper *The Woolwich Herald* put it, a good deal more grandiosely: 'We rely completely on the patriotism of the workers of these islands for the sustained maximum industrial endeavour that is vitally requisite for the attainment of that victory in which our kinsmen of all classes are freely risking life and limb at sea and on the battlefield.'[45]

Nevertheless, the tolerance towards civilian men, and especially towards war workers of military age, should not be exaggerated. The distribution of war service badges and armlets suggests that even working garb did not entirely exempt this section of the population from verbal assaults (and from the attention of recruiting sergeants). However, it was the appearance of affluence in working people, and particularly in munitions workers,[46] that aroused the greatest hostility: just like the 'nut' who paraded his lack of involvement in the war effort, the supposedly newly well-off worker, able to afford new clothes and to indulge in previously unheard-of consumption practices, was seen as refusing to participate in the national sacrifice demanded by the war. His material well-being and supposedly leisured life-style were contrasted with the suffering of combatants, and their willingness to make even the 'ultimate sacrifice'. According to 'Truthful James', writing in the *Woolwich Gazette* in 1915, 'it is perfectly nauseating to meet large numbers of young fellows of fighting age perambulating the neighbourhood, lackadaisical loungers, with just sufficient energy to toy with a cigarette and encourage the insipid smiles of perambulating flappers ... It is no less nauseating to notice the number of young men wearing war badges.' Work in the Arsenal, he added, provided not only the opportunity to dodge recruitment, but 'The big pay ticket ... is another attraction. These young men get wages out of all proportion to their worth.'[47] More than thirty years later, Harry Farshaw added anti-Semitism to the mixture, when he described how his clothing workshop had been staffed during the conflict by Jewish immigrants from Russia, Rumania and Poland,

---

[43]   *Tit-Bits*, 5 June 1915.

[44]   MacDonagh, *In London During the Great War*, p. 56. See also *Punch*, 22 September 1915.

[45]   *The Woolwich Herald*, 2 April 1915.

[46]   In women as well as men.

[47]   *Woolwich Gazette and Plumstead News*, 24 August 1915. See also published responses in *Woolwich Gazette and Plumstead News*, 31 August 1915. One of these supported Truthful James's position, while the other, from 'W.A. Mechanic', pointed out that if more 'places of amusement' had been available, Arsenal workers would not have been seen in public so much. 'And the big pay ticket what would it be without overtime and the present cost of living?'

Figure 3.4   Men doing their duty: munitions work. *Punch*, 2 August 1916. Courtesy of the Bodleian Library, University of Oxford, N.2706 d.10.

making overcoats 'for our soldiers in France'. According to Farshaw, these workers had been able to earn 'good money, and I've seen them swaggering down Market Street, hat at rakish angle, loudly dressed, cigar in corner of mouth, hell's of fellars; whilst those for whom they made coats were knee-deep in mud'.[48]

Many contemporaries were more impressed by the material rewards of civilian work in wartime, rather than its contribution to the war effort. Between 1914 and 1916 Charles Robert Quinnell served with the Ninth Battalion of the Royal Fusiliers. In March 1916 he was granted seven days' leave, which he spent at home in Woolwich Arsenal. Being interviewed in 1975, he recalled that at the time Woolwich 'was a very, very busy place with munitions workers and the place just hummed with activity. And there was plenty of money about … some of the munitions makers were getting four, five, six pounds, which in those days was a lot of money … to me they were wealthy because I was still on the old bob-a-day stunt.' A friend of his took him for an evening out at the Woolwich Hippodrome, and then on to a pub, where – a sure sign of affluence – he drank a succession of double whiskeys. Quinnell could not afford to keep up, and refused his friend's offers to pay for him: 'I wouldn't have it'. Although his tone was sad rather than bitter, he nonetheless felt that a gulf had opened up between combatants and munitions workers: 'with the young fellows in the army we were a race apart from these civilians'.[49] Others made their anger clearer: according to a disapproving Bill Horrocks, during the war Bolton men in reserved occupations became 'the aristocrats of labour … and … could afford Sunday suits', at a time when most local homes had their 'own roll of honour nailed to a wall, giving the names of the lads who had died'.[50] These men, many contemporaries agreed, were not only making no sacrifices, but were actually profiting from war, and using these profits to indulge in selfish and inappropriate consumption practices. It was in this context of 'doing well' out of the war, that another distinctive wartime figure become partly enmeshed with that of the 'shirker': the 'profiteer'.[51]

Profiteering and wartime consumption

In 1915, as it became clear that the war would not be a brief one, the semi-official policy of 'business as usual' in economic affairs was replaced by an emphasis on the

---

[48]   H. Farshaw, *Stillage Makes his Way* (John Sherratt and Son, Attrincham, 1948), p. 123.

[49]   Sound Archive, Imperial War Museum (IWM Sound), Interview transcript, 554, Charles Robert Quinnell, 1975.

[50]   B. Horrocks, *Reminiscences of Bolton* (Neil Richardson, Manchester, 1984), p. 20. See also P. O'Mara, *The Autobiography of a Liverpool Slummy* (The Bluecoat Press, Liverpool, n.d. [c. 1933]), p. 128; Bourke, *Dismembering the Male*, pp. 105–6.

[51]   J.-L. Robert, 'The image of the profiteer', in Winter and Robert (eds), *Capital Cities at War*, pp. 104–32. The term 'profiteer' has become associated with individuals who enriched themselves through wartime industrial activities. However, during the First World War the term was frequently used rather more indiscriminately, to indicate anybody, male or female, who was seen to be 'doing well' out of the conflict.

PUNCH, OR THE LONDON CHARIVARI.—February 7, 1917.

A PLAIN DUTY.

"WELL, GOODBYE, OLD CHAP, AND GOOD LUCK! I'M GOING IN HERE TO DO
MY BIT, THE BEST WAY I CAN. THE MORE EVERYBODY SCRAPES TOGETHER FOR
THE WAR LOAN, THE SOONER YOU'LL BE BACK FROM THE TRENCHES."

Figure 3.5   Men doing their duty: investing in war loans. *Punch*, 7 February 1917.
               Courtesy of the Bodleian Library, University of Oxford, N.2706 d.10.

need to redirect goods and resources from civilian to military use.[52] For civilians, this translated into calls to rein in consumption and exercise thrift. Any cash surplus was to be invested in one of the war loan schemes.[53] Far from exercising such restraint, many contemporaries believed that so-called 'profiteers' simply set out to make money out of the war in any way they could. According to Caroline Playne, in 1917 the 'continuous babble about "equality of sacrifice"' made even more obvious 'the sacrifices accruing to war traders, investors and government officials'.[54] A year later, A. Hamilton Gibbs was recovering from being gassed in a quiet seaside town, which he called the 'Funkhole of England', and 'where never a bomb from airship ... disturbed the sunny calm'. The hotels, according to him, were 'full of moneyed Hebrews, who only journey to London by day to make more money ... [They were] shopkeepers who rejoiced in the war because it enabled them to put up their prices two hundred per cent.'[55] At least among some combatants, there was a feeling that 'at home people liked the war and were not anxious to end it. People like miners, factory hands and government contractors', who, according to Philip Gibbs, not only were not fighting, but were all making money and – most importantly – spending it freely in an orgy of hedonistic consumption, 'while Tommy Atkins ... made a little go a long way in a wayside estaminet before jogging up the Menin Road to have his head blown off'.[56]

The profiteer was portrayed as a man (and less frequently as a woman) who saw the war as an opportunity, not only to make money, but also to spend it lavishly – and

---

[52] Dewey, *War and Progress*, chapter 2. In 1916 the War Office had purchased the home, Australia and New Zealand wool clips, effectively controlling the provision of wool both for military and civilian textile manufacturing. A year later a Cotton Control Board was set up, enforcing a uniform 60 per cent of pre-war capacity across the industry, and rationing out available cotton. See also A. Marwick, *The Deluge: British Society and the First World War* (The Bodley Head, London, 1965), p. 251.

[53] Marwick, *The Deluge*, pp. 39–44; S. Pollard, *The Development of the British Economy 1914–1950* (Edward Arnold, London, 1962), pp. 42–3. Pollard argued that the real watershed in government policy occurred in 1916. See also Hilton, *Consumerism in Twentieth-Century Britain*, chapter 2; J. Lawrence, M. Dean and J.-L. Robert, 'The outbreak of war and the urban economy: Paris, Berlin and London in 1914', *Economic History Review*, vol. 45, no. 3 (1992), pp. 564–93; Bourne, *Britain and the Great War*, chapter 8; D. French, 'The rise and fall of "business as usual"', in Burk (ed.), *War and the State*, pp. 7–31. Propaganda also emphasised the economic advantages of investing in war savings: Slogans included: 'Are you saving for the children? Save for their Education and Give them a Start in Life', or 'Old age must come. So prepare for it by investing in War Savings Certificates'. IWM Art, First World War Posters, PST / 441 and PST / 2737, n.d.

[54] C.E. Playne, *Britain Holds On 1917, 1918* (George Allen and Unwin, London, 1933), p. 63.

[55] Hamilton Gibbs, *The Grey Wave*, p. 265. For an even-handed assessment of business practices during the First World War, see J.S. Boswell and B.R. Johns, 'Patriots or profiteers? British businessmen and the First World War', *The Journal of European Economic History*, vol. 11, no. 2 (1982), pp. 423–45. See also Waites, *A Class Society at War*, pp. 99–105; 221–31.

[56] P. Gibbs, *Realities of War* (Hutchinson, London, 1929; first published 1920), pp. 338–9. See also Marwick, *The Deluge*, p. 218; Bourke, *Dismembering the Male*, p. 107. Combatants were not alone in expressing hostility towards profiteers. For discontent among industrial workers, see Hilton, *Consumerism in Twentieth-Century Britain*, p. 57. For the issue of profiteering in socialist and labour politics, see J. Bush, *Behind the Lines: East London Labour 1914–1918* (Merlin Press, London, 1984), especially pp. 81–3; 141; 145–6.

invariably vulgarly. Indeed, the journalistic and popular image of the profiteer owed much to pre-war and well-established representations of the rich capitalist, whose visible signs of affluence included a fat stomach, frock coat, top hat, spats and cigar. A further element was on occasion the supposedly Semitic features[57] (Figure 3.6). This was a middle-aged man whose sartorial practices were seen as reprehensible not because they were indulged in at the expense of wife and children, but rather because they were at the expense of the country as a whole. Like the shirker's, the profiteer's appearance and consumer practices proclaimed his lack of involvement in the national sacrifice demanded by the war.

It seems likely that most people would have been aware that this much-despised figure was not the actual representation of real individuals, but was rather the personification of a 'problem': the problem not only of profit-making, but also of consumption in wartime. The excesses of journalistic profiteers and shirkers were clearly ethically unacceptable, and thus easy to condemn. However, outside the pages of the press, the boundary between acceptable and unacceptable wartime consumer practices was not always firm, and was the subject of constant re-negotiation.[58] All could be outraged by images and tales of wild extravagance at a time of widespread (if not life-threatening) shortages and of mounting casualties. In 1915, for example, the *Daily Mail* reported that working-class people were 'warming themselves in the sun of affluence', buying luxury items such as pianos, gramophones and motorbikes.[59] Extreme forms of behaviour, whether real or imagined, were of course easy to condemn. More difficult was the day-to-day negotiation between the pressure (and indeed often the desire) to exercise thrift, and the need to maintain a minimum level of necessary expenditure.

The example of clothing was characteristically complex: to what extent were all purchases of clothes – and particularly of menswear – perceived as unpatriotic waste? At the outbreak of war, the trade journal *Men's Wear* had warned that the clothing trade, and especially the 'small struggling tradesman', would be hard hit by the conflict, which would bring in its train lessening demand and slack trade: at 'times of great national emergency and even peril, clothing is looked upon more in the nature of a luxury'.[60] Official and semi-official propaganda certainly included expenditure on clothes among the diversions of resources from the war effort, which it was considered necessary to minimise. An advertisement of 1917 by the National

---

[57]   *The Sketch*, 25 November 1914; *Punch*, 9 February 1916; 13 June 1917; *The Bystander*, 27 June 1917.

[58]   J. Winter, 'Paris, London, Berlin 1914–1919: capital cities at war', in Winter and Robert (eds), *Capital Cities at War*, especially pp. 19–20.

[59]   *Daily Mail*, 1 February 1915. Quoted in Marwick, *The Deluge*, p. 42. At the other end of the social scale, see, for example, the satirical portrait of two 'club knuts', in *The Sketch*, 15 September 1915.

[60]   *Men's Wear*, 8 August 1914. See also *The Outfitter*, 15 August 1914. On the general reluctance to consume and spend money in the first month of the war, see R.D. Blumenfeld, *All in a Lifetime* (Ernst Benn, London, 1931), pp. 6–12. A more sanguine view was taken, for example, by *The Tailor and Cutter*, 13 August 1914; 27 August 1914.

War Savings Committee, for example, called upon both men and women to 'wear old clothes, old boots, old dresses, and invest what you will save in the War Loan'.[61]

Many came to believe, as a result, that to be too 'well-dressed', to wear clothes that were too obviously new, too smart and well-looked-after, was ethically unacceptable for the duration of the war. According to *Men's Wear*, some people considered that for men to be interested in tailors' booklets and fashion plates at a time of war was 'effeminate, soft, dandical-criminal'.[62] The county court judge Spencer Hogg may well have been one of these people. When in 1918 a young man who had received compensation for an accident applied to the court for a lump sum of money to enable him to buy a 'new rig-out' for Whitsuntide, claiming that his clothes were now more than a year old, the judge was unsympathetic: 'Don't you know that during war-time people have stopped rigging themselves out in new clothes at Whitsuntide? ... you will have to wear your clothes more than 12 months. You must do like the rest of us, and wear your old clothes.'[63] While hostilities lasted, people made sure that their clothes lasted 'double as long as they used to do in the days of Peace and Plenty'.[64] According to Caroline Playne, calls to continue buying clothes as normal, in order to keep the clothing trades afloat, were largely ignored. Indeed, 'it was considered bad taste to wear good clothing, new things were taboo. Those accustomed to dress well must manage to look shabby. Nice clothes must be sold and got rid of to help win the war'[65] (Figure 3.7).

Walking through the streets of London's West End in the Summer of 1916, Michael MacDonagh noted the great drabness and shabbiness of civilian clothes. The cause, he believed, could be found on the city's walls and hoardings. Recruiting posters had largely been replaced by economy posters, calling upon citizens to spend less and save more. 'Accordingly it is the mode to assume a studied air of personal untidiness. Trousers with baggy knees and frayed edges indicate that

---

[61]   *News of the World*, 11 February 1917. See also Playne, *Britain Holds On*, p. 48. For similar appeals see *The Oxford Times*, 17 July 1915; *Reading Mercury*, 15 July 1915; *The Tailor and Cutter*, 9 March 1916. See also posters announcing an 'Exhibition of war economy dress', or calling upon the public to 'Salvage – save!', IWM Art, First World One Posters, PST / 2710 and PST / 5232, n.d. Of course, food was the commodity most strongly focused on in wartime debates about consumption. Hilton, *Consumerism in Twentieth-Century Britain*, chapter 2; R. Van Emden and S. Humphries, *All Quiet on the Home Front: An Oral History of Life in Britain During the First World War* (Headline, London, 2003), chapter 7; Winter, *The Great War*, pp. 215–29; Trentmann, 'Bread, milk and democracy'; T. Bonzon and B. Davis, 'Feeding the cities', in Winter and Robert (eds), *Capital Cities at War*, pp. 305–41; P.E. Dewey, 'Nutrition and living standards in wartime Britain', in R. Wall and J. Winter (eds), *The Upheaval of War: Family, Work and Welfare in Europe, 1914–1918* (Cambridge University Press, Cambridge, 1988), pp. 197–220; Waites, *A Class Society at War*.

[62]   *Men's Wear*, 26 October 1918.

[63]   *The Tailor and Cutter*, 23 May 1918.

[64]   Miles, *Untold Tales of War-Time London*, p. 75.

[65]   C.E. Playne, *Society at War 1914–1916* (George Allen and Unwin, London, 1931), p. 231. See also C.S. Peel, *How we Lived Then 1914–1918: A Sketch of Social and Domestic Life in England During the War* (John Lane, The Bodley Head, London, 1929), p. 6; Blumenfeld, *All in a Lifetime*, pp. 37–8; *Punch*, 19 January 1916.

The Bystander, November 13, 1918   289

Profit-tears

THE PROFITEER *(lamenting the shortage of raw material)*: "Yes, this would 'a been a good war if we could 'ave 'ad it in peace-time"

Figure 3.6   War profiteers. *The Bystander*, **13 November 1918. Courtesy of the Bodleian Library, University of Oxford, N.2705 d.161.**

you are ... "doing your bit" to win the war'. Eighteen months later he observed that 'the war has made the male section of us careless about dress. Men's fashions have been suspended "for the duration".'[66] Unsurprisingly, the tailoring trade press had little sympathy for those they called 'war economy cranks' who advocated the wearing of old clothes. This was a practice that merely showed 'a simulation of patriotism'.[67] However, cynicism was not limited to those involved in the menswear trade. According to the journalist R.D. Blumenfeld, in London society circles in 1916 'there is a great deal of humbug underneath all this war-time economy'. After all, 'Nothing gives you more kudos ... nowadays than to appear at dinner in shabby evening clothes and a collar with obvious fringes protruding from its edges. "Now, there's a patriot for you", they say. "He used to be the best-dressed man. Look at him now. He's doing it for the war". Thus you achieve fame cheaply and with honour.'[68]

NOVEMBER 24, 1915.]   PUNCH, OR THE LONDON CHARIVARI.   425

WAR ECONOMY.

Lady Sybil de Vere. "Do LOOK AT THOSE EXTRAORDINARY PEOPLE. THEIR CLOTHES ARE QUITE NEW!"
Sir Hugo. "ROTTEN BAD FORM!"

Figure 3.7   'War economy' and the 'cult of shabbiness'. *Punch*, 24 November 1915. Courtesy of the Bodleian Library, University of Oxford, N.2706 d.10.

---

[66]   MacDonagh, *In London During the Great War*, pp. 118–19; 122; 246. See also *Punch*, 19 January 1916.

[67]   *The Tailor and Cutter*, 2 March 1916. See also 15 June 1916.

[68]   Blumenfeld, *All in a Lifetime*, pp. 55–6. See also the more measured comments in ibid., pp. 105–6. For a satirical view of 'Economy in dress' see also *Punch*, 12 April 1916.

In any case, the extent of this so-called 'cult of shabbiness' should not be exaggerated. Firstly, it is impossible to tell where patriotism ended and necessity began. When during the war the Sixth Earl Spencer 'abandoned his high starched collars and replaced them with a scarf carefully wound round his neck to look like a collar', this may have been 'a gesture to the grave situation', but may equally have been due to the difficulties of obtaining starch.[69] The popularity of the shabby look seems to have been limited to upper-middle-class (or even upper-class), and indeed metropolitan milieus. Indeed, to be too well dressed may have raised eyebrows in certain circles, but to be badly dressed certainly did not ensure respectful treatment. When William Linton Andrews, the news editor of *The Dundee Advertiser*, enlisted in the early months of the war, there were not enough uniforms to go round, and recruits were forced to wear the civilian clothes they had joined up in. Andrews had decided that it was not worth ruining his best clothes, and had enlisted in an old golf jacket, tennis shirt and flannel trousers. He was shocked to find out how differently he was treated when he 'went out in shabby and dirty war clothes! Even in wartime, the cold shoulder replaced a smiling welcome' once he no longer looked 'well and prosperous'.[70] Despite 'the pretence that everyone is "at the Front"', *The Tailor and Cutter* pointed out that even in spring 1915 plenty of men still required 'smart and up-to-date clothes'.[71]

Munitions workers and working-class extravagance

Unsurprisingly, perhaps, tales of wild spending sprees among the working class tended to focus on munitions workers. According to John Gray, then a schoolboy growing up in London, the average wage of munitioners was eight pounds a week: 'Little wonder that grand pianos were bought and furs, silk and jewellery by those who but a short while before had been pawning to carry on'. Apparently, munitions workers could easily be spotted in a crowd, with their 'gaudy suits and caps', and their 'money-to-burn manners'.[72] Nevertheless, the image of the affluent munitions worker who in 1918, wearing a natty suit, with a flower in the lapel and cigar in hand, could buy a whole salmon for 50 shillings, since 'Fourteen quid a week takes a bit o' getting through', arguably owed more to journalistic and comic exaggeration

---

[69] Norfolk Federation of Women's Institutes, *Norfolk Within Living Memory* (Countryside Books and Norfolk Federation of Women's Institutes, Newbury, 1995), p. 102.

[70] W. Linton Andrews, *Haunting Years: The Commentaries of a War Territorial* (Hutchinson, London, n.d. [c. 1930]), pp. 14–15.

[71] *The Tailor and Cutter*, 15 April 1915. See also 22 April 1915. It has been estimated that, between 1914 and 1918, 53 per cent of British men of military age were enlisted in the armed forces. Gregory, 'Lost generations', p. 59.

[72] J. Gray, *Gin and Bitters* (Jarrold Publishers, London, n.d. [c. 1938]), pp. 104–5. See also M. Moynihan (ed.), *Greater Love: Letters Home 1914–1918* (W.H. Allen, London, 1980), p. 199; R. Roberts, *The Classic Slum: Salford Life in the First Quarter of the Century* (Penguin, Harmondsworth, 1974; first published 1971), pp. 199–200; but also p. 207; Blumenfeld, *All in a Lifetime*, pp. 118–19.

than to reality (Figure 3.8).[73] Despite the talk of working-class extravagance, there remained plenty of people for whom shabbiness was a necessity, rather than a more or less patriotic choice.[74]

Jonathan Manning has suggested that the wartime wage rates enjoyed by munitions workers were certainly better able to keep up with price inflation than those of other workers. However, even taking overtime payments into account, it is difficult to imagine munitions workers – either male or female – regularly indulging in wild spending sprees. Overall, between 1914 and 1918 the retail prices of consumer goods more than doubled (and continued to rise sharply until 1920). Price rises were even steeper for clothing and, as Figure 3.9 shows, the actual quantity of clothing sold during the conflict declined by more than 30 per cent, only beginning to recover after 1918. Thus, for example, the engineering fitter who in 1914 had earned (the relatively good wage of) 40 shillings a week, by December 1918 would have brought home roughly twice this sum (exclusive of overtime payments).[75] However, the suit that in 1914 he could have bought for 30 shillings, in 1918 would have cost him twice as much, or perhaps even more. In 1914, for example, the London-based mail order firm of Catesby's was advertising its inexpensive 'Burlington' suit for 37s 6d, which could be ordered by post and paid for in weekly instalments. In 1916 the price of the same suit increased to 40 shillings, and then to 55s in 1917. After this date, advertisements coyly stopped mentioning prices until the spring of 1919, when the 'Burlington' was offered for the astonishing price of £5 10s.[76] At the more expensive end of the market, price increases were equally spectacular. Before the outbreak of war, Harry Hall advertised their suits and overcoats for prices starting at 63s. The starting price increased to 3 ½ guineas

---

[73] *Punch*, 16 October 1918.

[74] The issue of wartime standards of living is a complex one: incomes, expenditure, the availability of services, the impact of factors like rent control or separation allowances, as well as more intangible issues such as bereavement, all need to be taken into account. Poverty certainly did not entirely disappear. See, for example, the casual dock workers, labourers and other 'marginal' workers considered in V. de Vesselitsky, *Expenditure and Waste: A Study in War-Time* (Ratan Tata Foundation, London, 1917). The impact of war on civilian standards of living is explored, for example, in Winter, *The Great War*; Winter and Robert (eds), *Capital Cities at War*; Waites, *A Class Society at War*; Stevenson, *British Society 1914–45*, chapter 3; J. Burnett, *A History of the Cost of Living* (Penguin Books, Harmondsworth, 1969), pp. 308–9; Marwick, *The Deluge*, pp. 123–30; 189–203.

[75] J. Manning, 'Wages and purchasing power', in Winter and Robert (eds), *Capital Cities at War*, pp. 255–85.

[76] *News of the World*, 26 July 1914; 4 October 1914; 2 May 1915; 7 May 1916; 4 February 1917; 2 September 1917; 24 February 1918; 30 March 1919; 27 April 1919. It was estimated that between 1914 and 1918 the prices of suits 'usually purchased by the working classes' had increased from 28s 6d to 60s, those of overcoats from 27s 4d to 46s 8d, and those of shirts (union flannel) from 4s 6d to 8s 2½ d. A.L. Bowley, *Prices and Wages in the United Kingdom, 1914–1920* (Clarendon Press, Oxford, 1921), pp. 64–6; Winter, *The Great War*, pp. 229–30. See also the estimates of price inflation in 'Retail prices of clothing', *The Ministry of Labour Gazette*, vol. 29 (April 1921), pp. 178–9; *The Tailor and Cutter*, 4 July 1918.

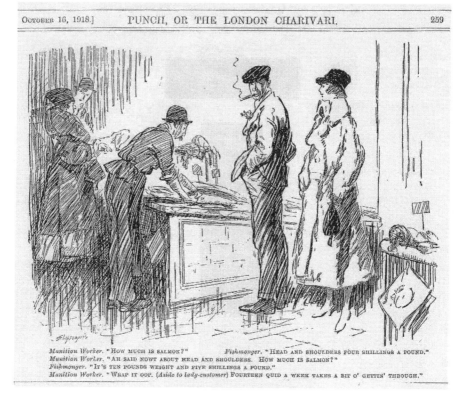

Munition Worker. "HOW MUCH IS SALMON?"   *Fishmonger.* "HEAD AND SHOULDERS FOUR SHILLINGS A POUND."
Munition Worker. "AH SAID NOWT ABOUT HEAD AND SHOULDERS. HOW MUCH IS SALMON?"
Fishmonger. "IT'S TEN POUNDS WEIGHT AND FIVE SHILLINGS A POUND."
Munition Worker. "WRAP IT OOP. (*Aside to lady-customer*) FOURTEEN QUID A WEEK TAKES A BIT O' GETTIN' THROUGH."

Figure 3.8   Munitions work and working-class extravagance. *Punch***, 16 October
1918. Courtesy of the Bodleian Library, University of Oxford,
N.2706 d.10.**

in February 1917, £4 4s in July 1917, £5 5s in February 1918, £6 6s in May 1918,
reaching £8 8s in December 1918.[77]

Overtime payments will have helped to make increased prices affordable.
However, even apart from the check on consumer activities caused by long and
exhausting hours of work, the shortages of materials, increasingly diverted to
military use, also effectively limited the opportunities for clothes purchase. As
Walter Gander, who was ten years old when the war broke out, explained, during the
conflict he was forced to wear clothes cast off by his brothers, 'because clothes in
those days were really hard to come by, and we wore more or less what we could get
– cut-down trousers and handed-down boots'.[78]

According to the trade press, demand for clothes in munitions centres remained
buoyant throughout the latter part of the war. In spring 1917, *Men's Wear* reported
that orders for the Easter holidays had for the first time since the outbreak of war

---

[77] *The Bystander*, 12 August 1914; 21 February 1917; 18 July 1917; 20 February 1918;
22 May 1918; 9 October 1918; 4 December 1918.

[78] N. Crowther (ed.), *I Can Remember ...* (Edward Arnold, London, 1976), p. 40.

been 'quite satisfactory'.[79] This was attributed to the fact that the 'war worker' now had some spare cash to spend on his own appearance. According to Henry Oxley, who between 1916 and 1917 worked as a munitions worker in Woolwich Arsenal, despite the very long hours, 'anybody in armaments they were like the modern car worker today. They were affluent ... we were paid in golden sovereigns'. Before the war he had worked as a silk warehouse clerk, and he found that in his new job his earnings were a good deal higher. As he explained:

> coming from a very small wage ... on to a wage which was sometimes four or five times higher ... one thought in terms of good suits, made to measure ... I felt I was having an uplift ... Of course, if one was able to buy new clothes it gives you a feeling of superiority over as you were, say two or three years before.[80]

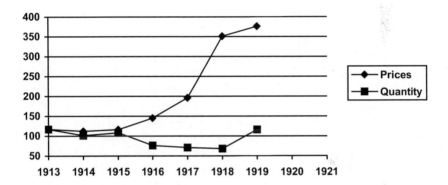

Figure 3.9   Price increases and quantity index of clothing in the UK, 1913–1919 (1900=100).
Source: **A.R. Prest with A.A. Adams,** *Consumers' Expenditure in the United Kingdom, 1900–1919* **(Cambridge University Press, Cambridge, 1954), p. 123.**

The new consumer opportunities offered by wartime conditions were by no means always viewed with embarrassment by those who were able to enjoy them, despite the widespread condemnation of extravagance. Walter Briggs and his friend, both Woolwich Arsenal munitions workers, celebrated their youthful leisure and consumption practices by composing a song, 'We are the two Woolwich Smashers'. Like any self-respecting young 'nuts', they sang: 'with the ladies we do cut a dash ... [they] do declare that we are debonair'.[81]

On the whole, however, these 'little flutters on new outfits' and other goods could hardly be described as extravagant.[82] As George Hodgkinson, who worked in a Coventry munitions factory, explained, by the end of the war wages had risen

---

[79] *Men's Wear*, 7 April 1917. Retailers' wartime strategies will be considered in Chapter 6.
[80] IWM Sound, Interview transcript, 716, Henry Oxley, 1975.
[81] IWM Sound, Interview, reel 1, 680, Walter Richard Briggs, 1975.
[82] *Men's Wear*, 7 April 1917; 12 May 1917.

as high as £15 per week: 'this was big money compared to what had been the level before'. However, increases in expenditure among munitions workers did not go on wild extravagances – the fur coats and lobsters of popular imagination – but on 'home comforts ... I don't think their living standards altered very much apart from that ... they were able to live ... as well as an average artisan ... better than some'.[83] There are indications, furthermore, that the exhortations to save money were not always ignored by munitions workers, and could actually engender an ambivalent attitude towards consumption. Henry Oxley could not remember any complaints about munitions workers flashing their money around during the conflict, and denied coming across any ill-feeling towards them on the part of combatants.[84] However, Patrick McGeown spent the war as 'a few-pounds-a-week man in a vital trade': steel smelting. He asked for no more, and 'didn't want anything extra, there was lots of scorn for war profiteers, and it was nice not being one of them'. Nevertheless, 'it wasn't too easy being a civilian in that first war. Old ladies with fearful bumps of righteousness were handing out white feathers to civilians who looked military age ... They never approached me, for which I thanked heaven, but I was always in dread of them and not even my arm band comforted me.'[85]

Moreover, if munitions workers were probably not as well-off as sections of the press and of the population would have liked to believe, it was also the case that some sections of the working class were actually impoverished during the war, most notably those not directly engaged in war work. The average wage of agricultural labourers, for example, had by 1920–21 more than tripled from their 1914 level. However, this advance was not quite as impressive as it sounds, as in the short term it actually failed to keep pace with price increases: it was only in mid-1918, after wage boards had been set up, that real wages regained their (often miserably low) 1914 level. Taking into account price inflation, a weekly wage of 46s in 1920 (in an occupation where there was little scope for overtime) would hardly have afforded a much more luxurious life-style than the 13s 4d of 1914.[86]

Understandably, then, the government's exhortations to practise economy and invest in the war funds could provoke anger and derision among agricultural workers and others not involved in war work. They certainly caused a good deal of resentment in Great Leighs, a village where, it was pointed out, nobody had ever done anything but practise economy, and 'where no one has any reserve to give or to invest'.[87] When, in 1917, Ernest Read Cooper, the Southwold town clerk, spoke at a village

[83]   IWM Sound, Interview transcript, 764, George Edward Hodgkinson, 1976.
[84]   IWM Sound, Interview transcript, 716, Henry Oxley, 1975.
[85]   P. McGeown, *Heat the Furnace Seven Times More* (Hutchinson, London, 1967), p. 98. It is also interesting to note that Elizabeth Flint's mother decided that the exhausting work, together with the long journey to and from Woolwich Arsenal, were not worth the cost of the piano that she wished to purchase with her wages. E. Flint, *Hot Bread and Chips* (Museum Press, London, 1963), pp. 83–90.
[86]   Marwick, *The Deluge*, p. 272; Dewey, *War and Progress*, pp. 41–2. James Whittaker desribed how his family's income did not keep up with price inflation. J. Whittaker, *I, James Whittaker* (Rich and Cowan, London, 1934), pp. 117–18.
[87]   Clark, *Echoes of the Great War*, p. 106. But see also A.S. Jasper, *A Hoxton Childhood* (Barrie and Rockliff: The Cresset Press, London, 1969), p. 102.

'Win the War' meeting, emphasising the need for economy, and dwelling 'upon the need to wear up all old clothes and destroy nothing', an old man at the back of the audience called out: "Ha' yew got an oud suit or tew, Master, cos I'll wear 'em for you", which caused much laughter'.[88]

To his audience, Cooper probably looked like a comfortably-off middle-class man, advocating a parsimony that he would never have to practise at first hand. It is significant, however, that wartime material pressures were by no means absent among the middle classes. Indeed, Jon Lawrence has suggested that during the war, non-manual earnings actually fell 'significantly' behind retail prices. At least for some sections of the middle-class salariat, this may well have meant a reduction in their disposable income, including, inevitably, that which could be spent on clothes. Although some undoubtedly benefited from the opportunities provided by the war economy, it was also the case that 'large numbers of previously prosperous individuals were forced to accept a much reduced standard of living',[89] a situation that may partly explain the bitterness towards munitions workers expressed in many sections of the wartime press.

Conclusion

Overall, between 1913 and 1918 the volume of civilian consumer expenditure in Britain fell by nearly 20 per cent, interrupting a period of growth that had stretched back at least as far as the 1870s. A remarkable quarter of this decline was due to a fall in clothing expenditure.[90] The trends in consumer behaviour, desires and expectations that lie behind these statistics are no doubt complex: the enlistment of almost five million men,[91] shortages, the diversion of textiles and labour to military use, as well as the resulting price increases, not always matched by wage rises, all no doubt played a part in reducing expenditure on clothes. Whether because of high prices, patriotic feelings, or fears of being thought a 'shirker' or a 'profiteer', or perhaps because of a mixture of all these and other factors, men all too often found that the best way to deal with the delicate question of wartime clothes purchase and consumption was, as one

---

[88] M. Moynihan, *People at War 1914–1918* (David and Charles, Newton Abbot, 1973), p. 205. The percentage increase in the wages of unskilled workers involved in war-related work, which often outstripped those of skilled workers, certainly sound impressive. However, it should be noted that the pre-war starting point had often been extremely low, and that average wages remained lower than those of skilled workers. Stevenson, *British Society 1914–45*, p. 79, table 2. See also pp. 78–82 for a discussion of wartime 'wages and living standards'; Dewey, *War and Progress*, p. 42; Marwick, *The Deluge*, p. 272.

[89] J. Lawrence, 'Material pressures on the middle classes', in Winter and Robert (eds), *Capital Cities at War*, pp. 229–54.

[90] Dewey, 'The new warfare and economic mobilisation', pp. 10–84, especially pp. 79–80. A further quarter was due to a fall in expenditure on food, and a third on alcohol. See also C. Lee, 'The service industries', in R. Floud and D. McCloskey (eds), *The Economic History of Britain since 1700. Vol. 2: 1860–1939* (Cambridge University Press, Cambridge, second edition 1994; first published 1981), p. 126.

[91] It has been calculated that 722,785 British servicemen died during the conflict. Dewey, *War and Progress*, pp. 23–4; Winter, *The Great War*, pp. 66–76.

irritated tailor put it: to 'press 'em and clean 'em and wear 'em again'. And when even that failed, 'wear 'em turned and the button-holes turned over again'.[92]

In a way, therefore, the war did bring about significant shifts in male sartorial behaviour. Practices that were commonplace before 1914 were no longer acceptable during the war: to be too well-dressed, even (or perhaps especially) in privileged circles, could be morally suspect. Elegant leisure-time clothes, particularly when worn by young men of military age, became tainted with associations of shirking and profiteering, as did any garments beyond the plainest working garb among the working classes. However, the continuities were arguably more significant than these short-term shifts. Firstly, menswear continued to be a matter of public assessment, and a way of constructing and reinforcing collective male identities, although ideas about which were the most desirable had inevitably changed, with military uniforms, even those of privates in obscure regiments, acquiring a new glamour. Even if one's clothes could not signal one's identity as a manly, patriotic combatant, it was still advisable to try and look as different as possible from press caricatures of 'shirkers' or 'profiteers'. Secondly, acceptable sartorial standards continued to be enforced through ridicule, verbal abuse and on occasion violence, although, in a reversal of pre-1914 practice, the enforcing frequently seems to have come from outside male peer groups, often even from female strangers. Finally, the local and contingent continued to be fundamental to sartorial decisions: the nut may have been driven out of Hyde Park and the streets of London's West End, but he seems to have found a congenial home in areas like Woolwich, a south-east London community with strong links to munitions-making. Here, buying a natty new suit was not necessarily seen as a sign of unpatriotic waste, but could be perceived as a reasonable reward for long hours of arduous and often dangerous war work. As civilian men went about their daily lives, they still had to negotiate the unstable boundary between acceptable and unacceptable sartorial practices, with others' potentially critical opinions very much in mind. In war as in peacetime, it was important to 'fit in'.

---

[92] Peel, *How we Lived Then*, p. 67.

Chapter 4

The Democratisation of Menswear? 1919–1939

How the war would change British society was an issue of absorbing interest to many commentators, both in the course and in the immediate aftermath of the conflict. How would the experience of war (and especially of combat), change ideas, practices, expectations, and indeed people themselves?[1] According to C.F.G. Masterman, to those living through it, whether as civilians or as combatants, the 'catastrophe' of war had 'seemed so immense, the loss of life and treasure so terrible', that many had feared that it would eventually spell the 'collapse of civilisation itself'. Not only would the impulse to work disappear, but consumption itself would become increasingly fraught with difficulties: 'Men would be found returning to the condition of a hungry mob, without hope or purpose, scrambling in the deepening darkness for the bare means of sustenance.'[2]

In a seemingly more light-hearted way, the impact of more than four years of war – and especially of the experience of active service in the armed forces – on male consumption, fashion and clothing styles was also debated. There was little agreement about the nature of the sartorial changes that the war could be expected to bring about. In October 1917, J. Wallace Black confidently asserted that returning soldiers 'have been living in drab clothes … for so long that there will be a revulsion of feeling in favour of clothes of brighter hue … lounge jackets of a "sloppy" cut will be in favour. The tight tunic has sickened the men of close-fitting garments, and they will demand something roomy.' On the other hand, a year and a half earlier, *The Outfitter*'s editor had asserted, equally confidently, that after the war loose-fitting lounge suits would no longer be fashionable, as young officers would have become used to close-fitting

---

[1]   See, for example, J. Lawrence, 'Forging a peaceable kingdom: war, violence, and fear of brutalization in post-First World War Britain', *The Journal of Modern History*, vol. 75, no. 3 (2003), pp. 557–89. The statistics are stark. Between 1914 and 1918 more than five million British men served in some capacity in the armed forces: around 22 per cent of the male population. In November 1918 the British Expeditionary Force still included a staggering 2,360,400 men. It has been estimated that around 722,000 British servicemen died in the course of the war (out of a total of 9.5 million combatant deaths). J. Bourke, *Dismembering the Male: Men's Bodies, Britain and the Great War* (Reaktion Books, London, 1996), pp. 15, 27; J.M. Bourne, *Britain and the Great War 1914–1918* (Edward Arnold, London, 1989), pp. 177–8. See also M. Roper, 'Between manliness and masculinity: the "war generation" and the psychology of fear in Britain, 1914–1950', *Journal of British Studies*, vol. 44, no. 2 (2005), pp. 343–62.

[2]   C.F.G. Masterman, *England After War: A Study* (Hodder and Stoughton, London, n.d. [c. 1923]), p. 3.

uniforms, and 'will not, when they return to civilian life, be able to endure the "roomy" type of coat'.[3] Despite these differences of opinion, all agreed that the conflict could hardly fail to have a notable impact. According to a contributor to *The Outfitter* in 1915, retailers trying to decide which shirts to stock were faced with uncertainty about when their youthful customers would be able to return to civilian life, as well as about what they would prefer to buy when they did, 'for the ideas of those who have been facing the music may have undergone a fundamental change'.[4] After the war, Stanley Casson certainly noticed the difference the first time he wore his new civilian suit: 'I felt as if I should fall to pieces. For so many years my waistline had been held firm by a belt and a close-fitting uniform and my legs in leggings, that no belt and soft trousers made me feel almost decadent'[5] (Figure 4.1).

For some ex-combatants, the 'sartorial' impact of war was straightforward, occasionally being responsible for opening up (even if only temporarily) previously unavailable opportunities for consumption. In 1918, for example, William Holt was sent to officer training school in Oxford. Before the war he had worked as a weaver, leaving school at the age of thirteen and joining the army at the outbreak of war. It was in Oxford that he enjoyed his first ever visit to a 'high-class tailor', where he treated himself to items such as 'an extra pair of riding breeches made from Bedford cord', and a British Warm overcoat. It was also in Oxford that he wore white flannel trousers for the first time in his life. 'When I first caught a glimpse of myself reflected in a shop window ... I could scarcely recognise myself, so great was the change they had made in my appearance, and so different the train of ideas they now started in my mind'.[6] Others, on the contrary, saw the shoddiness of the demob suit and the lack of material rewards at the end of the conflict as symbolic of a lack of recognition of their sacrifices, and of broken wartime promises. One of the ex-combatants interviewed by Stephen Humphries in the early 1980s commented scornfully:

> They'd said we were fighting for a better country, we'd be well looked after, but it was all propaganda. They soon forgot you. When we come out they give us an old army shirt, army pair of boots, army pair of grey socks, army overcoat an' a Martin Henry suit of clothes, which was the same as what they used to bloody wear in the Union.[7]

Even as khaki gradually disappeared from the streets and from shop windows after the end of hostilities, the demob suit and other items of army kit continued to act

---

[3]   *Men's Wear*, 13 October 1917; *The Outfitter*, 17 February 1916.

[4]   *The Outfitter*, 6 March 1915.

[5]   S. Casson, *Steady Drummer* (G. Bell and Sons, London, 1935), p. 268.

[6]   W. Holt, *I Haven't Unpacked: An Autobiography* (George G. Harrap, London, 1939), p. 78. See also the fictionalised accounts in H. Williamson, *A Test to Destruction* (Sutton Publishing, Stroud, 1997; first published 1977), pp. 235–9; G. Orwell, *Coming Up for Air* (Penguin Books, Harmondsworth, 1984; first published 1939), pp. 111–12; 125–6.

[7]   S. Humphries, *Hooligans or Rebels? An Oral History of Working-Class Childhood and Youth 1889–1939* (Basil Blackwell, Oxford, 1981), p. 187. For criticism of the demob suit, see *Men's Wear*, 29 September 1917; 8 February 1919; *The Tailor and Cutter*, 7 September 1916; 4 March 1920. But see also the more positive assessment in *Men's Wear*, 25 January 1919.

The Man She Married

IN ANOTHER GUISE

Figure 4.1   'The man she married': back to civvies. *The Bystander*, **15 January 1919. Courtesy of the Bodleian Library, University of Oxford, N.2705 d.161.**

as a reminder of the war, a reminder that ex-combatants and others literally carried
with them wherever they went. The twenty-one-year-old Vic Cole was demobbed in
1918 as medically unfit for further service. When the Armistice was announced he
spent the day drinking 'with men I had never seen before', but eventually, 'in my ill-
fitting suit, with cloth cap and heavy boots, I arrived home to the quiet, orderly and
peaceful atmosphere of Gipsy Hill', his grandmother's home.[8] Both garments and
memories could be passed on to others. Edward Blishen's first coat had been made
from his father's old military overcoat. 'It was often talked about: how it was cut
down by a jobbing tailor, and how dashing it was, this miniature form of the khaki
my father had worn throughout the Great War.' According to Blishen, together with
the overcoat, 'the war itself was cut down for me, as a small set of anecdotes my
father told, and certain objects that were kept in cupboards throughout the house', a
monocular and a swagger stick among them.[9]

For their part, fashion and dress historians have tended to emphasise the changes
to menswear styles after 1918, referring particularly to the greater informality and
'relaxed' nature of male clothing in the latter period.[10] Many contemporaries would
have agreed. According to Arthur Harding, after the war

> Clerks … appeared at work with flannel trousers and sports jackets instead of black jacket and
> striped trousers. They were done with tradition. I knew that, because when I was wardrobe dealing
> I was always being offered striped trousers, and you couldn't sell them for love nor money.[11]

On returning to his job as a bank clerk in 1919, the ex-officer R.H. Mottram
described himself in a bemused tone as being at the time a 'man of thirty … dressed
in "tweeds" with a soft collar, for we never resumed the black coat and starched shirt
of perfect clerkdom'.[12] From the perspective of a more exhalted social circle, Count
Harry Kessler observed a similar phenomenon. In 1922 the cosmopolitan German

---

[8]   R. Van Emden and S. Humphries, *All Quiet on the Home Front: An Oral History of
Life in Britain During the First World War* (Headline, London, 2003), p. 290. The damaged
and mutilated bodies of many ex-combatants provided another starkly visual reminder of the
war. See Bourke, *Dismembering the Male*, chapter 1. In 1928, almost 2.5 million men were
still in receipt of a war disability pension. J. Stevenson, *British Society 1914–45* (Penguin,
Harmondsworth, 1990; first published 1984), p. 94.

[9]   E. Blishen, *Sorry Dad* (Allison and Busby, London, 1984; first published 1978),
p. 23. Demobbed soldiers could either keep their army overcoats or return them to any railway
station and receive a pound in exchange. G. Coppard, *With a Machine Gun to Cambrai*
(Papermac, London, 1986; first published 1980), p. 134. In 1920, army overcoats, dyed blue,
were being sold for 25s each. *News of the World*, 11 January 1920.

[10]   See, for example, T. Edwards, *Men in the Mirror: Men's Fashion, Masculinity and
Consumer Society* (Cassell, London, 1997), p. 17; N. Tarrant, *The Development of Costume*
(Routledge with National Museums of Scotland, London, 1994), p. 101; D. de Marly, *Fashion
for Men: An Illustrated History* (B.T. Batsford, London, 1985), p. 125; P. Byrde, *The Male
Image: Men's Fashion in Britain 1300–1970* (B.T. Batsford, London, 1979), pp. 90–92.

[11]   R. Samuel, *East End Underworld: Chapters in the Life of Arthur Harding* (Routledge
and Kegan Paul, London, 1981), p. 267.

[12]   R.H. Mottram, *Another Window Seat or Life Observed: vol. 2 1919–1953* (Hutchinson,
London, 1957), p. 15.

aristocrat returned to London after an absence of more than eight years, and treated himself to an evening at the theatre. To his 'astonishment', he noticed that at least half the men in the stalls were wearing lounge suits, while most of the remainder were dressed in dinner jackets. Only five or six individuals were 'in tails'. This was 'a real revolution or, more accurately, the symptom of such'.[13]

Nevertheless, to observe the occurrence of changes in clothing styles is not the same as demonstrating that these were somehow 'caused' by the war. After all, items such as lounge suits and plus-fours were already popular in the Edwardian period, and were perceived to form part of a trend towards greater 'informality' that pre-dated the outbreak of hostilities. For example, *The Gentleman's Magazine of Fashion* was noting the impact on men's dress of 'the growing taste for athletic sports', and the 'growing desire for ease and comfort, for freedom of movement' as early as 1885.[14] More generally, although with some notable exceptions, such as the popularity of trench coats or of 'woollies',[15] it is often impossible to identify a straightforward link between the war and specific changes in patterns of consumption. It is quite possible that, as Joanna Bourke has suggested, 'many men took their wartime sartorial experiences back home with them', but it is not always easy to see what exactly they did with them.[16] Even contemporaries were often baffled. Soon after the end of the war, Alec Waugh spent a quiet Saturday with his father watching a cricket match. So often during the conflict, a large part of which he had spent as a prisoner of war, he 'had been told, in the Press, from the pulpit, in political debate, that nothing could be the same again', that it seemed 'strange to come back and find so little change upon the surface'. To an outside observer, 'my father and I can have looked little different. He looked the same to me.'[17]

Difficult as it was and is to identify a convincing link between the conflict and specific changes in male consumption, it is even more difficult to believe that the war, with its hardships, suffering, and – for some – opportunities, made no difference at all. Accordingly, this chapter will be concerned with changes and discontinuities across the 'boundary' of the First World War, even if no attempt will be made to assert that these changes were 'caused' by the war. Chapters 1 and 2 explored the pressures and influences that affected male sartorial decisions, which, I suggested, continued to be as relevant in 1939 as they had been in 1880. Of fundamental importance, these chapters argued, was the need, desire and pressure to fit, even if only temporarily, into a particular mould of masculinity and a generally male peer group, although

---

[13]　H. Kessler, *The Diaries of a Cosmopolitan: 1918–1937* (Phoenix Press, London, 2001; first published in Great Britain 1971), p. 203.

[14]　*The Gentleman's Magazine of Fashion*, January 1885. Christopher Breward notes, furthermore, that 'the tailoring legacy of the 1860s could ... be said to have prioritised an emphasis on producing clothing marked by ease of fit to the exclusion of stylistic or decorative considerations.' C. Breward, *The Hidden Consumer: Masculinities, Fashion and City Life 1860–1914* (Manchester University Press, Manchester, 1999), p. 29.

[15]　*The Outfitter*, 8 May 1920; *Men's Wear*, 3 February 1923.

[16]　Bourke, *Dismembering the Male*, p. 208.

[17]　A. Waugh, *Early Years* (Cassell, London, 1962), p. 141. See also R. Graves and A. Hodge, *The Long Weekend: A Social History of Britain 1918–1939* (Abacus, London, 1995; first published 1940), p. 40.

factors such as financial pressures, the rejection of the breadwinner role or the powerlessness of childhood could ensure a lack of conformity to prevailing 'codes'. These pressures, Chapter 3 suggested, remained relevant during the conflict, even though there were certain changes in the sartorial models that were seen as most desirable, and in the ways that conformity was enforced.

Within this overall framework, the present chapter shifts the focus, and considers the extent and nature of changes in menswear consumption in the two decades that followed the end of the war. After briefly discussing the thorny issues of incomes and prices, questioning whether and how far the inter-war period saw increasing numbers of men becoming better able to afford decent, varied and good-quality clothing, the chapter then focuses on the question of sartorial 'democratisation'. Did the inter-war years see a process of 'modernisation' that allowed even men from relatively humble backgrounds to look like their 'betters'? Or, from a different perspective, did all men increasingly tend to look the same? The final part of the chapter then turns its attention to two groups of men who, in very different ways, have gained a significant place in discussions of inter-war consumption, the former as 'non-consumers', the latter as increasingly enthusiastic, and possibly even 'affluent', consumers: the unemployed and the young. How far – this chapter concludes – did their sartorial experiences, expectations and desires support the notion of a new inter-war consumerism, providing a key stage towards Britain's development as a fully-fledged 'consumer society'?

Incomes, prices and affordability

In the very early 1920s, it seemed that it was going to be the middle classes' standard of living that would suffer the most from the economic dislocations brought about by the war, as salaries and incomes failed to keep pace with the rising cost of living. It was middle-class lives, Masterman lamented in 1923, that would in the future be characterised by 'the scraping together of oddments, etc., into clothes, with the willing acceptance (in contrast to previous proud rejection) of gifts of second-hand apparel from relations and friends'.[18] It certainly seems that in the immediate aftermath of the war some sections of the middle class found it difficult to maintain their pre-war standard of living. In 1922 Harry Kessler observed that the exclusive shops of London's West End were 'as good class and elegant' as they had been before the war. 'But there is no longer the astounding amount of bustle and luxury as in 1914 ... It can be sensed that the country has become poorer and the shoppers rarer.'[19]

The situation was especially stressful for those lower-middle-class salaried workers, such as the many clerical employees, who even before the war had experienced some difficulties in meeting all the demands on their purses. However, the latter part of 1920 saw the beginning of a period of sharp price deflation, accompanied by a reduction in wages, but generally not in middle-class salaries.

---

[18]   Masterman, *England After War*, p. 59. See also R. McKibbin, *Classes and Cultures: England 1918–1951* (Oxford University Press, Oxford, 2000; first published 1998), p. 53; B. Waites, *A Class Society at War: England 1914–1918* (Berg, Leamington Spa, 1987), pp. 81–5.

[19]   Kessler, *The Diaries of a Cosmopolitan*, p. 203.

Stevenson and Cook thus point out that 'Between 1920 and 1939 the cost of living index fell by a third, with one of the most dramatic declines occurring in the early 1930s'.[20] As a result, despite the introduction of a tougher taxation regime, the inter-war period saw the majority of the middle class returning to a position where they could enjoy a comfortable surplus income, although it has been suggested that for families with an income of less than £500 a year, margins continued to be tight.[21] According to C.S. Peel, between 1914 and 1918 the annual expenditure on clothes of a family composed of husband, wife and two young children living on an income of £300 a year, had increased from £22 to £44. 'The cost of clothes, boots and repairs is a nightmare these days, and it is in this direction that our £300-a-year family practises its strictest economy, and allots but £10 a head ... this may seem an absurdly low figure, but many families are obliged to make it suffice.'[22] Despite such examples of hardship, it is worth noting that throughout the inter-war period, the 'average' middle-class family enjoyed twice the income of an 'average' working-class family, and – significantly – spent roughly twice as much on clothes: the 12-guinea suit offered by high-class tailors in the late 1920s may have been out of the reach of most middle-class men, but the 6½-guinea suit sold by the 'ordinary middle class tailors' could be afforded by most without too much difficulty.[23]

Middle-class men were also much less likely than their working-class counterparts to suffer from periods of unemployment. Indeed, they were generally far less affected by the changes and dislocations of the inter-war economy than were many sections of the working class. This is not to suggest that for the working class as a whole the inter-war years were a period of unrelieved economic bleakness. Although after 1920 wages began to fall rapidly from their war-time peaks, prices seem to have fallen even more steeply.[24] Between 1923/4 and 1934 wages stabilised, and did not fall anywhere near as rapidly as prices did during the post-1929 slump. In 1935, furthermore, wages

---

[20]   J. Stevenson and C. Cook (eds), *Britain in the Depression: Society and Politics 1929–39* (Longman, London, 1994; first published 1977), p. 26. There were exceptions to the picture of renewed middle-class affluence. Between 1924 and 1934, for example, the earnings of teachers fell by 12 per cent. J. Burnett, *A History of the Cost of Living* (Penguin Books, Harmondsworth, 1969), p. 311.

[21]   McKibbin, *Classes and Cultures*, pp. 61–2. Taking into account wartime price inflation, the fact that the average earnings of male bank clerks rose from £142 in 1911–13 to £368 in 1935 may not have been as impressive as it would seem at first sight. J. Benson, *The Rise of Consumer Society in Britain 1880–1980* (Longman, Harlow, 1994), p. 25.

[22]   C.S. Peel, *How We Lived Then 1914–1918: A Sketch of Social and Domestic Life in England During the War* (John Lane, The Bodley Head, London, 1929), pp. 181. Peel estimated that for a family on an income of £500 a year, clothes expenditure increased from £33 to £60.

[23]   McKibbin, *Classes and Cultures*, pp. 70–72. See also J. Benson, *Affluence and Authority: A Social History of Twentieth-Century Britain* (Hodder Arnold, London, 2005), p. 25; Stevenson, *British Society 1914–45*, pp. 129–34. In 1927 the 'ordinary middle class tailors', 'not so low as the 50s man and not so high as the 12 guineas man', offered suits costing between 4½ guineas and 10 guineas, the average price being 6½ guineas. *Men's Wear*, 12 February 1927.

[24]   The exception to this trend were miners, who suffered real wage losses throughout the inter-war period. McKibbin, *Classes and Cultures*, pp. 114–15. Peter Dewey presents a rather less positive picture than Ross McKibbin of working-class incomes in the 1920s. He suggests that between 1920 and 1924 the real wages of fully employed workers fell by 4 per cent (of miners by 19 per cent),

began to rise, gathering pace most notably after 1938. It has been estimated that in 1938 average real wages were one-third higher than on the eve of the First World War.[25] Taken together, these statistics suggest that; particularly in the 1930s, the real incomes of most working-class men and women who were in full and regular employment in the inter-war period (with some notable exceptions, such as miners) improved considerably from their pre-1914 level. To this should also be added the positive impact on inter-war incomes of significantly smaller-sized families.[26]

Rising real incomes, distributed among fewer family members, resulted in increasing opportunities for consumption for many sections of the population in full-time employment, both working- and middle-class. It has been estimated that in 1938 consumers' expenditure (at constant 1938 prices) had increased by almost a third from its 1913 level, having already more than doubled between 1870 and 1913 (at 1900 prices).[27] It also seems that a lower proportion of the family income had to be spent on the essentials of food and rent than before the war: 'a working-class family in 1914 had typically spent about 60 per cent of its income on food and a further 16 per cent on rent, by 1937–8 these figures had fallen to 35 per cent and 9 per cent respectively'.[28] That said, it is more difficult to assess whether part of this increased disposable income was devoted to the purchase of a greater quantity or better-quality menswear than was the case before the war. Figure 4.2 reveals that both the average price and the quantity of men's and boys' clothing sold in the UK reflected the vicissitudes of the inter-war economy. As prices fell from their wartime and immediate post-war heights,[29] the

---

although they rose by 6 per cent between 1924 and 1929 (miners' fell by a further 5 per cent). P. Dewey, *War and Progress in Britain 1914–1945* (Longman, London, 1997), pp. 91–2; 143–5.

[25]   Stevenson and Cook (eds), *Britain in the Depression*, p. 26; Stevenson, *British Society 1914–45*, pp. 116–18.

[26]   McKibbin, *Classes and Cultures*, pp. 114–19; Benson, *The Rise of Consumer Society*, p. 13; D. Gittins, *Fair Sex: Family Size and Structure, 1900–1939* (Hutchinson, London, 1982), especially chapter 2. Matthew Hilton has noted, however, that the government's cost-of-living index calculations reflected 'poorly the common purchasing expectations and routines of the average working-class family', which may have led to exaggerated estimates of real income gains. M. Hilton, *Consumerism in Twentieth-Century Britain: The Search for a Historical Movement* (Cambridge University Press, Cambridge, 2003), pp. 112–13.

[27]   C.H. Feinstein, *National Income, Expenditure and Output in the United Kingdom 1855–1965* (Cambridge University Press, Cambridge, 1972), pp. T14–16. See also the analysis of changing patterns of spending *and* saving in Benson, *Affluence and Authority*, chapter 2; Stevenson, *British Society 1914–45*, chapter 4.

[28]   Stevenson and Cook (eds), *Britain in the Depression*, p. 26. But see also Benson, *The Rise of Consumer Society*, table 3.3, p. 63: here it is suggested that between 1913 and 1937 the proportion of family expenditure on clothing remained unchanged at 10 per cent.

[29]   It should be noted that by the end of the 1920s the price of clothes was still more than double its pre-war level. 'The cost of clothing for working-class families in London [was] ... from 2¼ and 2½ times its cost in 1889–91'. H. Llewellyn Smith with L.C. Marsh, 'Cost of living', in H. Llewellyn Smith (ed.), *The New Survey of London Life and Labour* (P.S. King and Son, London, 1931), pp. 87–90. See also *The Outfitter*, 22 March 1930. According to Rowntree, in 1937 a family of five's minimum expenditure on clothing that 'provides just what is necessary to keep the body warm and dry, and to maintain a moderate respectability [with] ... nothing allowed for mere show', had increased from the 5s a week of 1914, to 8s a week (3s for the husband,

quantity of men's and boys' garments sold steadily increased until the 1929 slump, which saw the beginning of a period of decline, both in prices and in quantity sold. They began to recover after 1932, although pre-1929 levels were not regained before the outbreak of the Second World War.

It is no easier to relate such national trends to individual circumstances in the inter-war period than it has been in relation to the pre-war years. Nevertheless, there is evidence to suggest that as prices fell, many consumers in full-time employment could begin to afford a bit of extra expenditure on dress. For the working-class family featured in the *New Survey of London Life and Labour*'s 'Eastern Survey Area' study, earning approximately the 'average' annual income of £187 a year in 1932, and without exceptional items of expenditure to contend with, an annual purchase of a new outfit for the paterfamilias – perhaps a 50s Burton suit – would not have been unthinkable. The *New Survey* found that 70 per cent of working-class families in regular employment 'had a margin of 20s weekly above the bare minimum'. It was acknowledged that 'no doubt the allocation of this margin varies from family to family ... [although] very likely more fuel and light are used, and more variety of clothes are bought'. In any case, as A.L. Bowley remarked, 'however used, this enlarged amount of free money is a very important and modern gain'.[30]

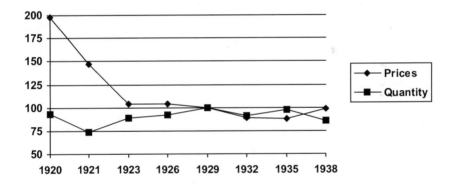

Figure 4.2   UK estimated average prices and quantity index, mens- and boyswear, 1920–1938 (1929 = 100).
Source: **R. Stone and D.A. Rowe, *The Measurement of Consumers' Expenditure and Behaviour in the United Kingdom 1920–1938* (Cambridge University Press, Cambridge, 1966), vol. 2, p. 13.**

1s 9d for the wife, 1s 1d for each child). B. Seebohm Rowntree, *The Human Needs of Labour* (Longmans, Green, London, 1937), pp. 116–17.

[30]   A.L. Bowley, 'Wages and family income', in Llewellyn Smith (ed.), *The New Survey*, pp. 60–69.

As is well known, however, not all sections of the population were able to benefit from the income deriving from regular employment. In the 1920s unemployment rates ranged between 10.6 and 12.7 per cent of the insured workforce, increasing during the post-1929 Depression period, and reaching a peak of 22.5 per cent of the insured workforce in 1932.[31] It has been estimated that inter-war unemployment was two to three times higher than before the war.[32] Furthermore, workers in certain industries (notably textiles, metals, mining and shipbuilding, as well as most waterside trades, building, fishing and road transport) and in certain regions (very roughly, outside the South East of England and the Midlands), were much more likely to experience both short and long spells of unemployment, while older and/or unskilled men were more likely to suffer from long-term unemployment, particularly in the 1930s. And although they were relatively regular, it is hard to see unemployment payments as permitting expenditure on more than the essentials of food, rent, fuel and clothing.[33] According to Ross McKibbin, between 1920 and 1939 these payments varied from 15s to £1, but for the most part an unemployed man could expect to receive around 17s a week. On average, unemployment benefits were 'only half the money value of a normal wage'.[34]

Overall, a far from insignificant section of the population remained excluded from any but the most basic of sartorial (and other) consumption. However, the inter-war period also saw the UK population as a whole newly able to spend unprecedented amounts of money on clothes and other consumer goods. It has been estimated that consumer expenditure per head of the population increased in real terms from £75 in 1910–14, to £93 in 1935–38.[35] Whether this increase actually amounted to a 'democratisation' of clothes consumption will be considered in the next section.

The democratisation of menswear?

Many inter-war commentators had little doubt that despite widespread unemployment, ever larger sections of the population were becoming able and willing to afford a new variety of mass-produced goods, and to indulge in new consumption-centred life-styles, often purchased on credit. According to Douglas Goldring, in the 1920s a whole class of black-coated workers had succumbed to the lure of novel and – in his eyes – valueless

---

[31] Historians disagree about what proportion of the workforce as a whole (rather than the insured section of the workforce, which in 1931 represented roughly 64 per cent of the total) was unemployed. It seems, however, that an average of 10 per cent of the population was unemployed throughout the period, increasing to over 15 per cent in the early 1930s. T. Hatton, 'Unemployement and the labour market in inter-war Britain', in R. Floud and D. McCloskey (eds), *The Economic History of Britain since 1700. Vol. 2: 1860–1939* (Cambridge University Press, Cambridge, 1994; first published 1981), pp. 359–61. See also Dewey, *War and Progress*, pp. 121–3.

[32] Hatton, 'Unemployement and the labour market', pp. 359–61; Stevenson and Cook (eds), *Britain in the Depression*, chapter 4.

[33] Dewey, *War and Progress*, pp. 126–30; 202–3.

[34] McKibbin, *Classes and Cultures*, pp. 116–17.

[35] Stevenson, *British Society 1914–45*, p. 124. See also S. Bowden, 'The new consumerism', in P. Johnson (ed.), *Twentieth Century Britain: Economic, Social and Cultural Change* (Longman, London, 1994), pp. 242–62.

commodities: 'Men drawing comfortable salaries were soon tempted to acquire not only their jerry-built villas, but cheap cars, wireless sets, furniture and other amenities on the "never-never" system.'[36] Not everybody saw the new goods and the new ability to purchase them in a negative light. Thomas Okey was delighted to observe in 1930 that the handyman who helped him out around the house and garden and maintained his car, was considerably 'better housed, better fed, better clothed' than he (a skilled workman) had been at his age, roughly half a century earlier. 'The "submerged" as they existed in Victorian times are but a memory ... [Among children] the improvement in physique, in clothing, in behaviour, is astounding.'[37]

What some commentators saw as the increasingly bland 'standardisation' of inter-war British society, with 'everything and everybody ... being ... swept into one dusty arterial road of cheap mass production and standardized living',[38] others tried to present as a new 'democratisation' of consumption. Powerful business interests, both in the manufacturing and in the distributive sectors, had a strong stake in the economic and social trends towards mass consumption. It is perhaps not surprising, then, that the 1930s saw the development not only of 'new forms of expertise for understanding the consumer' (most notably, perhaps, market research techniques), but also related 'attempts to channel his or her desires to a mass-produced chain of packaged pleasures'.[39] As far as the menswear trade was concerned, Katrina Honeyman

---

[36] D. Goldring, *The Nineteen Twenties: A General Survey and Some Personal Memories* (Nicholson and Watson, London, 1945), p. 26. See also A. Taylor, '"Funny money", hidden charges and repossession: working-class experiences of consumption and credit in the inter-war years', in J. Benson and L. Ugolini (eds), *Cultures of Selling: Perspectives on Consumption and Society Since 1700* (Ashgate, Aldershot, 2006), pp. 153–82; S. O'Connell and C. Reid, 'Working-class consumer credit in the UK, 1925–60: the role of the check trader', *Economic History Review*, vol. lviii, no. 2 (2005), pp. 378–405; P. Scott, 'The twilight world of interwar British hire purchase', *Past & Present*, no. 177 (2002), pp. 195–225. See also the changed attitudes towards credit observed in R. Roberts, *The Classic Slum: Salford Life in the First Quarter of the Century* (Penguin, Harmondsworth, 1974; first published 1971), pp. 224–5. But see also S. Reynoldson, B. Woolley and T. Woolley, *Seems So! A Working-Class View of Politics* (Macmillan, London, 1911), who observed as early as 1911 that working people's aspirations had in the recent past increased enormously.

[37] T. Okey, *A Basketful of Memories: An Autobiographical Sketch* (J.M. Dent and Sons, London, 1930), p. 143. A similar opinion was voiced, for example, by H. Coote, *While I Remember* (Spottiswoode, Ballantyne, London, 1937), p. 102; G. Lansbury, *My Life* (Constable, London, 1928), p. 283. The shifting attitudes towards consumerism that lay behind twentieth-century policy and protests are explored in Hilton, *Consumerism in Twentieth-Century Britain*. See also Benson, *Affluence and Authority*, especially part 1; Benson, *The Rise of Consumer Society*; J. Carey, *The Intellectuals and the Masses: Pride and Prejudice among the Literary Intelligentsia, 1880–1939* (Faber and Faber, London, 1992), p. 22; M. Nava, *Changing Cultures: Feminism, Youth and Consumerism* (Sage Publications, London, 1992), p. 187; Stevenson, *British Society 1914–45*, pp. 127–8.

[38] J.B. Priestley, *English Journey: Being a Rambling but Truthful Account of what One Man Saw* (Penguin, Harmondsworth, 1977; first published 1934), p. 67; see also pp. 376–80 for his well-known critique of cheap mass-produced consumerism. See also P. Balfour, *Society Racket: A Critical Survey of Modern Social Life* (John Lang, London, n.d. [c. 1933]), chapter 10.

[39] Hilton, *Consumerism in Twentieth-Century Britain*, p. 184. See also J. Greenfield, S. O'Connell and C. Reid, 'Gender, consumer culture and the middle-class male, 1918–39', in

has shown how a number of Leeds-based multiple tailoring firms, of which the best-known was Montague Burton, used relatively sophisticated marketing techniques, as well as mass-production and distribution methods, to spectacular effect, eventually capturing – it has been estimated – almost one-third of the interwar market for men's tailored outerwear.[40] In 1937 Montague Burton stated (and possibly sincerely believed): 'thanks to the tailoring evolution' that his firm had 'set in motion ... today clothes no longer divide the masses from the classes. Masters and men rub shoulders in the crowd and nobody can tell one from the other ... By putting good clothes within the reach of all [Montague Burton] ... have made democracy a living force.'[41] A year later, Sir Henry Price, the owner of the Fifty Shilling Tailor multiple concern, told the Leeds Publicity Club that even 'the poorer kind of working man to-day has a smart lounge suit, a good warm overcoat, perhaps even a dinner jacket or tails'.[42]

However, what Burton and others saw as a new and dignified sartorial democracy, with ever greater numbers of men increasingly able to afford decent garments, many saw as a purgatory of shoddy, mass-produced uniformity, with little to choose between the factory-produced suits that could be bought from one of the multiples, and the 'depressing' flannel trousers and tweed coats described by Giles and Esmond Romilly in 1935 as the 'Englishman's uniform'.[43] If business interests representing multiple concerns sought to emphasise the benefits of the new sartorial democracy, those behind independent, and especially bespoke, tailors, responded by lamenting that the present 'age tends to uniformity and mass production in clothes; personality is apt to be swamped by a depressing sameness'.[44]

Writing in 1946, Osbert Sitwell considered that most of the people to be seen on London streets at the beginning of the century would have looked 'both more smart and more shabby than they are today'. Although 'whole crowds were clothed in frock-coats and top hats [and] entire armies were crowned with bowlers', differences in class and income had been more obvious: 'the poor, men equally with women,

---

A. Kidd and D. Nicholls (eds), *Gender, Civic Culture and Consumerism: Middle-Class Identity in Britain, 1800–1940* (Manchester University Press, Manchester, 1999), pp. 183–97.

[40]   K. Honeyman, 'Style monotony and the business of fashion: the marketing of menswear in inter-war England', *Textile History*, vol. 34, no. 2 (2003), pp. 171–91; K. Honeyman, *Well Suited: A History of the Leeds Clothing Industry 1850–1990* (Pasold Research Fund and Oxford University Press, Oxford, 2000), especially chapter 3. See also S. Levitt, 'Cheap mass produced men's clothing in the nineteenth and early twentieth centuries', *Textile History*, vol. 22, no. 2 (1991), especially pp. 188–90. The six largest Leeds-based multiple tailors supplied roughly 50 per cent of the suits bought by British men in the inter-war period. K. Honeyman, 'Following suit: men, masculinity and gendered practices in the clothing trade in Leeds, England, 1890–1940', *Gender & History*, vol. 14, no. 3 (2002), pp. 430–31.

[41]   M. Burton, *Globe Girdling* (1937), quoted in Honeyman, 'Following suit', p. 429.

[42]   *Men's Wear*, 5 November 1938.

[43]   G. Romilly and E. Romilly, *Out of Bounds* (Hamish Hamilton, London, 1935), p. 106. See also K. Silex, *John Bull at Home* (George G. Harrap, London, 1931), pp. 150–51. Inter-war complaints of dull style monotony were not new. See, for example, Bourke, *Dismembering the Male*, pp. 198–209.

[44]   *The Tailor and Cutter*, 7 February 1930.

showed their distress more plainly ... unkempt, their clothes and boots torn'.[45] No such ambivalence can be found in Fred Willis's nostalgic picture of the Edwardian era as 'the last of that period of individuality which used to be such a marked feature of English life'. In his 1948 memoir, he scorned any notion of sartorial democracy. He suggested that all the men who in the pre-1914 period 'had ... money and time gave a good deal of attention to the clothes ... [they] wore'. As a result, not only their tailors, but also their hatters, hosiers and bootmakers went to some trouble to create 'something really distinctive' for them, putting together 'an ensemble that was the antithesis of the mass-produced figures seen about the streets to-day'. Even those without much money would have made an effort with their appearance, while 'To-day ... workmen look like the tramps of fifty years ago. But we have all changed in this respect and seem quite content with any mass-produced ready-made clothing that the clothes salesman chooses to let us have.'[46]

Unsurprisingly, unlike those of such – often elite – observers, the views of the actual consumers of inexpensive, mass-produced clothing are a good deal more elusive; no doubt, they would also have been extremely diverse. Nevertheless, there are indications that mass-produced menswear, far from being perceived as shoddily uniform, could be a source of great pleasure and satisfaction to the wearer, even if it was not necessarily associated with the high-minded sentiments of consumer democracy voiced by Montague Burton and others. Douglas Pope suggested in 1937 that among the poor, the clothes of 'the younger married people' soon became shabby, until the very 'thought of appearing in anything new in public amuses and embarrasses them', fearing that they would be sneered at for looking different from 'their less fortunate fellows'. Occasionally, however, new 'suits, coats, and frocks do find their way into the poverty-stricken wardrobes of these people'. These garments may have been 'cheap', but significantly, they were also 'new', and 'beautiful', provoking a sense of pride in their wearers, and helping them 'to overcome their self-consciousness'.[47] Similarly, every Sunday evening in the early 1920s G.A.W. Tomlinson 'would sally forth in all the glory of my cheap ready-made suit, and cloth cap with the tip broken and pulled down over one eye in the approved style, to stroll up and down the main street in order to "click"'.[48]

In any case, despite all the talk of democratisation or of standardisation, there continued to exist considerable material and cultural constraints on consumer choice, reflected in the appearance of men with different incomes and belonging to different social and class backgrounds. George Orwell may have commented in 1937 that the 'manufacture of cheap clothes', together with 'the general softening of manners' had toned down 'the surface differences between class and class', but the democratisation of

---

[45] O. Sitwell, *The Scarlet Tree* (Macmillan, London, 1946), p. 12.

[46] Willis himself worked as a hatter in an exclusive West End shop. F. Willis, *101 Jubilee Road: A Book of London Yesterdays* (Phoenix House, London, 1948), pp. 19–20. See also C.H. Middleton, *Village Memories: A Collection of Short Stories and Reminiscences of Village Life* (Cassell, London, 1941), p. 76.

[47] D. Pope, *Now I'm Sixteen: An Autobiography* (J.M. Dent and Sons, London, 1937), p. 75.

[48] G.A.W. Tomlinson, *Coal-Miner* (Hutchinson, London, n.d. [c. 1937]), p. 78.

menswear was far from a done deal in the inter-war years.[49] The photographs taken by Bill Brandt and others are an eloquent testimony to the continued relevance of clothes as markers of class identity, providing a striking visual evidence that was echoed by many contemporaries.[50] In 1920, Robin Douglas, then still under 18, enrolled in the 'Boy Service' of the RAF. On meeting his fellow recruits at Glasgow railway station, the differences in background between them were immediately obvious to all present. Douglas's clothes and suitcases were surveyed by the others 'with considerable disfavour', as was his felt hat, while 'my clean collar and tie were an affront'. The dislike was mutual: 'I didn't particularly care for cloth caps, dirty mufflers where collars should have been, and an atmosphere of "unwashedness" '.[51]

Differences in appearance could provoke considerable bitterness. Alex Granger acidly compared the clothes of an unpleasant headmaster ('a good breakfast in his belly, a smart suit and lovely polished shoes') with his own 'broken down clogs ... scruffy pair of trousers and ... jacket that had been handed down'.[52] Clifford Steele was the son of a miner who could only obtain work at irregular intervals. As a result, there were times when as a schoolboy he was forced to wear 'a patch on my behind'. This, he considered, 'brought you down just under that level you could tolerate', particularly in view of the fact that 'at that time so much emphasis was put on appearance. You were graded – this was the thing – Even if it was silent.'[53] Such grading could be based not only on garments' quality, but also on their style – or lack of it. When A.G. Macdonnell visited an exclusive golf club, Cedar Park, in the 1920s, he was 'painfully conscious' of standing out from all present, not only because of the shabbiness of his flannel trousers (which bagged at the knee) and golfing coat (which had 'a shine at one elbow and a hole at the other'), but also because his coat was an old-fashioned 1914 blue, while most of the other men wore 'purple jumpers and green jumpers and yellow jumpers and tartan jumpers'.[54]

Whether accepted matter-of-factly, resented or despised, sartorial differences continued to exist and continued to matter.[55] It was not simply that the clothes of a minority of down-and-outs stood out from those of the rest of the population, although

----

[49]   G. Orwell, *The Road to Wigan Pier* (Heinemann Educational, London, 1965; first published 1937), p. 133. See also Priestley, *English Journey*, pp. 325–6. On the 'democratisation' of dress, see also Honeyman, 'Following suit', pp. 426–46; Honeyman, *Well Suited*, pp. 53–4; J. Harris, *Private Lives, Public Spirit: Britain 1870–1914* (Penguin Books, London, 1994; first published 1993), pp. 9–10.

[50]   B. Joy and N. Warburton, *The Photography of Bill Brandt* (Thames and Hudson, London, 1999). See also, for example, F. Donaldson, *Those Were the Days: A Photographic Album of Daily Life in Britain* (J.M. Dent and Sons, London, 1983); J. Symons, *Between the Wars: Britain in Photographs* (B.T. Batsford, London, 1972).

[51]   R. Douglas, *16 to 21* (A.M. Philpot, London, n.d. [c. 1925]), p. 72.

[52]   A. Granger, *Life's a Gamble* (New Horizon, Bognor Regis, 1983), p. 1.

[53]   N. Gray, *The Worst of Times: An Oral History of the Great Depression in Britain* (Wildwood House, London, 1985), pp. 132–3.

[54]   A.G. Macdonnell, *England, their England* (Macmillan, London, 1933), pp. 129–30.

[55]   See also, for example, J. White, *The Worst Street in North London: Campbell Bunk, Islington, Between the Wars* (Routledge and Kegan Paul, London, 1986), p. 71; G.R. Lamb, *Roman Road* (Sheed and Ward, London, 1950), pp. 57–8.

they did. It was also the case that social and economic inequalities continued to be reflected in men's, children's, and no doubt women's, dress. As Sidney Day pointed out, he may have 'looked scruffy in me hand-me-downs', but he hardly stood out. In his neighbourhood, 'you weren't a boy unless yer arse was hanging out of yer trousers'.[56] For their part, 'most members of the middle class believed that there were certain standards in dress, housing, and diet from which they could deviate only with loss of status'.[57] And if most middle-class men would have had no wish to lose such status by looking as if they might belong to the working class, it is doubtful whether many working-class men would normally have looked anything other than what they were. Only an expert would have been able to tell that a 'typical' single-breasted Burton suit of the 1930s had double-breasted revers, giving it 'a touch of commonness ... showing ... that the suit did not come from a good tailor'.[58] However, most people would have been able to identify it for what it was: a good, solid, even smart, but definitely working- or lower-middle-class suit. Ken Ausden's father and uncle George both worked for the railways in Swindon in the 1930s. Both had 'same grey eyes, hollow cheek, bony jaw. Same sort of short-back and sides haircut, stooped shoulders, Burton's 3-guinea Sunday suit'. By the 1930s, the Burton suit had acquired a certain cultural currency: it was a known – and class-specific – entity.[59]

Furthermore, not all the products of Leeds clothing factories could equal the quality of the best that Burton could offer. Richard Hoggart acknowledged that firms such as Montague Burton, Sumries and Weaver to Wearer produced garments for almost all types of market, 'from the near-bespoke to the cheap and nasty'. However, he believed that at least as far as West Riding working-class men were concerned, the 'cheap shiny suit' was the most they could aspire to. His own first suit had cost 30 shillings (a price which admittedly may well have classed it among the 'cheap and nasty'). It had been:

> a dead, greyish thing, the cheap cloth hard at birth and destined to shine within weeks, the sort which any West Riding mill worker or ready-made clothing worker, using an eye for quality which they could not often apply to their own purchases, would instantly recognise for what it was. Even at 30 bob it was not good value.[60]

Many working-class men would have shared Hoggart's unhappiness at wearing such a garment. Indeed, there is a good deal of evidence to suggest that when extra disposable income became available, the purchase of new, better quality and more stylish clothes followed quickly: 'doing well' or 'prospering' would normally also rapidly find a sartorial expression. After the war, for example, one of Walter Greenwood's contemporaries 'made good'. Accordingly, he was 'transformed'.

---

[56]   S. Day, *London Born* (Fourth Estate, London, 2004), p. 24.

[57]   McKibbin, *Classes and Cultures*, p. 102. For the continued importance of dress in marking class differences, see also Stevenson, *British Society 1914–45*, p. 343.

[58]   H. Amies, *The Englishman's Suit* (Quartet Books, London, 1994), p. 29.

[59]   K. Ausden, *Up the Crossing* (BBC, London, 1981), p. 162. See also L. Heren, *Growing Up Poor in London* (Phoenix, London, 2001; first published 1973), pp. 49–50.

[60]   R. Hoggart, *A Local Habitation: Life and Times 1918–1940* (Chatto and Windus, London, 1988), pp. 78–9.

When Greenwood bumped into him, 'he was smartly dressed and, though the evening was warm, he wore a light overcoat, tailored, with a velvet collar'. His newly jaunty and impressive image was completed by 'a black bowler set at an angle'.[61] Doing well may often have led to the purchase of new and 'better' clothes, but this should not necessarily be interpreted as a desire to achieve a 'middle-class' look. After all, as J.B. Priestley pointed out, there was a large section of the population who did 'not want their friends and neighbours to think they are suddenly "trying to be posh"'. They would 'die of shame if they were discovered by their acquaintances conveying soup to their mouths above a stiff white shirt'.[62]

For some men, improved inter-war incomes provided new opportunities for clothes consumption. However, as in the pre-war period, the priority for boys and men was not to try and adopt a new 'democratic', or indeed middle-class, look, but rather to 'fit in' with one's immediate, often contingent, and overwhelmingly male, locality and peer group. The punishment for those who failed to conform to the sartorial 'rules' continued to be as harsh as it had ever been.

A consumer modernity?

In the eyes of many contemporary observers and commentators, the supposed growth of sartorial democracy (or as others saw it, standardisation) could only be understood as part of a wider process of 'modernisation' of British society, a process whose onset was often dated to the war. After all, this was the 'universally acknowledged historical benchmark against which relative changes in condition could be measured'.[63] Whether they looked upon it with approval or misgivings, many observers considered that the process of 'modernisation' was reflected in the adoption of new clothing styles and in a new fashion-consciousness, as well as in the introduction of new American-influenced leisure practices. This was thought to be especially the case among the young, with their enthusiasm for American popular music, films and dances.[64]

In the 1930s the teenaged Bob Copper, the son of a Sussex farm labourer, found a job working in the village barber's shop. Even in the context of rural Sussex, the sense

---

[61]   W. Greenwood, *There Was a Time* (Jonathan Cape, London, 1967), p. 161. See also H.K. Hales, *The Autobiography of 'The Card'* (Sampson Low, Marston, London, n.d. [c. 1936]), pp. 240–44.

[62]   Priestley, *English Journey*, p. 99. For the desire not to dress 'too well', see also chapters 1 and 2. Although see also A. Green, *Growing up in Attercliffe: Honey with a Ladle, Vinegar with a Teaspoon* (New City, Sheffield, 1981), p. 35. Green considered that among working-class young men, 'the fashions reflect[ed] those of the well-to-do'.

[63]   Waites, *A Class Society at War*, p. 84.

[64]   For a discussion of inter-war leisure and recreation that considers not only changes, but also continuities, see, for example, Stevenson, *British Society 1914–45*, chapter 14. The relationship between modernisation, Americanisation and distribution systems is thoughtfully analysed in V. de Grazia, 'Changing consumption regimes in Europe, 1930–1970: comparative perspectives on the distribution problem', in S. Strasser, C. McGovern and M. Judt (eds), *Getting and Spending: European and American Consumer Societies in the Twentieth Century* (Cambridge University Press, Cambridge, 1998), pp. 59–83.

of change was strong: 'There was a new, forward-looking way of thinking. The old order was indeed changing.' This was 'a fast-developing world of petrol-driven and electrical power, mass-production and the insidious but strong social influences from America'. Such trends were reflected in the changing dress of the rural population: 'From the hob-nails and corduroy of earlier days, we were being converted to more fashion-conscious clothes.' Copper's older cousin, who also worked as a barber, epitomised this 'new spirit':

> He was a stylish dresser with his colourful Fairisle, v-necked pullover, 24-inch bottomed Oxford bags in silver-grey flannel and his 'winkle-picker' brown brogues with side panels of white buckskin. His hair was combed straight back and plastered down with Arizona Viola till it shone like the flanks of a well-groomed horse.[65]

Although clearly a good deal less enthusiastic about them, C.H. Middleton would have recognised such developments. Writing in 1941, he looked back with longing to an unspecified time ('the past') when country people 'knew little or nothing of the so-called luxuries and artificialities which paint modern life in such bright and attractive colours'. He was saddened by the disappearance of 'traditional' garments like striped leather collars and corduroy trousers: 'The villagers buy their clothes in the shops, and look and dress very much the same as townspeople do, and it hasn't improved them.'[66]

However, the extent to which the inter-war years were unique in being characterised by a perception of a 'speeding-up' of modernisation, with its attendant changes in patterns of clothes consumption, should not be exaggerated.[67] In 1904 Gertrude Jekyll was already lamenting the passing of old styles of clothing, such as the smock-frock, among the labouring population of rural West Surrey. All the 'workpeople' were now 'clothed in a dead-level of shabbiness', having succumbed to the temptation of 'cheap' and 'shoddy' 'modern' suits, which offered 'a pretence of fashion', but which quickly acquired a 'sordid, shameful, degraded appearance'. According to Jekyll, 'Every sort of folly or absurdity is committed by these poor people in this insane striving to be what they think is "fashionable"'.[68]

In his autobiography, Fred Gresswell tried to explain the attraction to a rural population of the newly fashionable suits so despised by Jekyll: 'They were not

---

[65] B. Copper, *Early to Rise: A Sussex Boyhood* (Heinemann, London, 1976), pp. 179–80. See also pp. 184, 210.

[66] Middleton, *Village Memories*, pp. 49, 75–6. See also L. Ugolini, 'Clothes and the modern man in 1930s Oxford', *Fashion Theory*, vol. 4, issue 4 (2000), pp. 427–46.

[67] The notion of 'modernity' and its relationship to nineteenth- and twentieth-century consumer cultures has recently been receiving a good deal of attention. See, for example, C. Breward and C. Evans (eds), *Fashion and Modernity* (Berg, Oxford, 2005); M. Daunton and B. Rieger (eds), *Meanings of Modernity: Britain from the Late Victorian Era to World War II* (Berg, Oxford, 2001); Breward, *The Hidden Consumer*; M. Nava and A. O'Shea, *Modern Times: Reflections on a Century of English Modernity* (Routledge, London, 1996); C. Breward, *A New History of Fashionable Dress* (Manchester University Press, Manchester, 1995), chapter 5.

[68] G. Jekyll, *Old West Surrey: Some Notes and Memories* (Longmans, Green, London, 1904), pp. 262–4.

strongly made, [but] they had better finish'. They were also available in a choice of colours, and had a 'new style'. Most importantly, both they and the multiple shops where they could be bought, were part of a wider spirit of 'new enterprise', which Gresswell dated to the 1890s.[69] Jack Jones also singled out the turn of the century, rather than the inter-war years, as a period of key consumer changes, reflected in the sartorial and leisure practices of his younger brothers. Billa and Frank were miners like their father, but were also 'men of the new era', who spent their money in different ways to the older generation: 'After work they dressed in a way which made them look like gentlemen of leisure who had been turned out by most exacting valets'. They did not join their father at the pub, but went 'to the dance, the stalls in the theatre, or for a game of billiards'. It was under their guidance that Jones acquired a new outfit that was 'something more twentieth century'.[70]

This is not to deny that the inter-war period was perceived by many as a particularly strong 'moment of modernity'. Indeed, for some – perhaps many – individuals, the experience of war brought about a sense of definite break with the past. Before the war Alec Waugh had assumed that he would live his life very much as his own father had, imitating his employment, leisure and consumption practices: 'I saw myself catching the same tube every morning; lunching in my club, returning late in the day; changing into a tweed suit, taking an hour's walk'. At least as far as Waugh was concerned, the war had made such a life unthinkable.[71] The extent to which his experience was 'typical' is difficult to assess. Indeed, the degree to which men and women's lives and outlooks more generally were changed by the war, have been the subject of much debate.[72] However, at least as far as menswear consumption was concerned, the inter-war period clearly was also a period of profound continuities with established patterns and practices. The garments worn may have changed, and new retail outlets may have emerged to cater for those men with some extra money to spend, but the main pressures on sartorial decisions had not changed: gender, ethnicity, class, age and location in time and place remained fundamental, as did the desire to avoid ridicule and censure. Furthermore, the extent to which a distinctively 'modern look' emerged in this period should not be exaggerated. The observer who considered Barrow furnace-men at work, for example, would have had a strange sense of their location in time. Peter Donnelly invited his readers to 'See that big man down there with a swallow-tail coat that his grandfather once wore for dignity;

---

[69]   F. Gresswell, *Bright Boots: An Autobiography* (David and Charles, Newton Abbot, 1982; first published 1956), pp. 107, 112, 115.

[70]   J. Jones, *Unfinished Journey* (Hamish Hamilton, London, 1937), pp. 123–4.

[71]   Waugh, *Early Years*, pp. 136–7.

[72]   Key works include Bourke, *Dismembering the Male*; J. Winter, *Sites of Memory, Sites of Mourning: The Place of the Great War in European Cultural History* (Cambridge University Press, Cambridge, 1995); S. Hynes, *A War Imagined: The First World War and English Culture* (Pimlico, London, 1992; first published 1990); J.M. Winter, *The Great War and the British People* (Palgrave Macmillan, Basingstoke, 2003; first published 1985); E.J. Leed, *No Man's Land: Combat and Identity in World War One* (Cambridge University Press, Cambridge, 1979); P. Fussell, *The Great War and Modern Memory* (Oxford University Press, Oxford, 1977; first published 1975); A. Marwick, *War and Social Change in the Twentieth Century: A Comparative Study of Britain, France, Germany, Russia and the United States* (Macmillan, London, 1974).

this one with a long overcoat, a battered trilby hat, a long staff which makes him look like a patriarch ... and little Noah, who maintains the old tradition of furnacemen and wears moleskin trousers'.[73]

Non-consumers? Dress and the unemployed

Throughout the inter-war period, large sections of the population were excluded from participating in anything that could even remotely be described either as a democratisation or a modernisation of consumption: the poverty caused by loss of earnings in old age, by the need to support a large (or even a small) family, by sickness, death, or by low and irregular wages, had by no means disappeared after the war. Herbert Allen's father was a farm labourer in Leicestershire. In Allen's household, even with a father in full-time employment, a large family and small wages meant dire living conditions, including the almost complete absence of access to new clothing. When a change of garment became absolutely necessary, this would be found on the second-hand stalls of Leicester market.[74] However, the men who were most visibly denied access to any but the most basic of consumer goods were the unemployed, often just at the stage in their lives when, as single young men, they should have started to gain access to better-quality clothes or, as middle-aged men, they were expected to support a family.[75] The 'flashily' dressed 'work-shy' man who was able to live well even if out of work, perhaps being 'mixed up with some betting concern', or supplementing the dole by keeping greyhounds, seems to have been very much a minority, if not an outright journalistic invention.[76] For most of the unemployed, the loss of income meant material deprivation, a deprivation directly reflected in their appearance.

In his 1945 autobiographical account of unemployment, Max Cohen painted a bleak picture of leaving the Unemployment Exchange in the early 1930s, having received the dole (as a young man under twenty-one, this amounted to 12s 6d a week), 'with your mind occupied with the vast amount of your needs and the small possibilities of gratifying them. Little things, that a person who is earning wages scarcely bothers about, have now assumed great ... significance in your thoughts'. Even tiny purchases, such as shoelaces or a razor-blade, could not be afforded, once rent and food had been accounted for: 'Your trousers are falling to pieces, they have been patched too many times; but you don't know how you are going to get another pair ... Your overcoat and jacket are shabby, worn, ragged? These are mere trifles.'[77] A skilled millwright emphasised the difficulties faced by a family (himself, a wife and a crippled daughter) living on a means-tested dole of 17 shillings a week: 'It means reducing your living

---

[73]   P. Donnelly, *The Yellow Rock* (Eyre and Spottiswoode, London, 1950), p. 130.

[74]   Gray, *The Worst of Times*, p. 141. For the 'survival of poverty', by no means always connected to unemployment, see Stevenson, *British Society 1914–45*, pp. 134–42.

[75]   For the link between unemployment and poverty, see Hatton, 'Unemployement and the labour market', pp. 363–7. See also Stevenson and Cook (eds), *Britain in the Depression*, chapter 9.

[76]   The Pilgrim Trust, *Men Without Work* (Cambridge University Press, Cambridge, 1938), p. 173.

[77]   M. Cohen, *I Was One of the Unemployed* (Victor Gollancz, London, 1945), pp. 102–3.

still further when you are already at your wit's end to know how to renew your collars and shirts and get a new pair of shoes.'[78] In some cases, mass unemployment closed off all but the most basic consumption opportunities to whole communities. According to R.L. Lee, this happened in the South Wales town of Merthyr Tydfil, when the Dowlais steelworks were closed down in the 1930s. Soon people

> began to look haggard and shabby, and drew what bits of clothes they had about them as if holding on to their last remnants of pride and respectability. Patched clothing was now an accepted thing ... A far cry indeed, from the days when the 'tallyman' leaned on the well polished wall ... [outside the entrance to the works] collecting dues from well filled pay packets.[79]

Robert Morgan also emphasised the hardships caused by pit closures in his native South Wales. New clothes became 'luxuries' that could rarely be purchased: they were 'patched and worn until they were smooth and threadbare'. For his part, Morgan believed that 'such deprivations were common to us all ... so there was very little embarrassment when appearances were strangely unfashionable'.[80]

However, the perception that others – particularly others who belonged to the same community – were not experiencing the same hardships, but on the contrary were actually doing rather well, could provoke a good deal of bitterness. Charles Graham's brother-in-law worked in the merchant navy, and used to come ashore in South Shields with fifty or sixty pounds in his pockets, a proportion of which he would spend on what to the rest of his family was the unimaginable luxury of 'a couple of new suits'. Graham reflected that 'It wasn't a slump for some. It was great. On the railways, in the post office, you were the elite, anywhere you had continuous employment.'[81] In 1926 Patrick McGeown was twenty-nine years old, and had been unemployed for months. His clothes had become so 'worn and shabby that I felt ashamed to meet acquaintances who were employed'. Sometimes, he added, 'I hated these people so much for their good fortune that I grew alarmed at my state of mind'.[82] Stella Davies recognised her family's good fortune in having become if not 'affluent', at least 'comfortably placed' in the inter-war years. They could enjoy their pleasant house and garden, and were able to acquire a car, a piano and a wireless. At a time of economic depression, when 'many of our friends were either out of a job or suffering a reduction in salary', they 'had a fair margin of income over necessary expenditure for visits to the theatre and concerts and we opened a deposit account at the bank'.[83]

It was not only comparisons with others' comfortable circumstances that served to highlight the hardships involved in the unemployed's loss of access to many consumer goods. According to Willy Goldman, one of the consequences of unemployment was

[78] H.L. Beales and R.S. Lambert (eds), *Memoirs of the Unemployed* (EP Publishing, Wakefield, 1973; first published 1934), p. 100.
[79] R.L. Lee, *The Town that Died!* (R.L. Lee, London, 1930), pp. 54–5.
[80] R. Morgan, *My Lamp Still Burns* (Gomer Press, Llandysul, 1981), p. 23.
[81] Gray, *The Worst of Times*, p. 109.
[82] P. McGeown, *Heat the Furnace Seven Times More* (Hutchinson, London, 1967), p. 117. See also, for example, Beales and Lambert (eds), *Memoirs of the Unemployed*, p. 233.
[83] C.S. Davies, *North Country Bred: A Working-Class Family Chronicle* (Routledge and Kegan Paul, London, 1963), pp. 233–4.

that the weekend lost any meaning. Unable to afford a 'best' suit, 'You couldn't even change into another suit of clothes. If you were so lucky as to possess a "new" suit you would be wearing it during the week, and it didn't make a change putting it on on Saturday.'[84] G.A.W. Tomlinson, on the other hand, emphasised the gradual erosion of any sense of worth and dignity caused by the progressive loss of all one's possessions. His books and his clothes were soon gone: 'It's all very well for people to say: "Clothes don't make a man", but "hospital blues"[85] and boots with cardboard in the bottoms, and feet without socks, and hunger that never stops gnawing at your inside, don't make a man, either.'[86]

The bitterness provoked by the inability to buy any new or decent clothes for oneself was intensified when it extended also to the paterfamilias' inability to provide adequately for his dependants. In 1938 the Pilgrim Trust noted that in some households the 'normal' arrangements had been reversed, and children in work supported the family, including a long-term unemployed father. The result was that in 'many such cases the home appears to represent two standards, the earning children being often smartly dressed and happy, while the fathers were shabby and suffering from a sense of their dependence'. It sometimes seemed as if they were almost trying to avoid 'making any effort to keep up appearances in case the children might think that they were drawing an undue share of the family income'.[87]

Once back in employment, furthermore, many men did not find it easy to start spending money again on items that might not seem absolutely essential. Having been back in work for a few months, for example, and having accumulated enough money with which to 'reclothe' himself, Max Cohen nevertheless found himself 'reluctant to do so, in spite of all my former yearnings and vows. My jacket was merely a soiled rag. But buy a new jacket? This was not really necessary. One could always at a pinch live with an old jacket, but one could not live without food or shelter.' The insecurity and poverty of two years of unemployment had changed his priorities, so that to buy new clothes appeared to be a waste of 'money on things which … seemed mere sops to convention and respectability'. However, having finally bought a new outfit, he realised that the 'cool', 'clean' and 'neat' new garments did not represent 'merely a surface change … they were a symbol of the vast process of regeneration that could take place once a hopeless … out-of-work had the chance to recover his lost self-confidence and self-respect'.[88]

---

[84]   W. Goldman, *East End my Cradle* (Faber and Faber, London, 1940), pp. 137–8.

[85]   'Hospital blues' refer to the bright blue trousers that had been used during the war to clothe injured soldiers. Large stocks were left over after the war, and were sold off cheaply. According to Tomlinson, manufacturers had continued to produce trousers on the same model, calling them 'hospital blues'. 'Lots of men wore them in the pit, but nobody dreamed of wearing them at any other time'. Tomlinson, *Coal-Miner*, p. 78.

[86]   Tomlinson, *Coal-Miner*, p. 79. In Tomlinson's case, the cause of his poverty was a strike, rather than unemployment.

[87]   The Pilgrim Trust, *Men Without Work*, pp. 147–8. See also J. Benson, *Prime Time: A History of the Middle Aged in Twentieth-Century Britain* (Longman, Harlow, 1997), pp. 102–3.

[88]   Cohen, *I Was One of the Unemployed*, pp. 236–7.

A new consumerism? Dress and youth

Almost a century since the end of the First World War, the notion of a 'lost generation' remains a powerful one, as does the belief that in some ways the conflict changed the lives of boys too young to be combatants almost as much as it had those of their older counterparts. According to Joanna Bourke, for example, 'a generation of men who had been too young to be actively engaged in military services grew up in a world in which certain aspects of "being a man" were believed to be threatened, and their aesthetics of the body reflected this perception'.[89] However, historians have only recently begun to devote attention to the experience of being a teenager – and especially a teenage consumer – in the 1920s and 1930s, and to question the extent to which this differed from the pre-war period. According to David Fowler, the inter-war period saw working-class teenagers and young adults developing new consumer habits, setting them apart both from contemporary adults and from their pre-war counterparts.[90] He suggests that the purchasing power of young and unmarried waged workers had increased enormously from pre-First World War levels. At the same time, teenagers over 14 or 15 were increasingly able to keep a substantial proportion (up to or even over 50 per cent) of their wages for personal use.[91] The result was that in many working-class families the young wage-earners 'would have holidays and outings and new clothes, while probably the parents, the mother certainly, stayed at home and wore old clothes'.[92]

Evidence of young wage-earners with money to spare is not difficult to find. As an apprentice tool-maker, Leslie Halward developed an interest in a variety of hobbies, ranging from boxing to listening to music. All required what apparently were to him affordable purchases, including a gramophone and records.[93] It may also have become both easier and more important to achieve a 'fashionable' appearance.

---

[89]   Bourke, *Dismembering the Male*, p. 19.

[90]   D. Fowler, *The First Teenagers: The Lifestyles of Young Wage-Earners in Interwar Britain* (The Woburn Press, London, 1995). See also Benson, *The Rise of Consumer Society*, especially pp. 164–70. Young male consumers, it would seem, are constantly being rediscovered. See, for example, B. Beaven, *Leisure, Citizenship and Working-Class Men in Britain, 1850–1945* (Manchester University Press, Manchester, 2005), especially chapters 3 and 5; F. Mort, *Cultures of Consumption: Masculinities and Social Space in Late Twentieth-Century Britain* (Routledge, London, 1996), pp. 22–8. Also J. Springhall, *Youth, Popular Culture and Moral Panics: Penny Gaffs to Gangsta-Rap, 1830–1996* (Macmillan, Basingstoke, 1998); H. Hendrick, *Images of Youth: Age, Class and the Male Youth Problem, 1880–1920* (Clarendon Press, Oxford, 1990); G. Pearson, *Hooligan: A History of Respectable Fears* (Macmillan, London, 1983). For a thought-provoking discussion of changing perceptions of what constituted a 'real' boy in inter-war US, see J. Grant, 'A "real boy" and not a sissy: gender, childhood, and masculinity, 1890–1940', *Journal of Social History*, vol. 37, no. 4 (2004), pp. 329–51.

[91]   Between 1906 and 1935, money wages for boys under 18 increased between 100 and 300 per cent. Fowler, *The First Teenagers*, pp. 93–8. However, Benson suggests that although 'adolescent purchasing power increased between the wars', a large proportion of their earnings continued to be handed over to their family. Benson, *The Rise of Consumer Society*, pp. 17–18.

[92]   Manchester University Settlement, *Ancoats* (1945), p. 15, quoted in Fowler, *The First Teenagers*, p. 95.

[93]   L. Halward, *Let Me Tell You* (Michael Joseph, London, 1938), chapter IX.

Among one group of young men in Manchester in the early 1930s, for example, 'if you could afford it you had trousers with a 24-inch bottom, with an inch turn-up. And if they were anything under 24 inches, you didn't want to know them. That was the fashion.'[94] The East India Dock Road, in London's East End, was the scene of many inter-war monkey parades. Boys wore 'the latest fashions of the day: Bulldog toe boots, block-shouldered jackets, a waistcoat, cut low at the front, pleated front silk shirt, a blue bow with white spots ... "peg-top" trousers ... in fact anything that was ... up to date with the trend of the time'.[95] According to Bob Copper, the older generation's 'cravats, winged collars and gold tie-pins seemed a world away from our open-necked shirts and Oxford bags'.[96] Robert Roberts believed that the new generation of post-war youngsters growing up in Salford may not have been better-off than their parents, but were otherwise completely different: 'The young men in their ever widening "bags" and double-breasted jackets, slicked and fresh, [were] a different race from their fathers.' 'Almost incidentally', they became 'the first "moderns" of the twentieth century'. It was difficult to determine what had caused this change, but 'dumbly one felt that the millions lying lately dead in Flanders had somehow made a contribution.'[97]

At the other end of the social scale, it was also claimed that certain groups of young men, such as (some) Oxford undergraduates, particularly in the 1920s, represented a new and 'modern' model of youth, recognisable by their distinctive clothing styles, which included canary-yellow hunting waistcoats, green velveteen trousers, brown suede shoes, and especially the bell-bottomed flannel trousers known as 'Oxford bags'. These were mostly elite young men like Brian Howard and Harold Acton, who adopted a self-consciously dandified identity, and 'who were, and saw themselves as originators of a new "aesthetic" phase in English culture, to be characterised by ornament and brilliancy, playfulness and youthfulness, and by a turning of the back on the old forms of seriousness and power'. The cultural impact of these 'children of the sun' should not be underestimated, particularly in creating, or reinforcing, an image of Oxford that remains powerful to this day, as a city of 'stone wall retreats where flanneled youths play croquet amidst the oak and the elm'.[98] However, continuities in sartorial consumption should not be underestimated. It was suggested in Chapter 2 that interest in clothes on the part of young men, especially those in waged work and without a dependent family, was accepted and viewed with a good deal of tolerance throughout the period covered by this book – with the very notable

---

[94] A. Davies, *Leisure, Gender and Poverty: Working-Class Culture in Salford and Manchester, 1900–1939* (Open University Press, Buckingham, 1992), p. 105.

[95] J. Blake, *Memories of Old Poplar* (Stepney Books Publications, London, 1977), p. 23. See also Day, *London Born*, pp. 66–7.

[96] Copper, *Early to Rise*, p. 210.

[97] Roberts, *The Classic Slum*, p. 224.

[98] J.E. Dougill, *Oxford in English Literature: The Making and Undoing of 'The English Athens'* (University of Michigan Press, Ann Arbor, 1998), p. 235, quoted in Ugolini, 'Clothes and the modern man in 1930s Oxford', p. 444. See also Graves and Hodge, *The Long Weekend*, pp. 122–4; H. Green, *Pack My Bag: A Self-Portrait* (The Hogarth Press, London, 1992; first published 1940), especially pp. 213–14; H. Acton, *Memoirs of an Aesthete* (Hamish Hamilton, London, 1984; first published 1948), pp. 110–66.

exception of the war years – even though sartorial excess had been, and continued to be, curbed by economic, social, and especially by peer group pressures. It should come as no surprise that the distinctive roll-top collar jumpers and suede shoes of the Oxford aesthetes of the 1920s were 'abominable to some men and women', and that this group of young men suffered both verbal and physical abuse at the hands of other undergraduates.[99] Although they may have captured the public imagination (and arguably continue to do so), these aesthetes belonged to a long line of men who self-consciously adopted a 'dandified' identity, but conclusions about inter-war teenage consumers can hardly be drawn from their experiences.

Overall, it seems clear that the consumption practices of most youths did not differ substantially from those of their pre-war counterparts, and did not entirely set them apart from contemporary adults. Indeed, trade commentators frequently noted the increasing tendency for children and teenagers to wear clothes similar in materials and design to those worn by adults: 'the boy with his flannels and sports coats, and in the cut of his overcoat is a replica of the man'. In 1927 a contributor to *Men's Wear* pointed out that: 'I notice year by year an increasing tendency for boys of 15 or older to buy their clothes on the "just like father" principle.'[100] Furthermore, the 'affluence' of young people between the wars should not be exaggerated, and neither should the amount of money left in their pockets once a contribution had been made to the family budget. In the eleven occupations examined by Fowler, for example, boys under 18 were earning between 16s 1d (in shipbuilding) and 37s 1d (in tobacco) a week, averaging around 23s a week. Assuming that around 50 per cent was handed over to the family budget, the sum left over was certainly not negligible (especially if compared with pre-1914 earnings), but hardly princely.[101] They may have been able to afford trips to dance halls and cinemas, where American film stars provided new sartorial models to emulate.[102] However, understandings of appropriate sartorial consumption did not change fundamentally.

Despite the claims made by Roberts and others, the consumer practices of most young people seem to have differed very little from those of their pre-war predecessors. In inter-war Attercliffe, the garments had changed: 'Oxford bags and plus-fours' had become 'firm favourites with the youths and young men', whose attitudes and mannerisms often owed a lot to film stars like James Cagney and George Raft. However, little else had changed: 'Most young people had one new outfit a year, usually around Whitsuntide', and mostly 'dressed as well as possible on their limited resources'.[103] For many, a fashionable appearance was as unattainable as it had ever been before the war. As one respondent told the historian Andrew

---

[99] Green, *Pack My Bag*, pp. 213–14; Graves and Hodge, *The Long Weekend*, p. 124.

[100] *The Tailor and Cutter*, 8 January 1925; *Men's Wear*, 22 October 1927. See also, for example, *The Tailor and Cutter*, 6 June 1930; *Men's Wear*, 2 February 1935; *The Outfitter*, 4 October 1930.

[101] Fowler, *The First Teenagers*, table 4.3, p. 182.

[102] White, *The Worst Street in North London*, p. 166; S. Bruzzi, *Undressing Cinema: Clothing and Identity in the Movies* (Routledge, London, 1997), pp. 72–5. By 1935 *The Tailor and Cutter* was publishing a regular feature on 'Clothes on the screen'. See also *The Tailor and Cutter*, 25 January 1935, for an emphasis on the impact of cinema on young men's dress.

[103] Green, *Growing up in Attercliffe*, p. 35; Fowler, *The First Teenagers*, p. 108.

Davies, describing his experiences of monkey parades in the early 1920s, he could not remember any particular fashion: 'I was rough and ready, I never had money to buy suits of clothes'.[104] Writing in 1981, Alfred Green observed that the really significant change had occurred not in the appearance of young people in the inter-war period, but in that of older men and women after the Second World War: 'The improvement in dress of people of all ages since the war is the most striking example of the higher standard of living we now enjoy'.[105] According to Louis Heren, during the weekend the teenagers of Shadwell, in London's East End, would get 'dressed up to go to a dance or the cinema, or just walk up West'. Their lives followed a pattern familiar from the pre-war period:

> They did not live or pretend to live a separate existence, but for a few years between leaving school and getting married they had a few shillings a week to spend on themselves. Most of it went on cigarettes, cinema and dance tickets, and clothes.[106]

Conclusion

Many contemporary observers saw the inter-war period as a period of fast and furious change, a time when consumer practices altered fundamentally, and in the eyes of many, for the worse. There is little doubt that demographic and economic trends, and most notably price deflation, favoured increased consumer expenditure, including on clothing, among men and youths in full employment. However, it is doubtful whether this amounted to a 'democratisation' of menswear, or whether these years can justifiably be seen exclusively as a special moment of modernity. The experiences of two groups of men, the unemployed and teenagers, show the limitations of a narrative that focuses solely on change and on new opportunities for consumption.

There is little doubt that the clothes commonly worn by most men in 1930 were very different to those of the 1880s, or even the 1900s. New garments had come onto the market and gained in popularity, most notably, perhaps, the made-to-measure three-piece Burton suit, but also colourful woollen jumpers, soft collars, tweed sports coats and comfortable flannel trousers. Nonetheless, sartorial continuities were just as notable as changes. Decisions about what to wear were still made with reference not simply to personal preference or a desire to express one's unique individuality. The consumer's (mostly male) peer group and the men or boys among whom he spent his days had as great an influence on sartorial choices in 1939 as they had sixty years earlier: by conforming, a man signalled his acceptance of a particular mould of masculinity and a particular way of being a man. The ridicule heaped upon inter-war dress reformers, for example, points to the continued unpleasant consequences of non-conformity. However, conformity continued to be local and contingent, its rules negotiated as men lived their daily lives. Unsurprisingly, in 1939 as in 1880, most boys and men preferred to spare themselves a great deal of trouble and embarrassment by

---

[104] Davies, *Leisure, Gender and Poverty*, p. 105.

[105] Green, *Growing up in Attercliffe*, p. 35.

[106] Heren, *Growing up Poor in London*, pp. 49–50. See also Beaven, *Leisure, Citizenship and Working-Class Men*, pp. 169–75.

making an effort to 'fit in'. In the late 1930s, Ralph Glasser had left his poorly paid job as a presser in a Glasgow garment factory to take up an Oxford scholarship. Sitting with other students in tutorials, he was painfully aware that most of them were wearing 'loose tweed jackets and flannel trousers … in varying shades of grey or dark blue, with cotton shirts and college ties; a few wore silk shirts in pastel shades'. Soberly attired in his 'grey worsted suit, my only one, bought in Burtons for fifty shillings … before leaving Glasgow', he 'felt staidly overdressed'. No one teased him, or made any reference to his appearance. Nonetheless, he hated looking different to everybody else, and became determined to acquire 'the uniform of tweed jacket and bags' as soon as he 'dared spend more money'. Unsurprisingly, it was not long before he did.[107]

---

[107] R. Glasser, *Gorbals Boy at Oxford* (1988), quoted in Ugolini, 'Clothes and the modern man in 1930s Oxford', p. 443. See also W. Woodruff, *Beyond Nab End* (Abacus, London, 2003), pp. 135, 158, 165.

PART II
Selling Menswear

Chapter 5

Tailoring and Manliness, 1880–1914

In 1861 the novelist and poet George Meredith, then in his early thirties, published a comic novel entitled *Evan Harrington: Or, He Would be a Gentleman*. The novel's humour derived from the protagonist's ambiguous identity as both a tailor and a 'gentleman', as well as from his sisters' desperate attempts to distance themselves from their family's tailoring background. Although only moderately successful at the time, and now almost forgotten, part of the novel's continued interest lies in the fact that the plot drew upon Meredith's own family history. His grandfather, Melchizidec Meredith (known as 'the great Mel'), had been one of the leading tailors and naval outfitters in Portsmouth, but had refused to fit into the mould of a 'provincial tradesman'. It was said that he had established friendly relations with the families of many local naval officers and gentry, mixing with them both as a dinner guest and on the hunting field. As a result, particularly in view of his famed reluctance to send out bills, he had lived far beyond his means and left large debts on his death in 1814. The life stories of his son Augustus and his grandson George, while less dashing, can also be understood as attempts to escape from a life of 'tailordom' and achieve the status of 'gentlemen': almost entirely unsuccessfully in Augustus' case, and with an impressive degree of success in George's.[1]

In a way, *Evan Harrington* can be read as Meredith's protest against the prejudice that denied nineteenth-century tradesmen in general, and tailors in particular, the status of 'gentlemen', and condemned them to being scorned by their social 'superiors'. After all, Evan 'considered himself as good a gentleman as any man living, and was in absolute hostility with the prejudices of society'.[2] Nevertheless, there is little in the novel to indicate that that author saw the tailoring trade as a desirable one, and much that suggested distaste: the protagonist only takes over the management of the family shop when forced to do so by the need to pay off the debts left by his dead father, and in the end escapes from tailoring by marrying into a gentry family. Indeed, if a conclusion can be drawn from all the myth-making, distorted facts and lacunae surrounding the Meredith family history, it is the low social status of all those involved in the tailoring trade, as obvious at the end of the novelist's life in the 1900s as it had been at the time of *Evan Harrington*'s first publication in 1861. As Siegfried Sassoon noted in his biography of George Meredith, although in his early years the novelist had been willing to draw upon his family's tailoring background, by the time he had acquired

---

[1]   G. Meredith, *Evan Harrington* (Constable, London, 1902; first published 1861); S. Sassoon, *Meredith* (Constable, London, 1948), pp. 1–3. See also *The Tailor and Cutter*, 6 March 1902, for a discussion of tailors as protagonists of novels.

[2]   Meredith, *Evan Harrington*, p. 124.

enormous eminence as 'the laurelled and Olympian sage of Box Hill ... he did not wish the tailor's shop to be talked about. Ordinary common sense dictated his decision'.[3]

For the elderly Meredith, as for his contemporaries, it seems to have been 'common sense' that dignity and eminence could not be reconciled with a tailoring background. To some extent, tailoring shared its uncertain status with the retail trade as a whole. In many Victorian and Edwardian minds, shopkeeping and trade – particularly small-scale shopkeeping – were associated with greed, narrow-mindedness and pettiness. No reader would have been in the least surprised that when the protagonist of George Gissing's 1891 novel, *New Grub Street*, decided to write a book set in 'the sphere of the ignobly decent', and dealing with the 'essentially unheroic' lives of people 'at the mercy of paltry circumstance', he should choose 'Mr Bailey, grocer', as his main character.[4] For many, shopkeeping represented the epitome of pettiness and insignificance. However, there seems to have been a contemporary perception that the status of tailoring and of tailors was even lower. Returning for a moment to George Meredith's novel, Evan's well-born lover Rose eventually discovers his tailoring background, and asks her friend Jenny 'if tailors were thought worse of than other tradesmen. Jenny, premising that she was no authority, stated she imagined she had heard that they were'[5] (Figure 5.1). Indeed, as the well-known saying, that 'nine tailors make a man' suggested, even tailors' claims to full masculinity could be open

---

[3]   Sassoon, *Meredith*, p. 37. The story of the Meredith family also throws an intriguing light on the issue of occupation as a primary source of identity for nineteenth-century British men. See also J. Tosh, 'Masculinities in an industrialising society: Britain, 1800–1914', *Journal of British Studies*, vol. 44, no. 2 (2005), pp. 330–35; A.J. Hammerton, 'The English weakness? Gender, satire and "moral manliness" in the lower middle class, 1870–1920', in A. Kidd and D. Nicholls (eds), *Gender, Civic Culture and Consumerism: Middle-Class Identity in Britain, 1800–1940* (Manchester University Press, Manchester, 1999), pp. 164–82; J. Tosh, *A Man's Place: Masculinity and the Middle-Class Home in Victorian England* (Yale University Press, New Haven, 1999); G. Crossick, 'Past masters: in search of the artisan in European history', in G. Crossick (ed.), *The Artisan and the European Town, 1500–1900* (Scolar Press, Aldershot, 1997), pp. 6–7. The fact that Meredith was the son of a tailor was still the subject of gossip as late as 1904. A. Bennett, *The Journals* (Penguin Books, Harmondsworth, 1984; first published in this edition 1971), p. 113.

[4]   G. Gissing, *New Grub Street* (Penguin Books, London, 1985; first published 1891), pp. 173, 243. Shopkeepers' status is discussed in J. Benson and L. Ugolini, 'Historians and the nation of shopkeepers', in J. Benson and L. Ugolini (eds), *A Nation of Shopkeepers: Five Centuries of British Retailing* (I.B. Tauris, London, 2003), pp. 5–7. But see also the often relatively high status of retailers within working-class communities, noted, for example, in C.P. Hosgood, 'The "pigmies of commerce" and the working-class community: small shopkeepers in England, 1870–1914', *Journal of Social History*, vol. 22, no. 3 (1989), pp. 439–60; J. Benson, *The Penny Capitalists: A Study of Nineteenth-Century Working-Class Entrepreneurs* (Gill and Macmillan, Goldenbridge, 1983), chapter 10. See also M.J. Winstanley, *The Shopkeeper's World 1830–1914* (Manchester University Press, Manchester, 1983). The best known fictional representations of small shopkeepers in this period were those penned by H.G. Wells. See especially H.G. Wells, *Kipps* (J.M. Dent, London, 1993; first published 1905); H.G. Wells, *The History of Mr Polly* (J.M. Dent, London, 1999; first published 1910).

[5]   Meredith, *Evan Harrington*, p. 172. According to the radical tailor Francis Place, writing in 1825, 'Gentlemen cannot associate with tradesmen ... much less with a *tailor*'. M. Thale (ed.), *The Autobiography of Francis Place* (Cambridge University Press, Cambridge, 1972), p. 250.

to doubt. As one contributor to the tailoring trade press wryly observed in 1891, 'we are the byword for effeminate helplessness and imbecile incapacity'.[6]

A few years earlier, John Pallister, a frequent contributor to the trade press, had tackled the same issue in an editorial of *The London Tailor*, complaining about 'the slander with which tailors have been assailed from time immemorial': that of being 'only the fractional part of a man'. According to Pallister, the most likely explanation for the contempt in which the trade was held was its apparent 'effeminacy', and the association of sewing with femininity. He attempted to counter this impression by emphasising the male ancestry of the needle trades, stating that before the reign of Charles I, women had only been involved in the production of clothes for private, domestic consumption. In the past, he asserted, 'the skilful handling of the needle [was] not thought to be in any way derogatory to the dignity of manhood'. Medieval tailors, organised in their craft guilds and fighting for 'civil liberty', had shown that they were not 'effeminate', but rather 'doughty knights of the thimble'.[7] Pallister's account of the history of the tailoring trade was hardly accurate. However, he was not alone in his belief that the low status and 'unmanliness' of tailoring were linked to sewing's association with women. These views were already being expressed eighty years earlier, when a tailor writing a pamphlet under the pseudonym of 'A Flint', had asked rhetorically why, if sewing was considered effeminate because 'the province of Women', were hosiers not also persecuted with the 'same silly malignancy of wit?' He questioned how far clothes-making could be considered 'feminine' anyway, pointing out the supposed absurdity of 'a woman cutting out a coat, or making a pair of Breeches'. The men who laughed at tailors, taunting them with being the ninth

---

[6]   *The Weekly Record of Fashion*, September 1891. See also *The London Tailor*, October 1912. A comparison between depictions of tailors and dustmen is revealing of very different styles and conceptions of working-class masculinity. B. Maidment, '101 things to do with a fantail hat: dustmen, dirt and dandyism, 1820–1860', *Textile History*, vol. 33, no. 1 (2002), pp. 79–97. The various notions of working-class 'manliness' are explored, for example, in E. Janes Yeo (ed.), Special issue: 'Working-class masculinities in Britain, 1850 to present', *Labour History Review*, vol. 62, no. 2 (2004); C. Hall, K. McClelland and J. Rendall, *Defining the Victorian Nation: Class, Race, Gender and the British Reform Act of 1867* (Cambridge University Press, Cambridge, 2000), chapter 2; P. Ayers, 'The making of men: masculinities in interwar Liverpool', and V. Burton, '"Whoring, drinking sailors": reflections on masculinity from the labour history of nineteenth-century British shipping', both in M. Walsh (ed.), *Working Out Gender: Perspectives from Labour History* (Ashgate, Aldershot, 1999), pp. 66–83 and 84–101; S.O. Rose, *Limited Livelihoods: Gender and Class in Nineteenth-Century England* (Routledge, London, 1992), chapter 6; P.J. Walker, '"I live but not yet I for Christ liveth in me": men and masculinity in the Salvation Army, 1865–90', in M. Roper and J. Tosh (eds), *Manful Assertions: Masculinities in Britain since 1800* (Routledge, London, 1991), pp. 92–112. One possible suggestion for the origin of the saying 'Nine tailors make a man' is that the term 'tailor' is an adaptation of 'teller', 'a *teller* being a stroke on the funeral bell, three being given for a child, six for a woman, and nine for a man'. *Brewer's Dictionary of Phrase and Fable* (Cassell, London, 1991; first published 1870), p. 1079. Whatever its origin, the derogatory meaning of the saying is very clear.

[7]   *The London Tailor*, 9 May 1885.

part of a man, were invited to meet them 'fist to fist … and they will soon convince you of that complete virility which their wives never disputed'.[8]

It is with this notional 'tailor' and his impact on tailoring workers' identities and experiences of work in the three decades before the outbreak of the First World War, that this chapter is primarily concerned. It firstly considers the qualities long associated with tailors and tailoring, all of which served to diminish their claims to 'manliness': tailors were believed to be if not actually crippled, then certainly physically weak, and poor almost to the point of destitution. As the century advanced, they also became associated less with political radicalism, independence and the disorder of 'traditional' workshop culture, and more with passive victimhood and 'sweating'. Furthermore, especially in the wake of a new influx of Jewish refugees from Eastern Europe in the 1880s, the trade as a whole came to be increasingly associated with – largely negative – connotations of Jewishness.

The second part of the chapter then concentrates more specifically on the men involved primarily in the 'retailing' side of the tailoring trade, paying particular attention to independents specialising in the made-to-measure trade. It begins by examining the attempts by – supposedly – sober, industrious and respectable cutters, salesmen and managers to overcome the long-standing association of the trade with pitiful unmanliness. It then goes on to consider their strategies for dealing with the threat posed at the turn of the century by enterprises such as glamorous 'brass and glass' shops, co-operatives, and other large-scale businesses. The odds, as will be seen, were stacked heavily against the 'small man'. However, this did not stop many late-Victorian and Edwardian independent retailers from attempting to reinvent themselves as manly, business-like, modern, skilled (or even gifted), and, above all, successful tradesmen.

Tailoring and unmanliness

Almost ten years before the publication of *Evan Harrington*, another – and very different – novel had appeared with a tailor as its central character: Charles Kingsley's *Alton Locke*. Early on in the book the reader is told that although highly intelligent, as a child Alton had been 'a pale, consumptive, rickety, weakly boy, all forehead and no muscle'. For this reason, when the time had come for a trade to be found for such a poor weakling, tailoring had been the obvious option. After all, 'have not clothes and shoes been from time immemorial the appointed work of such?'[9] Kingsley's choice

---

[8]   A Flint, *The Tailor's Answer to the Late Attacks Upon their Profession from the Stage and Press* (Wake, London, 1805), pp. 6–7. See also Thomas Carlyle's satirical depiction of tailors and tailoring in *Sartor Resartus: The Life and Opinions of Herr Teufelsdröckh* (Chapman and Hall, London, 1901; first published in book form 1836), pp. 230–32. On the history of medieval clothing trades see, for example, F. Piponnier and P. Mane, *Dress in the Middle Ages* (Yale University Press, New Haven, 1997; first published 1995); N.B. Harte and K.G. Pointing (eds), *Cloth and Clothing in Medieval Europe: Essays in Memory of E.M. Carus-Wilson* (Heinemann and Pasold Research Fund, London, 1982). See also C. Richardson (ed.), *Clothing Culture, 1350–1650* (Ashgate, Aldershot, 2004).

[9]   C. Kingsley, *Alton Locke: Tailor and Poet* (T. Nelson and Sons, London, n.d.; first published 1850), p. 15.

DRAWING THE LINE.

Old Caddicombe (Retired Bone-boiler).—"LOOK HERE, FITZNOB, WE MUST PILL THIS MAN JONES IS PUTTING UP. THE FELLOW'S IN TRADE. MUST KEEP THE CLUB SELECT."

Fitznob.—"DON'T SEE THAT MATTERS SO MUCH. YOU WERE IN TRADE ONCE, YOU KNOW. WHAT'S HIS NAME?"

Old Caddicombe.—"ANSER. HE'S A TAILOR."

Fitznob.—"ANSER? THE BRUTE'S GOT A BIG BILL AGAINST ME. QUITE RIGHT, CADDICOMBE, PILL HIM. WE MUST KEEP THE CLUB SELECT."

Figure 5.1   'Drawing the line': tailors' low status. *Fun*, 12 December 1883. Courtesy of the Bodleian Library, University of Oxford, N.2706 d.13.

of words, suggesting that the association of physical weakness and tailoring was a long-standing one, is significant. After all, shoe- and clothes-making were two of the few sedentary trades open to working-class boys, tailoring in particular being almost unique in not requiring physical strength: 'a boy seldom became a tailor unless he was too much of a cripple for the mill, or too weak in the arm for the forge'.[10] The association of tailoring with weakness was sufficiently well-known for Samuel Butler to mock it in his semi-autobiographical novel *The Way of All Flesh*, mostly written in the 1870s and early 1880s. Butler had Ernest Pontifex, the hapless protagonist, decide to 'convert' to Christianity his upstairs neighbour, a tailor called Mr Holt, partly because 'once converted, he would no longer beat his wife at two o'clock in the morning, and the house would be much pleasanter in consequence'. Having determined on this course of action, Ernest carefully prepared his arguments: 'But the man was a great hulking fellow, of a savage temper, and Ernest was forced to admit that unforeseen developments might arise to disconcert him. They say it takes nine tailors to make a man, but Ernest felt that it would take at least nine Ernests to make a Mr Holt.'[11]

In reality, like the fictional Mr Holt, not all tailors were physically crippled or even particularly weak, but there was a perception, which proved remarkably tenacious, that, as a commentator put it in 1891, 'anything would do for a tailor, and the biggest cripple or the most confirmed idiot were out of place unless they were converted into tailors'.[12] Even healthy men – it was stated in 1886 – were turned into cripples with 'pale face[s] and cramped gait' by the work, and especially by the long periods spent sitting cross-legged, a posture derided as 'unhealthy, undignified, lazy, demoralising, humiliating and ludicrous'.[13] Physical strength was not as important in defining an individual's manliness among the skilled sections of the working class as it was among unskilled occupations, and a weak or even crippled physique would not necessarily have detracted from a man's standing in the local community.[14] Even when not as intimidating as Mr Holt, the 'little tailor' was by no means always a pushover. According to Norman Nicholson, his tailor father's appearance had resembled that of H.G. Wells's Kipps: a small man, 'his face was pale and wore much of the time a surprised, rather scared look'. However, the timid expression was highly misleading, as 'he knew very well how to take care of himself and would not be put upon by anybody'.[15] Nevertheless, there is no doubt that the association of tailoring with physical (and mental) weakness was a tenacious one, which did nothing to raise the trade's status.

---

[10]   *The London Tailor*, September 1909.

[11]   S. Butler, *The Way of All Flesh* (Wordsworth Classics, Ware, 1994; first published 1903), p. 212.

[12]   *The Weekly Record of Fashion*, March 1891. See also 4 April 1885.

[13]   *The Tailor and Cutter*, 16 September 1886. The notion that tailoring weakened men was dismissed, for example, by *The London Tailor*, February 1903.

[14]   See, for example, F. Gresswell, *Bright Boots: An Autobiography* (David and Charles, Newton Abbot, 1982; first published 1956), pp. 87–8. For the link between working-class manliness and physical strength see, for example, J. Bourke, *Working Class Cultures in Britain, 1890–1960: Gender, Class and Ethnicity* (Routledge, London, 1999; first published 1994), pp. 41–5.

[15]   N. Nicholson, *Wednesday Early Closing* (Faber and Faber, London, 1975), p. 38.

Furthermore, derogatory eighteenth- and nineteenth-century representations of tailors made much of how their weakness and lack of manliness was supposedly also reflected in their dealings with women, especially with wives and lovers. Although frequently depicted as lustful, tailors were also usually portrayed as losing out, hurt and humiliated, from their encounters with women.[16] This strand of humour had not entirely disappeared by the end of the nineteenth century. In a music-hall song performed by Marie Kendall at the turn of the century, for example, the tailor Bill Johnson was described as 'The ninth part of a man / Which was often thrown up to him by his missis Mary Ann / She'd only let him sleep at night in the ninth part of the bed'. On one occasion, however, Bill managed to assert his manliness, making use of his role as the family bread-winner: 'On Saturday night he came home "tight" and told his wife / "Ninth" part of a man you've called me … Here's the ninth part of my wages, eh? / How do we go now?'[17]

A strong association with poverty also often accompanied images of physically weak tailors. In reality, there was a considerable diversity of earnings among those involved in the tailoring trade. According to a Board of Trade Report of 1909, the average weekly wage of (male) bespoke tailors in London (calculated on the basis of an average working week of four days) was 28s 5d. However, this obscured the considerable differences within the trade: cutters' average wage was 57s 5d, and could be as high as 73s 3d; while journeymen tailors' average was considerably lower, at 26s 6d; and machinists' even lower, at 22s 5d. Cutters, particularly in high-class trades, were among those able to earn relatively well, while it was among the army of journeymen tailors, machinists and pressers, male and female, that real hardship could be found, with low wages and seasonal unemployment a constant threat.[18] In the 1880s the writer A.E. Coppard's father had managed to obtain skilled tailoring work in the Brighton army barracks, where he made officers' uniforms. But as his son pointed out, 'tailoring was not an enriching profession and unemployment

---

[16] See, for example, B. Smith, 'The hen peckt husband' (1768), in S. O'Connell, *The Popular Print in England 1550–1850* (British Museum Press, London, 1999), figure 1.4, p. 13; 'The tailor and the treacle cask' (J. Harkness, Preston, 1840–66); 'Tailor and trooper' (n.k.); 'The tailor done over' (Bebbington, Manchester, n.d. [nineteenth century]); 'The sailor and the tailor' (J. Jennings, London, 1790–1840), all Bodleian Library Broadside Ballads, University of Oxford. Also available at www.bodley.ox.ac.uk/ballads, the *allegro* catalogue of ballads.

[17] A. Hall, H. Costling and S. McCarthy (authors and composers), *How Do We Go Now?* (Francis, Day and Hunter, London, n.d. [c. 1900]). For the reality of conflict and discord in late eighteenth- and early nineteenth-century plebeian households, see A. Clark, *The Struggle for the Breeches: Gender and the Making of the British Working Class* (University of California Press, Berkeley, 1995), especially chapter 5.

[18] J. Morris, *Women Workers and the Sweated Trades: The Origins of Minimum Wage Legislation* (Gower, Aldershot, 1986), p. 32. See also S.P. Dobbs, *The Clothing Workers of Great Britain* (George Routledge and Sons, London, 1928), p. 108. In the mid-eighteenth century, Richard Campbell had remarked that, while 'foremen' could earn good wages, the 'mere working' tailors were 'as numerous as locusts … and generally as poor as rats'. R. Campbell, *The London Tradesman* (London, 1747), p. 192. In 1887, it was estimated that the average wage of cutters was £3 a week. *The Weekly Record of Fashion*, May 1887.

was endemic'. Eventually he was laid off, and forced 'to give up militancy and slave at home making uniforms for policemen until he died'.[19]

Radicalism and sweating

Throughout the nineteenth century, whether the intention was to mock or to sympathise, it was commonplace to portray tailoring workers as thin, unkempt and ragged. In the case of Robert Cruikshank's illustrations to the 1836 edition of the satiric play *The Tailors: A Tragedy for Warm Weather*, the aim was clearly the former.[20] In this mock-heroic play, which saw journeymen tailors pitted against their masters, both sides were portrayed as ridiculous: thin to the point of emaciation, dressed in rags, and armed with the instruments of their trade, rather than 'proper' weapons, they provided an unsubtle parody of the heroes of 'serious' drama. However, although the obvious poverty of the tailors in Cruikshank's illustrations continued to be relevant to representation of late Victorian and Edwardian tailors, in other ways the emphasis changed. Although not meant to be taken seriously, Cruikshank's tailors were still at least potentially threatening to good order, their actions evoking a continuing tradition of political radicalism, and the empty tankards strewn on the floor an aggressive and often disruptive male workshop culture built around drinking rituals.[21] Neither of these was exclusive to the urban context: in the 1870s, the public house in the Suffolk village of Bungay 'was the working man's Parliament ... and

---

[19]   A.E. Coppard, *It's Me O Lord!* (Methuen, London, 1957), p. 28. For tailors' wages, including a discussion of the impact of the 1909 Trades Boards, see also A.J. Kershen, *Uniting the Tailors: Trade Unionism Among the Tailors of London and Leeds, 1870–1939* (Frank Cass, Ilford, 1995), pp. 49, 51, 118–19, 121, 195–7; J.A. Schmiechen, *Sweated Industries and Sweated Labour: The London Clothing Trades, 1860–1914* (Croom Helm, London, 1984), especially pp. 161–79; G. Crossick, *An Artisan Elite in Victorian Society: Kentish London 1840–1880* (Croom Helm, London, 1978), pp. 110–13.

[20]   Anon. [Samuel Foote], *The Tailors: A Tragedy for Warm Weather* (Joseph Thomas, London, 1836). First performed in 1767, the main aim of the play was not to mock tailors, but rather to satirise contemporary drama: tailors were chosen as the central characters because of their seemingly obvious unheroic character. For the play's history, see ibid., especially pp. 5–7.

[21]   It is perhaps not a coincidence that this edition of the play should appear in 1836, only two years after the collapse of a well-publicised strike by 9,000 London tailors for higher wages, shorter hours and the abolition of piecework and homework. B. Taylor, *Eve and the New Jerusalem: Socialism and Feminism in the Nineteenth Century* (Virago, London, 1991; first published 1983), pp. 114–17. For the drinking culture of early nineteenth-century tailoring workshops, see Anon. [T. Carter], *Memoirs of a Working Man* (Charles Knight, London, 1845), pp. 71–4, 123. For artisanal culture more in general, see Crossick, 'Past masters', pp. 1–40; I. Prothero, *Radical Artisans in England and France, 1830–1870* (Cambridge University Press, Cambridge, 1997); Clark, *The Struggle for the Breeches*; G. Crossick and H.-G. Haupt, *The Petite Bourgeoisie in Europe, 1780–1914* (Routledge, London, 1995); I. McCalman, *Radical Underworld: Prophets, Revolutionaries and Pornographers in London, 1795–1840* (Cambridge University Press, Cambridge, 1988).

nine times out of ten the Miller was chosen as Prime Minister – the Speaker either the Village Tailor or one of the Snobs [shoemakers]'.[22]

By the end of the nineteenth century, however, representations of tailors had lost much of this aggressiveness and political content, replaced by a far greater emphasis on pathos. Taken out of his urban workshop and domesticated, the bland 'little tailor' became a suitable character for the children's books of the late Victorian and Edwardian periods. 'Tinker tailor Nicholas', for example, worked on his own, and despite being rather lonely, 'whistled and sang, or smoked and smiled, all day. At evening he'd go for a walk outside the city … and talk to the birds and bunnies, who knew he was kind and good, and let him come up quite near them'.[23] It is difficult to account with any certainty for this change. It may have accompanied a real decline in the drunkenness and disorder of 'traditional' workshop culture, and an increase in 'respectable' behaviour on the part of tailoring workers. According to one trade journalist, writing under the pseudonym of 'County Palatine', by 1890 the so-called 'cock-and-pie' tailors of mid-century had become a thing of the past: contemporary workers supposedly had more 'self-respect and self-restraint'.[24] It may also have been the case that there was a decline in the opportunity for such disruptive behaviour, as all-male workshops were replaced by outwork and homework (and to a limited extent by factory work) in the course of the nineteenth century. As a result, 'the new race of tailors will scarcely stand all the nonsense of the good (?) old times'. Indeed, the pace at which they were forced to work did not allow for such distractions, except when work was slack, a time when in any case they would not have the 'money to spare for such foolery'.[25]

That said, a drink-based work culture had certainly not entirely disappeared by the end of the nineteenth century, and the experiences of the teetotal Oxford tailor Henry Chandler give an indication of the continued pressure on individuals

---

[22]   G. Baldry, *The Rabbit Skin Cap* (The Boydell Press, Woodbridge, 1984; first published 1939), pp. 211–12.

[23]   Anon., *Tinker Tailor* (Henry Frowde and Hodder and Stoughton, London, n.d. [c. 1912]), n.p. See also Anon., *The Tailor and the Crow: An Old Rhyme with New Drawings by L. Leslie Brooke* (Frederick Warne, London, 1911); B. Potter, *The Tailor of Gloucester* (Frederick Warne, London, 1903); E. Vredenburg, *Tinker Tailor* (Raphael Tuck and Sons, London, n.d. [c. 1914]), pp. 22–33. It is interesting to note that the much more threatening tailor depicted in Heinrich Hoffman's *Struwwelpeter*, first published in 1845, had, like the other characters in the book, initially been intended to parody the bogeymen of traditional fairy-tales. See M. Warner, *No Go the Bogeyman: Scaring, Lulling and Making Mock* (Chatto and Windus, London, 1998), pp. 33–4.

[24]   *The Gentleman's Magazine of Fashion*, November 1890.

[25]   Anon., 'Tailoring and bootmaking in central London', in C. Booth (ed.), *Life and Labour of the People in London* (Macmillan, London, 1893), vol. IV, pp. 143–4. See also *The Gentleman's Magazine of Fashion*, February 1890. For a positive assessment of the effect of the factory environment on tailoring workers, see *Men's Wear*, 29 March 1902. The nature, extent and causes of the shift towards a more 'respectable' behaviour on the part of artisans are some of the themes explored by Clark, *The Struggle for the Breeches*. See also Hall et al., *Defining the Victorian Nation*, chapter 2; Rose, *Limited Livelihoods*, especially pp. 138–53; Taylor, *Eve and the New Jerusalem*, especially chapter 4; G. Stedman Jones, *Languages of Class: Studies in English Working-Class History 1832–1982* (Cambridge University Press, Cambridge, 1983), chapter 4.

to conform. In September 1879 he attended the annual feast of one of the firms he worked for. The dinner was held in a public house, and although – as he put it in his diary – 'there is a great deal done and said which I strongly object to', he did not want to 'appear exceptional' by complaining, and was even tempted to accept a cigar, not because he particularly wanted it, but 'from a desire to appear like all the others'. Despite his attempts to blend with the rest, he was teased by his dinner companions for drinking water rather than spirits: 'one asked "who was drinking the weak stuff" … another hinted at it being beyond endurance, at seeing it on the table a third merrily expressed a desire to "knock it over" but I appeared not to hear…' and somehow he managed to get through the difficult evening.[26]

Arguably, it was the renewed scandal in the 1880s over the 'sweating' of workers (among whom clothing workers featured prominently), which was more influential than any actual change in work culture in giving new impetus to the image of tailors, both male and female, as tragic, but essentially unthreatening victims. Theirs were the 'pathetic bewildered lives upon which the burden of overwork rests from childhood to old age'.[27] Their response to exploitation was portrayed as passive. In his study of Leeds slipper-makers and tailors, for example, Robert Sherard called upon 'men of heart' to consider how their 'lounge coat and fireside slippers' had been made with 'the tears of the women and the gaunt despair of the men'. Male workers, it seems, did not go as far as to shed tears, but nevertheless allowed themselves to be exploited without rebelling. Indeed, part of the pathos of their situation was their complete dependence on the 'sweater' for their very survival. Particularly at slack times of the year, 'no matter what the conditions are on which the work is offered, they must eagerly accept it'.[28] The often minute subdivision of tasks, it was emphasised, made tailoring skills superfluous, while starvation wages made it impossible for married male workers to support themselves, let alone discharge their obligation to look after their families. Pathetic images were presented to the newspaper-reading public of whole families being forced to toil at garment-making, in what was – explicitly or

---

[26]   Oxfordshire Record Office, Oxford, Diary and Notebooks of Henry Chandler of Grandpont, Oxford, 1872–c.1945, P408/J/I, H. Chandler Day Book, 13 September 1879.

[27]   G. Tuckwell, 'Preface', in R. Mudie Smith (ed.), *Sweated Industries: Being a Handbook of the Daily News Exhibition* (Bradbury, Agnew, London, 1906), p. 10. Sweating, if understood as work for miserable wages and long hours in poor conditions, was of course not a new phenomenon in the 1880s. The term 'sweating' itself had already been in circulation since at least the 1840s, when tailors had used it in an attempt to find expression to the changes taking place within their trade. In the 1880s, however, there seems to have been a new willingness on the part of the middle class (or at least a section of the middle class) to question accepted understandings of the causes of poverty, and their relationship with waged work. Part of what Beatrice Webb described as 'the humanitarian upsurge of the eighties', which both resulted in and further fuelled a whole series of 'social investigations', was a renewed concern over the 'sweating' of workers, and particularly outworkers and homeworkers. Schmiechen, *Sweated Industries*, especially pp. 134–5. See also B. Harris (ed.), *Famine and Fashion: Needlewomen in the Nineteenth Century* (Ashgate, Aldershot, 2005).

[28]   R.H. Sherard, *The White Slaves of England* (James Bowden, London, 1897), pp. 137–8; A. Sherwell, *Life in West London: A Study and a Contrast* (Methuen, London, 1897), pp. 101, 86–120. On the question of artisans' increasingly limited 'independence', see Crossick and Haupt, *The Petite Bourgeoisie*, pp. 2, 4.

implicitly – considered a perversion of the home's role as a domestic haven.[29] By the outbreak of the First World War, the whole of the tailoring trade had become tainted by the association with sweating,[30] and although images of 'bondage' and 'slavery'[31] may have been useful in arousing the public's sympathy for these workers' plight, they were hardly designed to impress with tailors' manliness and self-reliance.

Tailors, it seems, and by extension all those involved in the tailoring trade, lacked most of the characteristics associated with late Victorian and Edwardian working-class manliness. Physical strength, skill (or a perception of skill[32]), the ability to earn a decent wage and thus to support their family, including a non-wage-earning wife, and even a semblance of 'independence', all eluded them. Of course, in reality very few working-class men would have achieved all such ideals,[33] but the extent of tailors' perceived failings is remarkable. Many, no doubt, especially among the sweated workers, felt degraded by their circumstances. As Mr Coyle, a Leeds slipper maker, explained to Robert Sherard, in a 'pitifully sad and depressed manner': 'I do feel the poverty of my house ... It makes me miserable to be so badly paid ... because it makes me feel that I am of no use in the world.'[34]

Tailoring and Jewishness

In a society in which anti-Semitism was arguably deeply embedded, tailoring was also strongly associated with Jewishness. This was nothing new. Beverley Lemire has shown how by 1800 clothes dealing and Jewishness were already 'so closely identified that they were often portrayed as one and the same thing, fusing into the single entity all the negative characterisations assigned to the two categories'.[35] However, the new influx of Jewish refugees in the late nineteenth century, escaping from the poverty and persecution of the Pale of Settlement, an area of almost 400,000 square miles lying on the border between Poland and Russia, meant that

---

[29]   Sherwell, *Life in West London*, chapter 8; J. Macdonald, 'Sweating in the tailoring trade', in Mudie Smith (ed.), *Sweated Industries*, p. 67. In reality, not all sweated work was necessarily unskilled, while homework was hardly a new phenomenon in the late nineteenth century.

[30]   Unfairly, at least according to *The Sartorial Gazette*, the official organ of the Master Tailors' Association of Great Britain and Ireland and the National Federation of Foremen Tailors' Societies. *The Sartorial Gazette*, May 1913.

[31]   *The Tailor and Cutter*, 25 February 1886; *The Outfitter*, 27 May 1887.

[32]   'Skill' is notoriously difficult to define. However, by the end of the nineteenth century the *perception* was that tailors had through subdivision and mechanisation for the most part lost the craft skill associated with an (arguably mythical) 'golden age' of artisanal production. J. Rule, 'The property of skill in the period of manufacture', in P. Joyce (ed.), *The Historical Meanings of Work* (Cambridge University Press, Cambridge, 1987), pp. 99–118; C. More, *Skill and the English Working Class, 1870–1914* (Croom Helm, London, 1980), pp. 181–2.

[33]   W. Seccombe, 'Patriarchy stabilized: the construction of the male breadwinner wage norm in nineteenth-century Britain', *Social History*, vol. 11, no. 1 (1986), pp. 53–76.

[34]   Sherard, *The White Slaves of England*, pp. 113–14. Despite his miserable circumstances, Mr Coyle's 'spirit of manly pride' made him refuse to work below the minimum rate that he set himself.

[35]   B. Lemire, *Dress, Culture and Commerce: The English Clothing Trade Before the Factory, 1660–1800* (Macmillan, Basingstoke, 1997), p. 75.

the issue acquired a new topicality. V.D. Lipman has estimated that around 100,000 Russian Jews settled in Britain between 1881 and 1905, and up to 50,000 between 1906 and 1914, adding their numbers to an existing Jewish population of roughly 60,000 in 1881. Most of these new arrivals settled around existing communities and in areas where employment opportunities were available, particularly in the clothing trades. By 1914, the 300,000 or so Jewish people living in Britain were overwhelmingly concentrated in London (c. 120,000), with substantial communities also flourishing in Manchester (c. 30,000) and Leeds (c. 20,000). Many of these new immigrants seem to have gravitated towards tailoring: in Leeds in 1891 around two-thirds of employed men of Russian-Polish origin worked in the clothing trades, while in London, in 1901, 60 per cent of Jewish men worked in tailoring. It has been estimated that whereas 3 per cent of male tailors in London were Jewish in 1861, by 1901 the proportion had grown to 36 per cent.[36] According to 'Passer-by', writing in *The Tailor and Cutter*, by 1910 the East End of London had become 'a Jewish colony', whose 'staple industry' was tailoring.[37]

By the last decade of the nineteenth century, the questions of Jewish immigration and of sweating had become inseparable: whether they emphasised the supposed propensity of Jewish people for sweating other workers, or for becoming sweated workers themselves, the result was that for most commentators, tailoring, sweating and Jewishness had become different sides of the same coin. As Jose Harris has observed, 'Jews were perceived as exemplifying the early Victorian virtues of capitalist accumulation' at a time when the 'virtues of patriotism and public spirit' were more generally valued.[38] As a result, as *Der Arbeiter Freund* (an anarchist-communist newspaper aimed at an Anglo-Jewish readership) remarked in 1893, the Shakespearean image of the Jew as a 'bloodthirsty money-percentnik' and the Dickensian version, of 'a thief who teaches little children the light-fingered skills', had been replaced by the 'little tailoring and footwear sweaters over whom the dunghill of the capitalist press pours its poisonous hatred'.[39] This may have been a reference to statements such as those made in the London paper *The Evening News*, which in 1885 confidently affirmed that nine out of ten tailoring sweaters were German Jews. The paper smugly congratulated itself on the fact that this 'nefarious middleman' was 'as foreign in race as he is in sympathy and conduct from the

---

[36]   V.D. Lipman, *A History of the Jews in Britain Since 1858* (Leicester University Press, Leicester, 1990), pp. 12, 45, 50, 57; A. Godley, *Jewish Immigrant Entrepreneurs in New York and London 1880–1914: Enterprise and Culture* (Palgrave, Basingstoke, 2001), pp. 40–41. See also K. Honeyman, *Well Suited: A History of the Leeds Clothing Industry 1850–1990* (Pasold Research Fund and Oxford University Press, Oxford, 2000), pp. 14–19; Kershen, *Uniting the Tailors*, pp. 8–11; Schmiechen, *Sweated Industries*, p. 36.

[37]   *The Tailor and Cutter*, 12 May 1910.

[38]   J. Harris, *Private Lives, Public Spirit: Britain 1870–1914* (Penguin Books, London, 1994; first published 1993), p. 237. Whether this means that late-Victorian anti-semitism was therefore not based 'on quintessentially ethnic grounds', as Harris suggests, seems questionable.

[39]   *Der Arbeiter Freund*, 1893, quoted in J. Buckman, *Immigrants and the Class Struggle: The Jewish Immigrants in Leeds* (Manchester University Press, Manchester, 1983), p. 8.

honest working-men of old England'.[40] Even those who questioned the accuracy of journalistic images of the 'gorgeous Hebrew with diamond rings and a big cigar', nevertheless shared the general assumption that Jewish immigration had been the catalyst for the 'introduction' of sweating in Britain.[41] As a Pitman manual on the British clothing trade published in 1920 explained in a matter-of-fact way (although significantly, without mentioning dates), newly-arrived Jewish workers, being not only poor, but also 'accustomed to the then very low standard of Continental living', had undercut British labour and introduced the practice of 'sweating'.[42]

Perhaps unsurprisingly, high-class tailoring establishments, more modest firms, independent retailers, co-operatives, manufacturers, department stores and multiples all shared a desire to distance themselves from accusations of being involved in the 'sweating' of workers (although it should be noted that such distancing rarely involved a commitment to the payment of nationally agreed minimum wages).[43] The 1907 catalogue of the Army and Navy Stores, for example, was careful to emphasise that 'none but experienced workmen' were employed in its tailoring department, and that 'all garments are made in workshops under the Society's supervision, and in accordance with the rules laid down by the Factory Act'.[44] Almost ten years earlier, the Manchester-based clothing factory of J.H. Hutt was praised for providing its employees with a variety of facilities, including dining-rooms, cloakrooms and lavatories, while in Leeds the local press made much of the new and 'modern' clothing factories' alleged difference from the older Jewish sweatshops,[45] a trend that was to become increasingly marked in the inter-war period.

In 1884, the editorial of one of the tailoring trade papers took the unusual step of acknowledging the involvement of some of the most exclusive London firms – and their clients – in a system that led to the exploitation of a veritable army of outworkers. It suggested that: 'if some of the high bred ones of this proud land saw the dens in which a good deal of West End London tailoring is done … they would … refuse to touch the very clothes they … wear in the company of people of the highest

---

[40]   *The Evening News*, reprinted in *The London Tailor*, November 1885. The tailoring trade press, which for the most part portrayed itself as the champion of 'English' tailoring, was often vitriolic in its anti-semitism. See, for example, *The Gentleman's Magazine of Fashion*, October 1894; *The London Tailor*, November 1885, December 1885, July 1886.

[41]   G.R. Sims, 'Sweated London', in G.R. Sims (ed.), *Living London: Its Work and its Play its Humours and its Pathos its Sights and its Scenes* (Cassell, London, 1902), vol. 1, pp. 53–4. See also B. Potter, 'The tailoring trade', in Booth (ed.), *Life and Labour*, vol. iv, pp. 37, 58–60.

[42]   B.W. Poole, *The Clothing Trades Industry* (Pitman and Sons, London, 1920), pp. 56–9. See also Sherwell, *Life in West London*, pp. 95–105; Dobbs, *The Clothing Workers*, p. 15.

[43]   *The Tailor and Cutter*, 6 November 1913.

[44]   A. Adburgham, *Yesterday's Shopping: The Army and Navy Stores Catalogue 1907* (David and Charles, Newton Abbot, 1969), p. 870.

[45]   N. Richardson (ed.), *Good Value and No Humbug: A Discourse on Some of the Principal Trades and Manufactories in Manchester in 1892* (N. Richardson, Swinton, 1982; first published 1892); Kershen, *Uniting the Tailors*, pp. 31–2. As Katrina Honeyman has amply demonstrated, pre-First World War Leeds factories and workshops were in reality mutually dependent. Honeyman, *Well Suited*, pp. 21–9.

refinement'.[46] Unsurprisingly, however, bespoke firms were not much given to such introspection, or to investigating the conditions that prevailed in the workshops where part or all of the tailoring process was regularly 'put out'. They preferred to emphasise the supposed link between sweated products and 'large "show" shops', patronised by working men and 'would-be swells', who were lured by the fashionable clothing exhibited in the windows at 'such wonderfully low prices'.[47] Indeed, with their demands for ever-lower prices, customers were thought to bear their share of responsibility for the practice of sweating. Rather than approaching with scepticism firms that made 'more brazen statements than anybody with any knowledge of tailoring could have the cheek to do', 'the public ... absolutely love it'.[48] Generally, however, the trade press agreed with other commentators that sweating was the result of a supposed 'Jewish' influence on tailoring. It was suggested that even that bastion of high-class bespoke tailoring, London's West End, was being invaded by Jews who 'swim up from the East End'. 'It was they' – claimed a contributor to *The Gentleman's Magazine of Fashion* in 1894, with more heat than evidence – 'who first started the cheapening of prices, the lowering of the standard of quality and wages and trimmings.'[49]

Selling menswear

As late-nineteenth-century writers protesting against the exploitation of tailoring workers recognised, most – especially urban – consumers would have had little or no contact with the actual makers of their clothes, with the exception in some establishments of the cutter. It was acknowledged, even if only implicitly, that the customer would usually interact with a go-between, who may or may not have a practical knowledge of tailoring and garment-making. That said, the boundary between 'makers' and 'sellers' of clothing was not always fixed and insurmountable. Practices varied between different firms. In the less exclusive end of the bespoke trade, for example, at busy times the cutter might be expected to help out with the sewing. When the shop was a small one, or when the tailoring department was only one part of a larger store that also sold outfitting items such as shirts, collars, ties, underwear and so on, it was considered 'imperative that the cutter be an all-round

[46]   *The Weekly Record of Fashion*, 20 February 1884.

[47]   *The Weekly Record of Fashion*, June 1886; *The Gentleman's Magazine of Fashion*, October 1891. The same point had been made several decades earlier by Charles Kingsley in *Cheap Clothes and Nasty* (William Pickering, London, 1850), especially pp. 20, 26.

[48]   *Men's Wear*, 9 December 1905. Consumers' responsibility was also emphasised by Mrs Bernard Bosanquet, *Rich and Poor* (Macmillan, London, 1896), pp. 151–2; Macdonald, 'Sweating in the tailoring trade'. But see also L.G. Chiozza Money, *Riches and Poverty* (Methuen, London, 1905), pp. 137–43, who suggested that the source of the problem of poverty was not the consumption of cheap goods, but rather the economy's over-reliance on the consumption of luxury goods by only a small proportion of the population.

[49]   *The Gentleman's Magazine of Fashion*, October 1894. See also C. Breward, *The Hidden Consumer: Masculinities, Fashion and City Life 1860–1914* (Manchester University Press, Manchester, 1999), pp. 102–3.

man to attend to the whole concern'. Although the actual sewing was generally left to others, the cutter could be called upon 'to measure, cut, try on, sell, keep the stock, do the buying, look after the books, manage the workmen, dress the window, and in the quiet time, call on customers'.[50]

Nevertheless, it was acknowledged in the trade that the distinction between making and selling clothes was a real one, as was the difference between 'front' shop and workshop activities. Norman Nicholson's father was apprenticed to a bespoke tailor in around 1890. 'He learned to sew ... and to carry out minor alterations ... He learned how to press and clean and smarten up a suit, and how to measure and fit on. He knew how to judge the quality of cloth.' However, his 'ambition' had always been 'in the retail side of the business, in the shop rather than the sewing room'. Soon he became his employer's 'chief counter assistant, well capable of attending to customers and dealing with commercial travellers and of supervising the running of the shop and the ordering of stock'. After fifteen years of careful 'planning' and 'scheming', he was able to fulfil his long-held ambition, and open his own shop.[51]

Reflecting the distinction between making and selling clothes, turn-of-the-century representations of the menswear salesman did not generally depict him as quite so ragged, weak and pitiful as the journeyman tailor. Nonetheless, he too was in many ways implicated in narratives, both old and new, that associated those involved in the tailoring and the clothing trade with weakness, poverty, Jewishness, and unmanliness. The salesman, cutter or shop owner who dealt with customers was almost invariably also portrayed as thin, narrow-shouldered and unmuscular. His posture was generally stooped, if not actually cringing. However, unlike the journeyman tailor (particularly the 'sweated' journeyman tailor), he was also usually depicted as impeccably and 'respectably' dressed in a formal dark suit. As seen in Chapter 1, just as collar, tie and dark woollen suit served to distinguish clerical workers from the mass of manual labourers, the same garments served to separate the 'respectable' retailers, cutters, shop assistants and some of the higher-class journeyman tailors from the ranks of the poverty-stricken, unskilled and sweated clothing workers.[52] Indeed, the absence of such garments provided a potent symbol of a menswear retailer's degradation. In the popular cartoons of *Comic Cuts*, for example, it was the second-hand clothes dealer, the itinerant seller, or the 'cheap' tailor who either wore loud, ostentatious and 'flash' garments, or was reduced to making do with ragged, patched clothes, and lacked one or more of the elements of a 'respectable' wardrobe, such as tie, collar, coat, or even shoes[53] (Figure 5.2). In addition, according to such representations, the

---

[50]   *Men's Wear*, 18 February 1905.

[51]   Nicholson, *Wednesday Early Closing*, pp. 37–9. See also British Library of Political and Economic Science Archives, London School of Economics (BLPES Archives), Papers of Charles Booth, Survey Notebooks, Booth B110, interview with Mr Frank Harris, secretary of Tailors' and Outfitters' Assistants Mutual Association, 20 May 1895, pp. 85–8; *The Gentleman's Magazine of Fashion*, December 1893; *Men's Wear*, 14 January 1905; *The London Tailor*, May 1912.

[52]   On the appropriate clothing for men in the 'appearance industries', see also P. McNeil, 'Macaroni masculinities', *Fashion Theory*, vol. 4, issue 4 (2000), pp. 391–2; Breward, *The Hidden Consumer*, pp. 104, 165.

[53]   *Comic Cuts*, 18 April 1903; 4 April 1908; 17 April 1912.

clothes seller's degradation could also be 'read' from his facial features, behaviour and speech. In particular, supposedly 'Semitic' features and accent were strongly associated with the lower reaches of the menswear market.[54]

Unsurprisingly, many of the shop assistants and cutters who worked in higher-class establishments were very keen to endorse the notional dividing line between themselves and less exclusive retailers. Most notably, perhaps, they did so by by stressing the importance of respectable clothing and of a dignified demeanour. After all, as Joseph Conrad observed in the novel *The Secret Agent*, expressing a widely-held view: 'In a commercial transaction of the retail order much depends on the seller's engaging and amiable aspect'.[55] In his autobiography, W.F. Fish recalled that in the 1880s, moving to a new job as a shop assistant in London's East End had meant that 'he had risen to the dignity of a black morning coat'. He acknowledged that from the vantage point of the 1920s the idea of a nineteen-year-old wearing a tail coat and a silk hat seemed absurd, 'but it was considered quite the thing then ... and ... I must confess that I rather fancied myself'.[56]

At the same time, however, as discussed in Chapter 1, the black coat could also be read as a sign of servility, and as symbolic of the unmanliness of making a living by selling menswear. Contempt towards 'counter-jumpers' and 'counter skippers', particularly those working in the textile and clothing trades, was wide-spread, as shop assistants themselves were very much aware.[57] Despite 'fancying himself' in his morning coat, Fish often felt jealous of men such as the soldiers in the Royal Horse Artillery, with their 'long legs, clanking spurs and shell jackets ... their's [sic] were manly lives, mine was pitifully unmanly'. Similar sentiments were expressed by Percy Redfern, who described how in the 1890s, when he was engaged as a shop assistant in a Huddersfield drapery shop, he had felt like 'an ill-paid, black-coated littleness, neither knight, squire nor good manual labourer'.[58] Furthermore, the reality of retailers' appearance did not always match up to ideals

---

[54]   *Comic Cuts*, 10 February 1894; 2 May 1903. For a useful study of anti-semitism and representations of the Jewish body, see S. Gilman, *The Jew's Body* (Routledge, London, 1991). See also M.C. Finn, 'Scotch drapers and the politics of modernity: gender, class and national identity in the Victorian tally trade', in M. Daunton and M. Hilton (eds), *The Politics of Consumption: Material Culture and Citizenship in Europe and America* (Berg, Oxford, 2001), pp. 89–107, for perceptions of the Victorian tally trader as 'Scotchman-as-Jew'.

[55]   J. Conrad, *The Secret Agent: A Simple Tale* (Penguin Books, London, 1990; first published in book form 1907), p. 46.

[56]   W.F. Fish, *The Autobiography of a Counter-Jumper* (Lutterworths, London, 1929), pp. 83–4. See also N. Hancock, *An Innocent Grows Up* (J.M. Dent and Sons, London, 1947), pp. 115, 120–22. For tailors scrutinising each other's clothing when they met, see *The Gentleman's Magazine of Fashion*, April 1887.

[57]   W.B. Whitaker, *Victorian and Edwardian Shop Workers: The Struggle to Obtain Better Conditions and a Half-Holiday* (David and Charles, Newton Abbot, 1973), p. 173. See also Benson and Ugolini, 'Historians and the nation of shopkeepers', p. 7; C.P. Hosgood, '"Mercantile monastries": shops, shop assistants and shop life in late-Victorian and Edwardian Britain', *Journal of British Studies*, vol. 38, no. 3 (1999), pp. 322–52.

[58]   Fish, *The Autobiography*, pp. 39–40; P. Redfern, *Journey to Understanding* (George Allen and Unwin, London, 1946), p. 36.

Figure 5.2   'He had seen stars before!' The old clothes' man and a dissatisfied customer. *Comic Cuts*, 27 October 1894. Courtesy of the Bodleian Library, University of Oxford, N.2706 b.2.

recommended by the trade press. In 1908 the *Men's Wear* editor complained that too many outfitters dressed like 'tramps': those who only managed a 'seedy-shabby' appearance were bad enough, but others were actually 'quite disreputable and a disgrace to their noble calling'.[59] The appearance of the young shop assistant Ernest Egerton Wood would undoubtedly have horrified him. As Wood explained in his autobiography, his tedious work in an outfitting shop was made even worse by his uncomfortable and ill-fitting clothes:

> My socks were always coming down ... My hands were always tensely curled up, trying to hold up my loose cuffs. The stiff loose shirt front was always trying to get through the opening of my waistcoat. One size of collar was too small and the next size was said to look too big. My shoes were heavy and clumsy.[60]

Nevertheless, despite such reprehensible examples, there was widespread agreement among menswear (and indeed other) retailers about the importance of a smart and dignified appearance. Perhaps most significantly, the appearance of 'modern' clothing workers was often brought up in the trade press to distinguish them not only from less reputable traders, but also from the so-called 'cock-and-pie' tailors of an earlier era, who had tramped the country in search of work, carrying with them the tools of their trade and 'wearing a double-breasted black surtout, the lapel pinned up, and a hat that would do for a concertina, and known by the name of the "rook"'.[61] It was not skill that served to differentiate 'old-fashioned' from 'modern' tailors. Indeed, many commentators had to admit that the old peddler-tailors had often been highly skilled, particularly in the intricacies of hand-sewing. Rather, it was clothing that was used as a symbol of the difference between modern, respectable 'tailors' and the older, more disorderly trade tradition, and to assert a notion of working-class manliness based upon characteristics of respectability, initiative, sobriety and industriousness. Those men who embraced such smilesian imperatives sought to distance themselves from the trade's traditional drink-based culture, with its 'low taste', and the 'drinking, maundering selfishness' of its adherents, in order to define a new and positive identity for themselves not solely as able craftsmen, but also as successful businessmen.[62]

---

[59]   *Men's Wear*, 8 February 1908.

[60]   E.E. Wood, *Is this Theosophy?* (Ryder, London, 1936), p. 56.

[61]   *The Weekly Record of Fashion*, 31 January 1883. See also *The London Tailor*, December 1909. One such 'pedlar-tailor' [*sic*] could still be found tramping the countryside near Shrewsbury in the 1880s, 'mending clothes at the farm houses, collecting rabbit skins, selling tapes, cottons, laces and other small articles'. J. Beard, *My Shropshire Days on Common Ways* (Cornish Brothers, Birmingham, n.d. [c. 1948]), p. 6.

[62]   *The Gentleman's Magazine of Fashion*, February 1890; January 1890. For master tailors' increasing tendency to operate as 'small business men untempted by the restrictions of the artisanal past', see Crossick, 'Past masters', p. 25. For the complex relationship between working-class respectability and drink, see P. Bailey, '"Will the real Bill Banks please stand up?" Towards a role analysis of mid-Victorian respectability', *Journal of Social History*, vol. 12, no. 3 (1979), pp. 336–53. As Alexandra Shepard points out in relation to early modern England, men who were excluded from dominant notions of working-class manliness could and did develop alternative understandings of masculinity. A. Shepard, 'Manhood, credit and patriarchy in early modern England, c. 1580–1640', *Past & Present*, no. 167 (2000), pp. 75–106.

Modern tailoring: artistic excellence and business skills

The menswear retailers who possessed 'business qualities', 'tact', and 'steadiness', and who strictly avoided the evils of 'intemperance' – it was stressed in the trade press – were the ones who would gain the ultimate prize: success in business[63] (Figure 5.3). Individuals who wholeheartedly embraced such views would undoubtedly have represented only a small minority of the trade. However, they were both active and vocal. Among the outcomes of their self-improving beliefs were the organisation of a myriad of trade societies, the publication of trade newspapers and manuals, as well as the establishment of a variety of training courses, both for tailors and for cutters. T.H. Holding, for example, one of the strongest upholders of such notions of 'manly industriousness', was in charge of a tailoring business in the West End of London, edited one of the trade papers (*The Weekly Record of Fashion*, from 1884) and managed a cutting school.

It was training, the establishment of appropriate institutions where this training could take place, and ultimately the granting of a recognised award, that were seen as essential to the revitalisation of the bespoke tailoring trade, and to the transformation of tailors and cutters from 'mere plodders', into 'artists' in their profession.[64] Indeed, among those employed in higher-class tailoring establishments, it seems to have been more important that their trade should be viewed as an 'art', even than as a 'science'. The section of the press representing the interests of the bespoke trade repeatedly called upon both cutters and journeymen tailors to make a special study of 'the artistic and the beautiful',[65] and not to enter business solely in the spirit of 'pure commercialism'. Their first thought, on receiving a commission, was to be not how much money could be made out of it, but 'how well and worthily can this be done'.[66] These high-sounding sentiments may seem absurd. Indeed, it is difficult to believe that many of those involved in the menswear trade would or could have taken them too seriously. In 1905, for example, the editor of *Men's Wear* (a journal that sought to represent not only the bespoke trade, but also clothiers, outfitters and hosiers) expressed his scepticism about rhetorical flights of fancy that claimed for cutters 'a place beside the gifted ones ... who affect the fine arts as a means of livelihood'. A good cutter, he acknowledged, was likely to possess a good deal of 'perseverance and ability', but should be content 'with his honourable title as a craftsman'. A few years later, the pretensions of 'the professional tailor de luxe', who invited guests into his '– er – consulting room, where I draft out the models, d'ye know, and I'll show you my diplomas', was gently mocked.[67]

---

[63]   *The Gentleman's Magazine of Fashion*, November 1893.
[64]   *The Gentleman's Magazine of Fashion*, March 1880. See also, for example, *The London Tailor*, June 1903. The frequent references to cutting as a 'profession' rather than as a 'trade' are also worthy of note.
[65]   *The Gentleman's Magazine of Fashion*, December 1889.
[66]   *The Gentleman's Magazine of Fashion*, April 1890. See also *The Weekly Record of Fashion*, 8 February 1882.
[67]   *Men's Wear*, 12 August 1905; *The Master Tailor and Cutter's Gazette*, November 1913.

1.—Hard work, low wages, poor prospects. 2.—Determines to succeed, sowrites for
Tailor and Cutter prospectus 3.—Arrives in London and takes a cab to Drury-lane.
4.—Is there taught Scientific, Artistic and Practical Cutting by competent masters.
5.—Goes back to home and beauty after being awarded a First-class Diploma.
6.—Obtains a situation as Cutter at a good salary. 7.—His prospects having thus
brightened to such an extent he feels justified in marrying. 8.—Continued success
enables him to start a business of his own makes a fortune.

**Figure 5.3   Hard work, respectability and business success. *The Tailor and Cutter*,
25 January 1900. By permission of the British Library, LD163.**

The claims made on behalf of turn-of-the-century bespoke tailors and cutters were undoubtedly inflated. However, they made sense in the context both of tailoring's long-standing low status, and of more recent developments in the menswear trade, developments that threatened bespoke tailors even in the last bastion of their trade: the made-to-measure suit.[68] The seriousness of this challenge before the First World War may have been overestimated by trade commentators. However, there certainly *was* a widespread feeling among independent retailers, and especially bespoke tailors, that their livelihood was threatened by changes that were quickly gathering momentum. By the 1880s the majority of men would normally have bought most items of clothing, including underwear, shirts, raincoats, ties and other relatively small garments ready to wear, generally from hosiers or outfitters. The exceptions were suits and, to a lesser extent, overcoats: when customers could afford them, made-to-measure versions were considered vastly preferable, and throughout the period considered in this book accounted for the bulk of the bespoke trade.

However, by the 1880s concern was frequently being expressed about the increasing popularity, especially among working-class men, of cheaper ready-to-wear suits.[69] From around 1900, furthermore, an even greater threat to the bespoke trade was perceived to be factory-produced 'made-to-measure' suits and overcoats, whereby customers' measurements were taken in a shop,[70] and then posted to another firm for the order to be made up in the nearest standard size.[71] No actual part of clothes production took place on the shop's premises. Indeed, by 1900 a growing number of retailers with no knowledge of tailoring were able to take 'orders for clothes, measure for same, send off to the factory ... get it baisted, and sent down to fit on'.[72] It seemed that 'every local grocer and draper keeps a few pattern books',

---

[68]   Shopkeepers' 'fight for survival' between 1890 and 1914 is explored in Winstanley, *The Shopkeeper's World*, part 2. For a useful comparison with the tobacco trade, see M. Hilton, 'Retailing history as economic and cultural history: strategies of survival by specialist tobacconists in the mass market', *Business History*, vol. 40, no. 4 (1998), pp. 115–37.

[69]   *The Tailor and Cutter*, 12 July 1883; *The Weekly Record of Fashion*, 4 June 1884; *The Gentleman's Magazine of Fashion*, June 1886; October 1891.

[70]   Or customers took their own measures, in the case of mail order firms.

[71]   B. Hesling's father, for example, opened a shop selling factory-made made-to-measure suits, supplied by the Savile Row Tailoring Co., Pudsey. B. Hesling, *Little and Orphan* (Constable, London, 1954), p. 7. See also *Men's Wear*, 19 April 1902; 10 June 1905; *The Outfitter*, 19 September 1914. For the development of mass-produced made-to-measure suits, see Honeyman, *Well Suited*, pp. 45–7; S. Levitt, 'Cheap mass-produced men's clothing in the nineteenth and early twentieth centuries', *Textile History*, vol. 22, no. 2 (1991), pp. 172–92, especially p. 188. Other firms sent 'travellers from door to door supplying suits on the demoralising instalment system, and getting them made up, principally, in the factory'. *The Master Tailor and Cutter's Gazette*, October 1910.

[72]   *The Tailor and Cutter*, 18 January 1900. See also BLPES Archives, Papers of Charles Booth, Survey Notebooks, Booth B110, interview with Mr Harradine, assistant at outfitters and tailors, Messrs. Samuel Bros, Ludgate Hill, 3 July 1893, pp. 99–103: 'Many so-called tailors never make a suit of clothes. They simply take the measures and send the paper to another firm who make the garments and allow a commission on the amount.' In his manual for retail drapers, Fred Burgess explained how such a business could be set up. F.W. Burgess, *The Practical Retail Draper: A Complete Guide for the Drapery and Allied Trades* (Virtue, London, 1912–14), vol. iv, pp. 23–5.

and could send orders off to be made up by a wholesale firm.[73] These garments were made not by skilled and experienced men working in workshops attached to shops, but – it was alleged – by unskilled girls using sewing machines, including steam-driven machines, and working in large-scale factories.[74] Bespoke tailors like Sumner Brown, who owned a small shop in the Lincolnshire village of Digby and 'was a very pleasant man and a good workman ... could not compete in his slow methods with machine-made suits at 25s each' sold by a multiple shop recently opened in Lincoln. 'There was a new style with the multiple suits and, although they were not strongly made, they had a better finish. They also offered other shades than the indigo blue which was Sumner's only line for Sunday wear.'[75]

According to commentators in the bespoke trade, changes in clothes production had been accompanied by equally spectacular – and threatening – changes in retailing. It was feared that the menswear trade would increasingly be dominated by the already popular 'colossal store system', with its cheap clothes, 'attractive showy windows' and extensive use of advertising.[76] These were firms with 'a large capital behind them ... which are worked in a cold, calculating spirit of profit-production', and which, through economies of scale and the insistence of cash payments, were easily able to undercut the prices charged by independent tailors and clothiers.[77] Of course, where some saw a threat, others saw an opportunity. According to Montague Burton, writing in 1932, turn-of-the-century London-based multiples like Lupinsky and Brandon, Lockwood and Bradley, and Rego Clothiers, which specialised in 30s made-to-measure suits, 'displayed considerable enterprise', not only in their manufacturing methods, but also in their retailing techniques. 'Their establishments were probably the brightest in Edwardian London. The yellow-flame carbon arc-lamps of those days were objectionable to the ascetic and to those who looked upon enterprise as akin to vandalism, but they made a warm, glowing picture with a background of glittering signs, ticket showcards, and large expanses of silvered glass.' Even the bespoke tailoring trade press was forced to admit that the buildings of firms like West End Clothiers, which in 1894 claimed seven London branches, were 'smart in style and decor, and the interior appointments admirable for the convenience of customers'.[78]

---

[73]   *The Tailor and Cutter*, 31 July 1913. See also *The Master Tailor and Cutter's Gazette*, February 1910.

[74]   *The Gentleman's Magazine of Fashion*, June 1886. The 'problem' of women's employment in the tailoring trades already had a long history. See, for example, Harris (ed.), *Famine and Fashion*; Honeyman, *Well Suited*, especially chapter 8; Lemire, *Dress, Culture and Commerce*, pp. 52–5, 73; Taylor, *Eve and the New Jerusalem*, chapter 4.

[75]   Gresswell, *Bright Boots*, p. 112.

[76]   *The Weekly Record of Fashion*, 17 August 1881; *The Gentleman's Magazine of Fashion*, June 1892. See also *The Weekly Record of Fashion*, May 1888. Large and showy 'cheap shops' were not a new phenomenon in the late nineteenth century. See T.C. Whitlock, *Crime, Gender and Consumer Culture in Nineteenth-Century England* (Ashgate, Aldershot, 2005), especially chapter 3.

[77]   *The Tailor and Cutter*, 3 January 1907. See also, for example, *The Master Tailor and Cutter's Gazette*, August 1895; October 1910; *Men's Wear*, 19 April 1902; 10 June 1905; *The Tailor and Cutter*, 12 July 1883; 11 September 1913.

[78]   *Men's Wear*, 6 February 1932; *The Tailor and Cutter*, 19 April 1894.

By the end of the nineteenth century, it was widely accepted that only the most venerable businesses could still be carried out 'as in the olden days ... in a semi-private house, distinguished as a place of trade ... only by the lettering on the gauze blind, which screened the shop from the street'. Especially in larger towns and cities, successful tailoring shops increasingly needed 'large plate-glass windows, with all their dazzle and luminosity of carbon lamps and crystal pendants', and rich and varied window displays.[79] Unsurprisingly, not all in the trade viewed these developments with misgivings. In 1887 one 'multiple retailer with seven shops in his locality' saw them as the opening of a new entrepreneurial opportunity. He told *The Outfitter*: 'People do not want a shop next door now-a-days. Big shops in busy parts, large windows and big stocks – these are needed more than ever.'[80] He at least was ready and willing to provide them. He was not alone: a year later, a correspondent to *The Weekly Record of Fashion* observed that in Liverpool, 'many of the trades that used to have private, quiet windows, much after the manner of the West End of London, have now inserted every square inch of plate glass they can, and have stocked their windows with tweeds and homespuns, mostly ticketed'.[81]

In this context, it made sense for high-class tailoring establishments to emphasise their uniqueness, and indeed superiority, by staking a claim for both the 'scientific' and the 'artistic' nature of their products, and the secondary importance of profit-making, in contrast to the cheaper and flashier 'glass and brass' shops. From this lofty perspective, they could dismiss all competitors as hopelessly inferior, irrespective of whether they sold ready-to-wear or made-to-measure garments, all of which were dismissed as 'slop, shoddy monstrosit[ies]' and 'stick-together rubbish'.[82] However, bespoke tailors' competitors were not slow in making similar claims. When David Lewis had established his first store in Liverpool half a century earlier, advertisements had unabashedly stressed the cheapness of the menswear for sale,[83] but by the end of the nineteenth century the tone of retailers' advertisements had changed, arguably at least in part because the term 'cheap' had become tainted with associations of 'nastiness'.[84] Although prices continued to be well in evidence, equally visible were claims about the high quality and good value of the garments for sale, which (it was emphasised) offered West End style, durability and the same overall quality as the best bespoke items, but at a fraction of the cost. Bespoke tailors may have argued that customers were fooled into buying worthless goods by shops' imposing – or flashy – appearance,

---

[79]   *The Tailor and Cutter*, 19 April 1894. See also *Men's Wear*, 9 September 1905. In reality, even in 'the olden days' not all tailoring shops had been so unostentatious, while unobtrusive shop windows had not entirely disappeared by the inter-war period. Poole, *The Clothing Trades Industry*, pp. 7–8.

[80]   *The Outfitter*, 13 May 1887.

[81]   *The Weekly Record of Fashion*, May 1888.

[82]   *The Tailor and Cutter*, 13 July 1905; *The Gentleman's Magazine of Fashion*, May 1886.

[83]   A. Briggs, *Friends of the People: The Centenary History of Lewis's* (Batsford, London, 1956), especially pp. 131–2.

[84]   *Progressive Advertising*, 22 November 1901; 21 February 1902. Kingsley, *Cheap Clothes and Nasty*.

but for their part, their competitors stressed, with 'blazing impudence', that expensive bespoke tailoring was no longer a necessary precondition to a good quality suit or overcoat.[85] As one exasperated observer pointed out, some of these firms' advertisements 'inform the public ... that they have decided upon becoming the benefactors of a suffering humanity ... they ... cease to be traders, and develop as philanthropists'[86] (Figure 5.4).

In reality, it is difficult to believe that there was not a gulf, obvious to most observers, between 'a thoroughly good suit, well-cut ... and sent home in a stout cardboard carton' costing two guineas or more, and a mass-produced, made-to-measure or ready-made garment costing 30 shillings or less.[87] Nonetheless, many within the bespoke trade were worried: it was widely accepted that cheap made-to-measure and ready-to-wear garments were a problem, particularly for those sections of the trade that depended on a working-class or lower-middle-class clientele.[88] In a significant reversal, in the decade before the First World War low prices began to be touted as a more important goal for those catering for this section of the market than aspirations to artistic excellence. As 'Another tailor' pointed out in 1910, 'the tailor ... [who] stands on his dignity and, with the inner consciousness of the superiority of his productions, endeavours to ignore the new competition', was bound to lose customers.[89] At least according to one commentator, writing in 1903, price competitiveness could only be achieved by adopting 'modern' methods of production, abandoning hand-sewing in favour of machine-sewing, and accepting that except for the very higher-class trades, the tailor who made a complete garment from start to finish was an anachronism: the process of making clothes needed to be subdivided as much as possible.[90] The language of natural selection was used to warn that 'the tailor of the future was the man who could adapt himself to circumstances', the 'circumstances' being the demand for cheaper clothes made much more quickly than could be done by 'the ordinary tailor'.[91] In 1907 an editorial in *The Tailor and Cutter* acknowledged realities, and stated that no man in his senses would suggest that cheap garments should be made by hand. They were rather to be made by machine, and made up 'on the subdivision principle', 'utilising girl labour as fully as possible'.[92]

---

[85]   *The Weekly Record of Fashion*, March 1890; L. Ugolini, 'Men, masculinities, and menswear advertising, c. 1890–1914', in Benson and Ugolini (eds), *A Nation of Shopkeepers*, pp. 87–92.

[86]   *The Outfitter*, 1 January 1887.

[87]   F. Willis, *101 Jubilee Road: A Book of London's Yesterdays* (Phoenix House, London, 1948), pp. 127, 134. See also L. Ugolini, 'Ready-to-wear or made-to-measure? Consumer choice in the British menswear trade, 1900–1939', *Textile History*, vol. 34, no. 2 (2003), especially pp. 203–8; Breward, *The Hidden Consumer*, p. 103. In 1914 most suits ranged in price between 35 shillings and 6 guineas. *The Tailor and Cutter*, 2 July 1914; 15 April 1915.

[88]   *The Tailor and Cutter*, 31 July 1913.

[89]   *The Sartorial Gazette*, February 1910.

[90]   *The London Tailor*, August 1903. See also Honeyman, *Well Suited*, p. 21.

[91]   *The Tailor and Cutter*, 18 September 1902.

[92]   *The Tailor and Cutter*, 24 January 1907.

Figure 5.4 **'Don't you envy the well-dressed man?' A parody of contemporary advertisers' claims.** *Judy*, **18 November 1903. Courtesy of the Bodleian Library, University of Oxford, N.2706 d.12.**

From the turn of the century onwards, the trade was constantly reminded that modern and competitive bespoke firms needed business 'flair' and 'knowledge' in order to challenge the success of 'palatial clothing establishments, or pushing up-to-date cash tailors': simply being a good craftsman was no longer enough.[93] After all, there were plenty of tailors who successfully competed with 'the ready-made trades, but they are on … a different level to the artist in apparel that prides himself on the excellence of his productions'.[94] For 'up-to-date' tailors working in the lower and middle sections of the trade, the techniques involved in selling clothes acquired a new importance, with a new stress on advertising, the sale of sidelines, window dressing and good salesmanship. While in 1886 one of the trade papers had lamented the fact that 'the premises of the new order of tailor become a show-room instead of a work-room',[95] by the turn of the century, tailors and other menswear retailers were strongly encouraged to devote as much attention to the 'retailing' side of their business as to the 'production' side. Advertisements, whether in the press, as posted circulars or window displays, were essential. As one anonymous contributor to *The Outfitter* put it in 'The Song of Success':

[93] *The Tailor and Cutter*, 3 January 1907; *Men's Wear*, 21 October 1905.
[94] *The Tailor and Cutter*, 23 January 1902.
[95] *The Weekly Record of Fashion*, July 1886.

In letters big and bold and round
The praises of my wares I sound
Prosperity is my estate
The people come
The people go
In one continuous surging flow ...
The secret of my fortune lies
In one simple fact ...
If I have goods, I advertise![96]

There was no reason, a letter to *The Sartorial Gazette* pointed out in 1910, why bespoke tailors should not imitate their competitors: 'If the unscrupulous sham tailor goes in for "brass and glass", let the genuine tailor do likewise, and lay himself out to attract custom ... If the same artificial tailor advertises (brazenly or otherwise) let the real tailor do the same thing.'[97] To be successful, a firm needed 'a splendid window in a favoured position', 'energetic and skilled travelling', and 'extensive advertising'.[98]

Those menswear retailers who wanted to attract the man of 'moderate means' had to work especially hard to attract his notice. This was the type of man – it was assumed – who bought new clothes only when strictly necessary, and 'sticks pretty well to the shop he is used to'. Attractive window displays were essential to convince this type of customer to change his habits. They therefore had to be 'distinctly fresh' and different both from previous ones and from those of competitors. It was only when the potential customer's attention had been caught, that 'the style and value of the goods themselves' would come into play.[99] When 'fully equipped with fittings and cleverly dressed with goods', the shop window would act as a magnet for customers.[100] Indeed, by 1905 it was claimed that 'even village tradesmen, living in parts remote, now strive to tempt stray passers-by by exhibiting their wares in as enticing a manner as they are able to command'.[101]

Inside the shop, successful businessmen took care not to overstock ('no live man will hoard up his ancient pieces'[102]) and offered sidelines such as hats, gloves,

---

[96]   *The Outfitter*, 1 January 1887. See also *The Tailor and Cutter*, 4 October 1894; *The Master Tailor and Cutter's Gazette*, February 1896.

[97]   *The Sartorial Gazette*, December 1910, a response to a letter published in ibid., November 1910.

[98]   *The London Tailor*, March 1907.

[99]   *Progressive Advertising*, 11 April 1902. See also *Men's Wear*, 15 March 1902.

[100]   *Men's Wear*, 18 January 1918.

[101]   *Men's Wear*, 14 October 1905. See also 5 February 1902; *The Tailor and Cutter*, 28 August 1913. The importance of attractive window displays and 'modern' business methods was a common theme also among retailers in other trades. See, for example, Anon., *How to Run a Shop at a Profit* (A.W. Shaw, London, 1916). For a discussion of the relationship between menswear retailers' shop window displays and masculine aesthetics, see Breward, *The Hidden Consumer*, pp. 128–43. See also S. Lomax, 'The view from the shop: window display, the shopper and the formulation of theory', in J. Benson and L. Ugolini (eds), *Cultures of Selling: Perspectives on Consumption and Society Since 1700* (Ashgate, Aldershot, 2006), pp. 265–92.

[102]   *The Tailor and Cutter*, 13 August 1891.

ties, or 'novelties', all of which were normally the province of the outfitter.[103] Good salesmanship, made up of a combination of appearance and behaviour, was also essential. The salesman 'should be a man of pleasant appearance and commanding aspect, a tall man for preference … He should have confidence in himself … the confidence should be borne of knowledge of his business, and every detail connected with it … salesmanship is an art'.[104] In more frank language, tailoring firms were warned that only if they employed 'intelligent and mannerly salesmen' could they be sure that customers would 'be received frankly, and served with civility'.[105]

Examples of good practice were constantly placed before trade journal readers, from the Cardiff clothiers who in 1887 had just moved to 'entirely new and commodious premises', where they had 'erected a stupendous sign, the letters of which are said to rival in size that of the famous *Tit-Bits* office in London', to The Manchester firm of high-class tailors J.S. Moss and Sons, who were singled out by *The Tailor and Cutter* in 1905 for the elegance and stylishness of their recently renovated premises. The old windows had been ripped out and replaced with 'a handsome range of shop fronts of striking and original design', while the interior had been 'newly fixtured with all up-to-date appliances' and mirrors. The floors had been 'covered with parquetry flooring in oak and walnut'. Overall, 'an air of luxury pervades this showroom'.[106]

Conclusion

In his presidential address to the National Federation of Foremen Tailors' Societies' conference in October 1913, Frank Coleman told his audience that 'I well remember the time when tailors … had no place of honour, as tradesmen, among other trades; when it was the prevailing opinion that any weakling or "no user" should be sent to be a tailor.'[107] Coleman spoke as if those days were in the past, but his confidence in tailors' new-found status seems to have been rather over-optimistic. On the eve of the First World War, most contemporaries would still have perceived the notion of a 'manly' tailor as a contradiction in terms. All those involved in the trade, whether as journeymen tailors, machinists, cutters, salesmen or managers, continued to be tainted by its association with physical weakness, poverty, sweating and Jewishness. 'Tailors' were still seen as something rather less than real men.

Unsurprisingly, this did not stop those involved in the menswear trade – including the independent bespoke tailors upon whom this chapter has concentrated – from attempting to 'assert' their manliness,[108] and to construct positive identities for

---

[103]   *The Tailor and Cutter*, 12 April 1894; 19 April 1894; 28 September 1905.

[104]   *The Tailor and Cutter*, 17 January 1907.

[105]   *The Weekly Record of Fashion*, January 1888.

[106]   *The Outfitter*, March 1887; *The Tailor and Cutter*, 13 July 1905. See also, for example, *Men's Wear*, 4 November 1905. There is also a good deal of evidence to suggest that many (perhaps most) shops fell far short of the ideal set out in the trade press. See, for example, *Men's Wear*, 21 October 1905; *The Tailor and Cutter*, 7 September 1905; *The Weekly Record of Fashion*, October 1890.

[107]   *The Sartorial Gazette*, October 1913.

[108]   The terms are taken from the title of Roper and Tosh (eds), *Manful Assertions*.

themselves and for their trade. Increasingly vocal sections of the trade sought to distance themselves both from tailoring's disreputable past and from the trickery, deceit and shoddiness of new competitors, thus trying to create a new image of tailoring based on notions of sober industriousness and canny business know-how. For high-class tailors, this purpose could best be served by emphasising their craft knowledge, scientific abilities and artistic sensibilities. For the less exclusive bulk of the trade, however, it was arguably more useful and realistic to stress the importance of business abilities, not only in the production of clothes, but increasingly also in the retailing side. The sober, respectable and up-to-date tailor, a businessman increasingly more at home in the shop than in the workshop, showed his true worth by taking on 'brass and glass' shops and other firms of 'untrained capitalists, who care nothing for the trade, but as a means of making money',[109] surviving and even prospering.

Despite their best efforts, however, things were not destined to get any easier for independent tailors in the inter-war years: far from receding, the competition of big business increasingly came to threaten the very livelihood and existence of the 'small man'. That said, in 1914 both large and small traders were faced with a very different challenge, and one that would inevitably distract attention from the problems of competition for the following four years. It is the difficulties and opportunities faced by the menswear trade during the First World War that will be the subjects of the next chapter.

---

[109] *The Weekly Record of Fashion*, December 1887.

Chapter 6

Menswear Retailing and War, 1914–1920

Between July 1914 and November 1918 the 'nut' of military age, more concerned with his material and sartorial possessions than with the country's war effort, became a byword for unpatriotism, unmanliness and shirking. At the same time, patriotic civilian consumers – both men and women – were called upon to 'do their bit' for the war effort by limiting as far as possible their consumption of non-essential goods, thus ensuring that these could be redirected to military use. Any cash surplus was to be invested in the war debt. The national economy campaigns provided an official sanction to many civilians' already marked reluctance to spend money on clothes and other 'surplus' commodities at a time of war. As Chapter 3 has shown, in the eyes of many, the purchase of new garments beyond a bare minimum acquired morally dubious connotations, as an activity that truly patriotic men (and women) should avoid for the duration.

For their part, from the moment war broke out in the Summer of 1914, menswear retailers seem to have been aware that the conflict was likely to bring a good deal of hardship to many of them, even once the initial wave of panic had subsided.[1] *The Tailor and Cutter* attempted to reassure its readers, reminding them that not all business would cease because of the war. After all, 'the everyday wants of the nation must still be supplied; the food and clothing must be provided from day to day, and the ordinary duties of business fulfilled by those who have not been called to arms'. It was only natural that in the first few weeks of war people's attention should be focused on events at the front, but this could not be expected to last too long. Soon the steady stream of war reports would 'lose their freshness, and then business will surely begin to resume its normal course again'.[2]

However, the tone of most of the trade press was a good deal gloomier. Tailors, it was feared, were likely to lose many of their best customers to the armed forces.[3] At the same time, civilian consumers would be reluctant to spend their money on clothes, especially if the conflict proved to be a long one, and prices started to rise: 'At such times of national emergency and even peril, clothing is looked upon more in the nature of a luxury'.[4] The worst hit were likely to be small tradesmen like 'the suburban tailor and the small country tailor', who had already been struggling for survival against the competition 'of their own class and that of the "ready-mades" purveyor'. By December 1914, their prospects looked bleak: not only had 'a considerable proportion of their

---

[1]   The first week of war saw a wave of orders to wholesalers being cancelled, among rumours of the almost total collapse of the trade. *The Outfitter*, 15 August 1914. It is interesting to note the absence of confidence in the trade press that the war would be over shortly, or 'by Christmas'.

[2]   *The Tailor and Cutter*, 13 August 1914; 27 August 1914.

[3]   *Men's Wear*, 3 October 1914; 30 October 1915.

[4]   *Men's Wear*, 8 August 1914. See also *The Outfitter*, 15 August 1914.

clients ... enlisted; what remain are "off" spending for the time being', both because wages had in many cases fallen, and because since the start of the conflict, the price of cloth had been rising 'steadily' and 'relentlessly'.[5]

In October 1914, it was estimated that the retail side of the menswear business had declined since the beginning of the war by between 50 and 75 per cent.[6] These figures may well have been an exaggeration, but they certainly reflected a widespread sense of despondency, and indeed despair, within a trade that even before the war had felt itself beleaguered from all sides.[7] It was acknowledged that 'we must all bear our burden ... to see the country through and settle the European bully'.[8] However, many asked themselves whether this would necessarily have to be at the cost of retailers' livelihoods. Would it prove possible to adopt strategies that would allow menswear traders in general, and independent bespoke tailors in particular, to survive, and even flourish in wartime?[9]

These are the questions that this chapter will seek to answer. It will firstly consider menswear retailers' short-lived attempts in the first months of war to portray shopping and 'business as usual' as a patriotic activity. It will then explore their – perhaps more realistic – efforts to tap into markets seemingly unaffected by the conflict, from servicemen to munitions workers, albeit in the context of increasingly serious shortages of materials and labour. Menswear retailers' particular take on official and semi-official 'economy' appeals will be considered next, before turning to assess the extent to which they were able to develop an acceptable model of menswear consumption in wartime. The chapter will then conclude by considering the ways in which the trade negotiated the difficult aftermath of war, amidst discontent about continued high prices, shortages, and increasingly bitter accusations of profiteering.

Business as usual?

In the weeks immediately following the outbreak of war, retailers were repeatedly advised by the trade press to appeal to consumers' sense of patriotism, calling upon them to continue to patronise their usual shops, so that British businesses would not collapse and working men would not be thrown out of work: 'every opportunity should be taken of emphasising the patriotic note in the window display'. In response to such advice, in September 1914 Dudley and Co., which described itself as a firm of 'ticket experts', were offering for sale a set of four 'patriotic showcards', all depicting the Union Jack and emphasising the importance of continuing to shop, 'to prevent British factories from closing down'. Another firm offered posters depicting

---

[5]   *Men's Wear*, 5 December 1914.
[6]   *Men's Wear*, 31 October 1914.
[7]   See Chapter 5.
[8]   *Men's Wear*, 8 August 1914.
[9]   The impact of the war on commercial and marketing practices has to date received very little scholarly attention. But see J. Winter, 'Popular culture in wartime Britain', in A. Roshwold and R. Stites (eds), *European Culture in the Great War: The Arts, Entertainment and Propaganda, 1914–1918* (Cambridge University Press, Cambridge, 1999), pp. 330–48.

the slogan 'British clothes for British men made by British labour'.[10] Retailers' press advertisements in the first few weeks of war made similar claims. The London-based H.C. Russell used a full-page advertisement in *The Tatler* to assert shops' and customers' unity of purpose: 'the Business Houses – together with the Shopping Public – must unite to care for all who are dependent for their livelihood upon the steady stream of trade, and they appeal to their customers to shop as usual during the coming months of anxiety'.[11] These sentiments were echoed by provincial traders, who in Oxford, for example, advertised under the common slogan of 'YOU can serve your country by shopping as usual, and so prevent unemployment'.[12]

It seems unlikely that many menswear retailers really made use of the crudely patriotic and military symbolism that in 1914 was ridiculed by a *Punch* cartoon, showing an outfitter selling 'Dirigible' and 'Super-dreadnought' collars, 'Torpedo' studs ('very strong') and 'Flotilla' pyjamas ('for hard wear'). A bathrobe was depicted as carrying a ticket stating that 'It's a long way to Tipperary. But it's a short way to the bathroom in this wrap', a pair of socks were 'the Allies. In these shades' (Figure 6.1). In fact, the real window displays described in the trade press in 1915 included few references to 'patriotic' devices of any sort.[13] In any case, even if adopted, their effectiveness seems open to doubt. Chapter 3 has shown the patriotic pressures that militated against civilian consumption in wartime, including menswear consumption, especially as the unofficial policy of 'business as usual' was set aside in 1915 in favour of the diversion of goods and resources from civilian to military use. It is difficult to believe that these pressures would not have carried more weight than the seemingly self-serving appeals to shop as usual originating from a menswear trade that hardly enjoyed a position of moral superiority and authority.[14]

There is little doubt that the most effective and lucrative option for businesses that wished to outlive the conflict was to follow the example of those clothing manufacturers who shifted production from civilian to military garments, and sought to have their names added to the War Office's tenders list.[15] Demand was certainly not lacking. In October 1914, for example, the firm of Robert Glanfield, a London wholesale manufacturer, announced that it had received an order from the government to supply uniforms for the new army, and was now seeking further suppliers. Tellingly, it was added that the uniforms were of simpler design than previous regulation dress,

---

[10] *The Outfitter*, 17 October 1914; 5 September 1914. See also *The Tailor and Cutter*, 8 October 1914.

[11] *The Tatler*, 2 September 1914.

[12] *The Oxford Times*, 15 August 1914. See also 8 August 1914.

[13] The *Punch* cartoon was reproduced in *Men's Wear*, 12 September 1914. See, for example, the window displays described in *The Tailor and Cutter*, 20 May 1915; 5 August 1915.

[14] For the low status of the pre-war menswear trade, see Chapter 5.

[15] Katrina Honeyman, for example, observes that Leeds-based clothing manufacturers did well out of the war. There is no reason to believe that manufacturers elsewhere did not find the conflict equally profitable. K. Honeyman, *Well Suited: A History of the Leeds Clothing Industry 1850–1990* (Pasold Research Fund and Oxford University Press, Oxford, 2000), pp. 54–5. Officers received an allowance with which to purchase their own uniforms and other accoutrements, while the ranks were provided with their kit directly by the armed forces.

and not too difficult to make, even for businesses with no previous experience of military work.[16] It would seem some firms quickly adapted to military work. Harry Hall, which in 1914 claimed two London branches, one in the West End and one in the City, had in July of that year advertised itself as '"the" coat and breeches specialist', as

Reproduced by special permission of the proprietors of "Punch."

CLOTHES OF THE PERIOD.

"I want some smart collars."

"Yessir. Mr. Simpkins, just bring me down an assortment of 'Dirigibles' and some 'Super-Dreadnoughts'."

Figure 6.1   'Clothes of the period': the menswear shop and patriotic display. *Men's Wear*, 12 September 1914. By permission of the British Library, LD178.

---

[16]   *Men's Wear*, 17 October 1914. See also ibid., 29 August 1914; *The Outfitter*, 8 August 1914; *The Tailor and Cutter*, 20 August 1914.

well as specialising in 'the cut of dress, morning and hunt suit'. Two months later, they had become '"The" military and mufti tailor', offering to provide officers' 'service dress' within 24 hours of receiving an order.[17]

The popular magazine *John Bull* lent its support to the notion that orders for army clothing should be spread more widely 'among the hundreds of small private tailors … whose trade has been brought practically to a standstill … The uniforms … would necessarily be superior to those more or less thrown together by the tired hands of underpaid girls in huge clothing factories, and the cost need not be very much greater.'[18] Notwithstanding such reassuring words, in reality the shift from civilian to military work was by no means always an easy one. Bespoke tailoring businesses with no expertise in the making of officers' uniforms, normally the purvey of a specialised section of the trade, could find the transition a difficult one, and were not necessarily trusted to do a decent job, at least in the first months of the conflict. So, although in 1914 many tailors and 'Universal Providers' displayed khaki serges and all kinds of military garments in their windows, 'they do not seem to have attracted the military classes, who are rather conservative, and prefer to patronise old-established tailors'.[19] Furthermore, those retailers with no workshops attached, who depended on separate firms to make up their orders, could hardly tender for government work. However, they could (and did) offer their services both to officers and to other servicemen seeking non-regulation items and extra garments not supplied by the armed forces. Just as before the war retailers had been able to send orders off to be made up by a separate firm, the same could be done during the conflict with orders for officers' uniforms. The London firm of G. Glanfield and Son, for example, offered this service to retailers in 1916.[20]

Unsurprisingly, such new entrants into the 'military' market aroused a good deal of hostility among established military tailors and outfitters. In 1917 Thresher and Glenny responded to the competition of such opportunistic entrants into the trade by emphasising that, unlike them, their firm could claim a long history as 'military tailors since the Crimean war'. They pointed out that 'kit after a kind can be got almost anywhere nowadays. But for kit of the right kind – right in detail and in quality – there's nothing like going to a firm whose military tailoring is not a mere flash-in-the pan.' This was clearly a reference to firms such as Harry Hall or Gamage's, a London department store specialising in leisure and sporting goods, which only a week after Thresher and Glenny's protest, was advertising in the same columns 'complete uniforms for officers in 48 hours'.[21] There may well have been some truth in established military tailors' and outfitters' warnings. Travelling for the first time to his barracks in the outskirts of Liverpool, Siegfried Sassoon was joined by 'another evidently new officer … My companion was far from orthodox in what he was wearing … His shirt and tie were more yellow than khaki. And his breeches were of a bright buff tint. His tunic was of the correct military tint, but it sat uneasily on his podgy figure.' He was greeted by the Adjutant with the haughty exclamation:

---

17   *The Sketch*, 8 July 1914; 23 September 1914.
18   *John Bull*, 26 December 1914. See also ibid., 6 March 1915.
19   *The Tailor and Cutter*, 10 September 1914.
20   *The Outfitter*, 4 March 1916.
21   *The Bystander*, 31 January 1917; 7 February 1917. See also *The Sketch*, 17 March 1915; 18 August 1915.

'*Christ! Who's your tailor?*' Sasson's 'own reception was in accordance with the cut of my clothes', which he had obtained from a high-class military tailor.[22]

A less disruptive and complex alternative than trying to tap into the trade for regulation military uniforms was for menswear retailers to add to their stock non-regulation military garments, and items that might conceivably be both of civilian and of military use. The *Punch* depiction in 1915 of 'the only way a truly patriotic tailor dare advertise mufti at the present time' may have been an exaggeration (Figure 6.2). However, the strategy of drawing attention to goods that had at least a *potential* military use had the further advantage of allowing retailers to gracefully side-step any accusations that they sought to encourage civilian consumption of non-essential goods in wartime.[23] In August 1914, for example, demand boomed for 'flannel goods suitable for service wear', either in khaki or army grey, especially shirts and underwear.[24] A month later, retailers were reminded that many soldiers 'no doubt, will be wanting an extra pair of khaki trousers, even a complete suit, and underclothing in addition to that

SKETCH OF HOUSE-PARTY (SHOWING LATEST DESIGNS IN AUTUMN SUITINGS); BEING THE ONLY WAY A REALLY PATRIOTIC TAILOR DARE ADVERTISE MUFTI AT THE PRESENT TIME.

Figure 6.2   Menswear advertising in wartime. *Punch*, 8 September 1915. Courtesy of the Bodleian Library, University of Oxford, N.2706 d.10.

---

[22]   S. Sassoon, *Memoirs of a Fox-Hunting Man* (Faber and Faber, London, 1989; first published 1928), pp. 260–61.

[23]   There were also instances where advertisements for civilian menswear portrayed potential customers as older men beyond military age. See, for example, *The Tatler*, 13 November 1918; *Men's Wear*, 21 August 1915; 19 May 1917; *The Tailor and Cutter*, 15 February 1917; 1 August 1918. It should be noted, furthermore, that both local and national press advertisements for civilian menswear steadily decreased in the course of the war, the main reason for this no doubt being businesses' need to cut expenditure.

[24]   *Men's Wear*, 15 August 1914.

supplied them by the Government'.[25] At various times in the course of the conflict, not only life-jackets, bullet-proof body shields and swords, but also more mundane leather jackets, puttees, breeches, caps, trench coats and other military-style overcoats, all appeared in tailors' and outfitters' press advertisements and shop windows, where the dominant colours were throughout the war drab khakis and greys. The London outfitting firm of Pearson Brothers in 1916 offered the 'Matta-Vest, which, worn *beneath* the uniform is quite unnoticed, yet ... will keep your body – the vital parts susceptible to dangerous chills, dry and cosy'. Customers were reassured that that the vest could be worn 'for Drill and on Parade without anyone *but you* knowing that you are protected against Rain'.[26]

Certain garments, such as woollens and trench coats, could be advertised and sold as 'military' goods, safe in the knowledge that they were also very popular among civilians.[27] Among the larger and better-established London retailers, Moss Bros, for example, offered their 'famous Moscow trench coat', the Civil Service Stores their 'Aquarius' mackintosh, Robinson and Cleaver their 'khaki shirts, handkerchiefs and collars', which, it was promised, 'will wear well and retain their colour', while Harrods offered 'woollies for wear under uniform' (although there clearly was nothing to stop civilians from buying and wearing them as well).[28] Retailers outside London were not slow in coming forward with a similar range of military, or double-use, garments. In Oxford, only a few weeks after the outbreak of war the department store Elliston and Cavell made 'a special feature of army flannels', and some months later could be found advertising 'soldiers' shirts, bed jackets and pyjamas'.[29] In November 1914, the Reading outfitter A.H. Bull announced a 'Great War sale': 'thousands of garments of comfort for winter wear ... for our gallant sailors and soldiers are offered at extremely low prices'[30]

Furthermore, retailers were not slow in realising that if the purchase of civilian clothing could be perceived as an unnecessary and unpatriotic diversion of resources away from the war effort, the same could hardly be said about civilians' acquisition of garments for soldiers, sailors and airmen serving their country overseas. Consequently, a variety of retailers soon began to advertise parcels of clothing for delivery to the British Expeditionary Force. The London store Marshall and Snelgrove, for example, offered a 21s parcel containing a brown cardigan, cap, mittens, socks, 'special hair brush', toilet requirements, boot laces, lighter and handkerchiefs', while the Junior Army and Navy Store offered, at a rather more modest 5s (which they emphasised represented only half the cost price), a pack that

---

[25]   *Men's Wear*, 12 September 1914. See also ibid., 7 November 1914; *The Tailor and Cutter*, 28 January 1915.

[26]   *John Bull*, 22 January 1916. See also *The Tailor and Cutter*, 12 October 1916; 2 November 1916; 21 November 1918.

[27]   On the popularity of 'woollies' see, for example, *Men's Wear*, 20 July 1918; *The Tailor and Cutter*, 7 June 1917.

[28]   *The Tatler*, 9 October 1918 (Moss Bros); 23 October 1918 (Civil Service Stores); *The Sketch*, 14 October 1914; 15 March 1916 (both Robinson and Cleaver); 28 March 1917 (Harrods).

[29]   *The Oxford Times*, 22 August 1914.

[30]   *Reading Mercury*, 7 November 1914.

included a cardigan, a pair of socks and a woollen muffler.[31] Spotting a further gap in the market, in October 1914 the London department store Shoolbred's offered 'Flannel shirts for the army. Cut out ready for making. To ladies who desire to render help in this form we offer UNMADE strong union flannel shirts.'[32]

Although there is no reason to believe that these offers were always entirely motivated by a cynical assessment of available markets and opportunities for profit-making on the part of hard-hearted retailers, there is no doubt that advertisements sought to play on friends' and relatives' fears about the safety and well-being of loved ones in the armed forces. In 1916, for example, the South London hosier and outfitter C.A. Latter appealed to customers thus: 'Your soldier needs all the protection he can get NOW. Send him a "Chemico" body shield, it may save his life.' Not only did it provide protection against shrapnel, but 'No bayonet, Lance or Sword can penetrate the protecting material'.[33] A recurrent theme was the notion that without the advertised goods, servicemen would suffer unnecessarily from the cold. The multiple outfitting firm of Hope Bros claimed that: 'No present will be more eagerly welcomed at the Front than a parcel of really warm clothing. The added comfort and protection will mean much to the men who are keeping watch, day and night, in trenches rimmed with ice – whose aim must be steady, though their fingers shake with cold.'[34] Less melodramatically, but in an equally manipulative vein, the Witney (Oxon) clothiers Valentine and Barrell called upon customers to be ready to welcome back wounded servicemen, 'by having ready useful and warm articles to comfort them in their sufferings'.[35]

Despite such efforts, however, it soon became apparent that retailers were faced with an even greater problem than customers' reluctance to buy: the increasing difficulty of finding good stock to sell. Shortages of cloth and dyes were being reported as early as the spring of 1915.[36] In 1917 *Men's Wear* observed that the war had brought about a fundamental change in the relation between retailers and wholesalers. Before 1914, the retailer had been able to 'pick and choose' his supplier of cloth. 'To-day ... [he] finds that he is no longer courted and caressed. The wholesale house has not the slightest difficulty in disposing of its stock.'[37] Prices, both of cloth and of finished garments, steadily increased, and continued to do so in the immediate aftermath of war, at least until 1920.[38] By 1917, shortages and rising prices were deemed to be so serious that the introduction of a 'standard suit',

---

[31]   *The Tatler*, 25 November 1914; *John Bull*, 15 January 1916. The issue of 'comforts' for the troops is briefly considered in C. Messenger, *Call to Arms: The British Army 1914–18* (Weidenfeld and Nicolson, London, 2005), pp. 469–71. Gifts to combatants are considered in M. Roper, 'Maternal relations: moral manliness and emotional survival in letters home during the First World War', in S. Dudnik, K. Hagemann and J. Tosh (eds), *Masculinities in Politics and War: Gendering Modern History* (Manchester University Press, Manchester, 2004), pp. 296–7.

[32]   *The Bystander*, 14 October 1914.

[33]   *Woolwich Gazette and Plumstead News*, 28 November 1916. C.A. Latter had shops in Plumstead and Abbey Wood, both in South London.

[34]   *Reading Mercury*, 5 December 1914.

[35]   *The Oxford Times*, 5 September 1914. See also, for example, *The Bystander*, 27 October 1915.

[36]   *Men's Wear*, 21 August 1915; *The Tailor and Cutter*, 1 May 1915; *The Outfitter*, 3 July 1915.

[37]   *Men's Wear*, 1 September 1917.

[38]   For war-time price increases, see Chapter 2, Figure 2.2.

produced under government control, but sold by private retailers (for cash only), was being seriously considered by the government. Sir Charles Sykes, director of the Wool Textile Control Department of the War Office, was put in charge of the scheme, and in June 1918 it was announced that ready-to-wear suits and overcoats would soon be available, ranging in price from 57s 6d to 84s, although by the end of the war only a tiny proportion of the proposed one million suits had actually reached the market[39] (Figure 6.3). In such a context of reduced markets and

The Clothing Queue.

Unpleasant possibilities if the shortage of outfitting gets much worse.

Figure 6.3   'The clothing queue': shortages of civilian garments. *The Outfitter*, 15 December 1917. By permission of the British Library, 183.

[39]   For the standard suit scheme, see *The Tailor and Cutter*, 22 November 1917; 2 May 1918; 13 June 1918; *Men's Wear*, 12 May 1917; 17 November 1917; *The Outfitter*, 1 September 1917; 24 November 1917; 8 December 1917; 8 June 1918; 18 January 1919. By 1919 made-to-measure suits were also being offered, and the prices retailers were to be allowed to charge had increased considerably. See also *The Tailor and Cutter*, 17 June 1920; 23 September 1920; 16 December 1920. Also Honeyman, *Well Suited*, pp. 54–5.

increasingly serious shortages, both of materials and eventually also of labour,[40] diversification acquired a new importance, with tailors being called upon to try strategies such as undertaking 'repairs and renovations', despite the fact that this would encroach 'on the preserve of the legitimate "codging tailor"'.[41] However, not all menswear retailers were prepared to give up the much more profitable market for new civilian garments without a fight.

Selling to the civilian consumer

Throughout the war years, the menswear trade press expressed agreement with the more general view that 'knuttism' in wartime was morally reprehensible and unpatriotic. In April 1915 *The Outfitter* concurred with other observers about the disappearance of the stylishly dressed young men so typical of the pre-war era, strutting along the streets of British towns and cities, and showing off their new spring outfits. The reasons for this absence were, firstly, 'that so many of the "species" are at the front', and secondly, 'that those remaining behind, aware that the "knut's" code of honour demands his presence in the firing line, feel that a display of "dress talent" is a little unseemly in the circumstances'. Two months later, *The Tailor and Cutter* expressed surprise and disapproval at the number of men of military age to be seen strolling in civilian clothes on London's Strand.[42]

Unsurprisingly, however, those traders whose livelihoods depended on the sale of civilian clothes were also keen to stress that not all sartorial consumption in wartime was unpatriotic and tainted with 'shirking'. In the summer of 1915 *Men's Wear* reported that 'trade is not good, but it is no worse than we can expect ... in view of the fact that everybody is being told that the whole duty of man is to save money'. While careful not to seem critical of the national economy campaign, the article emphasised the hardship that menswear retailers had been suffering since the beginning of the war, and pointed out that, although 'the patriotic trader puts his country first ... he does hope that people will not be too drastic in cutting down their expenses'[43] (Figure 6.4). Traders' protests were not always entirely disregarded. In 1915, for example, after complaints by Luton straw hat manufacturers, a recruiting poster showing a straw boater and a khaki cap, under the heading 'Which ought you to wear?', was modified so that

---

[40] See, for example, the appeal to clerks and sales assistants to enlist made in *News of the World*, 28 March 1915. See also *The Oxford Times*, 28 December 1918, for the case of Gunner F.G. Mullins of the Royal Marine Artillery, an Oxford tailor and outfitter, who left the shop in the hands of his wife while he was in the armed forces.

[41] *The Tailor and Cutter*, 17 August 1916; 21 September 1916. Tailors were not without competition in this area. In 1916, for instance, the British Tailoring and Repairing Company responded to an economy poster that made the appeal: 'Don't buy new clothes needlessly. Don't be ashamed of wearing old clothes in war-time', by adding 'Especially as no one will know them for old clothes if you let us keep them in order'. *John Bull*, 13 May 1916.

[42] *The Outfitter*, 24 April 1915; *The Tailor and Cutter*, 1 July 1915. Of course, it is difficult to assess how much this was simply a case of paying lip-service to the dominant opinion.

[43] *Men's Wear*, 10 July 1915. See also *The Tailor and Cutter*, 19 August 1915.

A Fashion Plate for 1918

(AS IT MIGHT BE).

1. Standard Suit, War Savings Coupon Pattern.
2. Disguise Uniform for Captain of Hush Boat.
3. Grocer's Tea Cosy Waistcoat and Sugar Cube Trousers.

Figure 6.4   **'A fashion plate for 1918', according to *The Tailor and Cutter*, 20 December 1917. By permission of the British Library, LD163.**

it also showed a variety of other hats.[44] Overall, however, as Chapter 3 has shown, patriotic calls on civilians to refrain from consuming, based on the notion of equality

---

[44]   *The Outfitter*, 12 June 1915. The poster was designed and printed by Sir Joseph Causton and Sons, of Eastcheap, London. Of course, even after the amendments, the message – that civilian headgear was associated with shirking – remained the same. For

of sacrifice, and of 'doing one's bit' for the war, would undoubtedly have carried a good deal more weight than the appeals of traders and retailers.

As the war dragged on, the tone of the trade press became less diplomatic and more intolerant of the type of person who believed that 'For a <u>man</u> to be interested in tailors' booklets and fashion plates "in times such as these" (he means, really, any times) is effeminate, soft, dandical-criminal'.[45] The supposed connection between old clothes and patriotism was ridiculed: 'the luckless tramp is at last coming into his own, and will shortly be acclaimed the chief of patriots ... As for the poor tailor he will have to put up his shutters, or convert his establishment into an old clo' emporium.'[46] In 1918 the trade press was still complaining that 'what purpose can be served by suggesting that people should walk about like tramps or animated scarecrows passes our comprehension'.[47]

Perhaps more constructively, attempts were also made to develop an alternative view of sartorial consumption in wartime. After all, there were still plenty of men at home who required 'smart and up-to-date clothes'.[48] Clothes – it was emphasised – were not a 'luxury': 'Not only ... our climate, but the needs of health, and the requirements of statutory enactments, demand that we should be decently clad'.[49] Economy and the purchase of cheap clothes were not the same thing: 'cheap clothing is the falsest kind of economy', warned *The Outfitter*'s editor. Just when munitions workers were earning good wages, 'why not do away for ever with the awful rubbish, the making of which has "sweated" the workers, squeezed the profits of the retailer almost to vanishing point, and which is so bad economically for the public to buy?'[50] As an advertisement for F. Morris and Co., a tailoring firm based in Woolwich Arsenal, one of the country's most important munitions centres, bluntly put it in 1916:

> There are still more than a negligible quantity of gentlemen who are not wearing military uniforms, and never will be. We cannot all be fighting men in the military sense. Those who are not wearing khaki will require clothing in fashionable garments. We say fashionable advisedly, for despite the War Savings' Committee suggestions, those who can afford to buy new clothes will do so, and ... will demand that they are made stylishly, and why not? Very few people will buy new clothes needlessly.[51]

Retailers' press advertisements made much of the fact that to practise true economy was not to purchase new clothes only when absolutely necessary – by which time, it was pointed out, steeply rising prices were likely to have shot through the roof – but to take advantage of bargains as soon as they were available. The Banbury outfitter T.E. Baker, for example, reminded his customers that to practise economy 'does not mean doing without necessities, but it does mean getting the utmost value for every

the symbolism of the straw hat, associated with loafing and shirking, see also, for example, *The Sketch*, 25 August 1915.

45   *Men's Wear*, 26 October 1918.
46   *The Tailor and Cutter*, 2 March 1916. See also 15 June 1916.
47   *The Tailor and Cutter*, 20 June 1918.
48   *The Tailor and Cutter*, 22 April 1915. See also 15 April 1915.
49   *The Tailor and Cutter*, 2 September 1915.
50   *The Outfitter*, 14 August 1915. The point was reiterated in *The Outfitter*, 2 October 1915.
51   *Woolwich Gazette and Plumstead News*, 28 March 1916.

penny you spend'. Fortunately for them, he was able to offer 'a very large and well-assorted stock ... at rock-bottom prices', because he had had the foresight to purchase his stock before the most recent rise in the prices of cotton and wool.[52] A few months later, Hepworths advertised their Oxford branch by warning that 'the man who doesn't see for himself what Hepworth have to offer him, is missing one of the best means to Economy in his personal expenses'.[53] Economy in wartime, menswear retailers stressed, meant seizing the moment, in the expectation that prices could only go up even further.

Although often acknowledging the difficulties of the wartime economy, advertisements also shared an emphasis on the continued importance of dressing as well as possible, and on the identity of interest between the consumer and the retailer, both seeking to do their best in difficult circumstances. Prospective buyers were invited to take advantage of their retailer's commercial acumen, especially his far-sighted purchase of woollens and other cloth in advance of price rises. In the early weeks of 1916, for example, a Woolwich Arsenal tailor announced that 'Before prices advanced J.J. Woodford grasped the situation and bought Large Supplies to safeguard his Customers' interests. YOU are thus able to buy your blue serge suit from Woodford's and save 25 per cent'.[54] In 1915 a Catesby's advertisement had made a similar point, offering suits and overcoats for sale for 30s, a 'special offer [which] only holds good until this lot of fabrics we've snapped up sells out'. The customer was called upon to 'think of saving ten bob and also securing the additional advantages of a fine West End "Burlington" suit ... made to your individual measures and with a money-back guarantee'.[55]

Good-quality and well-made civilian clothes were not, it was stressed, a luxury. Writing in *Men's Wear*, Sesquip (himself in uniform), further emphasised the importance of maintaining 'a proper pride in one's personal appearance. Such a pride ... is no mean factor in building up human character and cheerfulness. It is a tonic thing'. As such, it was essential to the maintenance of morale: 'I bet my hat that many men now in hospital ... often find a source of real pleasure in picturing to themselves the nice suits of fancy pattern they will have made to stun the girls as soon as opportunity offers'.[56] Among civilians, 'to be smart and well dressed is to be alert and optimistic, and active and energetic', all essential wartime qualities.[57] Indeed, 'to advise people to appear shabbily dressed is to lower the business capacity of the nation, to take away the people's self-respect, to lower the moral tone generally, and' – it was added, apparently almost as an afterthought – 'to ruin the tailoring trade, which is already in grave difficulty'.[58]

In this, however, the menswear trade found itself at odds with mainstream opinion, where there does seem to have been a degree of agreement about the wartime association between an excessively well-groomed appearance, shirking and profiteering. Some

---

[52]   *The Banbury Guardian*, 23 November 1916.
[53]   *The Oxford Times*, 17 March 1917. See also, for example, *Punch*, 8 May 1918; *The Woolwich Herald*, 9 July 1915.
[54]   *Woolwich Gazette and Plumstead News*, 25 January 1916.
[55]   *News of the World*, 21 November 1915.
[56]   *Men's Wear*, 26 October 1918. See also 17 February 1917.
[57]   *The Tailor and Cutter*, 2 March 1916.
[58]   *The Tailor and Cutter*, 9 March 1916. See also 30 March 1916; *The Outfitter*, 21 August 1915; *The Sketch*, 31 May 1916.

within the trade took up the challenge with relish. As a contributor to *Men's Wear* pointed out, 'if customers must economise it is our business to try to manage things so that they will have to economise on something different from clothes'. In wartime, it was stressed, good salesmanship acquired an even greater importance than in normal circumstances. After all, 'Every Briton believes in keeping the flag flying, but when buying clothing and outfitting he is still influenced by his own personal wants, tastes, and fads ... It is to these we have to appeal rather than to patriotism.'[59] The good salesman could still manage to effect sales, since 'even in wartime ... the Winter Man, whether spectacled professor, natty clerk, thrifty farmer, or prosperous artisan, is still susceptible to your influence if he is sure of your interest'. An interest, that is, not in 'making money ... but your human interest in his tastes and comforts'.[60]

For those retailers based in areas where munitions factories were present, the relatively well-off munitions workers were singled out as an important potential market at a time of crisis: dungarees, overalls, knitted goods and other items of work gear for 'mechanics and munitions workers' made their appearance in press advertisements, particularly in the latter half of the war, in a marked contrast to the almost complete absence of images of manual workers before 1914.[61] In December 1914 it was pointed out that 'Woolwich may safely be described as one of the wealthiest spots in England at the present moment', although it was added that 'much money is no good unless it is well spent'. In May 1916 the Woolwich Chamber of Commerce reported that 'the increase in the garrison, the influx of workers into the Royal Arsenal and local works, and the high rate of pay earned by those engaged in munitions work, have combined to create an atmosphere of great prosperity'. 'The year', it was added, had proved 'a prosperous one for the traders of the borough'.[62]

Furthermore, it was observed with satisfaction that munitions workers were using their new-found relative prosperity to buy more than just items suitable for work. In April 1917 the trade press reported that orders for the Easter holidays had been quite satisfactory. This was attributed to the fact that 'the war-worker' now had a little spare cash, and was 'prepared to look at the amount he shall spend on his own clothes in the same light as ... boots for his children, furniture for his home, and bonnets for his wife', although his 'little flutters on new outfits' could hardly be described as extravagant. The notion circulating at the time in the mainstream press, that 'dress hogs' were making extravagant purchases of wool, was strongly rejected.[63] But even while carefully emphasising their modest nature, the right of munitions workers to enjoy their new purchases was defended: 'the poorer working-class that formerly wore mended clothes no longer do so. The wages they are earning enables them to purchase new clothes.' This was not seen in the trade press as a sign that – supposed – unprecedented riches

---

[59]   *Men's Wear*, 3 October 1914.

[60]   *Men's Wear*, 6 November 1915. See also *The Tailor and Cutter*, 27 April 1916.

[61]   See, for example, *The Banbury Guardian*, 11 July 1918; *News of the World*, 9 January 1916; *Reading Mercury*, 10 March 1917; *Woolwich Gazette and Plumstead News*, 4 January 1916. On pre-war advertising, see L. Ugolini, 'Men, masculinities, and menswear advertising, c. 1890–1914', in J. Benson and L. Ugolini (eds), *A Nation of Shopkeepers: Five Centuries of British Retailing* (I.B. Tauris, London, 2003), pp. 87–92.

[62]   *The Woolwich Herald*, 4 December 1914; 12 May 1916.

[63]   *Men's Wear*, 7 April 1917; 12 May 1917.

had gone to workers' heads. Rather, it was 'to their credit and self-respect ... [that] they have risen to the occasion, and instead of visiting the second-hand clothes dealer they now patronise the tailor'.[64] After all, it was in everybody's best interests that workers should be well dressed, fed and housed, so that 'their labour capacity may be sustained at the standard requisite to the great and urgent necessities of the war'.[65]

It was further emphasised, albeit rather defensively, that the retailer who provided such workers with their new apparel had nothing to be ashamed of. On the contrary, he was to be commended. Traders' right to run profitable businesses, even in wartime, without running the risk of being condemned as unpatriotic profiteers, was defended:

> The live man [by which was meant the retailer who had bought his stock well in advance of price increases] who has not been afraid to take his courage in both hands [unlike the 'business "slackers"'] has had the good time of the war in a business sense. The man who has made profit legitimately, by sheer industry and pluck, should not be regarded as an Ishmael. He should not be confounded with the 'profiteers' who have taken every opportunity to batten on the nation's agony.[66]

In occasional moments of candour, it was acknowledged that after all, 'the making of a profit is the essential point for the trader in a business transaction'. However, it was generally recognised that a rhetoric that only stressed entrepreneurial skills and money-making would not go down well in a wartime environment where business practices were increasingly under the spotlight for evidence of profiteering.[67] Retailers were thus urged to make clear to their customers that 'no undue profits are being made by the retail outfitting trade at the present time'. Rising prices, they were to emphasise, were not due to profiteering, but rather to the sharply rising costs of scarce labour and materials.[68]

In any case, the extent to which munitions workers and other civilian consumers could make up for wartime lost markets should not be exaggerated. It has been estimated that

---

[64]   *The Tailor and Cutter*, 20 June 1918. See also *Men's Wear*, 29 March 1919.

[65]   *The Outfitter*, 25 March 1916.

[66]   *The Outfitter*, 13 November 1915. However, it was acknowledged in the trade press that it was not always easy to make a clear distinction between retailers making a proper profit and those guilty of profiteering. *The Outfitter*, 30 June 1917.

[67]   M. Hilton, *Consumerism in Twentieth-Century Britain: The Search for a Historical Movement* (Cambridge University Press, Cambridge, 2003), chapter 2; F. Trentmann, 'Bread, milk and democracy: consumption and citizenship in Britain, c. 1903–51', in M. Daunton and M. Hilton (eds), *The Politics of Consumption: Material Culture and Citizenship in Europe and America* (Berg, Oxford, 2001), pp. 129–63; J.-L. Robert, 'The image of the profiteer', in J. Winter and J.-L. Robert (eds), *Capital Cities at War: Paris, London, Berlin 1914–1919* (Cambridge University Press, Cambridge, 1999; first published 1997), pp. 104–32; B. Waites, 'The government of the Home Front and the "moral economy" of the working class', in P.H. Liddle (ed.), *Home Fires and Foreign Fields: British Social and Military Experience in the First World War* (Brassey's Defence Publishers, London, 1985), pp. 175–93; J.S. Boswell and B.R. Johns, 'Patriots or profiteers? British businessmen and the First World War', *The Journal of European Economic History*, vol. 11, no. 2 (1982), pp. 423–45.

[68]   Mark-ups in outfitting 'normally' ranged, depending on the goods, between 20 and 25 per cent, 25 and almost 34 per cent, or – when retailers could get away with it – 34 and 50 per cent. *The Outfitter*, 17 March 1917.

between 1913 and 1918 total civilian expenditure in Britain fell by nearly 20 per cent, a quarter of this decline being due to a fall in clothes purchasing.[69] It was acknowledged in the summer of 1917, for example, that despite the 'finery in munitions centres, thousands of men are still poorly dressed', a sign of the persistence of those 'class distinctions which the war has not altered, and never will abolish'.[70] Most importantly, shortages of stock effectively limited the amount of trade that could be done, irrespective of the volume of demand. In 1915 the retailers of Waltham Cross were able to report a buoyant trade, which thanks to the presence of munitions factories had roughly doubled from its pre-war levels. However, 'the public have not yet appreciated the difference the war has made to the supply of many articles … and that they must put up with what they can get, rather than the special shade or fabric they require'.[71]

The aftermath of war

Anybody – either within the menswear trade or outside it – who had expected that the end of the war would see a rapid easing of shortages and a general lowering of prices, was doomed to disappointment. According to Robert Graves and Alan Hodge, as men returned to civilian life after the Armistice and needed to replenish their wardrobes, 'demand was so great and so sudden that the resulting shortage induced a sharp rise in prices'.[72] In February 1919 it was reported in the trade press that clothing prices were still double their pre-war levels, but that demand nevertheless remained strong: 'with so many officers replenishing their mufti wardrobes, and so many civilians desirous of smartening themselves after practising economy in dress during the war, the West End tailors are exceedingly busy.[73] Prices did not begin to fall until 1920, a year in which expenditure on men's and boys' wear reached a record peak of almost £281 million, as demobilised soldiers were forced to buy civilian garments regardless of high prices. In 1921 expenditure fell sharply to just over £164 million, reflecting both price deflation and (possibly) the fact that most of the necessary post-war purchases had by then been made.[74]

Having been demobbed at the end of the war, F.E. Baily found that prices were very high and many goods remained unavailable. Nevertheless, 'one had no clothes and it was necessary to buy more', despite the fact that they were 'sold expensively, and the

[69]　P. Dewey, 'The new warfare and economic mobilisation', in J. Turner (ed.), *Britain and the First World War* (Unwin Hyman, London, 1988), pp. 79–80.

[70]　*Men's Wear*, 25 August 1917.

[71]　*Men's Wear*, 18 September 1915. On shortages of materials for munitions workers' clothes, see *The Outfitter*, 20 November 1915. See also Chapter 3 for a discussion of munitions workers' wartime clothes consumption.

[72]　R. Graves and A. Hodge, *The Long Weekend: A Social History of Britain 1918–1939* (Abacus, London, 1995; first published 1940), pp. 67, 69.

[73]　*Men's Wear*, 22 February 1919. On post-war prices, which slowly began to fall from their peaks of 1920, but never returned to their pre-1914 levels, see Chapter 4.

[74]　These figures refer to the whole of the United Kingdom. R. Stone and D.A. Rowe, *The Measurement of Consumers' Expenditure and Behaviour in the United Kingdom 1920–1938* (Cambridge University Press, Cambridge, 1966), vol. 2, p. 13.

choice of materials ... [was] small'.[75] On his discharge from the army, Ifan Edwards had been given a choice between two pounds and a civilian suit, 'and having seen a victim in one of these suits I hurriedly asked for the money. I wasn't going to look like that if I could help it.' However, he soon had to bite the bullet, and 'went along ... to a popular tailors' and enquired the price of an outfit. The cheapest suit was ten pounds, cash down, and it *looked* cheap.' Nonetheless, he had no choice but 'to buy everything ... at home I had neither shirt nor sock nor collar ... The prices', he continued:

> were frightening, and my appearance when I had been dressed up by the tailor was more frightening still ... I caught sight of myself in the mirror and I nearly cried. I could never go out like that; it was humiliating. But the tailor was patting and pulling and murmuring approval as he licked me into shape ... fifteen pounds went west in that shop, and another two in the boot shop.[76]

In May 1919, R.D. Blumenfeld noted in his diary that pawnshops were currently doing a roaring trade, while 'the old-clothes merchants have almost got to the end of their tether, for no one now sells old clothes in view of the fact that new ones are so dear. Think of a standard suit of clothes for men costing £11. That is £1 more than we used to pay for the best evening dress clothes!'[77]

A year after the end of the war, Ashley Sterne wrote in *Tit-Bits* that 'I was needing some warm winter shirts very badly, and seeing some in a shop window at bargain prices, I drew a few thousand pounds out of the bank and called on the hosier.' He was offered a shirt which, he was assured, was made of 'Solid wool fleeced from the solid lamb. No mint sauce or other alternative substance used in their manufacture. Take this one in your hand and stroke it. I felt it. It was solid lamb right enough. I pinched it. It baa'd.'[78] Not everybody was prepared to see the funny side. In 1919, in his evidence to the Select Committee on High Prices and Profits, Sir Auckland Geddes raised the awful spectre of

> people who were ... superficially in quite a small way of business ... blossoming forth into quite a new manner of living. We have had instances of quite small persons in the haberdashery trade suddenly finding themselves in a position of being able to buy an estate of several hundred acres in the country, and we assume that their profits are now greater than they were when they had to live in a few rooms over their shop.

If the president of the Board of Trade could be found voicing such opinions, it is hardly surprising that newspapers were soon 'full of wild accusations of demobilised officers being the victims of unscrupulous profiteering tailors'.[79]

Such accusations of war profiteering were not directed only at the menswear trade. Indeed, in 1919 the government was forced to respond to the growing discontent over high prices and shortages (with food featuring prominently, especially as wartime

[75] F.E. Baily, *Twenty-Nine Years' Hard Labour* (Hutchinson, London, n.d. [c. 1935]), p. 153.

[76] I. Edwards, *No Gold on My Shovel* (The Porcupine Press, London, 1947), pp. 13, 15.

[77] R.D. Blumenfeld, *All in a Lifetime* (Ernest Benn, London, 1931), pp. 122–3.

[78] *Tit-Bits*, 29 November 1919.

[79] Select Committee on High Prices and Profits, *Special Report from the Select Committee on High Prices and Profits ...* (HMSO, London, 1919), vol. 5, p. 293; *Men's Wear*, 1 March 1919. See also ibid., 15 March 1919; *The Outfitter*, 3 January 1920. An assessment of British businesses' conduct during the war is found in Boswell and Johns, 'Patriots or profiteers?'.

controls were progressively abolished) insistently voiced by the popular press, the Consumers' Council, labour organisations, and by 'ordinary' consumers. It did so by passing into law a Profiteering Act. As a result, a Profiteering Act Department was established within the Board of Trade, and was charged with investigating allegations of 'unreasonable' profits on the sale of consumer goods, both retail and wholesale (with powers to set maximum prices), and with gathering information on trusts. Local government bodies were empowered (although not compelled) to set up profiteering committees, responsible for investigating complaints against local retailers, and tribunals, where appeals could be heard. [80]

The Profiteering Act has certainly not received a good press, and has been dismissed both by contemporaries and by historians either as ineffective and unnecessary, or as a stratagem to deflect criticism of the government's lack of action over continued high prices. Predictably, the menswear trade's response to the Act was also unenthusiastic. A year after the Armistice, the editor of *Men's Wear* pointed out that the trade was prepared to 'tolerate the Profiteering Act on the ground that it is intended to protect the poor against paying unreasonably high prices for their necessities'. However, they were infuriated by 'the suggestion that the Act is also intended to help the well-to-do to save money'. If retailers' profits were to be so questioned and curtailed, he continued, then surely those of 'well-paid professional men' should also have been investigated.[81]

Supposedly 'anti-profiteering' commercial ventures were met with particular scorn. In 1920, the shop opened in a blaze of publicity on London's Strand by the Conservative MP Mr Mallaby-Deely, for example, loudly proclaimed its intention of 'smashing' the profiteers, by demonstrating that high quality clothes *could* be produced and sold cheaply. This was to be achieved through 'the employment of "mass" production to obtain "mass" consumption'.[82] In the opinion of the menswear trade press, these were simply 'cheap clothes at cheap prices'. As a *Men's Wear* contributor commented acerbically, 'That value for money is given ... may be admitted, but the money being so little the value is necessarily in proportion'.[83] Furthermore, the shopkeeper who Mallaby-Deely and his admirers characterised as a 'profiteer' was viewed by the trade press as a victim of circumstances outside his control, a 'tradesman who understands his craft, and who finds it difficult, these days, to make both ends meet'. His merchandise was in a different category – hence more expensive – to the 'factory clothing' sold in the Strand shop[84] (Figure 6.5). This was reiterated by the *Financial Mail*, which reported in 1920 that 'the small tailor in the High Street' was discovering 'that the few hundred pounds of capital employed in his business is becoming daily more difficult to turn over profitably'. As a small-scale employer of labour and buyer of material, he could not enjoy the

[80]   Hilton, *Consumerism in Twentieth-Century Britain*, pp. 73–5. The act was allowed to lapse in 1921.

[81]   *Men's Wear*, 8 November 1919.

[82]   *Financial Mail*, 20 March 1920. On Mallaby-Deely's scheme, see also *The Times*, 27 February 1920; 28 February 1920; 10 March 1920; 13 March 1920.

[83]   *Men's Wear*, 6 March 1920; *The Outfitter*, 6 March 1920.

[84]   *The Tailor and Cutter*, 15 April 1920. See also ibid., 7 October 1920. In April 1920 a tailor was charged in Bow Street Police Court with smashing the plate-glass window of Mallaby-Deely's shop. *The Outfitter*, 17 April 1920. See also ibid., 18 September 1920.

same economies of scale as his larger competitors, a problem that was to become increasingly acute in the inter-war years.[85]

Conclusion

There is little doubt that the issue of profiteering aroused a good deal of bitterness on both sides of the argument, and that it related directly to fundamental wartime debates about appropriate consumption and commercial practices, about equality of sacrifice and about the role of the state in safeguarding the interests of consumers, especially among the poor, during a period of national emergency. It was also the case that these issues did not suddenly disappear in November 1918. Siegfried Sassoon dryly observed that his military tailor had 'chatted his way courageously through the War; "business as usual" was his watchword … when I last saw him, a few months before the Armistice, he was still outwardly unconscious of the casualty lists which had lost (and gained) him such a legion of customers'.[86] It is difficult to believe that accusations and perceptions of profiteering, or at least of traders doing well out of the war, did not leave at least some legacy of bitterness in the relationship between retailers and consumers in the years immediately following the end of the war.

THE STRAND, IF OTHER M.P.'s FOLLOW "SUIT."

Figure 6.5   Anti-profiteering commercial ventures. *Men's Wear*, 6 March 1920. By permission of the British Library, LD178.

---

[85] *Financial Mail*, 20 March 1920.
[86] Sassoon, *Memoirs of a Fox-Hunting Man*, pp. 259–60.

However, it also seems to be the case that the development of the menswear trade in the inter-war period owed less to the impact of new debates over the nature of private traders' 'reasonable' profits, either in wartime or under 'normal' circumstances, and a good deal more to trends already well in evidence before the outbreak of hostilities. As market share in the menswear trade shifted increasingly away from independent to large-scale concerns, even in that last bastion of the bespoke tailor, the suit, debates over the acceptability of wartime commerce and profits slowly faded from the headlines. According to a trade press contributor, writing in October 1920:

> There is no disguising the fact that many men have lost faith in their tailors. Perhaps the profiteering agitation has something to do with it, but the root cause is that the percentage of tailors turning out dependable garments at a reasonable price is small. We are saying nothing about profits, because it is not profits which rule the situation, but efficiency of production.[87]

As this commentator acknowledged, it was not concerns about the excessive profits allegedly made by tailors during the war, but about the quality and value of their products, which drove men to seek alternative sources of clothing. To independent tailors' dismay, such sources were to become ever easier to find in the inter-war period.

---

[87]   *The Outfitter*, 9 October 1920.

Chapter 7

The Struggle for Survival, 1920–1939

In the course of the three decades preceding the outbreak of the First World War, vocal and active sections of the menswear trade had sought to develop a new image of tailoring, one characterised by qualities of sober and business-like industriousness. Their aims had been to counter the well-established association between the trade and poverty, unmanliness and sweating, as well as to respond to the popularity of new retail outlets, including so-called 'brass and glass' shops.[1] These concerns were temporarily side-lined during and in the immediate aftermath of the war, but by the second half of the 1920s, as prices fell and issues of wartime profiteering faded from the headlines, the question of trade competition gained a renewed prominence and sense of urgency.[2] Fears were increasingly voiced that the menswear trade was undergoing a process of change that would eventually threaten the very livelihoods of independent retailers, particularly bespoke tailors. There was little agreement (at least initially) as to whether the greatest threat was posed by the wholesale bespoke or by the ready-to-wear trades, by the tally trade or by the impressive-looking branch shops of large multiple concerns. However, it was widely acknowledged that mass-production, marketing and distribution systems and techniques were disastrously affecting the 'small man', especially in the last bastion of the bespoke trade: the suit.

Some inter-war commentators sought to demonstrate that the situation was not as gloomy as most independent menswear traders and their supporters believed. Writing in *The Financial News* in 1935, B.O.W. Roskill pointed out that between them, Montague Burton and Prices Tailors had come to dominate the market for made-to-measure suits priced at 50 shillings. However, he added that 'It is doubtful … whether the multiple shop companies in the bespoke tailoring trade account for much over 10 per cent of the total turnover in men's and boys' wear'.[3] The ready-to-wear trade accounted for about 50 per cent of this total turnover, with around 10 per cent being sold in department stores. There were also 'a fairly large number of chain stores and multiples selling men's and boys' ready-made wear, although suits and overcoats constitute only part of their range'. Co-operative stores were also 'responsible for a considerable sale of ready-made clothing, but by far the most important group, either in the bespoke or ready-made

---

[1]   See Chapter 5.

[2]   See also S. Phillips and A. Alexander, 'An efficient pursuit? Independent shopkeeping in 1930s Britain', *Enterprise and Society*, vol. 6, no. 2 (2005), pp. 278–304; A. Alexander, J. Benson and G. Shaw, 'Action and reaction: competition and the multiple retailer in 1930s Britain', *The International Review of Retail, Distribution and Consumer Research*, vol. 9, no. 3 (1999), pp. 245–59.

[3]   Although this is not made entirely clear, Roskill seems to be dealing only with men's and boys' outerwear (suits and overcoats), rather than with the whole of the menswear market.

section of the trade, are the small independent outfitters, of whom there are many thousands throughout the country'. Overall, Roskill concluded that 'of the total consumption of men's and boys' clothing, about half ... is sold "ready made" chiefly by small outfitters, large chain stores and multiples, department stores and co-ops, while, of the other half, the retail bespoke tailors have the lion's share and the bespoke tailoring multiples the rest'.[4] There were still opportunities for independent outfitters to flourish. According to a 'Special correspondent' to *Man and his Clothes*, the '"chain" system' was more applicable to the tailoring than to the outfitting section of the trade. 'The power of the multiple system depends greatly on the standardisation of the manufacturing processes which ... is far more workable with tailoring than outfitting'. In the case of the latter, 'so many diverse units of merchandise must be stocked that it is almost impossible for one firm economically to manufacture them or any large part of them', thus forfeiting the advantages of vertical integration.[5]

However, even acknowledging that outfitters may have been less vulnerable than tailors to competition from multiples and other large retailers, Roskill's snapshot view of the contemporary menswear market still failed to take into account the rapid erosion of independent retailers' overall market share, steadily passing into the hands of department stores, co-operatives and, most notably, multiples. Such erosion had been taking place at least since 1900, but had gathered significant pace since the end of the war: in 1900 independents still controlled between 92 and 95.5 per cent of the market in men's and boys' wear, leaving multiples with between 2 and 3.5 per cent. However, by 1939 independents' share had fallen to between 55 and 62 per cent, multiples' having increased to between 28 and 32 per cent (Table 7.1).

Table 7.1   Proportion of total sales of mens- and boyswear in Britain, 1900–1939.

Source: **J.B. Jefferys, *Retail Trading in Britain 1850–1950* (Cambridge University Press, Cambridge, 1954), p. 315.**

Year	Co-ops	Dept. Stores	Multiples	Others
1900	1.5 – 3 %	1 – 1.5 %	2 – 3.5 %	92 – 95.5 %
1910	2 – 3.5 %	2 – 3 %	4 – 5 %	88.5 – 92 %
1920	2.5 – 3.5 %	3 – 4 %	8.5 – 10 %	82.5 – 86 %
1930	3 – 4.5 %	5 – 6 %	20.5 – 24 %	65.5 – 71.5 %
1939	4 – 6 %	6 – 7 %	28 – 32 %	55 – 62 %

---

[4]   West Yorkshire Archive Service, Leeds (WYAS), Burton Archives, Box 36, Press Cuttings, *The Financial News*, 11 April 1935.

[5]   *Man and his Clothes*, September 1928. However, a number of outfitting multiples also flourished in the inter-war years. Among these were Hope Bros, Horne Brothers (with 15 London shops and 7 in 'the chief provincial towns') and Austin Reed Ltd (with shops in London and in 8 'chief provincial towns'). WYAS, Burton Archives, Box 36, Press Cuttings, *The Financial News*, 11 April 1935. See also *The Outfitter*, 18 April 1936.

Even in an expanding market, the shift was a worrying one, and was especially significant as regarded the last remaining mainstay of independent bespoke tailoring, the made-to-measure suit, with a relatively small number of huge companies, many of them based in Leeds, eventually coming to dominate this section of the market. By the late 1930s, according to *Garment Worker*, 'Leeds multiple firms were said to supply 20 per cent of the nation's requirements of men's and boys' wear'.[6] The figures are even more impressive if outerwear is considered separately from other garments: Katrina Honeyman, for example, has suggested that by the 1930s, 'over sixty per cent of all suits sold in Britain were made and marketed by a handful of Leeds "multiple tailors"'.[7] Contemporaries could hardly be blamed for believing that this trend would continue to gather pace, leading to the eventual demise of independent menswear retailers, both in the bespoke and in the ready-to-wear sections of the trade, replaced by branch shops tied to large concerns, selling clothing produced (mostly by female labour) in large-scale factories.

This chapter will explore the impact on retailing practices and identities of such a rapid and, for many, fearsome change. It will firstly consider the differing opinions expressed within the trade about the place of independent menswear traders in the 'modern' commercial environment. As firms competed for market share, ideas concerning the value and qualities of the commodities they sold, as well as about consumer demand, became central to debates over the current and future state of the trade. After examining these ideas, the chapter will shift its attention to other issues that were believed to have an impact on consumer choice. Business practices, the look, location and atmosphere of the shop, as well as the character of the salesmanship on offer, were all accorded renewed importance both by independents and by large-scale retailers, with the notion of the 'modern' becoming a key reference point to attitudes towards commercial practices and strategies. The chapter will then conclude by questioning whether such tumultuous changes within the menswear trade were mirrored by equal changes in the status of the tailoring trade and of 'tailors'. On the eve of the Second World War, did it still take nine tailors to make one man?

Tailoring and the modern consumer

Although not necessarily unsympathetic to what was generally agreed to be the plight of independent retailers, particularly that of small bespoke tailors, a significant section of the trade believed their demise to be inevitable. In 1938, for example, *The Tailor and Cutter* published a brief series of articles on 'The tailoring trade: past and present'. The author observed that until the second half of the nineteenth century, 'the craft, especially in country districts, had changed little for centuries'. It was the arrival of 'steam, the sewing machine, and electricity' that had fundamentally changed clothes production, with the sewing machine, in particular, bringing about

---

[6]   Quoted in K. Honeyman, *Well Suited: A History of the Leeds Clothing Industry 1850–1990* (Pasold Research Fund and Oxford University Press, Oxford, 2000), p. 118.

[7]   Honeyman, *Well Suited*, p. 3. See also A. Alexander, 'The Evolution of Multiple Retailing in Britain, 1870–1950: A Geographical Analysis', unpublished PhD, University of Exeter (1994).

'the gradual evolution of a craft into a manufacture'. During the war, furthermore, 'many things went into the melting pot ... and the tailoring trade with them'. As many of 'the better paid workmen, artisans, members of the lower middle-class' were no longer able to afford the prices charged by bespoke tailors, they had 'gone over to the ready-to-wear trade', and had found themselves well-satisfied with it. The future – for this commentator – was clear, and indeed inexorable: 'Those who imagine in some vague way that the bespoke will right itself and win back its lost provinces are labouring under a delusion ... Economic laws, political measures, the trend of fashion, and the spirit of the time all tend in the same direction – to substitute a manufacture for a craft.'[8] He was not the only contributor to the trade press to believe that the eventual demise of the independent tailor was inevitable. Fifteen years earlier, a *Men's Wear* writer had similarly suggested that such a demise was part of a wider process of historical progress, and of 'the passing of the old order and the coming of the new', in the same way that horse-drawn coaches had been substituted by motor-cars, or steam trains by electric trains.[9] In other words, by the inter-war period many believed that the small-scale bespoke tailor was rapidly and inevitably becoming obsolete.[10]

In the opinion of many trade commentators, while the bespoke tailor continued with his anachronistic practices, his competitors were busy fulfilling a 'modern' demand that would not otherwise have been satisfied. A 1923 *Men's Wear* editorial pointed out that the success of the 'tally-man' was due to the fact that he met a 'public want': 'payment by instalment suits the poorer classes, and ... [as] the majority of people are honest', they conscientiously tried to keep up with repayments.[11] In general, retailers selling mass-produced menswear, whether made-to-measure or ready-to-wear, satisfied a demand for inexpensive garments of decent quality and appearance. Clothing factories, it was suggested, were 'the result of modern ideas to meet the demand for cheap clothing, for a large number of people earn wages inadequate to provide the means for the purchase of bespoke trade clothing'. Businesses specialising in mass-produced made-to-measure suits had 'met a real need and are in line with the evolutionary march of progress'.[12] According to the couturier Hardy Amies, multiple tailoring received a huge boost after the war, 'when thousands of officers and temporary gentlemen came back to civilian life. Wardrobes had to be made or renewed. Gentlemen bespoke their suits, but to have them made by hand was too expensive ... multiple tailoring satisfied a need and was wildly successful.'[13]

In 1931 A. Emil Davies speculated that multiple shops like Montague Burton, The Fifty Shilling Tailors and Rego Clothiers had been doing relatively well even during the post-1929 Depression because 'people who have previously bought

---

[8]   *The Tailor and Cutter*, 15 July 1938; 22 July 1938.

[9]   *Men's Wear*, 22 September 1923.

[10]   See also, for example, Anon., 'The clothing trades', in H. Llewellyn Smith (ed.), *The New Survey of London Life and Labour* (P.S. King and Son, London, 1931), vol. 2, 'London industries', especially p. 256.

[11]   *Men's Wear*, 21 April 1923. On the tally trade, see also *Men's Wear*, 30 June 1923; 25 May 1935.

[12]   *The Tailor and Cutter*, 8 January 1920; *Men's Wear*, 26 May 1923.

[13]   H. Amies, *The Englishman's Suit* (Quartet Books, London, 1994), p. 30.

their goods from specialised private traders are finding it necessary to buy more standardised articles'.[14] According to 'Anglo-Saxon', writing in 1935, the impact of mass-produced garments on men's fashions could hardly be over-estimated: 'to-day many are best served as regards style and value by taking advantage of the great skill and technique employed by the big producer'.[15] Some were prepared to take the argument further. In 1930 Joseph Greenaway, *The Outfitter*'s 'advertising specialist', suggested that large stores, 'with their attractive window displays and informative advertising', not only catered for, but actually *created* demand: they suggested 'to the public entirely new ideas of living that increase their desires and automatically bring about mass production to meet mass demand'. In Greenaway's view this was an entirely desirable development, as 'modern methods of production and selling' had been successful in bringing 'the fine styles of Savile Row ... within the means of practically every man in the British Isles'.[16]

Unsurprisingly, such opinions did not go uncontested. Many protested that the big businesses that threatened the livelihoods of independent retailers did not successfully satisfy a latent demand but rather they cunningly duped consumers into making unwise and unsatisfactory purchases. In a sense, therefore, the idea was accepted that multiples and other large retailers were able to arouse consumers' acquisitive desires, and create 'new' demand. However, the outcome was portrayed as unfortunate, or even calamitous for the hapless customers, especially for the younger, 'modern', generation of men, who were unable to 'appreciate the value of quality as ... [their] fathers did'.[17] There were 'good reasons to assume' that those buying clothes on the instalment system 'do not realise how much they are charged for the credit granted them', and risked finding themselves deeply in debt.[18] However, the greatest ire was reserved for the wholesale bespoke trade and multiple retailers such as Burton's and the Fifty Shilling Tailors, in particular for their heavily advertised mass-produced made-to-measure suits. As 'A Northern Tailor' bluntly put it, 'Take a walk along your main street, and look in the multiple "tailors'" windows. You will find them bristling with bare-faced lies'.[19]

The ease and frequency with which people were fooled by misleading advertisements was a constant trade press refrain, although supporters of factory-produced clothes were at pains to stress the knowledgeable and newly demanding nature of contemporary, 'modern', consumers. After visiting the Burton's factory, for example, Rosslyn Mitchell remarked that 'A generation ago the men of this country who had not large means were content with second-hand clothes ... style

---

[14]   WYAS, Burton Archives, Box 36, Press Cuttings, *Everyman*, 28 May 1931.

[15]   *Men's Wear*, 6 April 1935.

[16]   *The Outfitter*, 15 February 1930.

[17]   *Men's Wear*, 7 February 1931. This seems an extraordinary claim, given Edwardian and earlier condemnations of popular but 'cheap and nasty' clothes. That the young dressed 'badly' was also stated, for example, in *The Tailor and Cutter*, 28 May 1925; *The Sartorial Gazette*, October 1932. However, in 1935 it was affirmed that 'Pride of appearance has very definitely become a habit with the younger people'. *Men's Wear*, 12 January 1935.

[18]   *Men's Wear*, 9 April 1927. For a more positive assessment of the tally trade, see *Men's Wear*, 30 June 1932.

[19]   *Men's Wear*, 26 February 1927; 14 April 1923. See also 11 May 1935.

and smartness were for the middle-classes ... to-day nothing will do but the best, the most up-to-date design and cut and no second-rate cloth': all these could be obtained from Burton's.[20] Such claims were derided by multiples' competitors, revisiting pre-war warnings about the ease with which consumers could be fooled by misleading advertisements and flash-looking shops. Consumers, it was reiterated, were so innocent and credulous that they accepted unquestioningly the statements made by 'certain of the large London stores and most of the multiple "tailors" ... of astounding and unprecedented bargains of clothing being offered at vastly below its usual price'.[21] Of such promises, which stressed that the price of the garments was far below their actual value, 'the only wonderful thing is the gullibility of the British public and the public press'.[22] Indeed, 'the public love to be shouted to and gulled. Not one man in ten is really a judge of clothes.'[23] Such statements did not always go unchallenged. They certainly exasperated W. Hughes, the manager of an unnamed multiple branch shop in Poole. In 1928 he pointed out in a letter to *Men's Wear* that the 'rapid strides' made by multiple tailoring businesses since the war were 'not due to "exaggerated and untrue" advertisements, or to the innocence and gullibility of the British public ... The reason is that a good article can be purchased at a reasonable price.' After all, he added, 'unless you give a customer entire satisfaction you will rarely get a repetition of his patronage, which refutes ... [the] suggestion that the public are being gulled by the multiple firms'.[24]

The commodity: bespoke versus mass-production

Arguments raged throughout the inter-war years in the trade and (to a lesser extent) mainstream press, in advertisements, in meetings of trade organisations, and – it was asserted – across shop counters, about the quality, style, finish and durability of the garments offered by competing firms. Disagreements about the relative value of bespoke and ready-to-wear, of individually-made and mass-produced garments, were of course not new.[25] However, by the second half of the 1920s these debates had acquired a new prominence: many independents recognised that their very livelihood was now at stake. Arguments already well-rehearsed in the three decades before the outbreak of war, stressing both the scientific and the artistic nature of high-class bespoke tailoring, were thus given a renewed airing in the inter-war years. Once again, it was emphasised that 'there is a world of difference between art and craftsmanship and manufacture', comparable to that between a cheap print and 'a real water-colour by a Master'.[26] Such rhetorical and practical commitment to

---

[20]   WYAS, Burton Archives, Box 36, Press Cuttings, *Paisley Daily Express*, 17 October 1932.
[21]   *Men's Wear*, 5 May 1923. See also, for example, 25 June 1927.
[22]   *The Outfitter*, 20 March 1920. See also, for example, 16 May 1925.
[23]   *Men's Wear*, 7 April 1923.
[24]   *Men's Wear*, 10 November 1928. See also *Men's Wear*, 20 October 1928.
[25]   L. Ugolini, 'Ready-to-wear or made-to-measure? Consumer choice in the British menswear trade, 1900–1939', *Textile History*, vol. 34, no. 2 (2003), pp. 192–213.
[26]   *The Tailor and Cutter*, 15 April 1920. See also, for example, *The Sartorial Gazette*, February 1927.

quality seems to have continued to stand in good stead to the most exclusive sections of the bespoke trade, as even supporters of the ready-to-wear trade were forced to agree that 'there is, of course, all the difference in the world between a Savile Row 14-guinea suit, and a 30s reach-me-down suit'.[27] Few doubted that high-class (and expensive) tailors in London's West End provided the discerning customer with anything other than 'a perfect-fitting garment of a distinctive character, moulded carefully to the form of the figure ... [and with a] beautiful soft finish'.[28] Savile Row tailoring continued to 'set the world standard of men's tailoring as authoritatively as the Rue de la Paix set the *fashion* for women'.[29] However, 'Savile-row cut and tailoring are one thing, and the cut and tailoring one expects and receives from the average bespoke tailor up and down the country are quite another story'.[30]

Indeed, it was this 'average bespoke tailor' who was most vulnerable to the competition of the ready-to-wear and mass-produced made-to-measure trades, and to their claims that the garments they sold offered equal – indeed, greater – style, quality and value.[31] At various times in the course of the inter-war period it seemed as if ready-to-wear and branded suits were set to parallel the success they were already enjoying in the US, and supersede the bespoke trade.[32] However, by the end of the 1930s it was widely acknowledged that the great success story of the inter-war period had proved to be the factory-produced made-to-measure suits sold in branch shops by multiple concerns such as Montague Burton and Prices Tailors.[33]

---

[27] *Men's Wear*, 11 August 1923.

[28] *The Tailor and Cutter*, 10 January 1930. See also 22 January 1925: 'quality is to be the real test in the future'. For high-class bespoke tailors' continued success in the inter-war years and beyond, see J.B. Jefferys, *Retail Trading in Britain, 1850–1950* (Cambridge University Press, Cambridge, 1954), p. 314.

[29] R. Graves and A. Hodge, *The Long Weekend: A Social History of Great Britain 1918–1939* (Abacus, London, 1995; first published 1940), p. 353.

[30] *Men's Wear*, 11 August 1923.

[31] Ugolini, 'Ready-to-wear or made-to-measure?'

[32] See, for example, *The Outfitter*, 27 March 1920; 9 October 1920; 19 July 1930; *The Tailor and Cutter*, 24 May 1935; F. Chitham, 'Some problems of the tailoring trade', in A.S. Bridgland (ed.), *The Modern Tailor Outfitter and Clothier* (Caxton Publishing, London, n.d.), vol. 1, pp. 6–8. Also M. Zakim, *Ready-Made Democracy: A History of Men's Dress in the American Republic, 1760–1860* (University of Chicago Press, Chicago, 2003). Thank you to Matthew Hilton for directing me to this book.

[33] In 1913 Burton's had 5 branches, which increased to 11 in 1914, 26 in 1916, 40 in 1919, 211 in 1925, 357 in 1930, 480 in 1935, and 595 in 1939. WYAS, Burton Archives, Box 117, Costings per shop 1919–1952; Box 149, Branch cash receipts, 1913–1916. See also Honeyman, *Well Suited*, p. 60; A. Alexander, 'Strategy and strategists: evidence from an early retail revolution in Britain', *The International Review of Retail, Distribution and Consumer Research*, vol. 1, no. 1 (1997), pp. 61–78. In 1930 Prices Tailors, the owners of the Fifty Shilling Tailors' shops, owned 109 'depots'. Two years later they bought Stewarts Clothiers Ltd, which brought an additional 130 shops. In 1939, they claimed more than 350 'depots in all principal cities and towns'. WYAS, Burton Archives, Box 36, Press Cuttings, *Yorkshire Evening Post*, 21 November 1930; *Men's Wear*, 6 February 1932; 29 October 1932; *The Cumberland News*, 18 March 1939. Unlike William Blackburn, the other pioneer, Joseph Hepworth (which sold mostly, but by no means exclusively, ready-to-wear suits and

'Mr. Average Man', constantly being told by huge advertisements in his newspaper that he could have a 'bespoke' suit for 50s, or even 37s 6d, had – it was lamented– flocked to these shops.[34]

Multiples were certainly not reticent about the claims they made for the quality and value of their garments. In 1933, for example, Burton's advertised their '4 guinea suit to measure for 45 shillings'. Addressing both 'young men and men who stay young', the advertisement suggested that 'In Springtime ... every young man's fancy turns to love – of being well dressed ... every young man can fulfil his dream and desire with but little cost, thanks to Montague Burton's Organisation'. The customer could expect 'Complete personal service, the most skilled of cutters, renowned quality of material, a wondrous choice of tints and tones in specially woven textures, dignity of style', all for a very reasonable price.[35] Burton's dinner jacket suit, available for 75 shillings, but 'worth' 7 guineas, was 'Correctly styled – tailored by skilled craftsmen. Perfect in fit and finish. The suit is no longer a luxury for the favourite few, but is priced reasonably enough for a modest income.'[36] Other firms made similar claims. William Blackburn made much of the cheapness (or 'value') of its products, but at the same time also emphasised their good quality: 'Our garments are cut on modern lines and every detail ... is carried out by craftsmen who understand the secret of well made clothes'. Indeed, 'every garment has that character which distinguishes the well-dressed man'.[37]

Responding to attacks from the bespoke section of the trade, Montague Burton asserted that 'the goods produced by the wholesale firms in Leeds and London and

---

outfitting items), continued to expand throughout the inter-war years. In 1926 the firm owned 250 branches, which by 1945 had increased to 313. Honeyman, *Well Suited*, pp. 76–7. For smaller Leeds-based multiples, including William Blackburn, see Honeyman, *Well Suited*, pp. 68–72. Also Jefferys, *Retail Trading in Britain*, pp. 295–321. For an estimate of the number of multiples in existence in 1928, see *Man and his Clothes*, September 1928.

[34] *Men's Wear*, 12 February 1938. See also ibid., 23 February 1935. Note that in 1938 it was feared that the increasing number of ready-to-wear suits stocked by independent outfitters would also prove to be a 'serious menace' to tailors. *The Tailor and Cutter*, 22 April 1938.

[35] WYAS, Burton Archives, Box 128, News Cuttings, *The Peterborough Advertiser*, 3 March 1933. Also *Evening Standard*, 28 April 1933; *Birmingham News*, 28 June 1924; *The Star*, 22 October 1937; *Perthshire Advertiser*, 26 February 1938.

[36] WYAS, Burton Archives, Box 192, Booklets and Sales Leaflets, 'Dress distinction' booklet (1933–4). For Burton's post-Second World War advertising campaigns, see F. Mort, *Cultures of Consumption: Masculinities and Social Space in Late Twentieth-Century Britain* (Routledge, London, 1996), pp. 134–44.

[37] WYAS, William Blackburn Records, G. Misc., 18 (11), Collection of brochures, Chester (1933); Leamington Spa (1936). See also K. Honeyman, 'Style monotony and the business of fashion: the marketing of menswear in inter-war England', *Textile History*, vol. 34, no. 2 (2003), pp. 171–91. The advertising strategies of inter-war tobacco manufacturers provide a useful comparison. M. Hilton, 'Advertising, the modernist aesthetic of the market place? The cultural relationship between the tobacco manufacturer and the "mass" of consumers in Britain, 1870–1940', in M. Daunton and B. Rieger (eds), *Meanings of Modernity: Britain from the Late Victorian Era to World War II* (Berg, Oxford, 2001), pp. 45–69. Also E. Furlough, 'Selling the American way in interwar France: Prix Uniques and the salons des arts menagers', *Journal of Social History*, vol. 26, no. 3 (1993), pp. 491–519.

elsewhere, though made by machinery, are as well tailored as those made by hand ... One result is that a working man can now afford to wear a well-tailored suit, and that you never see him reduced to wearing second-hand clothes, cast off by the rich.'[38] More realistically, a 'Special correspondent' to the *Stock Exchange Gazette* reported in 1932 that Burton's and Prices Tailors' success was partly due to the fact that 'it is only natural' that working-class men 'should look round not so much for the last word in superiority of style and cut as much as for the very cheapest suit that can be obtained provided it is of serviceable quality and style'.[39]

Indeed, despite the advertising claims made by multiples like Burton's or the Fifty Shilling Tailors, their customers were mostly to be found among the lower middle and respectable working classes. Although certain multiple outfitters – most notably Austin Reed – 'traded up' in the inter-war years, 'The multiple tailors admit that they can cater to one section of the population only: roughly those men earning £200 a year or less in the great industrial areas ... the poorer clerks and industrial labourers'.[40] Other multiples aimed at a still more modest market. Marks and Spencer garments, for instance, were 'a synonym of extreme cheapness'.[41] Generally, even the best mass-produced garments could hardly compete with Savile Row products.[42] However, just at a time when earlier certainties within the trade that masculine fashions could always be traced back to the shops, streets, clubs and leisure sites of London's West End evaporated, the style and look of Burton's suits proved to be highly popular, especially among younger men.[43] In 1935, Southcott shop managers complained to headquarters that they were 'not holding the young men's bespoke trade, because we do not seem to be able to give him that distinctive "City" cut which our competitors were able to give them'. Two years later, a number of the firm's managers were still pointing out that the Leeds factory did not seem able to provide them with the 'smart', or 'Burton' cut that their younger customers wanted, with its fairly broad shoulders and well-defined waist and hips. As the Wakefield manager explained, because of this, 'he had long since been obliged to leave the young man's

---

[38]   WYAS, Burton Archives, Box 36, Press Cuttings, *Yorkshire Evening Post*, 11 September 1925. See also *Men's Wear*, 13 January 1934; R. Redmayne, *Ideals in Industry: Being the Story of Montague Burton Ltd 1900–1950* (Montague Burton, Leeds, n.d. [c. 1950]), p. 81. See Chapter 4 for claims that multiples like Burton's were contributing to a new 'democratisation' of clothes consumption.

[39]   WYAS, Burton Archives, Box 36, Press Cuttings, *Stock Exchange Gazette*, 29 July 1932.

[40]   *Man and his Clothes*, September 1928. The connotations of class associated with mass-produced garments are explored in Chapter 4.

[41]   E. Blishen, *Sorry Dad* (Allison and Busby, London, 1984; first published 1978), p. 148.

[42]   Amies, *The Englishman's Suit*, p. 29.

[43]   In 1925 it was confidently stated that 'the West End of London sets the fashions for the rest of the country'. *The Tailor and Cutter*, 19 February 1925. But see also *The Tailor and Cutter*, 21 November 1930; 7 June 1935. A good deal of attention was devoted to the issue of 'fashion' by the trade press, and particularly to the question of how and why certain fashions developed. The aim, ultimately, was to develop methods whereby trends in menswear styles could be predicted, and therefore more easily and quickly supplied. Market research, it was believed, would play a central role in this context. See, for example, *Men's Wear*, 28 November 1931; 9 February 1935; 8 January 1938; *The Sartorial Gazette*, May 1927; July 1927.

trade alone'. Eventually it was decided that the head cutter, clearly somewhat at a loss, 'should get one of Burtons' suits and see if the firm cannot give the Branches what they ask for in the matter of the Burton type of "City" cut & style'.[44]

The shopping experience: independent tailors

The style and quality of the goods offered by various firms were central to inter-war debates about the relative advantages of shopping for clothes with the 'small man' or with the big business, be it department store, co-op shop or multiple branch. However, it was also acknowledged that when men came to choose where to buy a new shirt, suit or socks, other considerations also played their part: the shopping experience the retailer could offer remained fundamental. In 1931, A.L.W. described how he had found in an isolated Yorkshire village a bespoke tailor seemingly 'undismayed by the growth of the multiple tailoring firms which offer a five-guinea suit for fifty shillings'. He obviously had few competitors within easy reach: 'Occasionally a young fellow … might go up to one of the towns and buy a "West End suit", but it usually was of little use for country wear, even on Sundays. Besides, the young men seldom had two guineas all at one time'. The local men had also given up buying their clothes by mail order, as the poor fit of these garments had 'soon damped the ardour of the enthusiasts'. Understandably, this village tailor saw no need to change his products (he had, for example, never made a suit of plus-fours, and did not intend to start doing so), or the look of his shop: his window was adorned by 'three pattern-bundles' and by a twenty-five-year-old style-plate. As 'nobody in that part of the country was ever in a hurry about fashion, he just left the picture where it was!' A.L.W. only had kind words for this Yorkshire 'craftsman' and his frankly antiquated and idiosyncratic business practices. However, it is doubtful whether he would have advised any of the readers of *Men's Wear* to follow his example.[45]

Indeed, continuing a trend already evident before the war, the inter-war trade press never tired of stressing the importance of 'good' and 'modern' business practices to ensure that independent retailers should not only survive, but even prosper. Multiple stores, with their 'Crystal Palace and chromium shop fronts, miniature arcades and a labyrinth of neon signs' may have been, in Cynicus's words, showy and worthless 'tinsel' in comparison to the independent bespoke tailor's solid 'gold'. However, the notion that the 'tailor-cutter', with his 'individual artistry' and 'dingy' shop had 'no fear of the multiple shop', and that he had 'no need of plate glass … or an effusion of … lights picking out his name', must by 1935 have rang very hollow to readers of *The Tailor and Cutter*.[46] On the contrary, most trade commentators agreed that the

---

[44]   Southcott was a relatively small Leeds-based multiple, with nine branch shops in 1931. WYAS, C.G. Southcott Co-partnership Ltd, Meeting of directors minute book (1920–1977), 31 January 1935; 30 January 1936; 21 January 1937. This bit of industrial espionage finally seems to have worked, and in 1938 managers expressed their satisfaction with the factory's efforts. Ibid., 3 February 1938.

[45]   *Men's Wear*, 29 August 1931.

[46]   *The Tailor and Cutter*, 12 April 1935. See also the varied responses to the question of 'How to stimulate business', in *The Sartorial Gazette*, January 1927.

small shopkeeper, content to sit in his obscure and unattractive shop, hidden from sight on a side-street, was destined to failure, whatever the quality of his wares. According to one trade commentator, there were in 1928 plenty of small shops that had failed to keep up with the times: 'Their stock is old-fashioned, their windows resemble those of junk shops, their interiors are dark and miserable, their clientele is dying off.' These were the shops – it was stressed – that sooner or later would fall victim to multiples' competition.[47]

The solution was to adopt 'modern' commercial practices. Advertising, it was emphasised, had become an absolute necessity. The language of psychology was increasingly used to reinforce a message already common before the war: that advertising not only alerted potential customers to a retailer's existence, but could actually influence consumers' behaviour: 'Thousands of men and women subconsciously ... [want] clothes. In everyone of us are wishes and requirements lying dormant ... waiting to be fished up from the dim and quiescent subconscious to the urgent conscious ... advertising is the clarion which reaches the far-off people, and the megaphone which is heard by the crowd.'[48] In the early 1920s, Henry Elliott was already cautioning small retailers that 'You may jeer at "brass and glass", but the truth is that these brass and glass shops make more profit and make it more easily.' These businesses, having carefully chosen their location, made sure that their windows and shop fronts were attractive and well-displayed, frequently employing 'men who have the gift necessary for this special work'. According to Elliott, small traders – and bespoke tailors in particular – did not seem 'to have grasped the value of an attractive display ... You may be able to do a good business with a dull and dingy window, but it is certain that you will do a much bigger business if the window be nicely decorated and ornamented and the goods shown really tastefully.'[49] In 1930 there still existed shops that decorated their windows solely with a wire blind, perhaps discreetly announcing the name of the firm in small gilt lettering, but it was only the most exclusive and prestigious firms that could afford not to advertise, and to scorn any attempt 'to attract the attention of passers-by to their wares'.[50]

Uncluttered styles of window display, with selected items artistically arranged, frequently around a particular 'theme', were increasingly associated with dynamic and modern business methods: 'the old styles of higgledy-piggledy display simply let folk know what was in a shop. The modern method focuses attention on goods in such a fashion that to see is to covet.'[51] Unusual, attractive and well-lit (ideally by electricity) window displays and shop fronts suggested to the potential buyer that 'the same enterprise, modernity and freshness are to be found' in the stock inside the shop[52] (Figure 7.1). Unfortunately, however, only too often the windows of the

---

[47]   *Man and his Clothes*, October 1928.
[48]   *The Tailor and Cutter*, 7 May 1925.
[49]   *Men's Wear*, 7 April 1923.
[50]   *The Tailor and Cutter*, 11 July 1930.
[51]   *The Tailor and Cutter*, 15 February 1935. See also *The Outfitter*, 19 June 1920; 20 June 1936.
[52]   *The Outfitter*, 15 March 1930. See also *Men's Wear*, 27 July 1935; *The Outfitter*, 18 October 1930; 20 June 1936.

independent trader were 'deadly, his merchandise often looks as if a good pressing would improve it, his tickets are lifeless ... instead of offering the bright new goods which almost every young and middle aged man now seeks, he continues to offer the same old drab patterns'. All things considered, he practically drove customers 'into the clutches of the "50s suit for 5d fraternity"'.[53]

Advice stressing the importance of advertising and of window displays for independent traders who wished to survive, and indeed flourish, had already been common before the war. However, the inter-war years also saw an increasing emphasis on the importance of shop interiors in the menswear trade, especially among outfitters.[54] As M.H. Deacon, a member of the British Association of Display Men, emphasised in 1923, once the potential customer had been lured into the shop, it was important that 'the good impression made by the window should not be neutralised owing to the interior being inconsistent with the exterior': to skimp on 'modern' fixtures, fittings and furnishings was a 'false economy'. Although, he continued, it had been asserted in the past that 'the average man shopper, for some psychological reason, objects to entering a

Figure 7.1　　Before and after: an old-fashioned and a modern shop-front. *Man and his Clothes*, **April 1928. By permission of the British Library, LD171.**

carpeted shop, or one that carries the appearance of elegance or ultra-smartness', this was no longer the case (if indeed it had ever really been): 'The discerning man to-day prefers to enter a shop that bears the hall-mark of smartness and the

---

[53]　*Men's Wear*, 5 February 1927.

[54]　On Edwardian shop interiors, see C. Breward, *The Hidden Consumer: Masculinities, Fashion and City Life 1860–1914* (Manchester University Press, Manchester, 1999), pp. 143–7. In 1936, A. Edward Hammond pointed out that, despite the advice of the trade press, most retailers continued to neglect interior display. *The Outfitter*, 5 September 1936.

atmosphere of efficiency, knowing full well that it is the reflection of the firm's methods as a whole.'[55] The distinction between 'modern' and 'old-fashioned' fixtures and fittings was key to setting successful, go-head businesses apart from their outmoded, struggling counterparts. The fitting rooms of 'many of the most up-to-date outfitters', for example, were equipped with 'a wall-case in the shape of a draw-out, sliding fitting, with opening sashes fronted with mirrors'.[56] In the main shop area, glass display cases and counters of various sizes, rather than open shelves and boxed goods, were considered indispensable for any up-to-date business, as were the fixtures and display stands around which smaller merchandise such as gloves, ties or handkerchiefs could be attractively arranged.[57]

Such glass and chromium counters and cases, it was emphasised, provided a new and modern visual element to men's shopping experience: not only did these fixtures make it easier for salesmen to access the merchandise, but customers could also look at the goods while waiting to be served. In 1925 the Cheapside branch of the outfitting firm of Hope Bros was extensively refitted. The shop carried 'A heavy stock of sports suits and flannels, but every garment is clearly seen and easily inspected'.[58] Like most of their competitors, Cooke's, a London-based firm of shopfitters, made this visual element the central theme of their advertising strategy, emphasising that their fittings placed 'every article … in full view of your customer, yet free from dust … the required article is easily seen by the assistant – no fumbling with dusty parcels whilst the customer waits'. The stock, they pointed out, would no longer be 'lying idle behind cupboard doors or under counters'; it would be 'ready for sale yet not exposed to dust and dirt'.[59] The reference to dirt was not accidental. Indeed, one of the chief characteristics generally perceived to distinguish 'modern' from 'old-fashioned' frontages and interiors was that the former were 'clean' and bright, while the latter were fusty, dingy and 'dirty'. Discussing an 'up-to-date' shop in a working-class district of East London in 1936, A. Edward Hammond denied 'that shabby shops are more suitable for the poorer district than clean, modern premises'. Almost ten years earlier, the recently-renovated Glasgow branch of Hope Bros was described as 'spacious, nicely arranged, hygienically heated and ventilated, clean and tidy, all conducive to good salesmanship'[60] (Figure 7.2).

In a well-run shop, the trade press emphasised, enticingly displayed merchandise, both in the window and within the shop, performed the fundamental function of arousing the potential customer's acquisitive impulses. However, it was recognised – rather regretfully at times – that commodities were not quite able to sell

---

[55]   *Men's Wear*, 4 August 1923. The British Association of Display Men was established in 1909. See S. Lomax, 'The view from the shop: window display, the shopper and the formulation of theory', in J. Benson and L. Ugolini (eds), *Cultures of Selling: Perspectives on Consumption and Society Since 1700* (Ashgate, Aldershot, 2006), pp. 265–92.

[56]   *Men's Wear*, 22 January 1927.

[57]   *The Outfitter*, 10 January 1920; 3 January 1925; 11 July 1925; 15 August 1936; *Men's Wear*, 30 July 1927.

[58]   *The Outfitter*, 12 September 1925.

[59]   *The Outfitter*, 19 September 1925. See also, for example, *The Outfitter*, 11 January 1930; 15 March 1930.

[60]   *The Outfitter*, 20 June 1936; *Men's Wear*, 18 June 1927.

themselves, and still required the input of a salesman to conclude the sales transaction. Customers may increasingly have been allowed to look at the merchandise more or less undisturbed, but this was a long way from self-service: the salesman's role as intermediary was still considered essential, and 'good' salesmanship fundamental to a successful business. Even when firms sold roughly similar goods, it was generally believed that 'one house will forge ahead of four or five competitors similarly placed'. This 'notable development' was 'due to the way clients have been handled'.[61]

In 1925 *The Tailor and Cutter* devoted a front-page article to a discussion of the selling practices that made for a 'successful tailoring business'. It began by stressing the importance not only of craft knowledge on the part of the salesman, but also of 'what constitutes elegant and beautiful attire', and of the various textiles used in the making of clothes, including 'the newest materials'. This, it was suggested, not only 'helps in offering wise advice' to customers, 'but there is an added feeling of pleasure and power in the possession of textile information'. Moreover, the cutter, salesman or manager 'should be conversant with the etiquette of dress, that he may advise his customers', as well as with 'suitable and fashionable collars, ties, hats, etc.'. The cutter should also be 'acquainted with the effects of varying styles of cut and patterns of material on different figures'. The aim was 'not merely to fit a customer, but to dress him with elegance and distinction'. Last, but certainly not least, were 'personality' and salesmanship: the ability not only to 'get on easy terms with those he does business with, but to sway them in their choice'.[62]

Indeed, although a technical knowledge of textiles, dress and fashion was clearly considered essential to good salesmanship, sales assistants' appearance and behaviour towards customers also continued to be perceived as crucial: while one assistant might behave as if he had 'been disturbed at some more alluring task, and looks upon the intruder as a necessary evil', another will convey 'the feeling that he is glad to see you and pleased to render service'. It is not difficult to guess which man was considered by the trade press to be more likely to succeed in business.[63] The relationship between buyers and sellers of menswear will be considered further in the final section of this book. However, it is worth noting here that in issues of salesmanship, as in display and advertising, the language of psychology was increasingly applied in the inter-war period to well-rehearsed trade press advice on how to successfully deal with the clientele, effect a sale and inspire customer loyalty. In 1920 A.B. Wakefield declared himself 'a diligent student of the principles of psychology as applied to salesmanship'. He stressed that in order to achieve success, salesmen needed to 'have an understanding of that branch of knowledge of the mind which we derive from a careful examination of the facts of consciousness. Indeed, the most successful salesmen to-day are men who know the laws of the human mind, and how the mind acts; what repels and what attracts.' This new terminology of

---

[61]   *The Tailor and Cutter*, 11 June 1925.

[62]   *The Tailor and Cutter*, 26 February 1925. For the 'small tailor' as 'dress expert', see *The Tailor and Cutter*, 28 February 1930. For knowledge of brands making the retailer 'an expert and not an automaton in distribution', see *Men's Wear*, 24 March 1923.

[63]   *The Tailor and Cutter*, 11 June 1925. See also *The Outfitter*, 19 April 1930. On salesmen's appearance, see, for example, *Men's Wear*, 13 September 1919; *The Outfitter*, 19 September 1936.

The Art of the Shopfitter

The hat dept. of Noel Bros. Ltd., Westminster, S.W., showing fixtures and sundry pieces of equipment in ancona walnut with new type disappearing flaps.

THREE NEW INTERIORS

The ground floor of Austin Reed's Oxford-street shop, looking towards the entrance.

A section of the first floor, with its large area of window lighting at the Oxford-street shop of Austin Reed, Ltd. The floor is mainly for the sale of shirts, pyjamas, underwear &c. The installations in each case were carried out by E. Pollard & Co., Ltd.

Figure 7.2   'The art of the shopfitter': three modern interiors. *The Tailor and Cutter*, 3 May 1935. By permission of the British Library, LD163.

'consciousness' and of the 'human mind' was applied to well-established advice about the shop assistant's need to anticipate and then accommodate customers' requirements and desires in a sales transaction.[64]

The shopping experience: multiples

In 1923 a contributor to *Men's Wear* claimed that customers were leaving multiple firms in droves, having found to their cost that these retailers' advertising claims did not match the reality of the merchandise they sold. Chastened, they were returning to independent traders: 'to the merchant tailor and the retail clothier, for fair value at a fair price plus a straight deal'.[65] However, his complacency was not widely shared. On the contrary, most trade commentators feared that small retailers were on the brink of disaster. They tirelessly stressed that good-quality and good-value merchandise, vigorous advertising, an attractive shop and effective salesmanship, were all fundamental to the establishment of a successful, modern business, which could withstand the competition of department stores, co-ops, firms that sent out agents to canvass for orders door-to-door, and especially of multiples. However, unfortunately for small shopkeepers, advertising, display and salesmanship were also key features of large businesses such as Burton's, the Fifty Shilling Tailors and Hepworth, who, in addition, were able to enjoy the advantages of economies of scale, of a cash-only trade, and of much larger advertising and display budgets.[66]

For their part, independent retailers' representatives argued that the smaller size of the independent shop could be turned to advantage, if it meant the opportunity to bring very important 'individual' and 'personal' elements to the business. Just as many contemporary commentators were lamenting the uniformity and monotony of contemporary consumer culture, independent bespoke tailors frequently stressed the individuality of their products.[67] In 1927, for example, *The Sartorial Gazette* published a full-page statement (intended to be cut out, framed, and displayed in the shop window), which concluded by reiterating: 'Genuine tailor-made garments embody style and individuality; while factory-made clothing presents "dead-level uniformity".'[68] According to Oliver Payne, writing in *The Tailor and Cutter*, this was the large stores' weak spot: the fact that they were 'most anxious to standardise their stock and their methods', with the result that many potential customers left department stores or multiples without making any purchase, having been unable to find exactly what they wanted among 'the standardised lines stocked by these organisations'.[69] Henry Elliott believed that 'the real chance the one-shop man gets

[64]   *The Outfitter*, 17 April 1920. See also *The Tailor and Cutter*, 11 April 1930. For a more sceptical approach to the psychology of salesmanship, see *The Outfitter*, 27 September 1930.

[65]   *Men's Wear*, 20 January 1923.

[66]   See, for example, *Men's Wear*, 6 January 1923: 'the big houses ... look upon five or ten thousand pounds [spent on advertising] as a fly in the ointment'; *Men's Wear*, 7 April 1923. The use of credit in the tailoring trade will be explored further in Chapter 9.

[67]   *The Tailor and Cutter*, 19 September 1930.

[68]   *The Sartorial Gazette*, January 1927.

[69]   *The Tailor and Cutter*, 31 May 1935.

is that he can pander somewhat more easily to the little peculiarities and special wants of his customers'.[70] 'C. W.-J.' pushed the argument further, and suggested in 1930 that nationally-advertised branded goods were not, and neither were they likely to become, popular as 'Clothes, being personal entities, must be sold in a personal way'. The 'personal quality' of shirts, collars, socks or ties was especially important to 'the man whose taste is reasonably well-educated. He prefers the shop where he can purchase clothes not so communist in their style, brand or get-up'.[71] At least some independent shops, such as the Wimbledon-based Bardales, successfully marketed themselves as catering for the customer who 'prefers to be treated as an individual in the matter of clothes'[72] (Figure 7.3).

Independent retailers, it was further asserted, were able to provide a uniquely customised service. Indeed, 'It is the personal relationship which tells with the small trader',[73] and 'personality remains the most valuable hidden asset on your balance sheet'.[74] As Austin Reed commented in his speech to the 1923 Clothing Exhibition, 'in many respects the individual was able, through the personal element, to give better service'.[75] In order to capitalise on this, the independent retailer 'must partake in all local affairs, he must constantly be in contact with customers, he must be a well-known man, and a popular man; he must be the final court of appeal on matters of men's dress in the locality'.[76] After all, the small retailer was not 'bound by cast-iron regulations laid down by head-quarters'. He could give the business 'proprietorial instead of managerial attention, and there is always an attraction to the customer in dealing with the owner of a business rather than with an employee'.[77] The customer, it was pointed out in 1930, was unlikely to be greeted by Mr 'Harrod' or Mr 'Whiteley' at the front door of his shop. The heads of such huge concerns could hardly know 'whether your settled taste is for one type of shirt or sock, or another. Not that his deputies take much interest in the matter either.'[78] As a *Tailor and Cutter* editorial observed: 'The large stores can show grandeur and space, indeed, they make a feature of display; but the friendliness and intimacy are to seek.'[79]

However, even independents' most ardent supporters had to admit that despite its inability to get 'to the heart of the shopper, the modern-minded big store' counterbalanced this 'by creating a warm "welcome-in-and-be-at-home" atmosphere about the place', whereby the customer could 'enjoy the delights of a club-like rest lounge, or perhaps the cool quiet of a roof garden'.[80] Indeed, despite the attempts of

---

[70]   *Men's Wear*, 7 April 1923.
[71]   *Man and his Clothes*, August 1930.
[72]   *Men's Wear*, 27 August 1938. See also *The Outfitter*, 24 January 1925.
[73]   *The Tailor and Cutter*, 8 January 1925.
[74]   *The Outfitter*, 8 February 1936.
[75]   *Men's Wear*, 24 March 1923.
[76]   *Man and his Clothes*, November 1928.
[77]   *Men's Wear*, 25 June 1927. See also *Men's Wear*, 26 March 1927.
[78]   *The Outfitter*, 8 February 1930.
[79]   *The Tailor and Cutter*, 31 January 1930. See also *Man and his Clothes*, November 1928.
[80]   *The Outfitter*, 8 February 1930.

Figure 7.3   Independent bespoke tailoring: 'Real tailoring'. *The Sartorial Gazette*, January 1932. By permission of the British Library, 125.

individual independent retailers such as Dudley Beck, a Chester tailor and outfitter, who in 1930 had a miniature golf course built adjacent to his shop, larger retailers were financially better placed to develop facilities that linked the shop to male leisure practices.[81] This was not always an unmixed blessing: in 1937, for example, the tenant of the cigarette kiosk at the basement of Burton's New Oxford Street branch warned head office that the building had become 'the haunt of gamblers', 'of women of doubtful character, the undesirable habitués of same, and characters known to the police'.[82] Overall, however, the provision of billiard halls in Burton's branch buildings or of lounges, restaurants and smoking rooms in department stores, proved both popular and profitable.[83]

For most retailers, independent or multiple, opportunities to add leisure facilities to the shop were limited by spatial (as well as financial) considerations. However, pleasant, well-maintained and 'modern' shops, located on prime commercial

---

[81]   *The Tailor and Cutter*, 10 October 1930.

[82]   WYAS, Burton Archives, Box 127, '300 branch file', 30 November 1937.

[83]   K. Honeyman, 'Following suit: men, masculinity and gendered practices in the clothing trade in Leeds, England, 1890–1940', *Gender & History*, vol. 14, no. 3 (2002), p. 440.

sites, were as important to large retailers' business strategies as to independents'. Photographs of Edwardian William Blackburn branch shops, or of Montague Burton's first shop, opened in Chesterfield in 1904, show that there was little to differentiate these, with their crowded window displays, large price tickets and garments festooned around the entrance, from any other cheap clothier aiming to attract a price-conscious clientele.[84] However, all this changed in the inter-war period, as multiples, with Burton's in the lead, paid increasing attention to the 'look' of their shops. By 1922 Burton's inspectors were being instructed to check that 'customers are properly and civilly served', that the shop was 'clean and inviting', stock 'properly dusted and kept neat', all the 'brasswork ... kept polished' and furniture, including chairs and mirrors, 'kept in good repair'. No detail was to be overlooked: 'Is edging cut off properly from window bottom paper?', inspectors were reminded to check.[85] In 1931 *Men's Wear* observed that Montague Burton's branches had 'been improving the tone of their displays considerably'.[86] A year later, a manual for branch managers underlined the new importance of window display, stressing that when well arranged, this 'is a greater selling force than all the newspaper publicity combined ... An ideal window display makes every garment look worth double'.[87] Equal, if not greater, attention was devoted to developing good salesmanship: 'the customer should be attended to in a business-like way ... when you speak do so with confidence, assurance and brevity'. 'Selling facts' were to be presented 'in such a way that your customer is persuaded that what you are offering him is undoubtedly all that you claim it to be'. Significantly, salesmen were reminded to take care of their appearance, since 'the personal element is strong in business'.[88] According to F. Chitham, a Harrods director, 'A salesman is not engaged merely to sell goods, but also to sell service, and to do this successfully he should know something of the technique of the trade'.[89]

The priorities of many large-scale retailers – advertising, display, and salesmanship – were the same as those of their independent counterparts, the difference being that they were generally able to invest a good deal more money on these than independent retailers. In 1930 it was suggested that recent developments in shopfitting had 'brought modern selling equipment and well-constructed shop fronts within range of the capital of the small retailer'. No longer was 'the well-planned, up-to-date shop ... the prerogative of the wealthy trader'.[90] However, this seems to have been an exaggeration: renovating shop interiors and exteriors remained a significant expense,

[84] WYAS, William Blackburn Records, C. Branches, 7(5) branch photographs, Stockton-on-Tees, n.d. [c. 1890]; Halifax, n.d. [c. 1890]; Brighton, n.d. [c. 1914?]; Castleford, n.d. [c. 1890] (reproduced also in Honeyman, *Well Suited*, p. 38); Middlesbrough, n.d. [c. 1890]; E.M. Sigsworth, *Montague Burton: The Tailor of Taste* (Manchester University Press, Manchester, 1990), opposite p. 40.

[85] WYAS, Burton Archives, Box 128, 'Inspectors' Manual', 1922, pp. 3, 10, 11.

[86] *Men's Wear*, 28 November 1931.

[87] WYAS, Burton Archives, Box 128, 'Manager's Guide', 1932, p. 37.

[88] WYAS, Burton Archives, Box 191, 'Clothing Classes Curriculum', 1935, pp. 24, 26. See also Box 250, 'Scientific Selling', 1927.

[89] Chitham, 'Some problems of the tailoring trade', p. 5. Chitham also emphasised the personal element and the 'intimacy' involved in tailoring.

[90] *Men's Wear*, 11 October 1930.

with no guarantee – despite the claims made in the trade press – that it would lead to increased sales. The amount of money invested by the larger multiples in the appearance of their shops gives some indication of the scale of the expenditure they could afford. In 1918, for example, Hepworth's 'retail plant' was valued at £27,000. This had roughly doubled by 1922, increasing to just over £100,000 in 1926 (by which time the firm had 250 branches), to almost £150,000 by 1932 and £220,000 by 1938.[91] The company's records indicate that expenditure was devoted both to the structural alteration of shops, and to the replacement of outdated fixtures and fittings. In 1925, for example, new linoleum, sofas, radiators, electric light, fascias, blinds and neon signs were all purchased. Smaller items included screens to form a fitting room in Cheltenham, a mahogany table and garment rails in Lincoln, mirrors and a showcase in Edinburgh. The Blackburn shop was more extensively renovated: the shop front was remodelled, a new window enclosure and fascia created, and electric light installed by the shopfitters Davis Ltd.[92]

However, even Hepworth's investment pales in comparison with Montague Burton's. In 1919 Burton's shop fixtures were valued at around £5,300 for 40 branches, or the relatively modest sum of £132.50 per branch. By 1925 the value had increased to £339,000 for 211 branches, or £1,607 per branch. After a dip in 1929 (to £231,000 for 333 branches, or £694 per branch), the value recovered, reaching a total of £394,000 for 434 branches in 1933, or £908 per branch.[93] Particularly in the 1930s, the opening of new Burton's shops generally followed an extensive programme of renovation and refitting. In 1933, for example, the shop front and interior of the new branch in Romford were redesigned by the Leeds firm of John Curtis and Son. The result was a 'modern' shop front, 'an extensive and uninterrupted expanse of glass for window display purposes, which affords the greatest opportunity to exhibit Suitings, Model Suits and Raincoats, and these may be viewed from any angle without obstruction, as would be the case with less modern forms of construction and design'. To this was added the 'inviting interior, spacious in extent, elegantly appointed, and completely equipped'.[94] By the 1930s, Burton's and other large-scale

---

[91]   WYAS, J. Hepworth and Sons Archives, Accounts, balance sheets, 1914–1939. In 1945 the firm had 313 stores. Honeyman, *Well Suited*, p. 65.

[92]   WYAS, J. Hepworth and Sons Archives, Plant Ledger, 1925–52. See also Honeyman, *Well Suited*, pp. 63–8; 77. As Honeyman points out, Hepworth shops specialised in outfitting, rather than tailoring, which helps explain the presence of garment rails and showcases.

[93]   It seems likely, however, that much of the annual expenditure on fixtures and fittings would have gone towards fitting out new branches. If this was indeed the case, then it can be calculated that between 1919 and 1920, roughly £900 was spent on each of the twenty new branches, £5,000 on each of thirteen between 1925 and 1926, and £2,700 on each of twenty between 1932 and 1933. WYAS, Burton Archives, Box 117, costing per shop, 1919–1952; balance sheets, 1917–1933. See also Sigsworth, *Montague Burton*, especially pp. 45–8. Honeyman has noted that Burton was an 'outstanding example' of a company that from the 1920s used its 'property assets as a major source of expansion finance'. Honeyman, *Well Suited*, p. 58. See also Alexander, 'Strategy and strategists'.

[94]   WYAS, Burton Archives, Box 128, News Cuttings, *The Romford Times*, 15 March 1933. This blurb was clearly written by the company. Compare it, for example, with the almost identical piece published in WYAS, Burton Archives, Box 128, News Cuttings, *The Bucks Free*

retailers' shops would have presented prospective customers with a modern exterior, characterised by extensive use of plate glass windows, recessed entrances (which extended the space available for display), an architectural up-to-the-minute lack of ornamentation and a skilful use of electric lighting: by 1938, 298 Burton's branches out of the almost 600 had some form of neon sign.[95]

Not many independents were able to afford expenditure on such a scale. In 1938 the Sheffield-based tailor Lew Harbour, who claimed 2,500 regular customers, spent thousands of pounds on improvements to his shop. These included the incorporation of 'an up-to-date fitting room which would do credit to a West-End tailor', and a 'Baronial Lounge', fitted with oak panelling and flooring, and complete with a tiger or bear skin on the floor. Nevertheless, Harbour, like other independent shopkeepers, such as the Rochester-based Featherstones, who 'realised the need for changing their shop-front to bring it into keeping with changing times and conditions', were clearly the exception, rather than the rule.[96]

Indeed, the tribulations of the small Leeds-based multiple C.G. Southcott, which in 1931 had nine branches (all concentrated in the north of England), shows something of the soul-searching that preceded even a fairly prosperous firm's decision to invest precious capital in shop improvements at a time of deep economic uncertainty. In 1933 Mr Southcott warned that something had to be done about the Goole shop, and suggested that £600 'should be spent on improving the shop front'. Although the company's directors agreed that the appearance of the shop needed to be brought 'up to date', in the end it was decided to postpone any work, until it was 'worthwhile'. However, a year later Mr Southcott was adamant that in the case of the Wakefield branch, 'it was absolutely necessary ... to bring this very old-fashioned shop up to date by putting in a new front, with new fixtures', and a tender of £1,482 by a firm of shopfitters had been accepted. Disappointingly, however, the work did not bear immediate fruit, and it was not until 1937 that the branch's takings slowly began to improve. Unsurprisingly, perhaps, the issue of shop improvements then fell off the agenda for the rest of the 1930s.[97]

The modern tailoring shop

Throughout the inter-war period, independent retailers were repeatedly called upon to adopt 'modern' trading and business methods in order to survive.[98] 'Modernity', after all, 'is nowadays regarded as the keystone of successful business, and

---

Press, 17 March 1933. See also a similar piece in WYAS, Burton Archives, Box 219, Newspaper Cuttings, *Epsom Courier and Ewell Times*, 10 July 1937. For an earlier example, see WYAS, Burton Archives, Box 219, Newspaper Cuttings, *Birmingham News*, 28 June 1924.

[95] WYAS, Burton Archives, Box 129, 'Neon Signs'.

[96] *Men's Wear*, 6 August 1938.

[97] WYAS, C.G. Southcott Co-partnership Ltd, Meeting of directors minute book (1920–1977), 27 April 1933; 25 January 1934; 11 April 1935; 30 January 1936; 21 January 1937.

[98] See also, for example, *The Outfitter*, 2 May 1925; 7 June 1930; *Men's Wear*, 7 September 1935.

old-fashioned retail premises and selling methods are for the most part being discarded'.[99] However, it is clear that as far as the menswear trade was concerned, it was multiples and department stores that were generally associated with an attractive and enticing image of modernity. Multiple branch shops were not as self-consciously 'modern' in conception, layout and design as many department stores' newly established 'man's shops', or as purpose-built stores such as Simpson Piccadilly, first opened in London in 1936 as a 'department store for men'.[100] However, they successfully established a distinctively contemporary and easily recognisable presence on the shopping street. As *The Joint Stock Companies' Journal* remarked in 1931: 'the large white buildings of modern design … in the principal streets of many cities and towns must be familiar to most members of the public'.[101] Their look, it was emphasised, set them apart from their independent counterparts. As Stanley Burton sought to make clear in the speeches he gave to mark the opening of new Burton's branches, the firm saw itself as participating in a move towards the architectural modernisation of commercial transactions: 'It is an easy matter to conform to the old mid-Victorian methods of trading, in tiny, confined, unhealthy shops, but to-day we celebrate the transformation of an ancient block … to a building of beauty and character'.[102]

Nevertheless, it would be misleading to suggest that there was a clear dividing line between old-fashioned, failing independent shops and thriving, modern multiples. First of all, there were plenty of unashamedly 'old-fashioned' independent shops that continued to be successful. The reason for this, it was suggested, was that 'the buying public is curiously constituted. For the most part it likes modernity – spacious shops, tastefully-dressed windows – crisp and smart (yet courteous) salesmanship, but, on the other hand, it retains a covert yet sincere regard for the old-fashioned'. The modern might have been 'gratifying' to contemporary tastes, but the old-fashioned was 'soothing'. Provided that the historic character of the shop was carefully constructed and marketed, it could provide the proprietor of a 'scientifically' old-fashioned business with a number of assets: 'a venerable building, a unique frontage … a good reputation, based upon many years of trading'.[103] Sidney Heath was one such businessman. His highly successful Swansea shop, located in a timbered building that had 'the quiet atmosphere of the Old World' and a 'Medieval'

---

[99] *Men's Wear*, 3 December 1927.

[100] For Harrods' man's shop see, for example, *The Outfitter*, 11 October 1930; *The Tailor and Cutter*, 24 October 1930. For Simpson Piccadilly, see B. Edwards, 'A man's world? Masculinity and metropolitan modernity at Simpson Piccadilly', in D. Gilbert, D. Matless and B. Short (eds), *Geographies of British Modernity: Space and Society in the Twentieth Century* (Blackwell Publishing, Oxford, 2003), pp. 151–67; *The Outfitter*, 2 May 1936. For another example of 'modernist shopfitting and display', see Walter Scott's shop in Regent Street, opened in 1935. *The Tailor and Cutter*, 12 July 1935. See also Austin Reed's flagship store, also situated in Regent Street, which in 1930 opened a 'Louis XIV room' and a 'Red lacquer room'. *The Outfitter*, 12 April 1930; *The Bystander*, 23 April 1930. Also B. Ritchie, *A Touch of Class: The Story of Austin Reed* (James and James, London, 1990).

[101] WYAS, Burton Archives, Box 36, Press Cuttings, *The Joint Stock Companies' Journal*, 30 September 1931. See also Honeyman, 'Following suit', p. 436.

[102] WYAS, Burton Archives, Box 219, Typescript of speech by Stanley H. Burton, Morecambe, 29 January 1937.

[103] *Men's Wear*, 3 December 1927. See also, for example, ibid., 15 October 1938.

character, was fittingly (if perhaps not in a historically accurate way) called 'Beau Nash House'. As *Men's Wear*'s 'Swansea Correspondent' pointed out in 1935, the architecture, interior and atmosphere of the shop all consciously sought to create a 'traditional', and indeed 'medieval', 'look'. Importantly, however, beneath the 'historical' surface was an efficient and modern business: 'There is nothing medieval about Mr Heath ... or his business methods. There is a modern style and efficiency throughout the general conduct of his business which has brought its reward in a large and satisfied custom'.[104]

Where possible, large-scale businesses were just as keen as their independent competitors to make use of the glamour of 'historic' buildings and interiors. Thus, in 1936 the Leeds-based manufacturer Joseph May and Sons, which specialised in high-class ready-to-wear clothing, opened a show-room in London's Regent Street to display their 'Maenson' models. Eschewing modern designs, they opted for a Regency setting, and decorated the display rooms with early eighteenth-century furniture, including 'mahogany tables for showing patterns ... [a] beautifully moulded genuine Adam mantelpiece ... a rounded mahogany cabinet, with gilt decorations ... small Georgian mirrors'. Overall, the impression was one of elegance and aristocratic good taste: 'One could picture the famous Beau [Brummell] quite at home in this room'.[105]

But most damagingly for independent bespoke tailors, many multiples were also able to successfully blend their modern frontages, up-to-date business methods and products with much of the atmosphere, look and feel of 'traditional' tailoring shops. The mahogany tables, mirrors, fashion plates, dark wooden shelves and panelling, even the tape measure around the salesman's neck, all followed the precedent set by bespoke shops.[106] Although no clothes production actually took place on the premises, the rolls of cloth on prominent display and the staff room marked 'cutters' room', all served to hint at bespoke craft work.[107] In 1928 a *Man and his Clothes* 'special correspondent' confidently asserted that multiple tailors' shops would never be able to achieve a proper tailoring 'atmosphere'.[108] However, there is little evidence that customers found the experience of buying their clothes from a chain any more ersatz than in a small independent shop whose own manufacturing had been partly or entirely entrusted to a separate firm. It is hard to blame them. At their best, multiples' premises would have looked like bespoke tailors' shops, except brighter, more spacious, tidier and better-organised, the fixtures and fittings more up-to-date, the frontage and window displays more modern and better lit. And the clothes, of course, were reasonably priced and not too bad-looking either.[109]

---

[104] *Men's Wear*, 22 June 1935. See also, for example, Lilly's, an independent Liverpool outfitter whose frontage had been 'carried out in the semi-Tudor style, with a painted sign hanging over the door bearing the head of a Georgian beau'. *Man and his Clothes*, March 1930.

[105] *The Outfitter*, 31 October 1936. For Joseph May and Sons, see Honeyman, *Well Suited*, pp. 288–9.

[106] See, for example, WYAS, Burton Archives, Box 219, Newspaper Cuttings, *Epsom Courier and Ewell Times*, 10 July 1937.

[107] Honeyman, 'Style monotony', p. 182.

[108] *Man and his Clothes*, September 1928.

[109] H. Levy, *The Shops of Britain: A Study of Retail Distribution* (Routledge, London, 1999; first published 1948), p. 89.

Conclusion

Experts surveying the menswear trade – and bespoke tailoring in particular – on the eve of the Second World War were struck with the extent of change since 1918. There was widespread concern that, although they had not quite triumphed yet, mass production, marketing and retailing would eventually swamp all small competitors. Paralleling these developments, the status of tailors and tailoring was also considered to have shifted. To some extent, this was interpreted as an improvement. By the inter-war period, the image of the semi-destitute, ragged and sweated Jewish tailoring worker, toiling in his own home for a pittance, had largely disappeared. Tailoring, it was believed, had been transformed into an industrial occupation, based in 'larger units of production' and protected by Trade Boards. The parliamentary acts of 1909 and especially the more comprehensive one of 1918 had 'improved the lot of the home-worker and indirectly helped to drive many home-workers into the factory'. Both the sweated tailoring homeworker and the radical – or drunken – artisan employed in a small workshop largely disappeared from contemporary discourses, replaced by the tailor as a factory worker, especially as 'the efficient, well-paid operatives in the mammoth factories of Leeds'. All in all, 'With shorter hours, higher real wages, and with less unemployment than many other workers, the clothing operative can no longer be regarded as the Cinderella of modern industry'.[110] Thus, in a sense, tailors had finally achieved the dignified status sought by many within the bespoke trade, even if not as 'artists' in the profession or as successful businessmen, but as factory 'hands'.

However, outside the factory, the status of those 'tailors' whose role was in the shop, selling garments and interacting with customers, remained more ambiguous. The menswear salesman portrayed in *Man and his Clothes* in 1928 as a 'thin, red-nosed gentleman, with fraying trousers, string-like tie, [and] soup-stained waistcoat', was only the latest of a long progeny of poor and depressed-looking 'tailors'. A little education and more money were needed – it was emphasised – to convert 'atrocities' into 'beings who would bring public appreciation and respect to the menswear business, as a trade and as a career'[111] (Figure 7.4). Two years later, G.F. Curtis acknowledged that there were still people who believed that shop assistants were in 'a lower social scale than, say, a clerk in an office', although they were – he stressed – a decreasing minority: 'the shop assistant of to-day is the captain of his own soul', and 'must not be ashamed

---

[110]   Anon., 'The clothing trades', p. 252; S.P. Dobbs, *The Clothing Workers of Great Britain* (George Routledge and Sons, London, 1928), pp. 4; 7; 201. See also, for example, W.H. Hulme, 'Tailoring as a vocation', in Bridgland (ed.), *The Modern Tailor*, vol. 1, pp. 9–15, especially p. 9; Redmayne, *Ideals in Industry*, p. 81. The reality of factory work was not so straightforward. As Katrina Honeyman has demonstrated in her work on the Leeds clothing industry, these images may have been accurate of the 'highly paid [male] cutters using increasingly sophisticated machinery', but not of the low-waged 'female machinists operating in sweatshop conditions redolent of the nineteenth century'. The latter represented between 70 and 80 per cent of the Leeds workforce, and generally earned wages less than half of men's. Honeyman, *Well Suited*, especially pp. 127, 129. See also *The Daily Herald*'s anti-sweating campaign in 1924 in Dobbs, *The Clothing Workers of Great Britain*, p. 186. On clothing workers' continued exploitation see A. Phizacklea, *Unpacking the Fashion Industry: Gender, Racism and Class Production* (Routledge, London, 1990).

[111]   *Man and his Clothes*, April 1928.

Figure 7.4   The menswear salesman: ninth part of a man? *Man and his Clothes,*
April 1928. By permission of the British Library, LD171.

of his calling'.[112] There is good deal of evidence to suggest that this was wishful thinking, as claims to manliness of both shop assistants and clerks continued to be seen as at the very least doubtful. Harry Hardcastle, the protagonist of Walter Greenwood's 1933 novel *Love on the Dole*, looked enviously upon engineering workers: 'He felt ashamed of himself ... All these boys and men wore overalls; *they* weren't clerks. They were Men, engaged in men's work.'[113]

That said, by the inter-war period retailers working in small independent tailoring shops were no longer perceived primarily as unmanly, but rather as anachronistic and out of step with 'modern' times. If before 1914 they had struggled to assert their manly credentials, by the 1930s they felt they were fighting for their very survival in the face of customers' apparent enthusiasm for the mass-produced garments sold by 'big business'. Not that everything was plain sailing for those retail workers employed by large concerns and multiple shops. In a sense, in fact, it was they who in the inter-war period inherited the mantle of the unmanly 'little tailor'.[114] Many of the younger shop

---

[112]   *Man and his Clothes*, February 1930.

[113]   W. Greenwood, *Love on the Dole* (Penguin Books, Harmondsworth, 1969; first published 1933), p. 19.

[114]   See also the continued anti-semitic prejudice directed at multiples, and especially at Burton's. In 1939, for example, a fascist organisation had taken to slashing the word 'Jew' on Burton's shop windows. WYAS, Burton Archives, Box 129, 'Window slashing and cutting', Letter from P. Pope, general manager, to chief constable, 6 December 1939. Also Honeyman, *Well Suited*, pp. 72–4.

assistants seem to have embraced a raffish, carefree and gregarious existence, in some ways reflecting the practices of an older, hard-drinking and overwhelmingly masculine culture associated with the tailoring workshop. According to Norman Hancock, for example, shop assistants' pay was often very low, but 'the less they earned the more freely they spent. They might be called counter-jumpers and white-collar wage-slaves, but in their manner of spending they were kings. Free, independent and individualistic; they enjoyed their leisure hours to the full.' Richard Hoggart's uncle Walter and his drinking cronies, all shop assistants, also sought to cultivate a rather raffish image. They were 'given to snap-brim trilbies and three-piece suits which for the first few months have a superficial smartness but then fray and become shiny'.[115]

Young sales assistants' carefree leisure and consumer practices could not disguise the fact that their working lives were characterised by dependence, insecurity and economic hardship, especially among those not so young workers with families to support. The 'man about town' image of masculinity became harder to maintain as the salesman grew older: 'This was an age when men were spoken of as being too old at forty, and ... such men would dye their hair, wear elastic-sided boots and even corsets, in a desperate attempt to preserve an illusion of vigour and youthfulness.' Hoggart's uncle Walter, who had spent all his working life as a salesman in a 'posh store', 'saying boo to no goose, in black jacket and pin-striped trousers, the perfect victim', eventually 'was unceremoniously ... sacked after a merger'.[116]

It is difficult to avoid the conclusion that by the end of the inter-war period most 'tailors' had not managed to transform themselves into the self-reliant, modern and industrious businessmen, able to compete successfully with 'big business', whose cause the trade press had so strongly championed. Tailoring workers may have been transformed from sweated victims into sturdy and self-respecting factory workers, but the same could hardly be said of menswear salesmen. As the editor of *The Outfitter* observed in 1930, sales assistants, particularly those in the soft goods trades, were regularly subjected to taunts 'of a sweeping and sarcastic nature, in that with few exceptions the average shop assistant has been portrayed as a person of mean intelligence, unhealthy, unsportsmanlike, in fact, an animal of a particularly nasty kind'. Frequently, 'artisans' were heard to refer 'to men who have just sold them half hose, neckties, etc., as "Phyllis", "Gladys", and so on'.[117]

It may no longer have needed nine 'tailors' to make one man, but it arguably still required nine sales assistants.

---

[115] N. Hancock, *An Innocent Grows Up* (J.M. Dent and Sons, London, 1947), pp. 123–4; R. Hoggart, *A Local Habitation: Life and Times 1918–1940* (Chatto and Windus, London, 1988), pp. 19–20.

[116] Hancock, *An Innocent Grows Up*, pp. 123–4; Hoggart, *A Local Habitation*, p. 16.

[117] *The Outfitter*, 30 August 1930.

PART III
Buying Menswear

Chapter 8

Shopping Decisions, 1880–1939

In 1890, the man who, finding himself in Oxford, decided to treat himself to an item of menswear, could choose from a variety of outlets, including at least five clothiers, eight outfitters, nine second-hand clothes dealers and more than a hundred tailors, as well as one breeches-, six shirt- and four robe-makers. If he came back in 1937, rather older but just as keen to shop, he could take his pick from considerably fewer tailors (sixty-two), second-hand clothes dealers (five) and shirt makers (four), but a greater number of clothiers (twelve), outfitters (twenty), and robe-makers (seven). In addition, he could visit one of the eleven hosiers and five athletic outfitters.[1] In reality, of course, this abundance of choice was more apparent than real. It was – at the very least – unlikely that a man, even a man with time, money and shoe leather to burn would move comfortably between second-hand clothes shop, high-class bespoke tailor, hosier and gentleman's outfitter, perhaps then popping in to have a look at some ready-made suits at a cheap clothier. There clearly did not exist a single male model and itinerary of clothes shopping, which encompassed all the available outlets and included all men.

Following in consumers' footsteps before they committed themselves to crossing the threshold of the shop, this chapter thus explores the pressures that played a part in influencing male shopping decisions and practices. It firstly considers the negative factors, those that stopped men from availing themselves of certain outlets and curbed their ability to shop freely. After considering the unavailability of supply, financial constraints and lack of purchasing power, other, perhaps less obvious factors, bound up with notions of age, gender and class will also be examined. The next section will then question whether such limitations to consumer choice amounted to a masculine disengagement from consumer culture and to an understanding of men as 'reluctant' or even non-shoppers. The chapter will conclude by focusing on the 'positive' factors that influenced male shopping practices, particularly routine, pleasure, knowledge, one-upmanship and sociability. It will suggest that all played a part in creating a more complex portrait of the male shopper than is generally acknowledged in the literature on consumption: an interested, engaged, well-informed consumer, for whom, in 1939 as much as 1880, the purchase and ownership of new clothes were key to the successful assertion of a manly identity.[2]

---

[1]   *Kelly's Directory of Oxford and Neighbourhood for 1890–91* (Kelly, London, 1890–91); *Kelly's Directory of Oxford and Neighbourhood for 1937* (Kelly, London, 1937).

[2]   The terms are once more borrowed from M. Roper and J. Tosh (eds), *Manful Assertions: Masculinities in Britain Since 1800* (Routledge, London, 1991).

The limits of consumer freedom

In his 1922 autobiography, R.W.S. Bishop, a doctor who spent the first two decades of the twentieth century working in moorland areas of Yorkshire and Derbyshire, painted an extremely bleak picture of isolation and lack of purchasing opportunities. He wrote of his patients: 'Thrift was a natural concomitant of an existence where there were no shops to tempt, or amusements to attract. There was a saying that when sixpence went over the local bridge it never returned.'[3] For those living in isolated rural areas, opportunities to shop around could be limited. According to Ernst Ambrose, in the Suffolk village of Long Melford in the 1880s and 1890s, it was to 'the Top Shop' that locals went to buy goods ranging 'from oil to groceries, from boots to hardware, clothes and medicine'. In Heathley, Norfolk, 'when the young bloods of the village wanted a new or Sunday suit they could get a ready-made one from a choice of patterns at Robert Addis' shop', the village 'general store'.[4]

That said, the extent to which rural areas were cut off from wider distribution networks should not be exaggerated. Garments could be ordered and obtained by post from specialist mail order firms, while it was by no means impossible to travel to larger villages or towns, where more shopping opportunities were available.[5] At the end of the nineteenth century, Fred Gresswell travelled up to Lincoln from the village of Digby 'on a half day excursion just to look in … [the] windows' of recently-opened multiples: 'a boot shop, a 25 shilling tailor and a cycle shop. They caused quite a sensation at the time.'[6] According to Tim Barnes, who grew up in a small Dorset village just before the Second World War, the decision to shop for clothes in the village shop could be dictated not simply by the lack of other opportunities, but also by a desire 'to avoid the time and expense of going to town'. Most importantly, the service available locally left nothing to be desired: 'You stated your requirement … and a telephone call produced a sample of 3 or 4 of the product for you to try at home and hopefully to choose'.[7]

Itinerant traders also brought commodities to communities beyond easy reach of shops. By the 1880s, the practice of 'whipping the cat', whereby tailors travelled across the countryside, carrying with them the tools of their trade, and stopped at farmhouses to make and repair clothing, using materials provided by the customer, had already largely died out.[8] However, the same was not true of all itinerant clothes

---

[3]   R.W.S. Bishop, *My Moorland Patients* (John Murray, London, 1922), p. 22.

[4]   E. Ambrose, *Melford Memories: Recollections of 94 Years* (Long Melford Historical and Archaeological Society, Long Melford, n.d. [c. 1972]), p. 16; M. Home, *Autumn Fields* (Methuen, London, 1944), p. 63.

[5]   R. Coopey, S. O'Connell and D. Porter, *Mail Order Retailing in Britain: A Business and Social History* (Oxford University Press, Oxford, 2005), chapter 1.

[6]   F. Gresswell, *Bright Boots: An Autobiography* (David and Charles, Newton Abbot, 1982; first published 1956), p. 15.

[7]   T. Barnes, *My Dorset Days* (Dorset Publishing, Sherborne, 1980), pp. 53–4.

[8]   For a description of the practice of 'whipping the cat' see, for example, *The Tailor and Cutter*, 7 March 1889; *The Master Tailor and Cutter's Gazette*, October 1913; G. Herbert, *Shoemaker's Window: Recollections of a Midland Town Before the Railway Age* (B.H. Blackwell, Oxford, 1948), p. 7.

dealing. John Beard recalled that in the 1880s a 'pedlar-tailor' called Charlie Breeze 'commenced to travel our parish [in the countryside near Shrewsbury], mending clothes at the farm houses, collecting rabbit skins, selling tapes, cottons, laces and other small articles'.[9] At the turn of the century, Harry Taylor recalled, a 'Braintree man would call Saturday evenings' at his family's house in Great Leighs, Essex, and ask 'if I wanted a pair of boots, or if father wanted any clothing'.[10] Twenty years later, in the countryside near Rottingdean, in Sussex, Mr Rumbold 'was one of the last travelling packmen of old. True his pack was contained in two gigantic and much-used cardboard suitcases posing as leather, but the astonishing array of pinafores, blouses, socks, shirts, handkerchiefs, ties, braces, pullovers and tweed caps ... would have stocked a small shop'.[11] In the first decade of the twentieth century, acting in some ways as the modern counterparts of the itinerant tailors of old, the tailor Frank Whynes travelled between the villages around Stowmarket, in Suffolk, taking orders for clothes among farm workers, as did Arthur Pluck and his father, travelling out from their clothier's shop in Stowmarket.[12]

However, even in areas where the supply of outlets was plentiful, the only purchasing opportunities affordable to a significant proportion of the population were clothing clubs, tallymen, jumble sales, charities and the second-hand market.[13] One of the reasons why B.L. Coombes left his native Herefordshire at the age of eighteen, shortly before the outbreak of the First World War, was that 'There was plenty of work at home, but little pay ... New clothes were very rare, and pocket-money was something to imagine ... I wanted good clothes, money to spend, to see fresh places and faces, and – well, many things.'[14] Ill-health, old age, unemployment or other misfortunes could have disastrous effects on the purchasing power of individuals, families, and even whole communities. In his autobiography, R.L. Lee described the effect of the closure of the Dowlais steelworks in the South Wales town of Merthyr

[9]   J. Beard, *My Shropshire Days on Common Ways* (Cornish Brothers, Birmingham, n.d., c. 1948), p. 6.

[10]   National Social Policy and Social Change Archive, Albert Sloman Library, University of Essex (NSPSC Archive), The Edwardians: Family Life and Work Experience Before 1918, oral history collection (The Edwardians), QD1/FLWE/C/10, interview transcript, Mr Harry Taylor, wheelwright.

[11]   B. Copper, *Early to Rise: A Sussex Boyhood* (Heinemann, London, 1976), p. 18.

[12]   G.E. Evans, *The Horse in the Furrow* (Faber and Faber, London, 1960), pp. 77, 79.

[13]   These are mentioned, for example, in F. Kitchen, *Brother to the Ox: The Autobiography of a Farm Labourer* (Penguin, Harmondsworth, 1983; first published 1940), p. 75; G. Foakes, *Between High Walls: A London Childhood* (Athena Books, London, 1974), pp. 15–16; Manchester University Settlement, *Ancoats: A Study of a Clearance Area. Report of a Study Made in 1937–1938* (Manchester University Settlement, Manchester, 1945), pp. 36–8; G. Bourne, *Change in the Village* (Gerald Duckworth, London, 1912), p. 64; *How the Casual Labourer Lives: A Report of the Joint Research Committee on the Domestic Condition and Expenditure of the Families of Certain Liverpool Labourers* (Liverpool Economic and Statistical Society, Liverpool, 1909); W.E.W. Collins, *Episodes of Rural Life* (William Blackwood and Sons, Edinburgh, 1902), pp. 256–72; A. Morrison, 'Family budgets no. 1: a workman's budget', *The Cornhill Magazine*, April 1901, pp. 446–56.

[14]   B.L. Coombes, *These Poor Hands: The Autobiography of a Miner Working in South Wales* (Victor Gollancz, London, 1939), p. 8.

Tydfil during the Slump. Townspeople were forced to radically change their shopping practices: 'Shops ... began closing down ... people ... began to look haggard and shabby, and drew what bits of clothes they had about them as if holding on to their last remnants of pride and respectability'. This was, he pointed out,

A far cry indeed, from the days when the 'tallyman' leaned on the well polished wall, opposite the Great Mill Gate, collecting dues from well filled pay packets. Those carefree days, when visits could be made to Picton and Morris, the general ironmongers, for all sorts of ware for the home ... Footwear galore at the Clog Shop, and loads and loads of things at Longstaffs the Bazaar.[15]

Inter-war pit closures in South Wales brought new hardships to communities that had previously by no means been affluent, but which now reached new depths of deprivation. As Robert Morgan explained, clothes shopping soon became a distant dream: 'Clothes and shoes were luxuries, so they were rarely purchased. Clothes were patched and worn until they were smooth and threadbare. Many boys and girls reached adulthood before they experienced the delight of wearing something absolutely new.'[16]

When money was tight, a range of strategies were deployed in order to obtain clothing without involving a cash payment, or having recourse to the 'formal' market. In 1939 Ken Ausden, the son of a Swindon railway man, began to play football every Thursday afternoon. In his autobiography, he described how he was finally able to obtain a jersey and boots: 'It took me three months of running errands for ha'penny a time to save up enough to buy Harold Briggs's boots, second-hand, for 1 and a tanner. And I dug old Mrs Crook's bit of back garden twice before she gave me her eldest son's old jersey.' His 'baggy, off-white shorts' were made by his mother, using an old sheet.[17] Garments could also be stolen or borrowed: whenever the opportunity presented itself, Arthur Harding's mother would steal clothes from church sales. More daringly, Sidney Day and his friend Ruddy spent most of the money they could cobble together on clothes, 'but generally if we needed new clothes we would break in somewhere and rig ourselves out'.[18]

More 'respectably', when Richard Hillyer's father (a cowman) had to travel up to London from the Northamptonshire village of Byfield to see a solicitor, he wore his own black coat, 'the one he had been married in ... but he had borrowed a pair of black trousers to go with it, because the check ones he had at his wedding wouldn't look right in

[15] R.L. Lee, *The Town that Died!* (R.L. Lee, London, 1930), pp. 54–5.

[16] R. Morgan, *My Lamp Still Burns* (Gomer Press, Llandysul, 1981), p. 23.

[17] K. Ausden, *Up the Crossing* (BBC, London, 1981), p. 189. See also J. Cummins, *The Landlord Cometh* (Queenspark Books, Brighton, n.d. [c. 1982]), p. 13. Such strategies are also considered, for example, in A. Taylor, '"Funny money", hidden charges and repossession: working-class experiences of consumption and credit in the inter-war years', in J. Benson and L. Ugolini (eds), *Cultures of Selling: Perspectives on Consumption and Society Since 1700* (Ashgate, Aldershot, 2006), pp. 153–82; B. Reay, *Microhistories: Demography, Society and Culture in Rural England, 1800–1930* (Cambridge University Press, Cambridge, 1996), pp. 120–25.

[18] R. Samuel, *East End Underworld: Chapters in the Life of Arthur Harding* (Routledge and Kegan Paul, London, 1981), p. 25; S. Day, *London Born* (Fourth Estate, London, 2004), pp. 66–7. See also W. Woodruff, *Beyond Nab End* (Abacus, London, 2003), pp. 92–3.

London nowadays'. Borrowing was not limited to the poor. The hunting illustrator Cecil Aldin was able to regularly borrow his better-known and better-off younger brother's 'top hats and tailcoats for weddings and funerals'. 'It is perhaps better', he suggested, 'to be a nonentity *with* these compensations than a celebrity with tailors' bills.'[19]

Clothes, especially less expensive garments, were also given and received as gifts. In the village of Long Melford, Christmas gifts were for the most part exchanged between adults, and tended to take the form of small items of apparel: 'a muffler or pair of braces, a belt or neck tie'.[20] In his autobiography, V.W. Garratt stressed the importance for his family's survival of the gifts received from a kindly downstairs neighbour: 'though poor herself she often brought extra things to nourish my mother, and the cast-off clothing of her own growing children found a new lease of life on our bodies'.[21] Indeed, the boundary between gift-giving and charity was not always a firm one. In the inter-war years, Molly Hughes's lawyer husband died suddenly, leaving her with little money and three young sons to support: the problem of how to clothe them was solved when 'an old friend who had precisely the same boys as myself, only a stage older, passed on their suits in excellent condition'.[22]

More often, garments were simply 'handed down', generally within a family, as the original owner outgrew them or was able to obtain new (or newer) items. As Joe Gormley, the son of a Lancashire miner, explained, echoing many other accounts: 'My elder brother John would get the new clothes, and they'd be passed to me as hand-me-downs, and by the time I'd worn them out there would have to be a new set for younger brother Bob. It wasn't too good a deal ... but then we were very poor.'[23] Garments were also made up at home. Ready-made children's clothes could certainly be bought from shops throughout the period: when the twelve-year-old Noel Coward began his acting career in 1911, he travelled between London theatres wearing a 'scrupulously pressed dinner-jacket suit', purchased from Lockwood and

---

[19]   R. Hillyer, *Country Boy* (Hodder and Stoughton, London, 1966), p. 114; C. Aldin, *Time I Was Dead: Pages from my Autobiography* (Eyre and Spottiswoode, London, 1934), p. vii. See also R. Kenney, *Westering: An Autobiography of Rowland Kenney* (J.M. Dent and Sons, London, 1939), p. 98.

[20]   Ambrose, *Melford Memories*, p. 27.

[21]   V.W. Garratt, *A Man in the Street* (J.M. Dent and Sons, London, 1939), p. 11. See also H.E. Palmer, *The Mistletoe Child: An Autobiography of Childhood* (J.M. Dent and Sons, London, 1935), p. 70.

[22]   M.V. Hughes, *A London Family Between the Wars* (Oxford University Press, Oxford, 1979; first published 1940), p. 10. Bill Horrocks also mentions the free clothing received by youths who joined the Territorials. B. Horrocks, *Reminiscences of Bolton* (Neil Richardson, Manchester, 1984), p. 18. Charities such as the Police Aided Clothing Society also provided free clothing, especially for children. See, for example, *How the Casual Labourer Lives*, p. 52.

[23]   J. Gormley, *Battered Cherub* (Hamish Hamilton, London, 1982), p. 2. See also, for example, N. Gray, *The Worst of Times: An Oral History of the Great Depression in Britain* (Wildwood House, London, 1985), pp. 80, 132–3, 141; Horrocks, *Reminiscences of Bolton*, p. 16; Gresswell, *Bright Boots*, p. 25; E. James, *Unforgettable Countryfolk: Midlands Reminiscences* (Cornish Brothers, Birmingham, n.d. [c. 1948]), p. 4; E. Wight Bakke, *The Unemployed Man: A Social Study* (Nisbet, London, 1933), p. 55.

Bradley on the Clapham Road.[24] However, the clothes of most working-class and many lower-middle-class children (and women) were adapted or made at home. A.E. Coppard was made a suit by his uncle, an ex-tailor with whom he was sent to live upon his father's death. These garments 'successfully dressed me despite an extreme roominess of trousers ... which sartorial effusion certainly caused me some twinges of uneasiness'.[25] When Sidney Day's father had

> finished with a pair of trousers he would give them to one of us boys ... If it was my turn he would put them on the table and tell me to lay on them. 'Up you go', he would say. Then he would chalk round me, cut round the outline and sew them up. They looked like nothing on earth.[26]

Generally, however, it was the women of the family, and especially mothers, who were most likely to make or mend children's clothing, often using material obtained from older garments.[27] M.K. Ashby's mother was noted for 'her Jones sewing machine and her ability to cut out clothes for any size or shape of woman or child and even to make a shapely jacket for a lad'.[28] W.H. Lax learnt to make do early on in life. His mother 'believed in darning, mending and patching until you could scarcely find the original garment. When I wanted a new pair of trousers, she replied by mending the old ones.'[29] These practices were by no means limited to the poorest sections of the population: according to G.S. Layard, writing in *The Cornhill Magazine* in 1901,

---

[24]   N. Coward, *Autobiography* (Mandarin, London, 1992; first published in this edition 1986), p. 29. See also L. Tregenza, *Harbour Village: Yesterday in Cornwall* (William Kimber, London, 1977), p. 162; F. Willis, *Peace and Dripping Toast* (Phoenix House, London, 1950), p. 49; J. Gray, *Gin and Bitters* (Jarrolds Publishers, London, n.d. [c. 1938]), p. 38.

[25]   A.E. Coppard, *It's Me, O Lord!* (Methuen, London, 1957), p. 43. Coppard was ten when his father died in the late 1880s. See also W. Holt, *I Haven't Unpacked: An Autobiography* (George G. Harrap, London, 1939), p. 25. Holt described how his grandfather, a tailor, had made his suits, obtaining the material either from old clothes handed down by his father, or from 'pieces of cloth bought by my mother at some bargain sale'.

[26]   Day, *London Born*, p. 23.

[27]   But see also M. Loane, *From Their Point of View* (Edward Arnold, London, 1908), pp. 147–8. According to Loane, 'most men draw the line at using a needle and cotton, but I have known many expert with a sewing machine'.

[28]   M.K. Ashby, *Joseph Ashby of Tysoe 1859–1919: A Study of English Village Life* (Cambridge University Press, Cambridge, 1961), pp. 107, 136. See also T. Thompson, *Edwardian Childhoods* (Routledge and Kegan Paul, London, 1981), p. 42; A. Jobson, *An Hour-Glass on the Run* (Michael Joseph, London, 1959), pp. 36–7; Garratt, *A Man in the Street*, p. 3. On home-dressmaking, see also B. Burman (ed.), *The Culture of Sewing: Gender, Consumption and Home Dressmaking* (Berg, Oxford, 1999); A. Davin, *Growing Up Poor: Home, School and Street in London, 1870–1914* (Rivers Oram Press, London, 1996), pp. 71, 136–7; A. Davies, *Leisure, Gender and Poverty: Working-Class Culture in Salford and Manchester, 1900–1939* (Open University Press, Buckingham, 1992), p. 61.

[29]   W.H. Lax, *Lax his Book: The Autobiography of Lax of Poplar* (The Epworth Press, London, 1937), p. 36.

among lower-middle-class families with annual incomes of between £150 and £200, '[the wife] must of course be her own and her children's dressmaker'.[30]

Women's willingness and ability to make up garments at home should not however be exaggerated: 'some women are very neat with joins and patches, while others cobble miserably, or not at all'.[31] H.H. Bashford's mother, an impoverished middle-class widow, kept a sewing box, but used it 'only for the purpose of necessary repairs, invariably put off to the last possible moment'. The only garment she ever tried to make from scratch was 'a mitten for a deep sea fisherman, of which she never began the fellow'.[32] Perhaps most importantly, adult men's and older boys' outerwear was usually considered beyond most women's dressmaking abilities. While H.G. Wells and his brother were growing up in the 1870s and 1880s, their mother had made all their clothes. However, they eventually reached the age when 'under the pressure of our schoolfellows' derision, we rebelled against something rather naïve in the cut'. Four decades or so later, George Ewart Evans was grateful that his South Wales school had no requirements about school dress for boys. This was just as well 'during the penurious twenties, for while the girls' slips could be tailored at home, homemade clothes for boys were a different matter'[33] (Figure 8.1).

In any case, it is clear that self-provisioning, however ingenious, could not satisfy all a family's clothing needs, particularly where outerwear, such as suits and overcoats, was concerned. For those with little disposable income, once the essentials of food, rent and heating had been paid for, dealers who offered relatively flexible credit arrangements and accepted instalment payments were an important source of clothing. By the turn of the century, John Blake's family had grown to seven children, all of whom 'required constant renewals of footwear and clothing'. Inevitably, this 'meant running up bills on the "never-never" with the tallymen, who took weekly payments off the main debt, plus interest'. Just before World War One,

---

[30] G.S. Layard, 'Family budgets no. 2: A lower-middle-class budget', *The Cornhill Magazine*, May 1901, pp. 655–66, especially pp. 660–61. See also, for example, H.G. Wells, *Experiment in Autobiography: Discoveries and Conclusions of a Very Ordinary Brain (Since 1866)* (Faber and Faber, London, 1984; first published 1934), p. 73.

[31] Morrison, 'Family budgets no. 1', p. 454. See also, for example, NSPSC Archive, The Edwardians, QD1/FLWE/4, interview transcript, Mr Knifton, maintenance engineer with London Omnibus Company.

[32] H.H. Bashford, *Lodgings for Twelve* (Constable, London, 1935), p. 17. According to Helen Bosanquet, writing in 1896, 'In these days of cheap materials a handy woman with the use of her needle can keep her family clad for almost incredibly little; but as a matter of fact nearly all Londoners buy their clothing ready-made.' Mrs B. Bosanquet, *Rich and Poor* (Macmillan, London, 1896), p. 86.

[33] Wells, *Experiment in Autobiography*, p. 73; G.E. Evans, *The Strength of the Hills: An Autobiography* (Faber and Faber, London, 1985; first published 1983), p. 50. Although most women would not have attempted to make older boys' or men's outerwear, they were generally responsible for their care and maintenance. It is perhaps also in the context of this responsibility that working-class women's practice of pledging their husband's Sunday suit to the pawnbroker should be seen. That said, there are plenty of instances of (especially single) men taking care of their own garments (for example by placing trousers under the mattress in order to press them back into shape), or taking them to the pawnbroker. See, for example, R. Douglas, *16 to 21* (A.M. Philpot, London, n.d. [c. 1925]), pp. 82, 127–8.

when A.S. Jasper and his brother needed suits for their sister's wedding, 'a local tallyman was contacted'.[34] Paradoxically, as Patrick McGeown explained, the poor could rarely afford the cheaper option of cash payments. 'The tallymen provided all the wearing apparel at our home, and in every home in Cowie Square ... We never grew rich enough to buy ready money. Craigneuk was so completely working class that my mother couldn't hope for real bargains in wearing apparel. There was no prosperous folk to do the needful at the jumble sales.'[35]

The second-hand trade filled another gap in the market. Growing up in Edwardian Birmingham, V.W. Garratt's Saturday evenings were generally spent accompanying his mother to the rag market, 'intent on the adventurous quest for bargains in that vast lumber-room of odds and ends, smoke and smells'. 'If', he continued, 'from my mother's efforts I came to wear a fresh pair of knickerbockers or a faded jacket, it was because my elder brother's clothes were not ready for the new lease of life on my own body. The law of inheritance in this respect was very strong in our family.'[36] That said, used clothes were not always associated with miserable necessity. At the turn of the century, Mr Bennett, a Chatham greengrocer, bought most of his suits second-hand. He generally frequented a shop where it was always possible to find 'gentry stuff ... real good suits ... bought down from London. That's where the fashion was ... that was the only way you could afford quality.'[37]

To some extent, used clothes, like home-made garments, were associated with childhood: new clothes were rarely purchased for non-wage-earning working-class children. According to Jim Bullock, none of the boys in his family 'ever had a new suit specially purchased for him while he was going to school'.[38] Indeed, whilst most consumers' freedom of choice in clothing matters was to varying extents limited by financial and other constraints, children from all social backgrounds had little or none at all, the responsibility for choosing where their

---

[34]   J. Blake, *Memories of Old Poplar* (Stepney Books Publications, London, 1977), p. 8; A.S. Jasper, *A Hoxton Childhood* (Barrie and Rockliff: The Cresset Press, London, 1969), p. 24. See also S. O'Connell and C. Reid, 'Working-class consumer credit in the UK, 1925–60: the role of the check trader', *Economic History Review*, vol. lviii, no. 2 (2005), pp. 378–405; P. Scott, 'The twilight world of interwar British hire purchase', *Past & Present*, no. 177 (2002), pp. 195–225; A. Taylor, *Working Class Credit and Community Since 1918* (Palgrave Macmillan, Basingstoke, 2002), especially chapters 3 and 4; G.R. Rubin, 'From packmen, tallymen and "perambulating scotchmen" to Credit Drapers' Associations, c. 1840–1914', *Business History*, vol. 28, no. 2 (1986), pp. 206–25. In 1900, it was estimated that menswear made up half of the British tally trade. Ibid., p. 214.

[35]   P. McGeown, *Heat the Furnace Seven Times More* (Hutchinson, London, 1967), pp. 32–3. Craigneuk is located 12 miles from Glasgow.

[36]   Garratt, *A Man in the Street*, pp. 69–71. See also C.E.B. Russell, *Manchester Boys: Sketches of Manchester Lads at Work and Play* (Neil Richardson, Manchester, 1984; first published 1905), p. 38; Thompson, *Edwardian Childhoods*, p. 17.

[37]   Quoted in M.J. Winstanley, *The Shopkeeper's World 1830–1914* (Manchester University Press, Manchester, 1983), p. 165. But see also Wight Bakke, *The Unemployed Man*, p. 55.

[38]   J. Bullock, *Bowers Row: Recollections of a Mining Village* (EP Publishing, Wakefield, 1976), p. 14. See also D. Pope, *Now I'm Sixteen: An Autobiography* (J.M. Dent and Sons, London, 1937), p. 74.

Six-year-old. "I SAY, GRANNIE, I THINK YOU'D BETTER STOP MAKING MY TROUSERS. LOTS O' TIMES TO-DAY I WASN'T SURE WHETHER I WAS GOIN' TER SCHOOL OR COMIN' 'OME."

Figure 8.1   The limits of women's dressmaking abilities. *Punch*, 6 September 1905. Courtesy of the Bodleian Library, University of Oxford, N.2706 d.10.

clothes (either used or new) were acquired most often lying with their mother.[39] As Mr Rook, the son of a navvy, pointed out, even once he had begun to earn money, ''course you see mother had to clothe us ... We couldn't buy it ourselves, well they couldn't give us the money to buy it.'[40] While growing up in 1930s and 1940s Homerton, George Cook only ever received one brand new suit. This was the result of a transaction that delighted him, but over which he had had no say: his mother had bought it from the local tallyman on behalf of another woman, who then decided she did not want it, and Cook was thus able to benefit from this unexpected 'dandy clothing'.[41]

A decade or so earlier, Peter Donnelly had equally 'been little more than a spectator on those gala days when my mother took me to buy a new suit or new boots'. Once in the shop, all the exchanges took place between his mother and the shop assistant, starting from the moment when his mother said: '"I want to see a suit to fit this boy". Always "this boy". The expression cut cubits from my stature.' No

---

[39]   E. Barker, *Father of the Man: Memories of Cheshire, Lancashire and Oxford, 1874–1898* (The National Council of Social Service, London, n.d. [c. 1948]), p. 68; F. Barton, *We'll Go No More A-Roving: An Autobiography* (Joiner and Steele, London, 1937), p. 29; M. Loane, *An Englishman's Castle* (Edward Arnold, London, 1909), p. 183.

[40]   NSPSC Archive, The Edwardians, QD1/FLWE/8, interview transcript, Mr James Rook, porter.

[41]   G.A. Cook, *A Hackney Memory Chest* (Centerprise Trust, London, 1983), p. 34.

attempts were made to discover Donnelly's own preferences. His role was a purely passive one, as the shop assistant started 'to slip coats on me, to prod me under the armpits, to turn me round, to make me stand back so that he and my mother could look at me dispassionately, as if I were a figure on a plinth'.[42] The freedom to choose where to shop for one's clothes could thus serve to mark the achievement of adult status. At eighteen, Ernald James had passed his teaching exams and become an 'Uncertified Assistant Master'. As a 'reward', he 'was permitted to buy a new pair of boots – to go to the shop personally and unaccompanied and make my own choice. How these apparently small things of life leave an ineffaceable impression. But it was a tremendous concession.'[43]

Shopping and status

The non-availability of supply, financial pressures and children's lack of autonomy all limited consumers' freedom to choose where to shop. At the same time, other considerations could also influence male shoppers' choice of outlet, and lead them to exclude certain options. It was often noted that most men seemed to dislike shopping in outlets associated with women and femininity, such as department stores or drapery shops. In 1927, the editor of *Men's Wear* observed, 'Notwithstanding the continued inroads which the drapery stores are making into the men's wear trade, the average man is still reluctant to shop in these great emporiums.'[44] Even when they entered 'men's shops' of department stores, most male customers still preferred to have 'direct access from the street to the clothes in which … [they are] interested', rather than having to 'drift through' a range of feminine departments[45] (Figure 8.2). However, gender was not the only factor at play in putting men off certain outlets. Issues of class and status were important too.

Indeed, it is clear that given a comfortable income, consumers were very unlikely to patronise outlets such as second-hand dealers or cheap clothiers. Examples of middle-class commentators' disgust with the commodities sold there, and especially with used clothing, are not difficult to find. In 1896 Helen Bosanquet observed that 'The adventures which … old clothes pass through in their transition from one set of backs to another are horrible to think of.'[46] Thirty years or so later, a down-on-his-luck Robin Douglas, having been forced to sell his underwear to a rag and bone merchant, watched in horrified fascination as his garments joined the other 'genuine

---

[42]   P. Donnelly, *The Yellow Rock* (Eyre and Spottiswoode, London, 1950), pp. 98–9.

[43]   James, *Unforgettable Countryfolk*, p. 48.

[44]   *Men's Wear*, 9 April 1927.

[45]   *The Outfitter*, 25 January 1930. See also K. Honeyman, 'Following suit: men, masculinity and gendered practices in the clothing trade in Leeds, England, 1890–1940', *Gender & History*, vol. 14, no. 3 (2002), pp. 433–4; B. Lancaster, *The Department Store: A Social History* (Leicester University Press, London, 1995), pp. 182–3.

[46]   Bosanquet, *Rich and Poor*, p. 58. See also C.H. Reilly, *Scaffolding in the Sky: A Semi-Architectural Autobiography* (George Routledge and Sons, London, 1938), p. 73. Reilly mentioned the 'strong stomach' needed to walk past the 'queer little Jewish shops' selling a mixture of second-hand clothing, oil and herrings in pre-First World War Liverpool.

bargains' on the dealer's stall.[47] When middle-class or more affluent consumers bought used items, these were often invested with connotations that sought to counteract their 'horrible' elements. The second-hand riding breeches bought at the turn of the century by Herbert Buckmaster on his way home from South Africa, allegedly enjoyed a reputable imperial lineage: they were 'a damn good pair of corduroy riding breeches, made by Rankin of Calcutta'.[48] The overcoat bought from Moss Bros by the country solicitor Alexander Pearson was 'a lovely bit of tailoring … it was made for poor Charlie (so and so) who was once a millionaire, but he's lost all his money racing, and now he's broke'.[49]

Alternatively, the affluent patronised 'cheap' retailers when they sought to 'disguise' themselves and their class background. In 1916, Stuart Cloete, then recovering from an injury inflicted at the battle of the Somme, 'bought a navy blue suit off the peg at some cheap shop' because he wished to blend in with the urban crowd, and 'drift about. It was much easier to do this if you were not well-dressed'.[50] The First World War saw the development of a thriving market in second-hand uniforms, which soldiers on leave made enthusiastic use of. This served partly to make up for the deficiencies of official channels, and partly, perhaps, to create sartorial identities that lay somewhere between those of combatants on active duty and civilians in mufti. Following the battle of Cambrai, for example, Jack Cummins returned home on leave wearing a 'filthy old uniform'. Having found out that 'owing to red tape' his battalion could not give him a new one, he 'bought a second-hand uniform somewhere very cheaply. Then I began to enjoy myself.'[51]

With a more overtly 'serious' intent, a visit to a second-hand clothes dealer was the first step taken by social explorers and writers, most notably Jack London and years later George Orwell, before entering unfamiliar plebeian areas such as 'the vast and malodorous sea' of the East End of London. It was in the used clothes shop that these middle-class men acquired the disguises necessary to blend in among the East Enders: in London's case, 'a pair of stout though well worn trousers, a frayed jacket

---

[47]   Douglas, *16 to 21*, pp. 175–6. The implication was that poorer consumers were less fussy and sensitive about matters of smell, dirt and hygiene. But see also, for example, Pat O'Mara's unflattering depiction of Paddy's Market, in his native Liverpool. It was here, he stated, that 'the refuse of Empire is bought and sold … frayed domestic and foreign underthings'. P. O'Mara, *The Autobiography of a Liverpool Slummy* (The Bluecoat Press, Liverpool, n.d. [c. 1934]), p. 2. For more recent attitudes towards second-hand clothes, see N. Gregson, K. Brooks and L. Crewe, 'Narratives of consumption and the body in the space of the charity / shop', in P. Jackson, M. Lowe, D. Miller and F. Mort (eds), *Commercial Cultures: Economies, Practices, Spaces* (Berg, Oxford, 2000), pp. 101–21.

[48]   H. Buckmaster, *Buck's Book: Ventures, Adventures and Misadventures* (Grayson and Grayson, London, 1933), p. 58.

[49]   A. Pearson, *The Doings of a Country Solicitor* (The Author, Kendal, 1947), pp. 57–8. For Moss Bros' carefully negotiated strategy of 'trading up' their second-hand and 'misfit' business, see W. Tute, *The Grey Top Hat: The Story of Moss Bros of Covent Garden* (Cassell, London, 1961).

[50]   S. Cloete, *A Victorian Son: An Autobiography 1897–1922* (Collins, London, 1972), p. 255.

[51]   Cummins, *The Landlord Cometh*, p. 36.

" Men do not like buying in a women's shop."

**Figure 8.2   'Men do not like buying in a women's shop.' *Man and his Clothes*,
              May 1930. By permission of the British Library, LD171.**

with one remaining button, a pair of brogans which had plainly seen service where
coal was shovelled, a thin leather belt, and a very dirty cloth cap'. The main challenge
had been to convince the shop assistant that despite looking like such an unlikely
customer, he really did wish to buy old clothes. Eventually 'a man in trouble, or a
high-class criminal from across the water, was what he took my measure for – in
either case, a man anxious to avoid the police'.[52]

Warwick Deeping's hugely successful 1925 novel *Sorrell and Son* vividly
illustrates the continued importance in the inter-war years of assumptions relating
to class and status in determining purchasing behaviour. The book's hero was an
unemployed ex-officer and 'gentleman' who, needing to support his son, accepted
a job as a shop assistant in an antique shop: in a telling order, this was described as
his final opportunity to 'save his last made-to-measure suit, his boy, and the remnant
of his gentility'. However, after the job fell through, he was forced to accept a (to
him) demeaning job as a hotel porter. Deeping then described how while Sorrell was
being measured for a porter's uniform, the tailor looked at 'the tailor's mark inside
the collar of his blue serge coat. That suit had been a post-war extravagance.' As it

[52]   J. London, *The People of the Abyss* (Isbister, London, 1903), pp. 24, 21. See also
G. Orwell, *Down and Out in Paris and London* (Penguin Books, London, n.d.; first published
1933), pp. 128–30.

was clearly impossible to believe that a porter could purchase a West End suit, the tailor simply assumed 'that Sorrell had been a valet or a porter at some flats, and that the suit had been passed on to him by some member of the aristocracy, moneyed or otherwise'.[53] Despite many commentators' talk of a 'democratisation' of fashion in the inter-war period, it nevertheless remained the case that to ignore the social stratifications involved in clothes shopping meant to defy well-rooted conventions. Edward Blishen's French schoolmaster made no secret of his habit of buying and wearing 'defiantly cheap clothes'.

> 'From Marks and Spencers', he'd say, indicating his yellowing trousers. 'Marks and Spencers' was then a synonym for extreme cheapness. 'I hope it interests you that I pay as little for my trousers as I can … get 'em *off the peg*. You're probably appalled, aren't you? Most of you, I suppose, are little snobs. On the way to becoming bigger snobs. Eh?'[54]

Men and shopping

When it came to buying their clothes, shoppers' options were limited by considerations such as a lack of accessible outlets and a shortage of ready money, as well as less quantifiable factors relating to age, gender and class. It remains to be seen whether these limitations amounted to a model of men as reluctant, or even non-shoppers. It is certainly difficult to believe that there did not exist plenty of men who, not being particularly interested in clothes, went shopping only when absolutely necessary, and then spent the minimum amount of time possible choosing and trying on garments, or whose shopping was done on their behalf by female relatives. According to Norman Hancock, it was farmers' wives who would come into his parents' drapery store in a pre-First World War small Somerset town. 'Some of them were in our shop for the greater part of the day selecting household goods, dress materials and underclothing for themselves, and caps, ties, and socks and suits for their husbands and sons, and even for the husbands and sons of their neighbours.'[55]

The disinterested and reluctant male shopper certainly was (and is) a stock character of the popular press. In 1899, for example, *Comic Cuts* published a series of sketches of 'the future', when men would be forced to read advertisements, inspect goods, and generally behave like stereotypical female shoppers. Male purchasing behaviour was contrasted (generally favourably) with women's: 'It's queer how different men and women are about dress. A man will stroll into his tailor's, order a new suit in five minutes, and think no more of the matter.' A man, it was suggested,

---

[53] W. Deeping, *Sorrell and Son* (Cassell, London, 1953; first published 1925), pp. 2, 68.

[54] E. Blishen, *Sorry Dad* (Allison and Busby, London, 1984; first published 1978), p. 148. The notion of an inter-war democratisation of fashion is discussed in Chapter 4. On Marks and Spencer, see R. Worth, '"Fashioning" the clothing product: technology and design at Marks and Spencer', *Textile History*, vol. 30, no. 2 (1999), pp. 234–50.

[55] N. Hancock, *An Innocent Grows Up* (J.M. Dent and Sons, London, 1947), p. 73. However, women could not necessarily be trusted to purchase clothes for men. See, for example, the music-hall song by J.S. Long (author) and K. Royle (composer), *She's Changed my Boots for a Set of Jugs* (Francis Brothers and Day, London, n.d. [c. 1888]).

would quickly look at a pattern and agree that 'Oh yes, that'll do send it round soon'.
A woman, however,

> will go to her dressmaker's every day for a week and stay there for hours ... trying to
> make up her mind about what style to have ... Then ... she'll spend another month being
> 'fitted' and 'altered' and goodness knows what else. Even then she's not satisfied with the
> dress when it does come home, though to the mere man it looks perfect.[56]

According to Leonard Sanders, writing in *Men's Wear* in 1905, hosiers all too often
made the mistake of treating their male customers as though they were women,
seeking 'to wheedle and ... to tempt when there is not an earthly chance of ...
succeeding, and there is great risk of giving offence'. Women shopped differently
to men: 'there is a special feminine pleasure in the knowledge that you are going
forth to be tempted ... the draper grows fat on it'. When men went to a hosier, on the
contrary, they already had a good idea of what they wanted to buy, and disliked being
'importuned' to make further purchases.[57]

Nevertheless, although it was (and is) often presented as such, it is difficult to
believe that a dislike of shopping was a 'natural' or essentially masculine attribute.
Not all male shoppers were either reluctant or disinterested. Indeed, the purchase of
commodities (small and not so small) for personal consumption was a more 'normal'
and acceptable part of men's everyday lives than is often admitted: shopping for
clothes and other items was by no means necessarily perceived as 'unmanly'.
While serving in France during the First World War, for example, Sidney Rogerson
unselfconsciously described an excursion to Amiens in 1916. The 'excuse' for
this 'was to procure some hair-oil, not the conventional English variety ... but the
highly perfumed yellow pomade one bought in little glass jars with gold labels.
Other requisites were a razor ... and some khaki collars.' Although his purchases
were few and relatively modest, 'my shopping took me a long time. There was so
much to see, so many temptations to squander money. It says something for my
self-control that after so long away from shops I did not succumb and buy for the
sheer joy of buying.'[58] Purchasing clothes, from a bespoke tailor or from other

---

[56]   *Comic Cuts*, 11 November 1899; 4 April 1903. See also, for example, *Fun*, 22 September
1896; *Comic Cuts*, 4 July 1908; *Tit-Bits*, 12 April 1930. Gender differences in purchasing patterns were
dealt with, for example, in *Progressive Advertising*, 11 April 1902; 5 September 1902; P. Nystrom,
The Economics of Retailing (The Ronald Press, New York, 1920; first published 1915), pp. 32–5; See
also E.D. Rappaport, *Shopping for Pleasure: Women in the Making of London's West End* (Princeton
University Press, Princeton, 2000), p. 128, for press representations of men hating and being useless
at shopping; C.P. Hosgood, '"Doing the shops" at Christmas: women, men and the department
store in England, c. 1880–1914', in G. Crossick and S. Jaumain (eds), *Cathedrals of Consumption:
The European Department Store, 1850–1939* (Ashgate, Aldershot, 1999), pp. 97–115.

[57]   *Men's Wear*, 15 July 1905. Sanders was the author of 'a series of articles in which a customer
unfolds the burden of his tale of woes against the men's wear retailer'. For opinions within the
trade, stressing men and women's different attitudes towards shopping, see, for example, *The Tailor
and Cutter*, 9 May 1889; *The Gentleman's Magazine of Fashion*, February 1881; September 1884;
March 1885; *Men's Wear*, 5 April 1902.

[58]   S. Rogerson, *Twelve Days* (Arthur Barker, London, n.d. [c. 1933]), pp. 148–9. As John
Tosh has pointed out, couples like Daniel Meinertzhagen, who spent most of his considerable

sources, was often a routine, but by no means necessarily unimportant part of many men's lives, although it was these routine shopping trips that were the least likely to be recorded in autobiographical material, and are therefore the most difficult to document. However, this does not mean that they did not take place. On a Sunday outing to the Isle of Sheppey at the turn of the century, B.G.A. Cannell and his wife decided to stop at an outfitting store. This visit was made memorable (and was therefore mentioned in Cannell's autobiography) only by the fact that in the shop they bumped into two of her brothers, who had just returned from South Africa, and were themselves stocking up on collars and ties.[59]

Understandably, it was 'special' purchases, especially those tied to specific events, that tended to be 'memorable', and therefore likely to be mentioned in autobiographical accounts. James Agate could well remember 'having my first boy's suit made by a tailor called Macbeth, and being firmly convinced that Shakespeare's character must be the tailor's grandfather or something of the sort', while Bruce Bairnsfather clearly recalled the excitement of visiting the regimental tailor upon being appointed Second Lieutenant in the Third Battalion of the Royal Warwickshire Regiment, and being rigged out 'with a set of suitable disguises'.[60] Understandably, J. Lewis May, the son of a London doctor, had particularly vivid memories of his first tailor. 'I had a tailor, my tailor, when I was five. My tailor was Mrs. Thompson. I was her customer ... and I have reason to believe that she had no other customers ... Mrs. Thompson was a sewing woman who used to come twice a week to our house.' She did her best to make him a sailor's suit:

> I knew it was a sailor's suit, because it had a whistle suspended from a piece of white cord round my neck. But it had knickerbockers, which no sailor ever wore that I knew of, and those knickerbockers were like no knickerbockers that anyone – sailor or no sailor – ever wore ... they were really truncated trousers ... And even that is not strictly accurate, for trousers have a front part and a back part, with a descending row of buttons, discreetly dissembled, down the front. With this emblem of maturer masculinity, it was then thought superfluous to endow me.[61]

Clothes purchasing, especially for major items such as suits or overcoats, was frequently associated with specific times of the year, and most notably Whitsun.

---

leisure time shooting, fishing, playing billiards and cards, and his serious-minded wife Georgina, confounded the stereotype of the frivolous, shopping-mad middle-class wife and hard-working, non-consuming husband. J. Tosh, *A Man's Place: Masculinity and the Middle-Class Home in Victorian England* (Yale University Press, New Haven, 1999), p. 67. See also C. Breward, 'Fashion and the man: from suburb to city street. The spaces of masculine consumption, 1870–1914', *New Formations*, no. 37 (1999), pp. 47–70.

[59]   B.G.A. Cannell, *From Monk to Busman: An Autobiography* (Skeffington, London, 1935), p. 62.

[60]   J. Agate, *Ego* (Hamish Hamilton, London, 1935), p. 130; B. Bairnsfather, *Wide Canvas: An Autobiography* (John Lang, London, 1939), p. 30. For other 'memorable' purchases, see Pearson, *The Doings of a Country Solicitor*, p. 17; S. Shaw, *Guttersnipe* (Sampson Low, Marston, London, 1946), p. 100; F. Anthony, *A Man's a Man* (Duckworth, London, 1932), p. 31; G. Brenan, *A Life of One's Own: Childhood and Youth* (Hamish Hamilton, London, 1962), p. 184.

[61]   J.L. May, *The Path Through the Wood* (Geoffrey Bles, London, 1930), pp. 62–4.

In the Suffolk countryside at the turn of the century, 'some of the old country folk' would buy new garments twice a year, in the spring and after harvest, 'when they'd been paid their harvest money'. As soon as he was old enough, Mr Keble, the son of a farm labourer, began to work at harvest time. At the end of five weeks of hard physical labour he was usually paid about thirty shillings. He would then go into Colchester with his father and brothers ('a red letter day') and 'buy some new clothing then and then had to wait until the next year' for the next opportunity. As a child in a late nineteenth-century Staffordshire mining village, Ernald James 'had one suit a year. It was purchased to fit with the highlight of the Chapel's year – the Sunday School Anniversary ... it took place, always, on Whit Sunday.'[62]

A new outfit often marked a special occasion, or a step in an individual's life-course. Before leaving for his preparatory school, for example, Herbert Buckmaster was taken to London by his mother to buy a school outfit at Swears and Wells.[63] Weddings, funerals, starting a new job, especially a first job, all frequently involved the purchase of new garments. In an unnamed mining village at the turn of the century, most young boys followed their older relatives down the pit: 'The week before a lad left school his mother would buy him a pair of white moleskin trousers in readiness for his work. This he would proudly wear as evidence to other envious youngsters that soon he would descend the pit, a man amongst men.' According to Thomas Jones, in late-nineteenth-century Rhymney, South Wales, funerals were important occasions, meant to be impressive. 'Clothes played a large and expensive part in the ceremony, and were a frequent origin of debt. There were three drapers in Rhymney', and although the Jones family depended on the company shop, 'we sometimes extended our orders for mourning to one or other of the three'.[64]

A new garment or outfit could also serve as both the symbol and the outcome of a change in financial circumstances. Just as hard times would quickly entail a loss of clothes to the pawnshop or the rag and bone man,[65] a windfall would often lead to the purchase of a new outfit. In the inter-war period, Maurice Levinson's neighbour, who despite working in a tailoring shop, wore 'ill-fitting clothes, and ... grease-stained cap', laughed at the idea that he should spend his gambling winnings on new clothes: 'Nothing like that ... I'm no sissy, you know'.[66] However, his attitude does not seem to have been typical; Levinson certainly thought it odd. Far from being a sign of unmanliness or 'sissyness', the purchase of new or 'better' clothes, however humble, was generally perceived as a mark of a successful, enviable manhood. In

[62] Evans, *The Horse in the Furrow*, p. 80; NSPSC Archive, The Edwardians, QD1/FLWE/1, interview transcript, Mr Keble, postman; James, *Unforgettable Countryfolk*, p. 4.

[63] Buckmaster, *Buck's Book*, p. 14. See also G. Romilly and E. Romilly, *Out of Bounds* (Hamish Hamilton, London, 1935), p. 48.

[64] M.G. Llewelyn, *Sand in the Glass* (John Murray, London, 1943), p. 41; T. Jones, *Rhymney Memories* (The Welsh Outlook Press, Newtown, 1938), p. 67. See also Jasper, *A Hoxton Childhood*, pp. 24, 26; Kenney, *Westering*, p. 85; J. Jones, *Unfinished Journey* (Hamish Hamilton, London, 1937), p. 67; Lee, *The Town that Died!*, pp. 124–5.

[65] M. Tebbutt, *Making Ends Meet: Pawnbroking and Working-Class Credit* (Leicester University Press, Leicester, 1983), for example pp. 16–17; 33. As a last resort, clothes could be sold outright. See, for example, M. Cohen, *I Was One of the Unemployed* (Victor Gollancz, London, 1945), pp. 41–4.

[66] M. Levinson, *The Trouble with Yesterday* (Peter Davies, London, 1946), p. 94.

the 1920s, a bursary as a pupil teacher made it possible for a proud George Ewart Evans to purchase a much-needed and wished-for suit and shoes. A few years earlier, when one of Willy Goldman's neighbours found local – and short-lived – fame as a boxer, this achievement quickly 'found a sartorial outlet. He wore decent clothes for the first time.'[67]

To some extent, as Chapter 4 has suggested, a distinction emerged in the inter-war years between those consumers in a position to benefit from the new shopping opportunities provided by rising real incomes, and those – most notably the unemployed – who were excluded. Men earning a decent and regular income were by no means reluctant to spend a proportion of it on new and attractive garments. A Carnegie United Kingdom Trust report on *Disinherited Youth*, based on research carried out in the late 1930s, observed that many of the unemployed 'to whom smart clothes were essential for a feeling of well-being and respectability suffered a moral defeat in having to lower their standard of dress ... a new suit and smart clothes belonged to success; second-hand clothes and odd garments belonged to failure'. 'Migrants returning to their native locality', the report continued, 'announce the success of their lives in the new areas by being smartly dressed. A well-dressed young man from Birmingham is a better advertisement for transference than all the efforts of the Ministry of Labour.'[68]

Making a choice: impulse, knowledge and sociability

Harry Blacker, who grew up in Bethnal Green, in East London, during and after the First World War, explained in his autobiography that within the local Jewish community the purchase of a new suit was a serious business, requiring a good deal of care and forethought. Standards were high: a made-to-measure suit was 'a must. Ready-to-wear was a nasty phrase in the Yiddish vocabulary.' Family and community networks were put to use, as 'Almost everyone in the quarter had a landsman or relative who was a tailor'. When Blacker himself reached the age of fourteen, his parents decided that he should have his first tailor-made suit. 'The first stage in the suit saga was the purchase of suitable cloth in the Lane. My parents had a landsman in the woollens' business who would sell us material at wholesale prices.' The next stage was a visit to the tailor: his father's cousin Oreh, who 'lived in the West End and was a high-class tailor making special orders for firms like Harrods'. At all stages of the process he was accompanied by both his parents, between whom the choice of material and style was largely made.[69]

Blacker's experiences of shopping for clothes were of course not 'typical'. However, they do highlight two important aspects of the purchasing process, which serve to qualify further the image of the reluctant and disinterested male consumer:

---

[67]   Evans, *The Strength of the Hills*, p. 50; W. Goldman, *East End My Cradle* (Faber and Faber, London, 1940), p. 102. See also Jasper, *A Hoxton Childhood*, p. 102.

[68]   Carnegie United Kingdom Trust, *Disinherited Youth: A Survey 1936–1939* (Carnegie UK Trust, Dunfermline, 1943), pp. 72–3.

[69]   H. Blacker, *Just Like it Was: Memoirs of the Mittel East* (Vallentine, Mitchell, London, 1974), pp. 68–70.

knowledge and sociability. That said, there is no doubt that in many cases, customers' choice of retailer – to the extent that choice was available – was a fairly casual and indeed spur-of-the-moment affair. Retailers certainly believed that male passers-by were no less susceptible than women to the lure of shop displays, although it has been suggested that lingering in front of shop windows could be misinterpreted as cruising.[70] Nevertheless, according to the author of a 1916 retailing manual, passers-by often had 'minutes to give to the business of window-gazing'. He praised a 'London tailor, with various London branches', who appreciated this, and aimed 'to give to every man who has such spare minutes a definite suggestion every time he gazes into his window'.[71] Alexander Paterson, writing in 1911, noted disapprovingly that, given the passion among South London working-class men for new clothes, 'it requires but a showy tailor's window, with offers of cheap ready-made suits, to tickle a young man's fancy into wild extravagance'.[72] At this end of the market, garments and cloth were frequently displayed outside the entrance, so that customers could be enticed into 'feel[ing] their quality' without immediately committing themselves by entering the shop.[73]

In Max Cohen's case, walking along a busy North London street in the 1930s, it was a tailor's tout, importuning him to ''ave a look at some of our suits', who more or less bullied him into 'looking' at the suits in the window and then entering the shop, despite the fact that 'even if I could have afforded to buy a suit, I would never have bought one at a shop that employed a tout'.[74] Although it is impossible to assess the proportion of shops that employed touts, their very existence was based on the assumption that men might stop to look at shop windows, and might then be enticed into entering the shop and making a purchase, once the ice had been broken by stock phrases such as: 'Would you care to try that coat on?', 'Looking for a suit this morning, sir?' or 'Coming in to see us to-day?'[75] In the 1930s, Alexander McRobbie's friend's father worked as a tout for a Glasgow store.

> Impeccably dressed, the dapper Mr Watson spent all day standing outside a tailors' shop. When a male window shopper showed any interest in the many suits displayed, Mr Watson would approach him and start chatting about the merits of the merchandise. He would tell the potential customer that he ... bought his clothes at this shop; that he knew the manager personally, and could organise a nice discount if the customer would like to come inside

[70] M.W. Turner, *Backward Glances: Cruising the Queer Streets of New York and London* (Reaktion Books, London, 2003), pp. 49–54.

[71] Anon., *How to Run a Shop at a Profit* (A.W. Shaw, London, 1916), p. 38. See also, for example, M. Rittenberg, *Selling Schemes for Retailers: Proved Methods which will Help the Retailer to do More Trade* (George Routledge and Sons, London, 1911), pp. 12, 47–8. Also Chapters 5 and 7 in this book.

[72] A. Paterson, *Across the Bridges or Life by the South London River-Side* (Edward Arnold, London, 1911), p. 38. See also G.J. Renier, *The English: Are they Human?* (Ernst Benn, London, 1956; first published 1931), p. 30.

[73] West Yorkshire Archive Service, Leeds (WYAS), William Blackburn Records, G. Misc., 21 (19), Centenary pamphlet (1967), n.p.

[74] Cohen, *I Was One of the Unemployed*, pp. 111–13. For the tactics employed by clothes retailers to lure unwary customers into their shops, see, for example, *Comic Cuts*, 20 May 1899.

[75] WYAS, Burton Archives, Box 250, 'Scientific Selling', 1927.

and try on a suit. Once in the shop, a sale was often made, usually on hire-purchase (2/6d deposit and 2/6d a week).

Mr Watson seems to have been remarkably successful: working on commission, he earned about four pounds a week.[76]

Impulse buying was by no means unheard of among men. In the inter-war years, Philip Allingham found himself earning plenty of money (as a palm-reader and fortune-teller) for the first time in his life: 'I bought a lot of new clothes ... It was pleasant to go into a shop to buy a shirt and then suddenly decide to buy two. I had only bought things singly before or had things bought for me by my mother.'[77] Having simply intended to accompany a friend who wished to buy a tie from a 'large shop', Lennox Kerr left the premises wearing an entirely new outfit: 'smart, single-breasted suit of a sort of mauve and grey mixture. I had a pale-blue shirt and collar and ... silk tie. My shoes were dark-brown and with pointed toes ... [a] silk handkerchief peeked from the breast pocket and I had a snap brim grey hat tugged over my neatly-trimmed hair.' It had all started when, his friend busy examining ties, he had 'touched a handkerchief with ... [his] fingers. It was silk and the stuff was cool and smooth.' He had felt 'ashamed of wanting a silk handkerchief, but the smooth material ... fascinated me. I bought it.'[78]

However, not all purchases were made on the spur of the moment. More time and attention were often devoted to the selection of garments than the conventional masculine stereotype allows. Lady Neish described how her husband would ask her to '"come into my study, I want to show you something." "Something" turned out to be trouser patterns, and after I had selected the one I definitely liked best ... he had chosen something completely different.' 'A man', she continued, 'will keep you twenty minutes talking about trouser patterns; will of course make his own selection in the end; but if you go into his room to ask him what you look like in your new gown, he will look up from his paper, saying "Oh, all right", and go on reading without having seen you.'[79]

Especially where more expensive garments were involved, a good deal of forethought was often required. Although not all consumers were as lucky as Blacker (or perhaps more accurately, as Blacker's parents) in having such good links to the tailoring trade, it was usual for a body of consumer knowledge to be put to use in the choice of retailer to be patronised. It is difficult to generalise about where and how this knowledge was acquired. Despite the conventional image of the male consumer as disinterested in 'commercial' information, especially press and other advertisements, menswear retailers did advertise widely, and were encouraged to do so by the trade press: newspaper advertisements, circulars and posters all sought to

---

[76]   A. McRobbie, *A Privileged Boyhood* (Richard Stenleke Publishing, Ochiltree, 1996), p. 48. On the use of touts, see also *Men's Wear*, 5 August 1905. *The Outfitter* condemned these as 'Eastern bazaar methods', which made men reluctant to stop and look at shop windows. *The Outfitter*, 6 September 1930.

[77]   P. Allingham, *Cheapjack* (William Heinemann, London, 1934), p. 121.

[78]   L. Kerr, *The Eager Years: An Autobiography* (Collins, London, 1940), p. 315.

[79]   Lady Neish, *A Scottish Husband: Making Cheerful Fun of One of Scotland's Best* (Robert Hall, London, 1940), p. 50.

inform, guide and influence consumer choice. Of course, this is hardly conclusive evidence that male consumers took any notice, or were influenced by this publicity. Furthermore, it seems clear that 'informal' channels of information, providing insights into the kind of service or product that they could expect to receive from particular retailers, were just as important as 'commercial' sources, if not more.

In the case of the American H.C. Chatfield-Taylor, who (as seen in Chapter 1) desperately wished to be taken for an English gentleman, such knowledge was acquired in a rather idiosyncratic way. Lodging at Long's Hotel in London's New Bond Street ('known as a bachelor's hotel'), he decided to 'patronise the tailors of Savile Row and Conduit Street in the order to which I heard their merits praised' in the hotel's coffee room.[80] At the other end of the social scale, in the case of Willy Goldman's boxer neighbour, the choice of tailor was influenced by his mother's anti-semitic prejudice, and her wish not to patronise a 'Jewish' shop.[81] On the other hand, the Gardiner family (themselves retailers), tended to patronise other Market Harborough shops whose owners were fellow Congregationalists: 'I suppose you were tied; you felt you'd like to go somewhere else, but if you wanted a suit you must go to Remington's say, or Elliott's, because they go to the chapel.'[82]

It is clear that while important, price was by no means always the only issue taken into consideration. A London engineer explained to Mass Observation in 1939 that when choosing a new suit, he began by inspecting 'tailors' windows and other men's styles and eventually decide on the kind of suit I want. I then go to the shop where I think I should get the best bargain and buy or am sold a suit similar to one I have chosen.'[83] William Woodruff received his first grown-up suit, complete with long trousers, on the occasion of his sister's wedding. His father took him 'to a shop called Weaver to Wearer, where I was measured for a suit of dark brown worsted wool'. The choice of shop was not accidental: not only was Weaver to Wearer known to be 'the cheapest tailor in town', but 'their cloth was thought to be better than that sold by the workers' Cooperative Store. Also, Weaver to Wearer gave me two fittings, at the Co-op I'd have got only one.'[84]

Male networks of information were vital in both selecting, and deciding whether to continue patronising, a particular outlet, and especially a particular bespoke tailor, as were the recommendations and advice received from (generally male) acquaintances, friends or relatives. Unsurprisingly, such networks did not always

---

[80]   H.C. Chatfield-Taylor, *Cities of Many Men: A Wanderer's Memories of London, Paris, New York and Chicago During Half a Century* (Stanley Paul, London, 1925), pp. 24–5.

[81]   Goldman, *East End My Cradle*, p. 102.

[82]   S. Mullins and D. Stockdale, *Talking Shop: An Oral History of Retailing in the Harborough Area in the Twentieth Century* (Alan Sutton, Stroud, 1994), p. 65. The importance of personal ties of patronage between tradesmen and customers are also stressed in M.C. Finn, *The Character of Credit: Personal Debt in English Culture, 1740–1914* (Cambridge University Press, Cambridge, 2003), p. 92. For an earlier period, see N. Cox, *The Complete Tradesman: A Study of Retailing, 1550–1820* (Ashgate, Aldershot, 2000), pp. 127–45.

[83]   Quoted in C. Horwood, *Keeping Up Appearances: Fashion and Class Between the Wars* (Sutton Publishing, Thrupp, 2005), p. 25.

[84]   W. Woodruff, *The Road to Nab End: A Lancashire Childhood* (Eland, London, 2000; first published 1993), p. 278.

work in a kindly and supportive way. On the contrary, sartorial knowledge could be used, more or less crudely, in order to establish one's superiority over the interlocutor. In his autobiography, H.K. Hales recounted how, having been to visit Arnold Bennett in 1923, the writer's 'eyes came to rest on my suit. "So you still go to Jennings?" he said. "Yes" I answered. "He's expensive, but he's good". "Not bad", said Bennett "not bad at-t-all".' For his part, Hales was of the opinion that Bennett's suit, despite probably costing 'a pretty penny', did not fit him well: 'Perhaps it was meant to be slack', he snidely suggested. 'Perhaps that was the one gentle hint of the artistic temperament which he permitted … All I could say to myself was that Jennings would not have passed a job like that'[85] (Figure 8.3).

Often, however, family members (especially fathers) and friends played a more constructive role. It was common for men to 'introduce' a friend, relative or acquaintance to 'their' tailor. Richard Wollheim's father, a successful theatrical impresario, 'liked introducing people to his tailor, and the only time I went there, which was in later life in order to get a dinner jacket I had inherited altered, the cutter greeted me suavely, and said, with the slightest bow, "I remember your father very well. He did us the honour of introducing to us Monsieur de Diaghileff"'.[86] With no close male relatives, Siegfried Sassoon's literary alter ego George Sherston relied on his kind-hearted friend Stephen's advice when it came to choosing which London tailor and bootmaker to patronise. It was Stephen who also taught Sassoon how to tie his hunting stock properly and suggested the type of head-gear appropriate for racing. When Sassoon decided to enlist at the start of the First World War, it was once again Stephen who wrote from the Front that 'since I was so keen on getting killed I might as well do it properly dressed, and gave me the name of his military tailor.'[87] Fathers frequently introduced sons to 'their' tailor. When Stuart Cloete obtained a commission and was gazetted to the Ninth King's Own Yorkshire Light Infantry, it was his father who took him to buy a uniform. Similarly, it was Joseph Millot Severn's father who went with him to the village tailor to have his first suit made.[88] Once Michael Hope and his brothers had reached 'public school age' they were given advice on dress by their father, a prosperous Birmingham manufacturer and a man who was always 'marvellously dressed, great flair for clothes, whether they were – smart clothes or –

---

[85]   H.K. Hales, *The Autobiography of the 'Card'* (Sampson Low, Marston, London, n.d. [c. 1936]), pp. 240, 242. Unwanted advice could of course be disregarded. See, for example, the fictionalised account in E. Waugh, *Brideshead Revisited* (Penguin Books, London, n.d.; first published 1945), pp. 28–9, 43.

[86]   R. Wollheim, *Germs: A Memoir of Childhood* (Black Swan, London, 2005; first published 2004), p. 189.

[87]   S. Sassoon, *Memoirs of a Fox-Hunting Man* (Faber and Faber, London, 1989; first published 1928), pp. 117, 132, 170, 259.

[88]   Cloete, *A Victorian Son*, p. 195; J. Millot Severn, *My Village: Owd Codnor, Derbyshire and the Village Folk When I Was a Boy* (The Author, Brighton, 1935), p. 131. See also the description of buying the first grown-up suit in R. Llewellyn, *How Green Was My Valley* (New English Library, Sevenoaks 1985; first published 1939), pp. 253–5, 274–7.

"I say, Cocky, *you* tell us where *you* gets ther biggest blowout for a bob, and *I'll* tell yer ther name of *my* tailor."

Figure 8.3 **'I'll tell yer the name of my tailor': passing on sartorial information.** *Judy*, **20 May 1903. Courtesy of the Bodleian Library, University of Oxford, N.2706 d.12.**

untidy clothes – he – somehow wore them with great air'. Eventually Hope 'was taken to his tailor when I should think when I was probably about 15'.[89]

In the young John Gray's case, it was his aunt (his mother had died when he was very young) who bought his suits, but another part of the process of acquiring a new outfit involved standing in front of his father (a publican) wearing the new garment, turning around for inspection and having the pockets 'wetted': 'into every pocket he would slip a farthing, which meant at least four or five. The suits were mostly of the "Norfolk" style, coat and knickerbockers, and there would be two pockets in either garment, with often three in the coat.'[90] Returning to Merthyr Tydfil shortly before the First World War after four years in the army, Jack Jones found his younger brothers, Billa and Frank, all grown up. Earning good money as miners, 'After work they dressed in a way which made them look like gentlemen of leisure … Fine linen they wore, and well-cut suits.' They looked on in disapproval as Jack was taken by their mother to buy his clothes from a local clothier, and eventually decided to take him in hand. They 'introduced' him to their tailor. 'They sighed as they said: "You shouldn't have let our mam put you into that reach-me-down. Of course mam has always gone there for our clothes when we were kids, but now – well look at it." The tailor shook his head sadly before taking my measures for something more twentieth century.'[91]

Not only did other men provide important shopping advice, but from an evening out with friends at the local Saturday market, to a visit with a friend or relative to a bespoke tailor, men by no means always shopped alone.[92] In 1934, twelve Lincoln College students visited the Oxford tailor Castell and Son to buy college silk ties, while a few weeks later the same number of Keble College students crowded into the shop to buy the flannel college scarf.[93] At around the same time, Sidney Day and his friend Ruddy would frequently go shopping together, buying items that took their fancy in shop windows. When they did not feel like spending their money (or had none to spare) they would break into a tailor's shop – also together – and grab as many garments as they could. They would then keep an outfit each, and sell the extra on.[94]

For some men, 'their' tailor was part of a network of male enclaves among which, especially in the pre-1918 era, they could spend much of their time. Consumption was here mixed up with sociability and leisure. On receiving a commission in the summer of 1914, for example, Gerald Brenan travelled up to London to be measured for a uniform by a Savile Row tailor. In the fitting room he bumped into his Uncle Charlie, who invited him for dinner at the Cavalry Club. The next stop for his uncle

---

[89]   NSPSC Archive, The Edwardians, QD1/FLWE/MUC/2019, interview transcript, Mr Michael Hope, director of family business.

[90]   Gray, *Gin and Bitters*, p. 38.

[91]   Jones, *Unfinished Journey*, pp. 123–4.

[92]   On Saturday evening markets see, for example, Davies, *Leisure, Gender and Poverty*, pp. 130–38; W. Rose, *Good Neighbours* (Green Books, Bideford, 1988; first published 1942), p. 82; Donnelly, *The Yellow Rock*, p. 42; A. Freeman, *Boy Life and Labour: The Manufacture of Inefficiency* (P.S. King and Son, London, 1914), p. 115; G.R. Sims, *How the Poor Live and Horrible London* (Chatto and Windus, London, 1889), pp. 81–2.

[93]   Oxfordshire Record Office, Oxford, Records of Castell and Son, Tailors and Robe Makers, Oxford, B22/A6/1, Customer Order Book, 1933–4.

[94]   Day, *London Born*, pp. 66–7.

was to a further male preserve, the Admiralty, to petition for a commission.[95] Brenan and his uncle clearly belonged to a small elite of wealthy consumers. However, the link between clothes purchasing, the tailor's shop and male sociability was not limited to these more exclusive sections of society. Despite complaints about over-friendly customers 'who would turn the cutting room into a gossip shop', many retailers were keen to encourage a sociable atmosphere in their shop.[96] The billiard halls frequently located above Burton's shops in the inter-war years were only the latest manifestation of the tailor's shop association with male sociability and leisure. In the pre-First World War Lincolnshire village of Digby, the tailor's shop, which overlooked the school, the saddler's, the grocer's and the post office, was 'the centre of village gossip'. In Cornwall, when members of the Tregenza family went to have a suit made to measure by Mr Hugo, the village tailor, 'There was none of your "Yes?" or "Can I help you?" with him. Welcoming us with a smile of recognition he would already be pulling the chairs round, and we would sit talking at first about anything except the purpose of our visit.'[97]

Conclusion

It would be absurd to suggest that all the men who grew up and grew older in Britain in the six decades before the Second World War loved shopping and spent most of their time discussing previous purchases or deciding where to buy their next outfit. However, the opposite presumption – that shopping for clothes played no part at all in men's lives – appears equally absurd. Most men had to devote at least *some* attention to their appearance, and plenty among them enjoyed both the process of purchasing new garments and that of owning them. That said, there undoubtedly were serious limitations to consumer 'freedom', resulting from insufficient incomes and a lack of suitable and convenient outlets. Furthermore, children rarely had a voice in the purchase of their garments, while certain shops were seen as the province of women or of 'other' men who belonged to different social backgrounds. There was no formal obstacle to men shopping in drapery stores, or to middle-class men buying a second-hand outfit from a market stall or a pawn-broker, but in practice, few did or wished to do so.

However, these limitations to consumer 'freedom' do not amount to a model of men as non-consumers and of shopping as an activity that could only be indulged in at the risk of appearing effete and unmanly. On the contrary, men could be found unselfconsciously window-shopping and enjoying the pleasures of impulse buying. A body of knowledge, whether acquired from commercial channels, from fellow consumers or from personal experience, was routinely put to use in making purchasing decisions, while (mostly masculine) networks of family, friendship and

[95]   Brenan, *A Life of One's Own*, p. 184. See also F. Anderson, 'Fashioning the gentleman: a study of Henry Poole and Co., Savile Row tailors 1861–1900', *Fashion Theory*, vol. 4, issue 4 (2000), especially pp. 407–8. On male enclaves and networks of sociability, see Tosh, *A Man's Place*, especially pp. 177–8.

[96]   *The Tailor and Cutter*, 5 July 1894.

[97]   Gresswell, *Bright Boots*, pp. 87–8; Tregenza, *Harbour Village*, p. 162.

sociability could both lead and keep a customer in a particular shop or shops. A successful shopping expedition, culminating in the acquisition of a smart and well-fitting garment, far from raising doubts about the customer's manliness, was more likely to lead to an enhanced sense of masculine self-worth: in the 1930s, when William Woodruff brought home his first grown-up suit 'in a big cardboard box', he 'felt like a millionaire'.[98]

---

[98] Woodruff, *The Road to Nab End*, p. 278.

Chapter 9

Making a Purchase, 1880–1939

Having endured months of unemployment in the 1930s, living 'from hand to mouth, budgetless, without calculations', there finally came a day when Max Cohen 'realised that I would have to buy myself a pair of trousers'. With much trepidation, he entered 'one of the cheap stores', where he purchased one of the only two items of clothing he was to buy in his first year of unemployment.[1] In a sense, this chapter follows in Cohen's footsteps, as it too finally crosses the shop's threshold, and focuses on what happened once the consumer had selected a particular outlet, whether on impulse, after some deliberation, or, as in Cohen's case, only when driven by absolute necessity. No attempt is made to describe or analyse all the diverse purchasing opportunities open to men in this period. Rather, the focus will be on the purchase of made-to-measure garments, generally (but by no means exclusively) from bespoke tailors. This is not meant to imply that purchasing a garment from a tailor was somehow 'typical' of clothes shopping generally. It is worth stressing once again that by the 1880s, most tailors were specialising in certain – albeit important – garments, especially suits and overcoats, leaving shirts, underwear, collars and other outfitting items to the ready-to-wear trade. Moreover, the experience of buying an outfit from a bespoke tailor would have been very different from, for example, negotiating the purchase of a second-hand item across a market stall, or acquiring garments by post from one of the mail order firms.

Crucially, however, the focus on the tailor's shop provides insights into two areas that have wider relevance for an understanding of male shopping practices and roles in the marketplace. Firstly, it sheds light onto the encounter and – literally – negotiation between buyer and seller, each side seeking to stamp the transaction with their own authority, and entering into a commercial relationship that often uneasily combined intimacy, trust and respect with embarrassment, one-upmanship and duplicity. Secondly, in the context of the challenge faced by 'traditional' retailing methods in the inter-war period, the tailoring trade provides an apt case study of the extent and ways in which the phenomenal rise of 'modern' businesses such as multiple stores modified shopping practices and experiences.

The chapter thus opens by setting the scene of the tailor's shop, a scene whose sober masculinity, it is argued, would have been both familiar and reassuring to most contemporary shoppers. Indeed, between the moment when he set foot in the shop and the moment when his outfit was ready, the customer could expect to go through a series of stages which, with minor deviations, were common to most bespoke tailors. After being greeted, he would be shown various lengths of cloth and his measures taken. He would be asked for any particular requirements, after which a deposit might

---

[1]   M. Cohen, *I Was One of the Unemployed* (Victor Gollancz, London, 1945), p. 106.

be requested and an appointment made for a 'try-on', during which the half-made suit could be checked for fit, and modifications made. The finished product would then be delivered or collected, and the bill either prepared, or the amount added to the customer's account.[2] This chapter will take a closer look at these various stages, paying particular attention to the differences between independent and multiple retailers. It will seek to reveal the pressures at play in the interaction between retailers and customers, and the complex negotiations involved in the seemingly simple matter of shopping for clothes. It will firstly explore the arguments involved in making a decision about the item to be ordered: who should have the final say about its look and feel? It will then go on to consider the uneasy intimacy of the measuring process, and will conclude with what potentially was the most serious flashpoint in the relationship between tailor and customer: the issues of credit and payment.

The setting: the tailor's shop

Describing his childhood in the East End of London in the inter-war years, Harry Blacker explained that, as a fourteen-year-old, he had been confused, as well as fascinated, by the whole process of being measured for his first suit, from the 'strange hieroglyphics' used to record his measurements, to the try-on, when 'bits of my suit … [were] speared with pins or wildly drawn upon with chalk'. What for him had been 'absolute agony', he ruefully added, 'was obviously normal procedure' for the tailor.[3] Blacker's bewilderment was not necessarily typical of most customers. Even before entering a tailor's shop, most boys and men would have had at least some awareness of the process involved in the purchase of a made-to-measure garment, and would have brought with them certain expectations about what would happen and what they would see once they crossed the threshold. These expectations would not generally have been disappointed. Indeed, by the 1880s the procedures involved in purchasing an item of men's wear were well-established and had become highly formalised, especially where the commodity in question was a bespoke suit or other garment. The gestures, behaviour and speech of tailors and shop assistants generally followed a set pattern and sequence[4] (Figure 9.1). As an apprentice at a gentleman's outfitters in Market Harborough in the 1920s, Mr Wimlett was told exactly how he should greet customers: 'If I met you at the door and I didn't know who you were, I should pass the time of day to you, "and what can I do to help you?".'[5] By the end of

---

[2]   The process is described, for example, in *The Tailor and Cutter*, 5 May 1920. See also *Illustrated Chips*, 15 October 1927; F. Anderson, 'Fashioning the gentleman: a study of Henry Poole and Co., Savile Row tailors 1861–1900', *Fashion Theory*, vol. 4, issue 4 (2000), pp. 405–26.

[3]   H. Blacker, *Just Like it Was: Memoirs of the Mittel East* (Vallentine, Mitchell, London, 1974), pp. 68–70.

[4]   Although, of course, there could be exceptions. For the ritual involved in serving the customer, see also M.J. Winstanley, *The Shopkeeper's World 1830–1914* (Manchester University Press, Manchester, 1983), p. 53.

[5]   S. Mullins and D. Stockdale, *Talking Shop: An Oral History of Retailing in the Harborough Area In the Twentieth Century* (Alan Sutton, Stroud, 1994), p. 5.

the nineteenth century, the rituals involved in buying clothes had arguably become part of contemporary cultural currency. An incident recounted in Henry Williamson's autobiography is revealing. After being demobbed at the end of the First World War, the writer had moved to Devon. One day, after going for his customary swim in the sea, he realised that he was being observed from the beach by a woman and a child. 'I took off my wet khaki tunic, wrung it out, knelt down to thump out the creases, afterwards standing up to fold it precisely and hang it, with an exaggerated gesture, as of a super-tailor, over my left arm.'[6]

For most people, both the retailer's behaviour and his shop would have been a familiar sight. Bob Copper and his family had never entered the tailor's shop in the Sussex village of Rottingdean, but could easily see the interior through the window: the garments at various stages of preparation, the 'mahogany counter surrounded by bales of suiting and rolls of buckram and striped cotton lining material', even the tape-measure placed around the tailor's neck, were all there to be seen by the 'small boys pressing their noses to the glass outside and watching him work'.[7] For those without such direct access to this spectacle, the contemporary press frequently provided images of tailoring shops. They appeared regularly in middle-class magazines such as *Punch*, whose readers would have had no difficulty in recognising them for what they were. They served, for example, as the background of political cartoons dealing with issues as diverse as Russia's request of a loan from France in 1905, Irish redistribution, and Lloyd George's 1913 budget. At the same time, the popular press also made use of the imagery and visual puns that tailoring shops offered in such abundance, rendering their interiors accessible even to those readers who were unlikely to be able to patronise them. In 1916 the reader of *Illustrated Chips* could enjoy a cartoon calling upon the customer: 'If you want any glad rags, try Baggs, the Casey Court tailor'. This may have been a not very subtle parody of a 'proper' tailoring shop, but nevertheless included all the necessary elements, however jumbled up. A machinist, cutter, presser, cashier and tailor, as well as shop assistants, were all present, variously assuring one customer of 'A beautiful fit!' or taking another's measures as '3 feet long and 2 feet thick'. Three years later, 'the Casey Court nibs ... [had found] a suitable occupation at last'[8] (Figure 9.2).

The right props, placed in an appropriately sober setting, together with the tailor or shop assistant's appearance, behaviour and speech, were necessary to 'make' a tailoring shop, in a way that most customers would have recognised and indeed expected. In 1938 'Successful tailoring' pointed out in *Men's Wear* that in order to sell made-to-measure garments, it was necessary for the shop to have 'the real tailoring atmosphere'. After all, 'You can't sell suits over the counter like ties or socks. The tailoring section needs a fit setting.'[9] Throughout the period covered by

---

[6]   H. Williamson, *The Sun in the Sands* (Faber and Faber, London, n.d. [c. 1945]), pp. 84–5. Williamson also used this incident in the semi-autobiographical novel *The Innocent Moon* (Sutton Publishing, Stroud, 1998; first published 1961), p. 195.

[7]   B. Copper, *Early to Rise: A Sussex Boyhood* (Heinemann, London, 1976), p. 46. This description refers to the 1920s.

[8]   *Punch*, 15 February 1905; 19 July 1905; 30 April 1913; *Illustrated Chips*, 15 April 1916.

[9]   *Men's Wear*, 30 July 1938.

16th. Century.   17th. Century.

18th. Century.   19th. Century.

(From Le Parisein.)   **THE TAILOR AND HIS CUSTOMER.**

From the 16th. to the 19th. Centuries.

Figure 9.1   'The tailor and his customer. From the sixteenth to the nineteenth
centuries.' *The Tailor and Cutter*, 24 January 1907. By permission
of the British Library, LD163.

this book, and as late as the 1930s, it was by no means unheard of to see a tailor hard at work in the shop, sewing or pressing garments. Perhaps ironically, however, the actual crafting of garments was not always necessarily a significant feature in the 'making' of a bespoke tailoring shop: cutting, sewing, pressing and all the other stages in the manufacture of garments could – and increasingly did – take place in separate factories, workshops, or workers' own homes. Of greater importance in the creation of a proper 'tailoring atmosphere' was the presence of 'props' that suggested craft work without the inconvenience, expense and disruption caused by its actual presence in the shop.

Figure 9.2 **'A suit-able occupation': the tailoring shop in the popular press.** *Illustrated Chips*, **10 May 1919. Courtesy of the Bodleian Library, University of Oxford, N.2706 b.4.**

Both large- and small-scale businesses routinely placed rolls of cloth, the low mahogany tables on which tailors had traditionally sat cross-legged as they worked, pattern books, even scissors and shears, in the shop, reflecting older images of what a tailor's shop should look like.[10] Moreover, it was widely acknowledged that these props had to be set against an appropriately sober and masculine setting, characterised by the use of dark wood in all the fixtures and fittings, and a lack of excessive ornamentation, with the exception, perhaps, of some well-arranged fashion plates.[11] As shown in Chapter 8, some retailers sought to make more of the masculine nature of the shop interior, linking it with other male spaces and leisure

[10]   See, for example the early nineteenth-century images in Bodleian Library, University of Oxford, John Johnson Collection of Printed Ephemera, Trades and Professions, 3 (54c); 'Tailor' engraving (n.d. [c. 1800]); Trades and Professions, 2 (23); 'Taylor' engraving (Tabart and co., London, 1806). Also available at www.bodley.ox.ac.uk/johnson.

[11]   The growing importance accorded to shop interiors in the inter-war period is considered in Chapter 7.

sites, or even seeking to disguise its commercial nature. Harrods' 'man's shop', for example, 'had something of the atmosphere of the man's club'.[12] However, most bespoke tailors would have looked exactly like what they were: shops *for* men and almost entirely staffed *by* men.[13]

Tailors and customers

Once the customer had entered the shop and had made his requirements known, the real negotiations began as, under the salesman or the cutter's guidance, he was invited to inspect various materials, his attention directed to the design and feel of the cloth, using both sight and touch. This was an important matter, with the retailer generally seeking to steer the customer towards more expensive options. Indeed, it is difficult to believe that Norman Nicholson's father, who owned and ran a tailoring shop in the small town of Millom, Cumbria, in the inter-war years, would have been as brusque with his other customers as he was with his son. When it came to choosing the material for a new suit, Nicholson was generally shown some patterns, 'but the choice would be limited and my parents had already decided what I should want'. Moreover, 'my father regarded it as mere affectation to take too much time considering such matters ... He'd look down at the patterns, with mildly contemptuous impatience', adding '"They're all the same, if there's any difference"'.[14] The approach adopted by Max Cohen's would-be tailor, on the other hand, was much more insinuating. He 'took a roll of cloth and demonstrated it to me lovingly, caressing it with his fingers. "See what a nice pattern," he wheedled'.[15] Similarly, customers were invited to inspect the cloth in multiple shops. Having entered a Burton's shop and asked for a 37s 6d suit, Jack Cook, the unemployed miner at the centre of Walter Brierley's 1935 novel *Means Test Man*, was invited to finger the end of a roll of grey cloth: 'Substantial, and you couldn't get a better wearing colour'. To Jack's comment 'seems good', the sales assistant responded that 'It is good, sir, I guarantee that, sir'.[16]

The exchanges that led to the eventual choice of pattern, cut, trimmings and other details could vary enormously, from the harmonious, to the business-like, to the down-right conflictual. Some customers entered the shop with a clear idea of the garments they wanted. A Mr Harvey's instructions to his Oxford tailor, for example, included a request that the trousers should have two-inch turn ups, as those of the

---

[12]   S. Callery, *Harrods Knightsbridge: The Story of Society's Favourite Store* (Ebury Press, London, 1991), p. 129. See also, for example, C. Horwood, *Keeping Up Appearances: Fashion and Class Between the Wars* (Sutton Publishing, Thrupp, 2005), p. 23.

[13]   The ways in which tailors adapted – if at all – in order to accommodate a female clientele is an area that would reward further investigation. Female staff members could include unobtrusive cashiers. See, for example, Mullins and Stockdale, *Talking Shop*, p. 46.

[14]   N. Nicholson, *Wednesday Early Closing* (Faber and Faber, London, 1975), p. 156.

[15]   Cohen, *I Was One of the Unemployed*, pp. 114–15. See also the more positive description in H. Williamson, *A Test to Destruction* (Sutton Publishing, Stroud, 1997; first published 1977), pp. 235–9.

[16]   W. Brierley, *Means Test Man* (Methuen, London, 1935), pp. 222–3.

last pair he had purchased had been too narrow, while the coat should not be too narrow over the hips and the rolls should not be pressed flat.[17] Other customers had much vaguer requirements, although the trade press never tired of emphasising to its readers that an essential requirement of 'good salesmanship' was the ability to ascertain and satisfy *all* customers' needs and wishes, however vaguely expressed, and indeed sometimes seemingly odd or daft. According to Mr Lovell, addressing a meeting of Liverpool tailors in 1889, it was vitally important to meet 'the whims and crochets of ... customers ... A cutter's main duty is to please his customer, whether he be a young man, or an old man, or one who considers every change in fashion as a sign of general degeneration'.[18] His words were echoed forty years later, their meaning unchanged, by Russell B. Hobson, who pointed out that 'It is inevitable that brain-storms will occur even in the most regular clients, unless they are carefully handled, and the whole art of the salesman should be devoted to giving satisfaction'.[19] The language of psychology and of 'scientific' salesmanship was increasingly used in the 1920s and 1930s to back arguments about the need to 'read' and understand customers, enabling the sales assistant to anticipate, and thus cater for and even influence their requirements. However, the meaning remained the same: retailers needed to put themselves in the customers' place, and indulge their foibles.[20] After all, understanding and then satisfying the customer was the key to commercial success: 'Sympathy can be remuneratively exercised during conversation ... By listening attentively to their complaints, or even to their troubles (when time permits), by noting their eccentricities of taste ... the interests of business are bound to be advanced.'[21]

Of course, there were limits, and in a seller's market a more cavalier attitude could be adopted. The busy summer holiday season, for example, 'is not the time to pander unduly to cranks', and as Burton's sales assistants were told: 'Avoid the man who is just out for a good gossip, there are a good many of this type about'.[22] These warnings aside, sales staff were frequently called upon not merely to identify customers' needs, but to actually mould their own appearance and personality in order to suit them. In Burton's shops, for example, managers were responsible for ensuring that both the porter and the sales assistants had 'clean chin, clean collars, clean boots and clean appearance'. But there was more to it than merely sprucing up the staff's appearance, important as that was.[23] According to W. Woodall, 'Height, build, manner and general appearance' were vital to successful selling, but retailers

---

[17]   Oxfordshire Record Office, Oxford (ORO), Records of Castell and Son, Tailors and Robe Makers, Oxford, B22/A3/1, 'T' Dept Order Book, 2 May 1912.

[18]   *The Tailor and Cutter*, 25 April 1889. See also, for example, *The Gentleman's Magazine of Fashion*, February 1883; ibid., August 1886; *The Tailor and Cutter*, 11 June 1925.

[19]   *The Tailor and Cutter*, 3 January 1930.

[20]   See also, for example, *The Tailor and Cutter*, 11 April 1930; 26 December 1930.

[21]   *Men's Wear*, 28 January 1905.

[22]   *Men's Wear*, 1 August 1908; West Yorkshire Archive Service, Leeds (WYAS), Burton Archives, Box 250, 'Scientific Selling', 1927, p. 14.

[23]   WYAS, Burton Archives, Box 128, 'Manager's Guide', 1932, p. 37.

also had to make sure that there was nothing in their habits and manner to arouse the dislike of men and women of any class.[24]

This was not an easy task. As a *Men's Wear* contributor pointed out in 1908, far from costing nothing, courtesy in business 'requires a very considerable expenditure of mental effort, which very few of us are capable of sustaining at all times'.[25] Mr Wimlett explained how maintaining a pleasant façade was both essential and very difficult: 'Greet your customers with a smile ... Never scowl, no matter how much they make you cross ... That was the worst thing I had to learn, how to be pleasant whether I liked it ... whether I hated the sight of the bloke who'd just come in ... You'd got to sink your personality.'[26] Part of the problem was the fact that all too often, customers' requirements seemed neither reasonable nor rational. In Percy Redfern's experience as a shop assistant in the 1890s, 'customers never failed to act awkwardly ... Customers hesitated, haggled, lied. They were ignorant, stupid, wayward, tedious. In them was meanness, greed and even treachery ... behind their backs, we could enjoy mimicking customers, and remembering them for sport.'[27] The customer who, despite all the salesman's efforts, was never satisfied was 'one of the pests of tradesmen ... It is no uncommon thing for men with round shoulders, lean arms, no waists, and spindle legs, to grumble at their Schneider because ... he does not transform their ugly carcases into models of the Apollo Belvedere.'[28]

The trade press was littered with references to customers' unreasonable behaviour and tailors' forbearance, from the customer who shouted and swore because he had been provided with a (perfectly normal) outside breast pocket, or 'too much loose cloth at the fork' of the trousers, or the customer who complained of badly fitting breeches (which it turned out he had simply been wearing twisted the wrong way round).[29] As far as the trade press was concerned, the customer was always wrong. Almost half a century later, similar complaints were still being aired. In 1938 'Sufferer' lamented the impossibility of satisfying the unreasonable customer who 'wants his suit for riding, golfing, shooting and walking; wants a smart close jacket with plenty of ease; wants an easy fit but will not have things loose; does not want ease, but must have a draped style'.[30]

---

[24]   *The Weekly Record of Fashion*, May 1887.

[25]   *Men's Wear*, 15 February 1908. See also, for example, *The Tailor and Cutter*, 20 March 1902; *The Gentleman's Magazine of Fashion*, November 1884; *The Master Tailor and Cutter's Gazette*, January 1910. For a discussion of the demands made on shop assistants, see J. Cushman, '"The customer is always right": change and continuity in British and American department store salesmanship, 1945–1960', in J. Benson and L. Ugolini (eds), *Cultures of Selling: Perspectives on Consumption and Society Since 1700* (Ashgate, Aldershot, 2006), pp. 185–213.

[26]   Mullins and Stockdale, *Talking Shop*, p. 5. See also P. Donnelly, *The Yellow Rock* (Eyre and Spottiswoode, London, 1950), pp. 100–102.

[27]   P. Redfern, *Journey to Understanding* (George Allen and Unwin, London, 1946), p. 27.

[28]   *The Outfitter*, 13 May 1887. For the customer as the tailor's 'demon' see, for example, *The Weekly Record of Fashion*, March 1887.

[29]   *The Gentleman's Magazine of Fashion*, September 1890; January 1894. See also, for example, *The Weekly Record of Fashion*, November 1886; *The London Tailor*, April 1909; *Men's Wear*, 30 April 1905.

[30]   *Men's Wear*, 30 July 1938. See also, for example, *The Tailor and Cutter*, 26 December 1930.

'Faddy customers', with their eternal and 'unjust complaints' haunted multiples as well as independents.[31] In 1930, *The Outfitter*'s editor provocatively suggested that assistants in large stores were a good deal more adept at using methods of tactful and sympathetic salesmanship than their independent counterparts. This, he believed, was the result of training, together with 'more than a soupçon of natural customer-understanding linked up with a trained mind as well'.[32] Indeed, chains such as Burton's publicly prided themselves in their 'scientific' methods of salesmanship, and their ability to satisfy all their customers' needs.[33] Behind the scenes, however, it is clear that the whole thrust of Burton's (and arguably, most other multiples') selling policy was to steer customers towards certain standardised choices, and to ensure that their requirements suited the company, rather than the other way round. This was to be done with a certain degree of subtlety: 'Persuasion', a 1935 training manual explained, 'is not meant to influence a customer to purchase something he doesn't want, but a presentation of your selling facts in such a way that your customer is persuaded that what you are offering him is undoubtedly all you claim it to be'. Successful salesmanship, staff were reminded in 1932, was not simply to identify what customers wanted, but 'the art of making people want what you have to sell'.[34]

Individual features and deviations from standard lines were more expensive for the company and customers were discouraged from requesting them. Each branch was provided with well-produced style books to be kept on the premises, which included pictures of all Burton's models currently available. By the mid-1930s, the company claimed that these volumes were 'complete and comprehensive, so that the average customer can reasonably be persuaded to select a style without deviation, thus avoiding possible errors'. After all, salesmen were told in 1927, although customers 'usually have a good idea of what they require' before they entered the shop, '75% will be persuaded to have what you suggest will suit, and be quite satisfied'.[35]

In a sense, then, independent tailors who sought to distance themselves from the mass-produced garments sold by large-scale organisations by stressing their ability to cater for all of their customers' individual needs, placed themselves at a disadvantage when faced with demanding or unreasonable customers: they too had to be satisfied. Indeed, whatever the immediate cause of customers' complaints, the true source of friction arguably was the unequal balance of power between customer and tailor, and the amount of effort the latter was expected to put into obtaining and then retaining the former's custom. Customers were seen as willing to exploit to the full the fact that retailers' livelihoods were dependent on their success in pleasing them. According to a contributor to *The Weekly Record of Fashion*, 'the petty despotic nature that some people display over business matters, but ... display

---

[31] WYAS, Burton Archives, Box 128, 'Manager's Guide', 1932, p. 22.

[32] *The Outfitter*, 19 April 1930.

[33] See, for example, WYAS, Burton Archives, Box 219, Newspaper Cuttings, *Epsom Courier and Ewell Times*, 10 July 1937; Box 250, 'Scientific Selling'.

[34] WYAS, Burton Archives, Box 191, 'Clothing Classes Curriculum', 1935, p. 24; Box 128, 'Manager's Guide', 1932, p. 43.

[35] WYAS, Burton Archives, Box 190, 'The Trend of Fashion' style book, 1934–36; Box 250, 'Scientific Selling', 1927, p. 15.

to a still greater extent in dealing with their tailors' was due to 'the want of honesty, principle and good nature which characterises people in their dealings with those dependent upon them'.[36] 'Many customers', the *Men's Wear* editor pointed out in 1905, 'like to try to perpetuate the old idea that tradesmen are their servants, as, of course, they are in some respects'. As a result, he added, it was especially important for a bespoke tailor 'to be an adept in the art of suiting oneself to the humour of his various patrons … because a successful tailoring business depends … on holding the connection'.[37]

However, not all bespoke tailors and menswear retailers dealt with this dependence on customers' whims by adopting a subservient attitude. Higher-class bespoke tailors, in particular, could – and did – deploy to good effect their trade knowledge and expertise, seeking to create a mystique that some customers found difficult to challenge. On occasion, such attempts were taken to extreme lengths, and customers were fed rather tall tales. In the 1930s the Cork Street tailor who was 'concocting' a suit for Anthony Gibbs, supposedly 'let slip that there was a special golf club … for tailors', where information about the sartorial habits of celebrities such as the Prince of Wales could – at a price – be obtained, while Alexander Pearson was told by a very distinguished tailor that there were 'certain secret signs by which those who are in the profession can tell the work of famous tailors'.[38] Even when not taken to these lengths, it was clearly in the interest of the tailor to emphasise his superior trade knowledge, in the expectation that, as a result, the intimidated customer would mould his requirements to fit the dictates of the tailor, and not the other way round. Gilbert Thomas, who after the First World War worked in his father's outfitting shop in Leicester, believed that 'the average buyer has but the vaguest idea of what he wanted, and was easily overborne by a show of authority coupled with blandishments and a little flattery'.[39]

After all, the trade was reminded in 1900, although the tailor was dependent on the customer for his livelihood, the customer went to 'his' tailor for 'advice, as well as attire … the client's comfort, his health and his appearance are to a large extent dependent on what he wears'. As a result, it was emphasised, it was only right that tailors' opinions on matters of dress should be accorded the same respect as those of doctors, architects or artists in their own fields of professional expertise.[40] T.H. Holding, delivering a lecture to Exeter 'Masters, cutters and men' in 1885, put it rather more grandiloquently. Directing himself particularly at cutters, he stressed that 'the whole outer man of England at the present time is almost entirely in the cutters' hands. Their character and reputation are, to a certain extent, in their hands. The cut of their clothes, the material, and the taste displayed, stand in many men's minds as importantly as their income. Therefore', he concluded triumphantly,

---

[36]   *The Weekly Record of Fashion*, September 1890. See also *The Gentleman's Magazine of Fashion*, June 1891.

[37]   *Men's Wear*, 5 August 1905.

[38]   A. Gibbs, *In My Time* (Peter Davies, London, 1969), p. 78; A. Pearson, *The Doings of a Country Solicitor* (The Author, Kendal, 1947), pp. 121–2.

[39]   G. Thomas, *Autobiography 1891–1941* (Chapman and Hall, London, 1946), p. 179.

[40]   *The Tailor and Cutter*, 5 April 1900.

'you are an important man.'[41] Cutters and craftsmen were not the only members of the menswear trade needing to be reminded of their importance, and have their confidence in dealing with awkward customers propped up. Chain-store salesmen may not have had any practical knowledge of clothes production, but as they were reminded in 1935: 'You are not only a vendor of garments, you are a seller of style and a purveyor of fashion. You are selling that which not only provides comfort but also enhances appearance.'[42]

This was not just empty rhetoric. The chapters in Part I of this book have sought to show the importance of dress in creating and sustaining male identities, and the punishment meted out to non-conformity: tailors could play an important role in ensuring that sartorial problems did not occur. Alexander Pearson's experiences show the possible dangers of overruling one's tailor's judgement. The London tailor who made his 'country' clothes had tried to warn him that the bright green and purple tweed material he had received as a gift from a friend might prove rather garish when made up into a suit. However, he had not pressed the issue, beyond stating 'Well, although it looks startling in Bond Street, it perhaps may be all right for Westmorland'. This proved not to be the case, and Pearson was teased unmercifully for his bright outfit. So much so, that in the end 'I sent it to Perth and had it dyed such a dull and sombre colour that it never again caused comment'.[43] Other customers wisely paid more attention to their tailor's advice, especially when it came to choosing garments with which they were not familiar. Novice soldiers' military uniforms and other accoutrements during the war were a good example. As soon as Siegfried Sassoon's military tailor had 'put ... [him] ... at ease I became as wax in his hands'. When the moment came to choose khaki shirts, '"You can't have them too dark", he insisted, when my eye wandered toward a paler pattern'. He was, it turned out, quite right.[44] In the semi-autobiographical novel *A Test to Destruction*, Henry Williamson had the young protagonist visit a military tailor, who tactfully steered him into making the 'correct' sartorial choices. Having immediately approved the cloth shown by the tailor, Phillip was then asked to choose between

'cloth rank badges on the shoulder straps, or gilt and enamel? ...They're in three sizes ... here we are, sir.' The smallest were scarcely more than a quarter of an inch across. 'I'll have this size, Mr Kerr.' 'In gilt or bronze?' 'Bronze.' 'They'll be hard to distinguish, sir. Perhaps you want that?' 'I think I'll have the medium size, in gilt.' 'That would balance up the jacket, sir. Now the buttons. You'd prefer the usual gilt, or leather? I always think that the smaller round leather button looks well with a fine serge cloth, particularly for a mounted officer'.

Unsurprisingly, having been steam-rolled so charmingly and effectively, Phillip could only reply meekly: 'Yes, I'll have leather buttons'.[45]

---

[41]   *The Weekly Record of Fashion*, 4 April 1885.

[42]   WYAS, Burton Archives, Box 191, 'Clothing Classes Curriculum', 1935, p. 27.

[43]   Pearson, *The Doings of a Country Solicitor*, pp. 77–8.

[44]   S. Sassoon, *Memoirs of a Fox-Hunting Man* (Faber and Faber, London, 1989; first published 1928), p. 260.

[45]   Williamson, *A Test to Destruction*, pp. 244–5.

Arguably, more was at stake for tailors than the ability to make customers spend a few more shillings than they had originally intended, or to silence their seemingly endless complaints. In 1891 a contributor to *The Weekly Record of Fashion* reminded tailors that 'we are the byword for effeminate helplessness, and imbecile incapacity … Perhaps there is no trade in which the members of it are more despised by the high and mighty of the land.' For this reason it was particularly important that they remember that 'there is no man, no professional man, and certainly no tradesman, on whom these high and mighty ones are more dependent for their passport into society, their standing in the community, their appearance before the public'.[46] By emphasising their authority over their customers, it was implied, not only did tailors and menswear retailers make their working lives easier and ensure that their businesses were successful, but also asserted their manliness in a way that countered the all too familiar saying that it took nine tailors to make one man. According to an 'Old Snip', 'tailoring, it is said, is not a manly business, and is very much despised. So far as you are concerned, make dead sure that nothing you shall do or say shall make you a supporter of that theory. Be a man first and then a tailor.'[47]

Many tailors were only too happy to obey this injunction. The relationship between Molly Hughes's barrister husband and his Cambridge tailor was very amicable. However, there was no doubt about who had the final say in sartorial matters: 'Mr. Neal paid periodical visits to his customers in London, told them what they wanted, and took orders'. On one such occasion, Arthur Hughes might be told that 'I want a new overcoat as well as a new suit. I suppose I do'.[48] In Aldous Huxley's 1923 novel *Antic Hay*, the protagonist, Theodore Gumbril, entered his tailor's shop confident that 'he really looked rather confident and distinguished … no, that he looked positively neat … in his black jacket and his musical-comedy trousers and his patent-leather shoes'. However, under the tailor's professional scrutiny, having been greeted with: 'I notice that the garments you are wearing at present, Mr Gumbril, look … a trifle negleejay, as the French would put it', he was forced to view his clothes 'through the tailor's expert eyes. There were sagging folds about the overloaded pockets, there was a stain on his waistcoat, the knees of his trousers were baggy and puckered … Yes', he had to conclude, 'it was all horribly negleejay'.[49]

Measures

Once the material had been selected and other details of the garment agreed, amicably or otherwise, it was time for the customer to be measured. Despite the fact that by the latter part of the nineteenth century measuring was undertaken – many tailors emphasised – on the basis of 'scientific' principles and using complex

---

[46]   *The Weekly Record of Fashion*, September 1891.

[47]   *The London Tailor*, October 1912.

[48]   M.V. Hughes, *A London Home in the 1890s* (Oxford University Press, Oxford, 1979; first published 1946), pp. 149–50.

[49]   A. Huxley, *Antic Hay* (Flamingo, London, 1994; first published 1923), pp. 25–6.

'systems', this was by no means always a conflict-free process[50] (Figure 9.3). At its best, the customer could feel that he literally was in the hands of an expert, whose arcane craft knowledge was being put to his service, and who was able to provide that most sought-after sartorial quality: a 'good fit'. Well-fitting garments not only followed the contours of a customer's body, but actually hid any physical defects and showed it to the best advantage.[51] The letters from satisfied customers collected by the Oxford tailoring firm of Castell and Son singled out the clothes' 'good fit' as the aspect considered most worthy of praise. As one customer put it in the late 1870s, 'the shirts fit very well and the trousers are as nice a pair as I have ever had'.[52]

At the same time, many customers were very much aware that, through the measuring process, all the details of their bodies were revealed to the tailor, and any defects, including those usually hidden away, were laid bare. Indeed, other private information could also unwittingly be revealed to the tailor: a *Comic Cuts* cartoon of 1908 showed a customer picking up his new suit from an obviously cheap shop. He innocently pointed to a tiny purse attached to his trousers, and asked the tailor what its purpose was. The reply was crushing: 'That's the cash-pocket you ordered, sir. I hadn't any personal reason to – er – suppose you'd got very much cash to carry in it'.[53]

However, it was the physical intimacy brought about by the process of measuring that could be the most troubling for the customer. The tailor's touch may have been physically uncomfortable. When taking the inside leg measurement, for example, the Burton's sales assistant would ask the customer to 'pull his trousers well up'. Then, a manual instructed, 'using the long metal end of your tape, place it as high up in the crutch as possible and continue to shoe heel'.[54] Nonetheless, it does not seem to have been the possible sexual overtones of the encounter that most troubled customers.[55] More difficult seems to have been the tailor's access to all the details of the customer's body, and the use that he could make of this knowledge. Even when there was no malicious intent, such as when Leo Tregenza's brother was told 'My gosh, boy, you'll be as big as your father soon', this public broadcasting of 'private' information could be embarrassing.[56] One customer, writing to an Oxford tailor to enquire if they had 'some up to date Day Shirts', pre-empted any criticism by ruefully admitting that 'I take a 19 inch collar, all my shirts are too small. I have got fat and ugly.'[57]

---

[50] W. Aldrich, 'Tailors' cutting manuals and the growing provision of popular clothing, 1770–1870', *Textile History*, vol. 31, no. 2 (2000), pp. 163–201.

[51] L. Ugolini, 'Ready-to-wear or made-to-measure? Consumer choice in the British menswear trade, 1900–1939', *Textile History*, vol. 34, no. 2 (2003), pp. 195–6.

[52] ORO, Records of Castell and Son, Tailors and Robe Makers, Oxford, B22/C1/1, Correspondence, 1868–1967, Albert A. Betham to Castell and Son, n.d. [c. 1870s].

[53] *Comic Cuts*, 27 June 1908.

[54] WYAS, Burton Archives, Box 128, 255, A Designer, 'Measuring Methods', July 1948, p. 12.

[55] Intriguingly, this seems to have been a later phenomenon. It is worth speculating whether it was connected to the decline of made-to-measure tailoring in the post-Second World War period.

[56] L. Tregenza, *Harbour Village: Yesterday in Cornwall* (William Kimber, London, 1977), p. 162.

[57] ORO, Records of Castell and Son, Tailors and Robe Makers, Oxford, B22/C1/1, Correspondence, 1868–1967, Oxford customer (illegible signature) to Mr Parrish, 9 March 1954. The writer explained that 'All my people were customers of your firm'.

TRYING ON A 1910 LOUNGE.

Figure 9.3   Trying on a suit. *The Tailor and Cutter*, 28 April 1910. By permission
of the British Library, LD163.

It was acknowledged in the trade press that not all retailers approached customers' bodies with sensitivity. Some cutters 'will poke here and feel there ... acting generally as if they were horse dealers or cattle buyers'. This was condemned as hugely objectionable (and as bad for business), as was the practice of shouting to the clerk '"head forward", "round back", "prominent blades" ... and generally detail such a list of disproportions that the customer might be excused for considering himself a candidate for a museum of living curiosities'.[58] The comic press was certainly full of jokes about tailors' tactless handling of their customers' bodies, from the tailor who asked a portly customer to hold one end of the tape, while he walked round him, to the older customer seeking reassurance that 'Measurements about the same as they used to be, Snippe?', being told 'Yes Sir. Chest a trifle lower down, Sir, that's all!', to the two tailors who used a customer's broad back to chalk a game of noughts and crosses.[59] Given the importance of a healthy, vigorous, and increasingly also youthful and slim physique to contemporary notions of manliness, it is not surprising to find that while they were being measured, many men would assume unnaturally 'manly' poses, puffing out their chest, or breathing in to reduce the size of their waist.[60]

At the same time, as well as being a butt for jokes, the customer's body could present the tailor with practical difficulties. It may have been fun to make a portly customer feel uncomfortable, but attempting to 'fit' him could turn out to be no joke. In his autobiography, W.H. Lax explained that being a small man had its compensations. 'One is that it gives happiness to others. I notice how my tailor rejoices to see me enter his shop. Only the other day I called to see him about a new suit. The effect upon his worn and worried face was magical.' He had been dealing with a 'Falstaffian' customer, more than 6 feet high and weighing at least 16 stone. His was a figure that 'filled itself with pride and his friends with wonder. But it filled the tailor with sorrow and pain ... he would be paid by the suit', and not by the amount of material used. When Lax 'appeared he instantly cheered up ... with the warmest welcome possible, he invited me in his inner sanctum ... I was ... a profitable friend, because I was a ... respectable height and weight'.[61] However, more difficult than the question of sheer bulk often proved to be that of ensuring a good 'fit', especially when the customer's body presented some physical peculiarities. J. Lewis May's dress suit shows how this could prove to be a challenge for both tailor and customer. The suit in question 'had this in common with some of our old cathedrals – its constituent parts were not all of the same date nor of the same design, nor again, to be quite frank, were they all of the same material'. The coat was not too bad, as it had belonged to his father, whose size

---

[58]   *The Tailor and Cutter*, 13 May 1897. See also, for example, 17 February 1910.

[59]   *Comic Cuts*, 9 December 1893; *Punch*, 5 June 1880; *The Tailor and Cutter*, 17 June 1938 (reproduced from *Today*). See also *Comic Cuts*, 10 January 1903; *Punch*, 5 June 1880; 17 October 1885; 24 August 1932; *The Tatler*, 29 July 1914.

[60]   The 'Major' of *To-day*, *Clothes and the Man: Hints on the Wearing and Caring of Clothes* (Grant Richards, London, 1900), pp. 29–31. See also, for example, I. Zweiniger-Bargielowska, 'The culture of the abdomen: obesity and reducing in Britain, *circa* 1900–1939', *Journal of British Studies*, vol. 44, no. 2 (2005), pp. 239–73.

[61]   W.H. Lax, *Lax his Book: The Autobiography of Lax of Poplar* (The Epworth Press, London, 1937), pp. 77–8.

was broadly similar to his. The waistcoat was slightly more difficult, as it had belonged to his thinner brother,

> But the trousers! ... They had belonged to my great-uncle. Nature had designed him on a generous scale ... Even Mr. Belbin, 'Tailor and Professed Trouser-Cutter' ... to whom my mother and I betook ourselves in this grave dilemma, looked momentarily disconcerted as his eye lighted on these surprising trousers, which, as they lay folded, leg to leg, upon his mahogany counter, presented the appearance of an enormous 'V'. However, he swiftly recovered his professional *sang froid* ... But apparently the task transcended the ability even of a Professed Trouser-Cutter. When he returned the suit, after the process of adaptation, the trousers could only be persuaded to confine themselves within the exiguous circumference of the waistcoat by being folded into pleats.

Unsurprisingly, 'the strain on the wearer was tremendous'.[62]

Multiple tailors publicly made much of the fact that their organisation and systems solved all the problems relating to measuring customers and providing a good 'fit'.[63] In 1938, a *Chain and Multiple Store* correspondent explained that when a customer was measured, the assistant noted on the order form not only essential information regarding cloth and measures, but also drew 'a word picture of the client's peculiarities; his approximate age is noted and a guess is made at his occupation. There is, consequently, no risk of a man of mature 60 receiving a suit cut to please a young blood of 21, although the cutter never sees the customer.'[64] In their publicity, Burton's claimed that 'In the Measuring Room, amidst comfortable surroundings, the necessary parts are taken with the utmost care. In this part of the tailoring art, Montague Burton are especially painstaking, for figures vary to an extent undreamt [*sic*] of by anyone not conversant with the business.' The firm's policy, it was stressed, was 'to give a perfect individual fit to every customer'.[65] The reality, however, was rather different. For instance, staff were warned by head office to avoid the time-consuming practice of providing 'try-ons'. 'Explain to the customer that by our scientific measure system this worrying process is unnecessary': the suit or overcoat was bound to fit perfectly, and would assuredly not require alterations.[66] Even when they had to bow to pressure and provide a try-on, staff were to tell customers, rather snidely, that 'the second and third fittings by the private tailor are for the most part unnecessary, and would entirely be eliminated if the cutter had measured and fitted perfectly the first time'.[67]

Despite such claims, providing a good individual fit was clearly as much of a challenge for multiples as for independents. Problems included the difficulty of

---

[62]   J.L. May, *The Path Through the Wood* (Geoffrey Bles, London, 1930), pp. 127–8. The trade press was full of advice on issues such as 'Cutting for disproportionate figures', 'Oddly shaped men', 'Waistcoats for corpulent figures', 'Easy-fitting lounge for industrial districts', and so on. *The Tailor and Cutter*, 11 November 1920; 3 December 1925; 12 September 1930.

[63]   As did most other men's wear retailers, including ready-wear and mail order firms.

[64]   WYAS, Burton Archives, Box 36, Press Cuttings, *Chain and Multiple Store*, 30 April 1938.

[65]   WYAS, Burton Archives, Box 128, News Cuttings, *The Romford Times*, 15 March 1933; *The Bucks Free Press*, 17 March 1933.

[66]   WYAS, Burton Archives, Box 128, 'Manager's Guide', 1932.

[67]   WYAS, Burton Archives, Box 128, 250, 'Scientific Selling', 1927, p. 23.

'conveying on paper … to the clothing factory an exact record of a customer's figure', since the old system of classifying figures was 'a relic of the days when the cutter himself took the measures, rather than a shop assistant with no practical knowledge of the craft'.[68] Similar problems arose at the 'trying-on' stage. According to Louis Richter, for those 'who are in that happy position of fitting garments of their own cutting and measures, the work is pleasing and easy. But to those whose knowledge of the fundamentals is nil, it is easier to grope in the dark of a strange room than to meet with success as a fitter.'[69] In 1935, even Burton's acknowledged the problem of conveying to the factory 'in accurate terms, the fit of a garment when an alteration is necessary', but the shop assistant had no knowledge of tailoring. To try and provide them with some guidance, a series of photographs were produced, which featured examples of 'square shoulders', 'sloping shoulders', 'erect figure', and so on. By the mid-1930s, classes in measuring techniques were a central feature of a six-week training course for shop staff.[70]

Payment

If the process of choosing patterns and styles, and then of being measured and fitted could generate conflict between tailor and customer, these spats paled into insignificance when compared to the thorny issue of payment. Harry Lauder's song *Calligan – Call Again!* well illustrates the possible sources of conflict between tailor and customer in the matter of payment in a trade largely dependent on credit:

> Now Calligan always used to make my clothes,
> And I always used to pay him so much a week … never did I suppose
> He'd prove himself a very nasty sneak
> Some time ago from Calligan a pair of pants I bought,
> But since I've had them trousers, well, my work has fallen short.

Calligan called with the bill, refused to go away, and 'swore he'd put the coppers on my track'. When the money was not forthcoming, he demanded the trousers back, although 'they were all that I had got to wear … Said I to him, "What shall I be without a pair of pants?" Said he: "A living picture – or else tableaux vivants".'[71]

Of course, cash payments were by no means unknown in the clothing trade. Although it is very difficult to generalise, it seems that they were most prevalent in the ready-to-wear and outfitting sections. Multiple shops also enjoyed the notable advantage over independents of being able to 'insist on a deposit with every order, and cash before delivery. A man will willingly, and without being the least offended,

---

[68]   *Man and his Clothes*, June 1934.

[69]   *The Tailor and Cutter*, 4 February 1938.

[70]   WYAS, Burton Archives, Box 128, 189, Private booklet, 'Guide to Defects and Figure Description', 1935, n.p.; Box 128, 191, 'Clothing Classes Curriculum', 1935. See also, for example, Box 255, A Designer, 'Measuring Methods', July 1948, p. 12.

[71]   H. Lauder, *Calligan – Call Again!* (Francis, Day and Hunter, London, n.d.), n.p. The issue of consumer credit is explored in M.C. Finn, *The Character of Credit: Personal Debt in English Culture, 1740–1914* (Cambridge University Press, Cambridge, 2003).

pay for a suit in a multiple shop before he has tried it on. The same man is insulted if a one-man shop proprietor asks him for payment some months after the suit has been delivered'. As a result, multiples were able to reap the benefits of 'quick returns, very few alterations, and no bad debts'.[72] The large sign prominently displayed in Burton's shops, stating 'Deposit with order. Cash before delivery. No discount' would have left customers with no doubt about what was expected of them in the matter of payment. Recalcitrant individuals were to be reminded that 'Under our system we buy for cash, sell for cash, and save the customer's cash'.[73]

In some cases, it was customers themselves who insisted on a cash trade. Arthur Pluck, a Stowmarket clothier, recalled how the Edwardian farm labourer

> wouldn't have a bill. He wouldn't trust a bill. Perhaps he couldn't understand it; couldn't add the separate items quickly enough. Some of the labourers came into the town only very rarely those days ... they were off their home ground, so they were very careful. So he'd have a pair of trousers; and he'd pay for it and put it to one side ... and so on until he'd got what he wanted.[74]

Nonetheless, most bespoke tailors operated on the basis of credit: it was rare for them to demand cash payments. As *The Tailor and Cutter*'s editor pointed out in 1925, 'credit is so rife, so inseparably connected with the bespoke trade, that nothing short of a miracle will banish it'.[75] This was so much the case, that on becoming a Labour MP in 1906, J.R. Clynes, an ex-Lancashire piecer, was offended by a note from a London tailor, who offered him 'a suit of clothes, suitable for wear among the most distinguished and lordly of my new Parliamentary opponents', for a cash payment of 50 or 60 sovereigns. 'Apparently', Clynes complained, 'Labour Members were not granted credit'.[76] At the same time, if it was difficult for tailors to demand immediate payment, it could also be awkward for customers to ask the cost of the clothes they were ordering. Not long before the outbreak of the First World War, Siegfried Sassoon travelled up to London to try on a new hunting outfit at a high-class tailoring establishment: 'to have asked the price of so much as a waistcoat would have been an indecency. But I couldn't help wondering, as I was being ushered into one of the fitting compartments, just how many guineas my hunting coat was going to cost.'[77]

---

[72]	*Men's Wear*, 7 April 1923. See also K. Honeyman, 'Following suit: men, masculinity and gendered practices in the clothing trade in Leeds, England, 1890–1940', *Gender & History*, vol. 14, no. 3 (2002), p. 431.

[73]	WYAS, Burton Archives, Box 118, 'Shops and Openings', 3 / 12 Opening of Montague Burton new tailoring establishment at Colchester, 1936; Box 128, 250, 'Scientific Selling', 1927, p. 20. Although note how, despite the rhetoric, co-op shops were forced to provide their customers with some form of credit. M. Purvis, 'Co-operative retailing in Britain', in J. Benson and G. Shaw (eds), *The Evolution of Retail Systems, c. 1800–1914* (Leicester University Press, Leicester, 1992), p. 125. It would not be too surprising to find that necessity forced at least some menswear multiples to do the same.

[74]	G.E. Evans, *The Horse in the Furrow* (Faber and Faber, London, 1960), p. 81.

[75]	*The Tailor and Cutter*, 16 July 1925.

[76]	J.R. Clynes, *Memoirs 1869–1924* (Hutchinson, London, 1937), p. 114.

[77]	Sassoon, *Memoirs of a Fox-Hunting Man*, p. 116.

From the retailer's point of view, the main difficulty lay in attempting to assess the credit-worthiness, reliability and good character of customers about whom they often knew little or nothing. Unsurprisingly, they could on occasion get it entirely wrong. The tailor who sought to sell Max Cohen a five-guinea suit, initially demanding a deposit of thirty shillings, then by quick degrees lowering the sum to half a crown, does not seem to have noticed his extreme shabbiness, which should have given some indication of his near destitution: 'It is true', Cohen wryly explained, 'that I happened to be wearing a new pair of bootlaces, but I doubt whether these gave me a more than usually opulent appearance.'[78] At the other end of the social scale, Castell and Son had to contend with a youthful clientele composed largely of undergraduates who were in Oxford only for a few years, before disappearing to other parts of the country or abroad. Some turned out, quite simply, to have been 'rotten', with one extreme case being 'rotten in jail'.[79]

Difficulties could arise even with well-known customers, especially when they introduced relatives, friends or acquaintances to 'their' tailor. A case held in the King's Bench of the High Court in February 1908 shows how the relationship of trust between tailor and customer could all too easily break down. The action was brought by Reid Bros, London- and Huddersfield-based tailors and outfitters, against Mr F.W. Wright, an obviously affluent regular customer, 'to recover £74 2s 6d for goods supplied to defendant on his account and at his request'. Mr Wright admitted liability for goods worth just over ten pounds, 'but denied that the rest had been ordered by him or delivered to him on his orders'. It turned out that just over two years earlier the defendant, 'who was well-known to the shop's manager' had come to the shop with 'one Durnback, who was about to go abroad, [and] ordered a large quantity of clothes'. 'Enquiries' concerning Mr Durnback had raised concern about his credit-worthiness, and the plaintiffs had refused to deliver the garments until they were paid for. 'Defendant then called at the plaintiff's shop and expressed his annoyance that Durnback's clothes had not been delivered to him ... he ... said he would pay for Durnback's clothes up to £100. The clothes were then placed in Durnback's portmanteau, and placed in a cab and driven away'. When sent the bill, however, Mr Wright had refused to pay, protesting that he had 'not unconditionally promised to pay', but only if Durnback had not. The judge was unsympathetic to the defendant's argument: the shop manager, he stated, had clearly suspected that 'Durnback was not worth a farthing', but 'Wright so believed in him that he was ready to make himself responsible'. He thus had to take the consequences, and was ordered to pay the outstanding sum plus costs.[80]

At its best, however, a relationship of mutual trust could be established between tailor and customer, whereby financial risk was counterbalanced by knowledge of the customer's character and financial circumstances, and assurance of continued custom.

---

[78] Cohen, *I Was One of the Unemployed*, pp. 111–16.

[79] ORO, Records of Castell and Son, Tailors and Robe Makers, Oxford, B22/F1/1, Bad Debt Book, 1893–1945. The firm's bad debts were passed on to a debt-recovering agency. The work of these agencies is another area of research that would surely reward further study. See, for example, Finn, *The Character of Credit*, pp. 295–300.

[80] *Men's Wear*, 22 February 1908. See also, for example, *Men's Wear*, 25 April 1931.

Soon after starting a career in the army, Franklin Lushington and a friend decided to spend their first evening in London out on the town. They had no money, but that particular problem was solved by his friend 'cashing a cheque at his tailor', who was clearly confident that it would be honoured.[81] In some cases, a relationship was established between tailor and customer that could last for decades. As an undergraduate at the beginning of the century, for instance, T.B. Tate purchased from Castell and Son suits and shirts, as well as a range of sports and outfitting garments. In the 1920s and 1930s, by then living at various addresses in India, he was still faithfully obtaining from them – and promptly paying for – college ties and the odd lounge suit.[82]

Generally, the main problem for tailors seems not to have been credit *per se*, or even simply bad debts, but many customers' laxity in paying their bills, and the sometimes very long delays before even part of the outstanding sum was settled. In his 1935 autobiography, the theatre critic James Agate explained that he had been in debt to various retailers since the age of seventeen. He had always 'paid in the long run', he added, although 'the run has had to be long, and the trouble has arisen through my contemplating mile races while shorter-sighted tradesfolk have had their eyes on sprints of a hundred yards'[83] (Figure 9.4). As Lord Harris told the historian Michael Winstanley: 'the tailor was the fellow who was renowned for having to wait for his money. By the time you wanted a new suit you'd probably just paid for the old one. It was really like deferred payment today.'[84] Understandably, such attitudes infuriated retailers. Norman Nicholson's father 'was lenient to those of his own creditors, whom he knew to be genuinely hard up'. However, 'he had nothing but contempt for what he called the "high-ups" who ran up bills they could not afford to pay', leaving tradesmen waiting for long periods of time before they were paid. Of 'the wife of the manager of one of our local industries' he would comment disparagingly: '"Look at her ... walking about like Lady Muck, and she hasn't paid for the pyjamas she gave her husband last Christmas"'.[85]

In 1889 a contributor to *The Tailor and Cutter* pointed out in resignation that tailors' difficulties in obtaining payment were inevitable: 'the wise man in the trade recognises the fact that to be too ... exacting in his demands will be to "offend" his customer and lose perhaps both his money and his trade'. Increasingly, however, this attitude was replaced by a determination to recover debts, including through the courts: the men who were 'so servile as not to ask for their accounts when they are due' were condemned.[86] The organisation of mutual protection associations among tailors, sharing information

---

[81] F. Lushington, *Portrait of a Young Man* (Faber and Faber, London, n.d. [c.1940]), pp. 147–9.

[82] ORO, Records of Castell and Son, Tailors and Robe Makers, Oxford, B22/F2/1, Ledger CH2, 1903–37.

[83] J. Agate, *Ego* (Hamish Hamilton, London, 1935), p. 18.

[84] Quoted in Winstanley, *The Shopkeeper's World*, p. 55.

[85] Nicholson, *Wednesday Early Closing*, p. 152.

[86] *The Tailor and Cutter*, 16 May 1889; *The Weekly Record of Fashion*, August 1887. See also *The Tailor and Cutter*, 18 January 1894.

about 'smooth-tongued, oily individual[s] who didn't pay their bills' was advocated, although (it was lamented) not often put into practice.[87]

Menswear retailers' exasperation was exacerbated by the fact that tailors' difficulties in the matter of payment clearly aroused little sympathy outside the trade. The comic press regularly used tailors' attempts to obtain payment from their customers, and the ruses adopted by the latter in order not to pay their bills, as the basis

CUSTOMER : "I've brought these trousers to be re-seated. You see I sit a lot."
TAILOR : "It's about time you brought your bill to be receipted, too. You know I've stood a lot.

Figure 9.4   'It's about time you brought your bill to be receipted': paying the tailor's bill. *Men's Wear*, 14 February 1931. By permission of the British Library, LD178.

for humorous sketches.[88] In part, these should be seen in the context of papers like *Comic Cuts*, *Fun*, or *Illustrated Chips*' celebration of the quick wits and resourcefulness of their characters, pitted against figures of authority (most notably policemen, but also tradesmen and shopkeepers). However, it is difficult to avoid the conclusion that the persistently low status of tailors and tailoring contributed to a perception that consumers, whether affluent, hard-up, or somewhere in the middle, need not treat their bills as a priority. If tailors could not be taken seriously, then

---

[87]   *The Gentleman's Magazine of Fashion*, February 1889. On trade protection societies, see T.C. Whitlock, *Crime, Gender and Consumer Culture in Nineteenth-Century England* (Ashgate, Aldershot, 2005), pp. 155–9; Finn, *The Character of Credit*, pp. 288–314.

[88]   *Comic Cuts*, 27 June 1903; 4 July 1908; *Fun*, 12 December 1883; *Illustrated Chips*, 15 May 1915; *Judy*, 12 August 1903; *Tit-Bits*, Summer Annual 1930, p. 73. There were cases in which the tailor could outwit the customer, although not necessarily in the matter of payment. See, for example, *Comic Cuts*, 2 January 1909. See also the character of 'Happy 'Ike, the old clo' man', portrayed as a wily old man, which regularly appeared in *Comic Cuts* in 1912.

– arguably – neither could their requests for payment. All too often, it was felt that tailors' claims were not taken seriously by county court judges either. It was hardly fair of them – Richard Roe pointed out in 1903 – to 'produce "roars of laughter" before an amused court at the expense of the tailor who vainly expects to get both law and equity in bringing some contemptible specimen of humanity up to scratch, because he refuses to pay his bill, or complains of some real or imaginary crease'.[89]

In Henry Williamson's semi-autobiographical novel *The Innocent Moon*, the protagonist's friend Julian arrived for a visit with two new suits. 'The two suits had cost nine guineas each; he had not yet paid for them. He had an idea, from occasional jokes in *Punch*, that the correct thing was never to pay one's tailor, for a few years anyway.'[90] As *Men's Wear*'s editor complained in 1905, 'there are men walking about to-day, well-dressed, … who often boast that they never pay for clothes. The alleged humorous Press is filled with "jokes" upon this subject.'[91] It is perhaps not surprising, then, to find that in the 1930s the Salford tailor Abe Sacks should have 'a chap handing the things out and collecting the money by the name of Jack Bennett, a well known local boxer'.[92]

Conclusion

In 1886 Mr D. Winstanley bought a suit of clothes costing £7 18s from the Cheltenham tailors Felton and Son. When the garments were delivered to his home, Mr Winstanley declared himself horrified by the coat, which he judged a 'disgraceful misfit' and refused to pay for the clothes. Unusually, the tailor then seems to have lost his temper, writing in a curt postcard to Mr Winstanley what most retailers no doubt thought: that the troublesome customer was seeing faults where none existed. Not only did Mr Felton express his complete confidence in the cutter's workmanship, but pointed out that 'the imaginary imperfections in the coat would vanish when he put it on'. Eventually, the matter was resolved in court, which found in the tailor's favour, although not before Mr Felton was rebuked by the judge for his rudeness to the customer.[93]

The relationship between tailor and customer did not often break down as completely as this. No doubt, most shopping expeditions were routine, even rather dull events. For most customers, the tailor's shop held few surprises, and even before crossing the threshold, they would have had certain expectations about what they would see and hear once they got inside. These were rarely disappointed, in multiple as well as in independent shops. Nonetheless, opportunities for conflict abounded. From the moment when decisions had to be made about the type of garment the customer wanted to order, to the moment when he had to reveal all, as his measures were taken, to the final moment when he – often reluctantly – had to part with his money, the

---

[89]   *The London Tailor*, June 1903. See also, for example, ibid., April 1907. Also Finn, *The Character of Credit*, pp. 252–64, 306–14.

[90]   Williamson, *The Innocent Moon*, p. 146.

[91]   *Men's Wear*, 4 March 1905.

[92]   R. Heaton, *Salford: My Home Town* (Neil Richardson, Manchester, 1982), p. 17.

[93]   *The Gentleman's Magazine of Fashion*, February 1886.

process of buying a made-to-measure suit, in an independent as much as in a multiple shop, involved some tricky negotiations between the customer and his tailor.

For his part, the tailor could deploy his professional expertise, or in the case of the chain-store shop assistant, arguments about his firm's highly developed business systems, in order to steer the customer towards making particular choices in the matter of cloth, cut or other details. Menswear retailers could also sneakily enjoy making customers feel uncomfortable during the measuring process, although awkwardly proportioned individuals could give them headaches too. Those who suffered most, perhaps, were those independent tailors who made much of their ability to satisfy all customers' individual requirements and to fit all shapes and sizes, a claim that was intended to set them apart from the purveyors of mass-produced clothes. That said, most customers would have noticed little difference between shopping for made-to-measure suits in an independent or a multiple shop: the rituals and procedures, as well as the look of the shop itself, were very similar, not least because multiples like Burton's actually modelled their outlets on 'traditional' bespoke shops. Or perhaps more accurately, customers would have noticed little difference until the matter of payment was broached. Indeed, many multiples' refusal to grant credit was arguably one of the greatest advantages they enjoyed over their independent counterparts, as was their avoidance of the problems of bad debt and delayed payments. Unlike most independents, they did not have to try and guess customers' credit-worthiness on the basis of what often was little or no information beyond manner and – rather ironically – dress and appearance.

Given the possible sources of conflict, it is not surprising that customers' feelings about the whole shopping process, as well as towards the commodity they ended up owning, could vary enormously, ranging from pride and pleasure, to disappointment and anger. When Huntly Gordon joined the Royal Military Academy in 1916, he went to an 'inexpensive' Edinburgh tailor to purchase a suit with which to travel down to London: 'Unfortunately when I came to try it on ... the trousers turned out to be too long and too tight, and the coat too big. However, knowing that within a few weeks this sorry misfit would be replaced by a well-fitted uniform, I put a good face on it and presented myself to [barracks]'.[94] Other dissatisfied customers were less forgiving. In 1895 Joseph Neave, a grocer's assistant in Aldbury, Hertfordshire, refused to pay for a suit of clothes, which he considered to be a misfit. When ordered to pay by the small claims court, Neave took revenge by inserting an advertisement in the local newspaper, offering 'For sale, a cheap misfit suit of clothes made by Ashby & co.'[95] Most customers, no doubt, were neither as unhappy as Neave nor particularly delighted with their sartorial experiences. A middle-class Mass Observation respondent's opinion in 1939 was probably typical of the attitude of many. He acknowledged that when buying clothes he usually let himself be guided by his tailor: 'He know more about it than I do ... [I] manage to look reasonably presentable, so suppose it's all right'.[96]

---

[94]   H. Gordon, *The Unreturning Army: A Field-Gunner in Flanders, 1917–18* (J.M. Dent and Sons, London, 1967), pp. 20–21.

[95]   *The Master Tailor and Cutter's Gazette*, November 1895.

[96]   Horwood, *Keeping Up Appearances*, p. 24.

Conclusion

Not long before the outbreak of the First World War, the youthful Archie Yuille had enthusiastically embraced the newly fashionable practice of wearing turn-ups at the bottom of his trousers. Not everybody was impressed. One Sunday afternoon he reluctantly visited one of his father's sisters. She 'looked at me and said – Archie – no gentleman walks into a lady's drawing room with his trousers turned up, turn them down at once'.[1] This was one rule of dress that poor Archie clearly knew nothing about. And yet, why should a young – or indeed, not so young – man not wear turned-up trousers, either in the presence of a lady or anywhere else? It is pretty obvious why society should seek to prevent and if necessary punish actions that leave clear victims, such as fraud or theft. It is not so obvious why apparently inconsequential practices, such as wearing turn-ups with a frock coat, or a coloured shirt with a morning coat, should have been condemned too.[2] After all, who were the victims here? The answer, perhaps, was everybody. If clothes and appearance contributed to fashioning the various collective male identities upon which contemporary society was based, it arguably followed that sartorial non-conformity implied both their rejection and a suspicious lack of allegiance to the social order.

Dress – this book has argued – was not a purely personal matter. Indeed, sartorial practices support Robert Connell's contention that 'personal life and collective social arrangements … are linked in a fundamental and constitutive way'.[3] It was not necessarily details such as the shape of a jacket, the colour of a shirt or the material of a pair of trousers that mattered, but rather, the very act of conformity. This does not mean that there was a single British model of manhood and masculine 'look' that all men were expected or sought to adhere to. Rather, there existed a set of local, contingent and more or less explicit sartorial standards, influenced by issues of gender, class, ethnicity and age, deviation from which meant to bring into question the very 'male solidarities and understandings of manhood which were woven into the complex tapestry of local male identities'.[4] It is not really surprising, then, that the enforcement of sartorial codes –

---

[1] National Social Policy and Social Change Archive, Albert Sloman Library, University of Essex (NSPSC Archive), The Edwardians: Family Life and Work Experience Before 1918, oral history collection (The Edwardians), QD1/FLWE/MUC/2011, interview transcript, Mr Archie Yuille, businessman. Compare with T.S. Eliot, 'The love song of J. Alfred Prufrock' (1917), in *The Complete Poems and Plays of T.S. Eliot* (Faber and Faber, 1982; first published in this edition 1969), pp. 13–17: 'I shall wear the bottoms of my trousers rolled …'. Many thanks to Philip de Jersey for this reference

[2] W. Macqueen Pope, *Twenty Shillings in the Pound* (Hutchinson, London, n.d. [c. 1949]), pp. 177–8.

[3] R.W. Connell, *Gender and Power: Society, the Person and Sexual Politics* (Polity Press, Cambridge, 1987), p. 17.

[4] P. Ayers, 'The making of men: masculinities in interwar Liverpool', in M. Walsh (ed.), *Working Out Gender: Perspectives from Labour History* (Ashgate, Aldershot, 1999), p. 75.

generally by ridicule, but occasionally by verbal and physical violence – was undertaken most zealously (although by no means exclusively, as Archie's aunt demonstrates) from *within* male peer groups: the boys and men encountered on a day-to-day basis in the neighbourhood, the pub, the school, the club, the workplace, and so on.

Despite this diversity, however, it was by no means the case that the sartorial choices of all groups of men enjoyed equal status, reflecting the fact that not all masculinities were equally powerful, not benefiting to the same degree from economic and political resources, opportunities for social mobility, education and knowledge, physical supremacy and last but certainly not least, claims to heterosexuality.[5] It may not be possible to identify a single 'hegemonic masculinity' and its related sartorial expression, but this does not mean that all ways of being a man enjoyed the same status and cachet. The male shop assistant's garb, for instance, while perfectly correct in the context of the shop, nevertheless enjoyed at best some very ambivalent connotations, reflecting shop workers' perceived servility and lack of manly independence, in sharp contrast to, for example, the slick elegance of the perfectly tailored and debonair English gentleman. Furthermore, sartorial judgements and preferences were not immutable. In this book, the most notable example of a shift in opinion was provided by the upheaval of the First World War, and the at least temporary discrediting of some forms of civilian attire – including some of the elements of 'gentlemanly' dress – in favour of military uniforms. And not just the glamorous service dress of officers in elite regiments, but also the mass-produced and often ill-fitting khaki uniforms of the ranks.

As far as men were concerned, far from being an irrelevance or a meaningless activity, clothes consumption played an important part in constructing and reinforcing collective male identities. At the most fundamental level, it served to assert men's difference from women. Men, few would have disagreed, did not wear dresses or other feminine garments. They certainly were not supposed to wear 'ankle length black lace frock, imitation leopard skin coat, blue silk underslip, pink knickers, gun metal stockings, ladies-size ... high-heeled shoes ... and a handbag containing rouge and powder puff', the garments a young transvestite was forced to wear at the judge's insistence during his trial for homosexuality in 1931.[6] At the same time, apart from reinforcing the boundary between the sexes, clothes consumption also contributed to establishing the legitimacy of a male group and of a particular way of being a man, based on often unspoken assumptions about what was appropriate wear at different times and in different places. When the costermonger in the popular music-hall song *The Coat 'urts Me Underneath the Arm* plied his trade wearing a comfortable

---

[5]   Robert Connell considers the relationship between masculinities and power, including the importance of consent to 'hegemonic masculinity', in Connell, *Gender and Power*, pp. 107–111, 184–6, although the main focus is on the relationship of power between men and women. See also J. Tosh, 'Hegemonic masculinity and the history of gender', in S. Dudnik, K. Hagemann and J. Tosh (eds), *Masculinities in Politics and War: Gendering Modern History* (Manchester University Press, Manchester, 2004), pp. 41–58; R.W. Connell, *Gender* (Polity Press, Cambridge, 2003; first published 2002), especially pp. 58–60; J. Tosh, 'What should historians do with masculinity? Reflections on nineteenth-century Britain', *History Workshop Journal*, issue 38 (1994), pp. 179–202.

[6]   A. McLaren, *The Trials of Masculinity: Policing Sexual Boundaries 1870–1930* (The University of Chicago Press, Chicago, 1997), p. 210. See also pp. 207–31.

guernsey jumper and corduroy trousers, he hardly attracted any attention. But when, in order to please an aunt whose money he wished to inherit, he took to wearing a top hat and frock coat, his troubles started: 'They come to me with orders in a nice sarcastic way; It's "Will the noble marquis kindly weigh a pound of beans?"'[7]

Conformity, this book has stressed, was ultimately enforced by the use of ridicule, verbal abuse and even physical violence. However, this should not lead us to underestimate the importance of willing – even enthusiastic – consent. The autobiographies and reminiscences used in this book were much more likely to record instances when the author or interviewee found himself at odds with the sartorial 'rules', rather than the times when they had themselves contributed to their enforcement, if only, perhaps, with a sarcastic remark or meaningful 'look'. There was no clearly defined group of correctly-dressed men or boys who sought to impose conformity on recalcitrant rebels. Indeed, men were even less likely to mention in their memoirs occasions when, simply and uneventfully, they had found themselves in agreement with the 'common-sense' consensus. For every 'Francey milord', 'gentleman collier' or University tutor dressed as a 'British workman',[8] there were plenty of others who thought their idiosyncratic style of dressing ridiculous, inappropriate or even infuriating. No doubt, many men chose to conform against their personal inclination, in order to spare themselves a good deal of trouble. However, plenty more were quite happy to fit in.

The pleasure and gratification that could be obtained from wearing 'approved' clothes were considerable. The garments in question need not have been anything special. Indeed, among rural villagers at the end of the nineteenth century, 'to put on clean clothes and lighter boots was itself an aid and inspiration to the spirit'.[9] However, when the clothes were new or better quality than usual, the pleasure was intensified further. Huw, the protagonist and narrator of Richard Llewellyn's novel *How Green Was My Valley*, wore his first grown-up tailor-made suit on the occasion of his sister's wedding: 'Royal, royal is the feeling, to be standing in your good long trews.' He could only catch a glimpse of his reflection in the tiny mirror in his bedroom, 'But I was feeling elegant, and that was enough for me. Even old Napoleon never felt so good, and when I went downstairs, very careful again, no Queen's Ambassador to the Court of the Tzar had more straightness in his back, or lift to his nose, or firmness to his feet, than I had.'[10]

[7]   W. Hastings, E. Bateman (authors) and A. Perry (composer), *The Coat 'urts Me Underneath the Arm* (Francis, Day and Hunter, London, 1901).

[8]   P. McGeown, *Heat the Furnace Seven Times More* (Hutchinson, London, 1967), p. 56; R. Davies, *Print of a Hare's Foot: An Autobiographical Beginning* (Seren, Bridgend, 1998; first published 1969), p. 73; C. Oman, *Memories of Victorian Oxford and of Some Early Years* (Methuen, London, 1941), pp. 207–8.

[9]   W. Rose, *Good Neighbours* (Green Books, Bideford, 1988; first published 1942), p. 82.

[10]   R. Llewellyn, *How Green Was My Valley* (New English Library, Sevenoaks, 1985; first published 1939), p. 290.

Nine tailors

In her exploration of the relationship between credit and masculinity in early modern England, Alexandra Shepard has observed that the many men who could not aspire to the 'economic independence and mastery' that were fundamental to dominant notions of manliness,[11] did not simply hang their heads in shame and accept their unmanly status in resignation. On the contrary, many among them developed alternative understandings of 'proper' masculinity, often based on 'drinking bouts, collective misrule and daring spectacles, and carefully calculated displays of violence, excess and disorder'.[12] The parallel with tailoring workers and menswear retailers is clear. Although in a very different way, they too responded to the trade's overwhelming association with pitiful unmanliness by trying to develop positive understandings of their role both as craftsmen and as retailers.

The terms and concepts they used were not novel or original. Notions of artistic skill, sober industriousness or up-to-date business know-how were hardly unheard-of. Furthermore, unlike the unruly and violent men considered by Shepard, they neither did, nor wished to, challenge the social order. The understandings of manliness developed by tailoring workers posed no threat (certainly no physical threat) to other men, or – significantly – women. Nevertheless, despite the apparent lack of forcefulness, such understandings served two useful functions for tailors who wished to construct positive identities for themselves and their trade. Firstly, in a changing economic and business context, they served to distinguish independents from their competitors, be they cheap 'brass and glass' shops, attractive-looking multiples or other big businesses. Secondly, they helped establish a boundary between the trade's past and its present. Geoffrey Crossick has suggested that myths about the past, and particularly about a golden age of artisanal production, have played a central part in the development of early modern and modern European craft identities: 'There had always been a better artisanal past, it seems, whether in the minds of craftsmen themselves or of those seeking to sketch a better future from an idealised artisanate.'[13] At the same time, as far as tailors and menswear retailers were concerned, myths and memories about the past served to set the serious, modern and successful craftsmen and businessmen of the present apart from the (supposedly) degraded, drunken and improvident 'cock and pie' tailoring workers of the not so distant past.

Of course, to observe the extensive use of such a rhetoric of business and craft manliness, and its links to wider contemporary concerns, such as the problems of sweating and competition, is a good deal easier than to measure its effectiveness. It arguably worked best for the small minority of high-class or 'Savile Row' tailors whose products and rituals could be invested with a special glamour and extra value that few dared dispute, even as (or perhaps especially as) mass-produced and distributed menswear gained increasing market dominance. In 1932, Sir Stephen

---

[11]   The cautious terms 'dominant notions of manliness' are mine: Shepard argues rather more strongly that these amounted to a 'patriarchal ideology'.

[12]   A. Shepard, 'Manhood, credit and patriarchy in early modern England, c. 1580–1640', *Past & Present*, no. 167 (2000), pp. 102.

[13]   G. Crossick, 'Past masters: in search of the artisan in European history', in G. Crossick (ed.), *The Artisan and the European Town, 1500–1900* (Scolar Press, Aldershot, 1997), p. 3.

Tallents, secretary of the Empire Marketing Board, published an influential leaflet, *The Projection of England*, where he argued that 'we ... must set ourselves to throw a fitting presentation of England upon the world's screen'. Tellingly, among the deeply conservative and yet uncontroversial 'medley of institutions and excellences' that he considered worth including were 'the arts of gardening and tailoring'.[14]

However, as far as the majority of menswear retailers, particularly small, independent retailers, were concerned, the gap between rhetoric and reality often proved too wide to be bridged. Sumner Brown, the owner of a tailoring shop in the Lincolnshire village of Digby, seemed to conform to the image of the pitifully weak tailoring worker, since 'unfortunately, he did not have the use of his legs and went about on crutches'. The reality was more complex: he was a hard-working and independent artisan and shopkeeper, who employed two journeymen tailors, took an active role in the social life of the village, and to some extent had managed to overcome his disability: 'Unaided he could get the cloth down from his shelves, measure and fit his customers'. He also paid some attention to the retail side of his business: his 'pleasant' shop's side-window 'had the only men's outfitting display in the village', although this usually consisted of some studs, a cap and a tie. At the same time, this does not mean that he conformed to the manly ideal of a modern and successful businessman. Like many other independent retailers, in the 1890s his business began to suffer from multiples' competition. 'Everybody was sorry for Sumner Brown when his trade declined as, being a cripple with no legs, he had nothing else to turn to ... he was a very pleasant man and a good workman, but he just could not compete in his slow methods with machine-made suits at 25s each.'[15]

Even when there was no glamorous competition in the vicinity, independent tailors often failed to impress. In his 1942 autobiography, Walter Rose had words of praise for all the craftsmen that had peopled the village of his childhood, each of whom 'was ensconced in a private knowledge of his craft'. The very notable exceptions were the tailors. He acknowledged that the villagers who depended on them for their attire were not easily pleased: 'only reliable workmanship could stand against the strong tide of local opinion, always voiced freely'. Nevertheless, he remained dismissive: 'male tailors ... sat cross-legged on benches, hand-stitching "leather-cloth" and corduroy, for so long that one wondered if their legs would ever have power to resume a leg's proper action. It seemed to me a job for which man was not intended; I never envied them, nor did I learn anything about their methods of work.'[16] In the Sussex village of Rottingdean in the 1920s, peering 'into the dimly lit interior' of the tailor's shop, 'you could see the hump-backed, bearded figure of Mr Trowbridge sitting like a gnome cross-legged on the wide, mahogany counter surrounded by bales of suiting ... with a tape-measure draped round his neck ... He sat there eternally, it seemed ... Poor Mr Trowbridge seemed to live a lonely and unenviable existence.'[17]

---

[14]   J. Richards, *The Age of the Dream Palace: Cinema and Society in Britain 1930–1939* (Routledge and Kegan Paul, London, 1984), pp. 248–9.

[15]   F. Gresswell, *Bright Boots: An Autobiography* (David and Charles, Newton Abbot, 1982; first published 1956), pp. 87–8, 107–15.

[16]   Rose, *Good Neighbours*, pp. 47–8.

[17]   B. Copper, *Early to Rise: A Sussex Boyhood* (Heinemann, London, 1976), p. 46.

Although not mentioned in so many words, the ghosts of the nine tailors continued to haunt a trade where small independent businesses were slowly but surely being squeezed out of existence. Ultimately, both cheerful tailors like Sumner Brown, or more forbidding ones like Mr Trowbridge, whose shop's 'silent and solitary gloom … seeped out even through the closed door',[18] often remained what they had always been: objects of pity.

Shopping

In 1893 – Arnold Bennett recounted in the novel *The Old Wives' Tale* – 'a new and strange man' came to live in the Potteries town of Bursley. He was the son of Bursley's leading tailor, and had been apprenticed in London before returning to his native town after his father's death. It was in Bursley that he made 'a fortune while creating a new type in the town'. Before his arrival, 'any cap was a cap in Bursley, and any collar was a collar', but soon:

> no cap was a cap, and no collar was a collar, which did not exactly conform in shape and material to certain sacred caps and collars guarded by the young tailor in his back shop … their sacredness endured for about six months, and then suddenly … they fell from their estate and became lower than offal for dogs, and were supplanted at the altar.

The new type of man created by the tailor could 'be recognised by its caps and collars, and in a similar manner by every other article of attire, except its boots', which the tailor did not sell.[19] Most tailors and menswear retailers could only dream of exercising such control over their customers' shopping practices and decisions: real consumers were by no means as malleable as their fictional counterparts. Still, this did not stop retailers from trying to stamp their authority on all stages of the purchasing process, nor customers from seeking to have their own way.

That said, to suggest that the relationship between tailor and customer should simply be understood as a power struggle is no doubt an exaggeration. This characterisation does not accurately reflect the often amicable and long-standing relationships that could develop between a friendly, pleasant tailor and a satisfied, promptly-paying customer. As Molly Hughes explained in 1946, her husband's tailor eventually became 'more of a friend than a tailor to both of us, taking genuine interest in the joys and sorrows of our life; and now his sons clothe my son Arthur in the same delightful way'.[20] It also does not reflect the routine, unremarkable nature of most shopping expeditions, such as the one with which this book has opened: the Birmingham lad in question went to a shop, bought a cap and tie and came home again, all with minimum fuss.[21] Furthermore, the exchanges between tailor and

---

[18]   Ibid., p. 46.

[19]   A. Bennett, *The Old Wives' Tale* (Penguin Books, London, 1990; first published 1908), pp. 300–301.

[20]   M.V. Hughes, *A London Home in the 1890s* (Oxford University Press, Oxford, 1979; first published 1946), pp. 149–50. There is little indication that Hughes had taken a similar interest in the tailor's family.

[21]   A. Freeman, *Boy Life and Labour: The Manufacture of Inefficiency* (P.S. King and Son, London, 1914), p. 113.

customer often followed such a well-worn and familiar pattern, that little space was arguably left for conflict, especially when credit was not an issue. As long as retailer and customer both played their parts, all generally went well. Sidney Day explained that when a customer entered one of 'the fifty bob tailors' shops' in the inter-war years, 'The tailor would show you a load of patterns and colours and when one took yer fancy you would stop him and say, "I like that one". Then he would get the tape out and measure you up. "Come back next week and have another fitting", he would say.' As far as Day was concerned, the result was a very satisfactory and 'beautiful' made-to-measure suit, which could be obtained for the very moderate cost of fifty shillings.[22]

Nonetheless, issues of power and authority cannot entirely be discounted from the shopping process either. From the customer's point of view, what was at stake was the achievement of a proper masculine appearance, which would ensure that he 'fitted in' with the other youths and men in his locality, would not be ridiculed, and in the best possible scenario, might actually be envied and admired. Few men, furthermore, had bottomless pockets from which to fund their sartorial efforts. Max Cohen experienced at first hand the horror of a semi-destitute man finding that the trousers he had just bought at 'one of the cheap stores', and which had cost him all the precious 'money I had for food' that week, were about six inches too big for him. It was only after he 'had engaged in a desperate argument with, apparently, every member of the staff, from the errand boy to the branch manager' that he was finally given another pair.[23]

From the retailer's point of view, his very livelihood was seen to depend on the ability to satisfy customers' whims, customers who all too often appeared unreasonable and duplicitous, if not actually dishonest, especially when it came to extracting money from them. Huge efforts might have to be made to obtain and retain custom, frequently also putting pressure further back in the distribution chain. Being interviewed as part of Charles Booth's investigation into the working and living conditions of the London poor in 1888, Harris Garfinkle, a small manufacturer specialising in bespoke work, complained about the short notice provided by many shops:

[Only] the previous Saturday, when he went to one of his shops, they had a coat that they wanted on Monday morning, so that the customer could attend a funeral. He said he could not do it, but was pressed, and was told that this was the first order the man had given and that he had three brothers whose orders would be obtained if this were done. He said that he would do it ...[24]

Making sure that all customers – including the rude and unreasonable ones – left the shop satisfied, having met all their requirements with 'energy, virility, sparkle and buoyancy', often proved to be a challenge.[25] In reality, the need to please customers could translate in a behaviour that appeared to be the very opposite of 'virile'. During

[22]   S. Day, *London Born* (Fourth Estate, London, 2004), p. 66.
[23]   M. Cohen, *I Was One of the Unemployed* (Victor Gollancz, London, 1945), p. 106.
[24]   British Library of Political and Economic Science Archives, London School of Economics, Papers of Charles Booth, Survey Notebooks, Booth A19, interview with Harris Garfinkle, 1888, pp. 92–3.
[25]   Montague Burton, 'Manager's Guide', quoted in K. Honeyman, 'Following suit: men, masculinity and gendered practices in the clothing trade in Leeds, England, 1890–1940', *Gender & History*, vol. 14, no. 3 (2002), p. 438.

his lunch break in 1937, a young Liverpool clerk went with a friend 'to a ready-made tailor store which I hoped would have a cheap hat'. He pointed out that the shop was 'very vulgarly ornately planned and the attendants are unpleasantly servile'. Once he had chosen and paid for his purchase, he found that the attitude of the sales assistants had noticeably changed. His friend 'noted that they were not nearly as fawning after you had bought something as before'.[26]

Men and menswear

When first conceived, the original title of this book was to be *Menswear and Manliness: Selling Men's Clothes in Britain, 1880–1939*. Having been struck by the extent of tailors' low status and lack of manly credentials, I wanted to find out whether it was possible to sell menswear without renouncing all claims to manliness. As it turns out, there *is* a good deal of manliness in this book, if by the term we understand 'those attributes which men were happy to own, which they had often acquired with great effort, and which they frequently boasted about – as in "manly character" or "manly figure"'.[27] Not least, manliness appears in tailors' and menswear retailers' attempts to develop a positive identity for themselves and their trade, often against considerable odds. Ultimately, however, this book says a good deal more about the experiences of being a man than about men's efforts to be manly. Buying, selling and wearing clothes, it has been argued, were all part of men's day-to-day lives in the six decades before the Second World War. As such, their engagement with sartorial consumption reveals a wealth of information about men's identities and experiences, and particularly about their relationships with other men: with fellow consumers, retailers and customers.

It is hoped that the opposite has also been shown: that consumption cannot be ignored when considering men's lives and identities. Buying and wearing, as well as selling clothes, this book has suggested, were not somehow alien to men and incompatible with masculinity. To suggest so means obscuring much that was taken for granted in boys' and men's lives, from the pleasure and worry of buying a new outfit, to the mortification of those whose appearance was mocked, to the discontent felt by the men who had to wear the same tatty or nondescript garments day after day. After all, if sartorial consumption did not matter, how is it possible to explain the priorities of a young man like Lennox Kerr? In his 1940 autobiography, he looked back fondly upon his younger self, growing up in the Scottish town of Paisley, where he worked in the local cooked meat factory. In 1915, the sixteen-year-old Kerr 'had a thousand standards of good behaviour. I had no ambitions except to learn how to season sausages. And to be one of the best-dressed chaps on the High Street.'[28]

---

[26]   H. Jennings and C. Madge (eds), *May the Twelfth Mass-Observation Day-Surveys 1937* (Faber and Faber, London, 1937), p. 386.

[27]   J. Tosh, *Manliness and Masculinity in Nineteenth-Century Britain* (Pearson Education, Harlow, 2005), p. 3.

[28]   L. Kerr, *The Eager Years: An Autobiography* (Collins, London, 1940), p. 20.

Bibliography

Books first published before 1939

Anon., *How to Run a Shop at a Profit* (A.W. Shaw, London, 1916).

Anon., *The Tailor and the Crow: An Old Rhyme with New Drawings by L. Leslie Brooke* (Frederick Warne, London, 1911).

Anon. [Samuel Foote], *The Tailors: A Tragedy for Warm Weather* (Joseph Thomas, London, 1836).

Anon., *Tinker Tailor* (Henry Frowde and Hodder and Stoughton, London, n.d. [c. 1912]).

Arlen, M., *The Green Hat: A Romance for a Few People* (The Boydell Press, Woodbridge, 1983; first published 1924).

Balfour, P., *Society Racket: A Critical Survey of Modern Social Life* (John Lang, London, n.d. [c. 1933]).

Bell, Lady, *At the Works: A Study of a Manufacturing Town*, (Virago, London, 1985; first published 1907).

Bennett, A., *The Old Wives' Tale* (Penguin Books, London, 1990; first published 1908).

Booth, C. (ed.), *Life and Labour of the People in London* (Macmillan, London, 1893).

Bosanquet, Mrs B., *Rich and Poor* (Macmillan, London, 1896).

Bowley, A.L., *Prices and Wages in the United Kingdom, 1914–1920* (Clarendon Press, Oxford, 1921).

Bowley, A.L. and Burnett-Hurst, A.R., *Livelihood and Poverty* (G. Bell, London, 1915).

Bridgland, A.S. (ed.), *The Modern Tailor Outfitter and Clothier*, 3 vols (Caxton Publishing, London, n.d.).

Brierley, W., *Means Test Man* (Methuen, London, 1935).

Burgess, F.W., *The Practical Retail Draper: A Complete Guide for the Drapery and Allied Trades*, 5 vols (Virtue, London, 1912–14).

Butler, S., *The Way of All Flesh* (Wordsworth Classics, Ware, 1994; first published 1903).

Cameron, W., *Common People* (Victor Gollancz, London, 1938).

Campbell, R., *The London Tradesman* (London, 1747).

Carlyle, T., *Sartor Resartus: The Life and Opinions of Herr Teufelsdröckh* (Chapman and Hall, London, 1901; first published in book form 1836).

Chiozza Money, L.G., *Riches and Poverty* (Methuen, London, 1905).

Conrad, J., *The Secret Agent: A Simple Tale* (Penguin Books, London, 1990; first published in book form 1907).

Crosland, T.W.H., *The Suburbans* (John Lang, London, 1905).

Deeping, W., *Sorrell and Son* (Cassell, London, 1953; first published 1925).

de Vesselitsky, V., *Expenditure and Waste: A Study in War-Time* (Ratan Tata Foundation, London, 1917).

Dobbs, S.P., *The Clothing Workers of Great Britain* (George Routledge and Sons, London, 1928).

Family Budgets: Being the Income and Expenses of Twenty-Eight British Households 1891–1894 (P.S. King and Son, London, 1896).

Flint, A, *The Tailor's Answer to the Late Attacks Upon their Profession from the Stage and Press* (Wake, London, 1805).

Flügel, J.C., *The Psychology of Clothes* (The Hogarth Press, London, 1930).

Freeman, A., *Boy Life and Labour: The Manufacture of Inefficiency* (P.S. King and Son, London, 1914).

Gissing, G., *New Grub Street* (Penguin Books, London, 1985; first published 1891).

Greenwood, W., *Love on the Dole* (Penguin Books, Harmondsworth, 1969; first published 1933).

Jennings, H. and Madge, C. (eds), *May the Twelfth Mass-Observation Day-Surveys 1937* (Faber and Faber, London, 1937).

How the Casual Labourer Lives: A Report of the Joint Research Committee on the Domestic Condition and Expenditure of the Families of Certain Liverpool Labourers (Liverpool Economic and Statistical Society, Liverpool, 1909).

Huxley, A., *Antic Hay* (Flamingo, London, 1994; first published 1923).

Kelly's Directory of Oxford and Neighbourhood for 1937 (Kelly, London, 1937).

Kelly's Directory of Oxford and Neighbourhood for 1890–91 (Kelly, London, 1890–91).

Kingsley, C., *Alton Locke: Tailor and Poet* (T. Nelson and Sons, London, n.d.; first published 1850).

Kingsley, C., *Cheap Clothes and Nasty* (William Pickering, London, 1850).

Llewellyn, R., *How Green Was My Valley* (New English Library, Sevenoaks 1985; first published 1939).

Llewellyn Smith, H. (ed.), *The New Survey of London Life and Labour*, 9 vols (P.S. King and Son, London, 1931).

Loane, M., *An Englishman's Castle* (Edward Arnold, London, 1909).

Loane, M., *From Their Point of View* (Edward Arnold, London, 1908).

London, J., *The People of the Abyss* (Isbister, London, 1903).

Macdonnell, A.G., *England, their England* (Macmillan, London, 1933).

Madge, C. and Harrison, T., *Britain by Mass-Observation* (Penguin Books, Harmondsworth, 1939).

The 'Major' of *To-day*, *Clothes and the Man: Hints on the Wearing and Caring of Clothes* (Grant Richards, London, 1900).

Masterman, C.F.G., *England After War: A Study* (Hodder and Stoughton, London, n.d., [c. 1923]).

Meredith, G., *Evan Harrington* (Constable, London, 1902; first published 1861).

Mr. Punch's History of the Great War (Cassell, London, 1919).

Mudie Smith, R. (ed.), *Sweated Industries: Being a Handbook of the Daily News Exhibition* (Bradbury, Agnew, London, 1906).

Nystrom, P., *The Economics of Retailing* (The Ronald Press, New York, 1920; first published 1915).

Orwell, G., *Coming Up for Air* (Penguin Books, Harmondsworth, 1984; first published 1939).

Orwell, G., *Down and Out in Paris and London* (Penguin Books, London, n.d.; first published 1933).

Orwell, G., *Keep the Aspidistra Flying* (Penguin Books, London, 1989; first published 1936).

Orwell, G., *The Road to Wigan Pier* (Heinemann Educational, London, 1965; first published 1937).

The Pilgrim Trust, *Men Without Work* (Cambridge University Press, Cambridge, 1938).

Poole, B.W., *The Clothing Trades Industry* (Pitman and Sons, London, 1920).

Potter, B., *The Tailor of Gloucester* (Frederick Warne, London, 1903).

Priestley, J.B., *English Journey: Being a Rambling but Truthful Account of what One Man Saw* (Penguin, Harmondsworth, 1977; first published 1934).

Priestley, J.B., *The Good Companions* (Heinemann, London, 1974; first published 1929).

Renier, G.J., *The English: Are they Human?* (Ernst Benn, London, 1956; first published 1931).

Reynoldson, S., Woolley, B. and Woolley, T., *Seems So! A Working-Class View of Politics* (Macmillan, London, 1911).

Richardson, N. (ed.), *Good Value and No Humbug: A Discourse on Some of the Principal Trades and Manufactories in Manchester in 1892* (N. Richardson, Swinton, 1982; first published 1892).

Rider Haggard H., *King Solomon's Mines* (Oxford University Press, Oxford, 1991; first published 1885).

Rittenberg, M., *Selling Schemes for Retailers: Proved Methods which will Help the Retailer to do More Trade* (George Routledge and Sons, London, 1911).

Rowntree, B.S., *The Human Needs of Labour* (Longmans, Green, London, 1937).

Rowntree, B.S., *Poverty: A Study of Town Life* (Macmillan, London, 1903; first published 1901).

Russell, C.E.B., *Manchester Boys: Sketches of Manchester Lads at Work and Play* (Neil Richardson, Manchester, 1984; first published 1905).

Select Committee on High Prices and Profits, *Special Report from the Select Committee on High Prices and Profits ...*, vol. 5 (HMSO, London, 1919).

Sherard, R.H., *The White Slaves of England* (James Bowden, London, 1897).

Sherwell, A., *Life in West London: A Study and a Contrast* (Methuen, London, 1897).

Silex, K., *John Bull at Home* (George G. Harrap, London, 1931).

Sims, G.R. (ed.), *Living London: Its Work and its Play its Humours and its Pathos its Sights and its Scenes*, 3 vols (Cassell, London, 1902).

Sims, G.R., *How the Poor Live and Horrible London* (Chatto and Windus, London, 1889).

Stutfield, H.E.M., *The Sovrainty of Society* (T. Fisher Unwin, London, 1909).

Thorne, G. *When it Was Dark: The Story of a Great Conspiracy* (Greening, London, 1904; first published 1903).

Tinker, B., *The Man who Stayed at Home* (Mills and Boon, London, 1915).

Veblen, T., *The Theory of the Leisure* Class (Dover Publications, New York, 1994; first published 1899).

Vredenburg, E., *Tinker Tailor* (Raphael Tuck and Sons, London, n.d. [c. 1914]).

Wells, H.G., *The History of Mr Polly* (J.M. Dent, London, 1999; first published 1910).

Wells, H.G., *Kipps* (J.M. Dent, London, 1993; first published 1905).

Wells, H.G., *Mr. Britling Sees it Through* (Cassell, London, 1917; first published 1916).

Wight Bakke, E., *The Unemployed Man: A Social Study* (Nisbet, London, 1933).

Books published after 1939

Adburgham, A., *Yesterday's Shopping: The Army and Navy Stores Catalogue 1907* (David and Charles, Newton Abbot, 1969).

Alexander, D., *Retailing in England During the Industrial Revolution* (The Athlone Press, London, 1970).

Amies, H., *The Englishman's Suit* (Quartet Books, London, 1994).

Appadurai, A. (ed.), *The Social Life of Things: Commodities in Cultural Perspective* (Cambridge University Press, Cambridge, 1992; first published 1986).

Ash, J. and Wilson, E. (eds), *Chic Thrills: A Fashion Reader* (Pandora Press, London, 1992).

Barnard, M., *Fashion as Communication* (Routledge, London, 1996).

Barnes, R. and Eicher, J.B. (eds), *Dress and Gender: Making and Meaning in Cultural Contexts* (Berg, Oxford, 1992).

Bailey, P., *Popular Culture and Performance in the Victorian City* (Cambridge University Press, Cambridge, 1998).

Beaven, B., *Leisure, Citizenship and Working-Class Men in Britain, 1850–1945* (Manchester University Press, Manchester, 2005).

Benson, J., *Affluence and Authority: A Social History of Twentieth-Century Britain* (Hodder Arnold, London, 2005).

Benson, J., *The Penny Capitalists: A Study of Nineteenth-Century Working-Class Entrepreneurs* (Gill and Macmillan, Goldenbridge, 1983).

Benson, J., *Prime Time: A History of the Middle Aged in Twentieth-Century Britain* (Longman, Harlow, 1997).

Benson, J., *The Rise of Consumer Society in Britain 1880–1980* (Longman, Harlow, 1994).

Benson, J., *The Working Class in Britain, 1850–1939* (I.B. Tauris, London, 2003; first published 1989).

Benson, J. and Shaw, G. (eds), *The Evolution of Retail Systems, c. 1800–1914* (Leicester University Press, Leicester, 1992).

Benson, J. and Ugolini, L. (eds), *Cultures of Selling: Perspectives on Consumption and Society Since 1700* (Ashgate, Aldershot, 2006).

Benson, J. and Ugolini, L. (eds), *A Nation of Shopkeepers: Five Centuries of British Retailing* (I.B. Tauris, London, 2003).

Boscagli, M., *Eye on the Flesh: Fashions of Masculinity in the Early Twentieth Century* (Westview Press, Oxford, 1996).

Bourdieu, P., *Distinction: A Social Critique of the Judgement of Taste* (Routledge, London, 1992; first published 1979).

Bourke, J., *Dismembering the Male: Men's Bodies, Britain and the Great War* (Reaktion Books, London, 1996).

Bourke, J., *Working Class Cultures in Britain, 1890–1960: Gender, Class and Ethnicity* (Routledge, London, 1999; first published 1994).

Bourne, J.M., *Britain and the Great War 1914–1918* (Edward Arnold, London, 1989).

Breward, C., *Fashioning London: Clothing and the Modern Metropolis* (Berg, Oxford, 2004).

Breward, C., *The Hidden Consumer: Masculinities, Fashion and City Life 1860–1914* (Manchester University Press, Manchester, 1999).

Breward, C., *A New History of Fashionable Dress* (Manchester University Press, Manchester, 1995).

Breward, C. and Evans, C. (eds), *Fashion and Modernity* (Berg, Oxford, 2005).

Breward, C., Conekin, B. and Cox, C. (eds), *The Englishness of English Dress* (Berg, Oxford, 2002).

Brewer's Dictionary of Phrase and Fable (Cassell, London, 1991; first published 1870).

Briggs, A., *Friends of the People: The Centenary History of Lewis's* (Batsford, London, 1956).

Brush Kidwell, C. and Steele, V. (eds), *Men and Women: Dressing the Part* (Smithsonian Institution Press, Washington, 1989).

Bruzzi, S., *Undressing Cinema: Clothing and Identity in the Movies* (Routledge, London, 1997).

Bruzzi, S. and Church Gibson, P. (eds), *Fashion Cultures: Theories, Explorations and Analysis* (Routledge, London, 2000).

Buckman, J., *Immigrants and the Class Struggle: The Jewish Immigrants in Leeds* (Manchester University Press, Manchester, 1983).

Burk, K. (ed.), *War and the State: The Transformation of British Government, 1914–1919* (George Allen and Unwin, London, 1982).

Burman, B. (ed.), *The Culture of Sewing: Gender, Consumption and Home Dressmaking* (Berg, Oxford, 1999).

Burnett, J., *A History of the Cost of Living* (Penguin Books, Harmodsworth, 1969).

Bush, J., *Behind the Lines: East London Labour 1914–1918* (Merlin Press, London, 1984).

Byrde, P., *The Male Image: Men's Fashion in Britain 1300–1970* (B.T. Batsford, London, 1979).

Callery, S., *Harrods Knightsbridge: The Story of Society's Favourite Store* (Ebury Press, London, 1991).

Carey, J., *The Intellectuals and the Masses: Pride and Prejudice Among the Literary Intelligentsia 1880–1939* (Faber and Faber, London, 1992).

Carnegie United Kingdom Trust, *Disinherited Youth: A Survey 1936–1939* (Carnegie UK Trust, Dunfermline, 1943).

Carter, M., *Fashion Classics: From Carlyle to Barthes* (Berg, Oxford, 2003).

Clark, A., *The Struggle for the Breeches: Gender and the Making of the British Working Class* (University of California Press, Berkeley, 1995).

Cohen, E., *Talk on the Wilde Side: Towards a Genealogy of a Discourse on Male Sexualities* (Routledge, London, 1993).

Cohen, S., *Folk Devils and Moral Panics: The Creation of Mods and Rockers* (Basil Blackwell, Oxford, 1987; first published 1972).

Collingham, E.M., *Imperial Bodies: The Physical Experience of the Raj, c. 1800–1947* (Polity Press, Cambridge, 2001).

Connell, R.W., *Gender* (Polity Press, Cambridge, 2003; first published 2002).

Connell, R.W., *Gender and Power: Society, the Person and Sexual Politics* (Polity Press, Cambridge, 1987).

Connell, R.W., *Masculinities* (Polity Press, Cambridge, 1995).

Coopey, R., O'Connell, S. and Porter, D., *Mail Order Retailing in Britain: A Business and Social History* (Oxford University Press, Oxford, 2005).

Cox, N., *The Complete Tradesman: A Study of Retailing, 1550–1820* (Ashgate, Aldershot, 2000).

Craik, J., *The Face of Fashion: Cultural Studies in Fashion* (Routledge, London, 1994).

Crossick, G., *An Artisan Elite in Victorian Society: Kentish London 1840–1880* (Croom Helm, London, 1978).

Crossick, G. (ed.), *The Artisan and the European Town, 1500–1900* (Scolar Press, Aldershot, 1997).

Crossick, G. and Haupt, H.-G., *The Petite Bourgeoisie in Europe, 1780–1914* (Routledge, London, 1995).

Crossick, G., and Jaumain, S. (eds), *Cathedrals of Consumption: The European Department Store, 1850–1939* (Ashgate, Aldershot, 1999).

Cunningham, H., *Children and Childhood in Western Society since 1500* (Longman, Harlow, 1995).

Darracott, J. and Loftus, B., *First World War Posters* (Imperial War Museum, London, n.d. [c. 1972]).

Daunton, M. and Hilton, M. (eds), *The Politics of Consumption: Material Culture and Citizenship in Europe and America* (Berg, Oxford, 2001).

Daunton, M. and Rieger, B. (eds), *Meanings of Modernity: Britain from the Late Victorian Era to World War II* (Berg, Oxford, 2001).

Davies, A., *Leisure, Gender and Poverty: Working-Class Culture in Salford and Manchester, 1900–1939* (Open University Press, Buckingham, 1992).

Davin, A., *Growing Up Poor: Home, School and Street in London, 1870–1914* (Rivers Oram Press, London, 1996).

Davis, B.J., *Home Fires Burning: Food, Politics, and Everyday Life in World War I Berlin* (The University of North Carolina Press, Chapel Hill, 2000).

Davis, F., *Fashion, Culture and Identity* (The University of Chicago Press, Chicago, 1992).

Dawson, G., *Soldier Heroes: British Adventure, Empire and the Imagining of Masculinities* (Routledge, London, 1994).

de Grazia, V. with Furlough, E. (eds), *The Sex of Things: Gender and Consumption in Historical Perspective* (University of California Press, Berkeley, 1996).

de Marly, D., *Fashion for Men: An Illustrated History* (B.T. Batsford, London, 1985).

de Marly, D., *Working Dress: A History of Occupational Clothing* (B.T. Batsford, London, 1986).

Dewey, P., *War and Progress: Britain, 1914–1945* (Longman, London, 1997).

Donaldson, F., *Those Were the Days: A Photographic Album of Daily Life in Britain* (J.M. Dent and Sons, London, 1983).

Dudnik, S., Hagemann, K. and Tosh, J. (eds), *Masculinities in Politics and War: Gendering Modern History* (Manchester University Press, Manchester, 2004).

Edwards, T., *Contradictions of Consumption: Concepts, Practices and Politics in Consumer Society* (Open University Press, Buckingham, 2000).

Edwards, T., *Men in the Mirror: Men's Fashion, Masculinity and Consumer Society* (Cassell, London, 1997).

Eicher, J.B. (ed.), *Dress and Ethnicity: Change Across Space and Time* (Berg, Oxford, 1995).

Eliot, T.S., *The Complete Poems and Plays of T.S. Eliot* (Faber and Faber, 1982; first published in this edition 1969).

Entwistle, J., *The Fashioned Body: Fashion, Dress and Modern Social Theory* (Polity Press, Cambridge, 2000).

Falk, P. and Campbell, C. (eds), *The Shopping Experience* (Sage, London, 1997).

Featherstone, M., *Consumer Culture and Postmodernism* (Sage Publications, London, 1991).

Feinstein, C.H., *National Income, Expenditure and Output of the United Kingdom 1855–1965* (Cambridge University Press, Cambridge, 1972).

Fillin-Yeh, S. (ed.), *Dandies: Fashion and Finesse in Art and Culture* (New York University Press, New York, 2001).

Fine, B. and Leopold, E., *The World of Consumption* (Routledge, London, 1993).

Finkelstein, J., *The Fashioned Self* (Polity Press, Cambridge, 1991).

Finn, M.C., *The Character of Credit: Personal Debt in English Culture, 1740–1914* (Cambridge University Press, Cambridge, 2003).

Floud, R. and McCloskey, D. (eds), *The Economic History of Britain since 1700. Vol. 2: 1860–1939* (Cambridge University Press, Cambridge, second edition 1994; first published 1981).

Fowler, D., *The First Teenagers: The Lifestyles of Young Wage-Earners in Interwar Britain* (The Woburn Press, London, 1995).

Fussell, P., *The Great War and Modern Memory* (Oxford University Press, Oxford, 1977; first published 1975).

Garber, M., *Vested Interests: Cross-Dressing and Cultural Anxiety* (Routledge, New York, 1992).

Garelick, R.K., *Rising Star: Dandyism, Gender and Performance in the Fin de Siècle* (Princeton University Press, Princeton, 1998).

Gilbert, D., Matless, D. and Short, B. (eds), *Geographies of British Modernity: Space and Society in the Twentieth Century* (Blackwell Publishing, Oxford, 2003).

Gilman, S., *The Jew's Body* (Routledge, London, 1991).

Gittins, D., *Fair Sex: Family Size and Structure, 1900–1939* (Hutchinson, London, 1982).

Godley, A., *Jewish Immigrant Entrepreneurs in New York and London 1880–1914: Enterprise and Culture* (Palgrave, Basingstoke, 2001).

Graves, R. and Hodge, A., *The Long Weekend: A Social History of Great Britain 1918–1939* (Abacus, London, 1995; first published 1940).

N. Gregson and L. Crewe, *Second-Hand Cultures* (Berg, Oxford, 2003).

J. Gronow and A. Warde (eds), *Ordinary Consumption* (Routledge, London, 2001).

Hall, C., McClelland, K. and Rendall, J., *Defining the Victorian Nation: Class, Race, Gender and the British Reform Act of 1867* (Cambridge University Press, Cambridge, 2000).

Harris B. (ed.), *Famine and Fashion: Needlewomen in the Nineteenth Century* (Ashgate, Aldershot, 2005).

Harris, J., *Private Lives, Public Spirit: Britain 1870–1914* (Penguin Books, London, 1994; first published 1993).

Harte, N.B. and Pointing, K.G. (eds), *Cloth and Clothing in Medieval Europe: Essays in Memory of E.M. Carus-Wilson* (Heinemann and Pasold Research Fund, London, 1982).

Harvey, J., *Men in Black* (Reaktion Books, London, 1995).

Hebdige, D., *Subculture: The Meaning of Style* (Routledge, London, 2003; first published 1979).

Hendrick, H., *Images of Youth: Age, Class and the Male Youth Problem, 1880–1920* (Clarendon Press, Oxford, 1990).

Hilton, M., *Consumerism in Twentieth-Century Britain: The Search for a Historical Movement* (Cambridge University Press, Cambridge, 2003).

Hilton, M., *Smoking in British Popular Culture 1800–2000: Perfect Pleasures* (Manchester University Press, Manchester, 2000).

Hinchberger, J.W.M., *Images of the Army: The Military in British Art, 1815–1914* (Manchester University Press, Manchester, 1988).

Hodgkinson, P., *Goth: Identity, Style and Subculture* (Berg, Oxford, 2002).

Honeyman, K., *Well Suited: A History of the Leeds Clothing Industry 1850–1990* (Pasold Research Fund and Oxford University Press, Oxford, 2000).

Horn, P., *The Victorian Country Child* (Sutton Publishing, Stroud, 1997; first published 1974).

Horwood, C., *Keeping Up Appearances: Fashion and Class Between the Wars* (Sutton Publishing, Thrupp, 2005).

Houlbrook, M., *Queer London: Perils and Pleasures in the Sexual Metropolis, 1918–1957* (University of Chicago Press, Chicago, 2005).

Humphries, S., *Hooligans or Rebels? An Oral History of Working-Class Childhood and Youth 1889–1939* (Basil Blackwell, Oxford, 1981).

Humphries, S. and Gordon, P., *A Labour of Love: The Experience of Parenthood in Britain 1900–1950* (Sidgwick and Jackson, London, 1993).

Hynes, S., *A War Imagined: The First World War and English Culture* (Pimlico, London, 1992; first published 1990).

Jackson, P., Lowe, M., Miller, D. and Mort, F. (eds), *Commercial Cultures: Economies, Practices, Spaces* (Berg, Oxford, 2000).

Jackson, S. and Moores, S. (eds), *The Politics of Domestic Consumption: Critical Readings* (Prentice Hall, London, 1995).

Janes Yeo, E. (ed.), Special issue: 'Working-class masculinities in Britain, 1850 to present', *Labour History Review*, vol. 62, no. 2 (2004).

Jefferys, J.B., *Retail Trading in Britain, 1850–1950* (Cambridge University Press, Cambridge, 1954).

Jenkins, D.T. and Pointing, K.G., *The British Wool Trade Industry 1770–1914* (Heinemann Educational Books and The Pasold Research Fund, London, 1982).

Jobling, P., *Man Appeal: Advertising, Modernism and Menswear* (Berg, Oxford, 2005).

Johnson, K.K.P., Torntore, S.J. and Eicher, J.B. (eds), *Fashion Foundations: Early Writings on Fashion and Dress* (Berg, Oxford, 2003).

Johnson, P. (ed.), *Twentieth Century Britain: Economic, Social and Cultural Change* (Longman, London, 1994).

Joy, B. and Warburton, N. *The Photography of Bill Brandt* (Thames and Hudson, London, 1999).

Joyce, P. (ed.), *The Historical Meanings of Work* (Cambridge University Press, Cambridge, 1987).

Kersh, G., *The Thousand Deaths of Mr Small* (Heinemann, London, 1951).

Kershen, A.J., *Uniting the Tailors: Trade Unionism Amongst the Tailors of London and Leeds, 1870–1939* (Frank Cass, Ilford, 1995).

Kidd, A. and Nicholls, D. (eds), *Gender, Civic Culture and Consumerism: Middle-class Identity in Britain, 1800–1940* (Manchester University Press, Manchester, 1999).

Kuchta, D., *The Three-Piece Suit and Modern Masculinity: England, 1550–1850* (University of California Press, Berkeley, 2002).

Lancaster, B., *The Department Store: A Social History* (Leicester University Press, London, 1995).

Leed, E.J., *No Man's Land: Combat and Identity in World War One* (Cambridge University Press, Cambridge, 1979).

Lemire, B., *Dress, Culture and Commerce: The English Clothing Trade Before the Factory, 1660–1800* (Macmillan, Basingstoke, 1997).

Levy, H., *The Shops of Britain: A Study of Retail Distribution* (Routledge, London, 1999; first published 1948).

Liddle, P.H. (ed.) *Home Fires and Foreign Fields: British Social and Military Experience in the First World War* (Brassey's Defence Publishers, London, 1985).

Lipman, V.D., *A History of the Jews in Britain Since 1858* (Leicester University Press, Leicester, 1990).

Manchester University Settlement, *Ancoats: A Study of a Clearance Area. Report of a Study Made in 1937–1938* (Manchester University Settlement, Manchester, 1945).

Mangan, J.A. and Walvin, J. (eds), *Manliness and Morality: Middle-Class Masculinity in Britain and America, 1800–1940* (Manchester University Press, Manchester, 1987).

Mansfield, N., *English Farmworkers and Local Patriotism, 1900–1930* (Ashgate, Aldershot, 2001).

Marwick, A., *The Deluge: British Society and the First World War* (The Bodley Head, London, 1965).

Marwick, A., *War and Social Change in the Twentieth Century: A Comparative Study of Britain, France, Germany, Russia and the United States* (Macmillan, London, 1974).

McCalman, I., *Radical Underworld: Prophets, Revolutionaries and Pornographers in London, 1795–1840* (Cambridge University Press, Cambridge, 1988).

McCracken, G., *Culture and Consumption: New Approaches to the Symbolic Character of Consumer Goods and Activities* (Indiana University Press, Bloomington, 1990; first published 1988).

McKibbin, R., *Classes and Cultures: England 1918–1951* (Oxford University Press, Oxford, 2000; first published 1998).

McKibbin, R., *The Ideologies of Class: Social Relations in Britain 1880–1950* (Clarendon Press, Oxford, 1994; first published 1991).

McLaren, A., *The Trials of Masculinity: Policing Sexual Boundaries 1870–1930* (The University of Chicago Press, Chicago, 1997).

McRobbie, A. (ed.), *Zoot Suits and Second-Hand Dresses: An Anthology of Fashion and Music* (Macmillan, Basingstoke, 1989).

Melman, B. (ed.), *Borderlines: Genders and Identities in War and Peace, 1870–1930* (Routledge, London, 1998).

Messenger, C., *Call to Arms: The British Army 1914–18* (Weidenfeld and Nicolson, London, 2005).

Miller, D. (ed.), *Acknowledging Consumption: A Review of New Studies* (Routledge, London, 1995).

Miller, D., *A Theory of Shopping* (Polity Press, Cambridge, 1998).

Miller, D., Jackson, P., Thrift, N., Holbrook, B. and Rowlands, L., *Shopping, Place and Identity* (Routledge, London, 1998).

Moers, E., *The Dandy: Brummel to Beerbohm* (Secker and Warburg, London, 1960).

More, C., *Skill and the English Working Class, 1870–1914* (Croom Helm, London, 1980).

Morris, J., *Women Workers and the Sweated Trades: The Origins of Minimum Wage Legislation* (Gower, Aldershot, 1986).

Mort, F., *Cultures of Consumption: Masculinities and Social Space in Late-Twentieth Century Britain* (Routledge, London, 1996).

Moynihan, M. (ed.), *Greater Love: Letters Home 1914–1918* (W.H. Allen, London, 1980).

Moynihan, M., *People at War 1914–1918* (David and Charles, Newton Abbot, 1973).

Muggleton, D., *Inside Subculture: The Postmodern Meaning of Style* (Berg, Oxford, 2000).

Mullins, S. and Stockdale, D., *Talking Shop: An Oral History of Retailing in the Harborough Area in the Twentieth Century* (Alan Sutton, Stroud, 1994).

Nava, M., *Changing Cultures: Feminism, Youth and Consumerism* (Sage Publications, London, 1992).

Nava, M. and O'Shea, A., *Modern Times: Reflections on a Century of English Modernity* (Routledge, London, 1996).

Nava, M., Blake, A., MacRury, I. and Richards, B. (eds), *Buy this Book: Studies in Advertising and Consumption* (Routledge, London, 1997).

Nixon, S., *Hard Looks: Masculinities, Spectatorship and Contemporary Consumption* (Routledge, London, 2003; first published 1996).

O'Connell, S., *The Popular Print in England 1550–1850* (British Museum Press, London, 1999).

Ogborn, M., *Spaces of Modernity: London's Geographies 1680–1780* (The Guildford Press, New York, 1998).

Orwell, G., *The Collected Essays, Journalism and Letters of George Orwell, vol. I. An Age Like This 1920–1940*, ed. S. Orwell and I. Angus (Penguin Books, Harmondsworth, 1970; first published in this edition 1968).

Paris, M., *Warrior Nation: Images of War in British Popular Culture, 1850–2000* (Reaktion Books, London, 2000).

Parker, P., *The Old Lie: The Great War and the Public School Ethos* (Constable, London, 1987).

Parkins, W. (ed.), *Fashioning the Body Politic: Dress, Gender, Citizenship* (Berg, Oxford, 2002).

Pearson, G., *Hooligan: A History of Respectable Fears* (Macmillan, London, 1983).

Pedersen, S., *Family Dependence and the Origins of the Welfare State: Britain and France, 1914–1945* (Cambridge University Press, Cambridge, 1993).

Phizacklea, A., *Unpacking the Fashion Industry: Gender, Racism and Class Production* (Routledge, London, 1990).

Piponnier, F. and Mane, P., *Dress in the Middle Ages* (Yale University Press, New Haven, 1997; first published 1995).

Pollard, S., *The Development of the British Economy 1914–1950* (Edward Arnold, London, 1962).

Powell, A., *A Question of Upbringing* (Mandarin, London, 1991; first published 1951).

Prest, A.R. with Adams, A.A., *Consumers' Expenditure in the United Kingdom, 1900–1919* (Cambridge University Press, Cambridge, 1954).

Prothero, I., *Radical Artisans in England and France, 1830–1870* (Cambridge University Press, Cambridge, 1997).

Rappaport, E.D., *Shopping for Pleasure: Women in the Making of London's West End* (Princeton University Press, Princeton, 2000).

Reay, B., *Microhistories: Demography, Society and Culture in Rural England, 1800–1930* (Cambridge University Press, Cambridge, 1996).

Redmayne, R., *Ideals in Industry: Being the Story of Montague Burton Ltd 1900–1950* (Montague Burton, Leeds, n.d. [c. 1950]).

Richards, J., *The Age of the Dream Palace: Cinema and Society in Britain 1930–1939* (Routledge and Kegan Paul, London, 1984).

Richardson, C. (ed.), *Clothing Culture, 1350–1650* (Ashgate, Aldershot, 2004).

Ritchie, B., *A Touch of Class: The Story of Austin Reed* (James and James, London, 1990).

Roper, M. and Tosh, J. (eds), *Manful Assertions: Masculinities in Britain Since 1800* (Routledge, London, 1991).

Rose, S.O., *Limited Livelihoods: Gender and Class in Nineteenth-Century England* (Routledge, London, 1992).

Roshwald, A. and Stites, R. (eds), *European Culture in the Great War: The Arts, Entertainment and Propaganda, 1914–1918* (Cambridge University Press, Cambridge, 1999).

Ross, E., *Love and Toil: Motherhood in Outcast London, 1870–1918* (Oxford University Press, Oxford, 1993).

Sanders, M.L. and Taylor, P.M., *British Propaganda During the First World War, 1914–18* (Macmillan, Basingstoke, 1982).

Sassoon, S., *Meredith* (Constable, London, 1948).

Schmiechen, J.A., *Sweated Industries and Sweated Labor: The London Clothing Trades, 1860–1914* (Croom Helm, London, 1984).

Scranton, P. (ed.), *Beauty and Business: Commerce, Gender and Culture in Modern America* (Routledge, New York, 2001).

Sennett, R., *The Fall of Public Man* (Cambridge University Press, Cambridge, 1974).

Shammas, C., *The Pre-Industrial Consumer in England and America* (Clarendon Press, Oxford, 1990).

Sigsworth, E.M., *Montague Burton: The Tailor of Taste* (Manchester University Press, Manchester, 1990).

Simkins, P., *Kitchener's Army: The Raising of the New Armies, 1914–16* (Manchester University Press, Manchester, 1988).

Sinfield, A., *The Wilde Century: Effeminacy, Oscar Wilde and the Queer Moment* (Cassell, London, 1994).

Springhall, J., *Youth, Popular Culture and Moral Panics: Penny Gaffs to Gangsta-Rap, 1830–1996* (Macmillan, Basingstoke, 1998).

Stedman Jones, G., *Languages of Class: Studies in English Working-Class History 1832–1982* (Cambridge University Press, Cambridge, 1983).

Stevenson, J., *British Society 1914–45* (Penguin, Harmondsworth, 1990; first published 1984).

Stevenson, J. and Cook, C. (eds), *Britain in the Depression: Society and Politics 1929–39* (Longman, London, 1994; first published 1977).

Stewart, M. and Hunter, L., *The Needle is Threaded: The History of an Industry* (Heinemann and Newman Neame, London, 1964).

Stone, R. and Rowe, D.A., *The Measurement of Consumers' Expenditure and Behaviour in the United Kingdom 1920–1938*, 2 vols (Cambridge University Press, Cambridge, 1966).

Strasser, S., McGovern, C. and Judt, M. (eds), *Getting and Spending: European and American Consumer Societies in the Twentieth Century* (Cambridge University Press, Cambridge, 1998).

Symons, J., *Between the Wars: Britain in Photographs* (B.T. Batsford, London, 1972).

Tarrant, N., *The Development of Costume* (Routledge with National Museums of Scotland, London, 1994).

Tawney, R.H., *The Attack and Other Papers* (Spokesman, Nottingham, 1981; first published in this edition 1953).

Taylor, A., *Working Class Credit and Community Since 1918* (Palgrave Macmillan, Basingstoke, 2002).

Taylor, B., *Eve and the New Jerusalem: Socialism and Feminism in the Nineteenth Century* (Virago, London, 1991; first published 1983).

Tebbutt, M., *Making Ends Meet: Pawnbroking and Working-Class Credit* (Leicester University Press, Leicester, 1983).

Thomas, K. (ed.), *The Oxford Book of Work* (Oxford University Press, Oxford, 1999).

Thompson, T., *Edwardian Childhoods* (Routledge and Kegan Paul, London, 1981).

Thornton, S., *Club Cultures: Music, Media and Subcultural Capital* (Polity Press, Cambridge, 1995).

Tosh, J., *Manliness and Masculinity in Nineteenth-Century Britain* (Pearson Education, Harlow, 2005).

Tosh, J., *A Man's Place: Masculinity and the Middle-Class Home in Victorian England* (Yale University Press, New Haven, 1999).

Tseëlon, E., *The Masque of Femininity* (Sage, London, 1995).

Turner, J. (ed.), *Britain and the First World War* (Unwin Hyman, London, 1988).

Turner, M.W., *Backward Glances: Cruising the Queer Streets of New York and London* (Reaktion Books, London, 2003).

Tute, W., *The Grey Top Hat: The Story of Moss Bros of Covent Garden* (Cassell, London, 1961).

Van Emden, R. and Humphries, S., *All Quiet on the Home Front: An Oral History of Life in Britain During the First World War* (Headline, London, 2003).

Waites, B., *A Class Society at War: England 1914–1918* (Berg, Leamington Spa, 1987).

Walkowitz, J.R., *City of Dreadful Delight: Narratives of Sexual Danger in Late Victorian London* (Virago, London, 1992).

Wall, R. and Winter, J. (eds), *The Upheaval of War: Family, Work and Welfare in Europe, 1914–1918* (Cambridge University Press, Cambridge, 1988).

Walsh, M. (ed.), *Working Out Gender: Perspectives from Labour History* (Ashgate, Aldershot, 1999).

Warner, M., *No Go the Bogeyman: Scaring, Lulling and Making Mock* (Chatto and Windus, London, 1998).

Watt, J. (ed.), *The Penguin Book of Twentieth-Century Fashion Writing* (Penguin Books, London, 2000; first published 1999).

Waugh, E., *Brideshead Revisited* (Penguin Books, London, n.d.; first published 1945).

Whitaker, W.B., *Victorian and Edwardian Shop Workers: The Struggle to Obtain Better Conditions and a Half-Holiday* (David and Charles, Newton Abbot, 1973).

White, J., *The Worst Street in North London: Campbell Bunk, Islington, Between the Wars* (Routledge and Kegan Paul, London, 1986).

Whitlock, T.C., *Crime, Gender and Consumer Culture in Nineteenth-Century England* (Ashgate, Aldershot, 2005).

Wiener, A., *Inalienable Possessions: The Paradox of Keeping-While-Giving* (University of California Press, Berkeley, 1992).

Wight, D., *Workers not Wasters. Masculine Respectability, Consumption and Unemployment in Central Scotland: A Community Study* (Edinburgh University Press, Edinburgh, 1993).

Williamson, H., *How Dear is Life* (Macdonald, London, 1984; first published 1954).

Williamson, H., *The Innocent Moon* (Sutton Publishing, Stroud, 1998; first published 1961).

Williamson, H., *A Test to Destruction* (Sutton Publishing, Stroud, 1997; first published 1977).

Willis, P.E., *Profane Culture* (Routledge and Kegan Paul, London, 1978).

Wilson, E., *Adorned in Dreams: Fashion and Modernity* (Virago, London, 1985).

Winstanley, M.J., *The Shopkeeper's World 1830–1914* (Manchester University Press, Manchester, 1983).

Winter, J., *Sites of Memory, Sites of Mourning: The Place of the Great War in European Cultural History* (Cambridge University Press, Cambridge, 1995).

Winter, J. and Robert, J.-L. (eds), *Capital Cities at War: Paris, London, Berlin 1914–1919* (Cambridge University Press, Cambridge, 1999; first published 1997).

Winter, J.M., *The Great War and the British People* (Palgrave Macmillan, Basingstoke, 2003; first published 1985).

Wrigley, N. and Lowe, M. (eds), *Retailing, Consumption and Capital: Towards the New Retail Geography* (Longman, Harlow, 1996).

Zakim, M., *Ready-Made Democracy: A History of Men's Dress in the American Republic, 1760–1860* (University of Chicago Press, Chicago, 2003).

Zweiniger-Bargielowska, I., *Austerity in Britain: Rationing, Controls and Consumption, 1939–1955* (Oxford University Press, Oxford, 2000).

Articles

Agnew, Lady, 'Family budgets no. 5: ten thousand a year', *The Cornhill Magazine*, August 1901, pp. 184–91.

Aldrich, W., 'Tailors' cutting manuals and the growing provision of popular clothing, 1770–1870', *Textile History*, vol. 31, no. 2 (2000), pp. 163–201.

Alexander, A., 'Strategy and strategists: evidence from an early retail revolution in Britain', *The International Review of Retail, Distribution and Consumer Research*, vol. 1, no. 1 (1997), pp. 61–78.

Alexander, A., Benson, J. and Shaw, G., 'Action and reaction: competition and the multiple retailer in 1930s Britain', *The International Review of Retail, Distribution and Consumer Research*, vol. 9, no. 3 (1999), pp. 245–59.

Anderson, F., 'Fashioning the gentleman: a study of Henry Poole and Co., Savile Row tailors 1861–1900', *Fashion Theory*, vol. 4, issue 4 (2000), pp. 405–26.

Anon., 'Tailoring and bootmaking in central London', in C. Booth (ed.), *Life and Labour of the People in London* (Macmillan, London, 1893), vol. IV, pp. 138–56.

Anon., 'The clothing trades', in H. Llewellyn Smith (ed.), *The New Survey of London Life and Labour* (P.S. King and Son, London, 1931), vol. 2, pp. 251–349.

Appadurai, A., 'Introduction: commodities and the politics of value', in A. Appadurai (ed.), *The Social Life of Things: Commodities in Cultural Perspective* (Cambridge University Press, Cambridge, 1992; first published 1986), pp. 3–63.

Ayers, P., 'The making of men: masculinities in interwar Liverpool', in M. Walsh (ed.), *Working Out Gender: Perspectives from Labour History* (Ashgate, Aldershot, 1999), pp. 66–83.

Bailey, P., 'Champagne Charlie and the music-hall swell song', in P. Bailey, *Popular Culture and Performance in the Victorian City* (Cambridge University Press, Cambridge, 1998), pp. 101–27.

Bailey, P., '"Will the real Bill Banks please stand up?" Towards a role analysis of mid-Victorian working-class respectability', *Journal of Social History*, vol. 12, no. 3 (1979), p. 336–53.

Baines, D., 'Population, migration and regional development, 1870–1939', in R. Floud and D. McCloskey (eds), *The Economic History of Britain since 1700. Vol. 2: 1860–1939* (Cambridge University Press, Cambridge, second edition 1994; first published 1981), pp. 29–61.

Barraclough Paoletti, J., 'Ridicule and role models as factors in American men's fashion change, 1880–1910', *Costume*, vol. 19 (1985), pp. 121–34.

Benson, J. and Ugolini, L., 'Historians and the nation of shopkeepers', in J. Benson and L. Ugolini (eds), *A Nation of Shopkeepers: Five Centuries of British Retailing* (I.B. Tauris, London, 2003), pp. 1–24.

Bet-El, I.R., 'Men and soldiers: British conscripts, concepts of masculinity, and the Great War', in B. Melman (ed.), *Borderlines: Genders and Identities in War and Peace, 1870–1930* (Routledge, London, 1998), pp. 73–94.

Bonzon, T. and Davis, B., 'Feeding the cities', in J. Winter and J.-L. Robert (eds), *Capital Cities at War: Paris, London, Berlin 1914–1919* (Cambridge University Press, Cambridge, 1999; first published 1997), pp. 305–41.

Boswell, J.S. and Johns, B.R., 'Patriots or profiteers? British businessmen and the First World War', *The Journal of European Economic History*, vol. 11, no. 2 (1982), pp. 423–45.

Bourdieu, P., 'Structures, *habitus* and practices', in *The Polity Reader in Social Theory* (Polity Press, Cambridge, 1994), pp. 95–110.

Bourke, J., 'The great male renunciation: men's dress reform in inter-war Britain', *Journal of Design History*, vol. 9, no. 1 (1996), pp. 23–33.

Bowley, A.L., 'Wages and family income', in H. Llewellyn Smith (ed.), *The New Survey of London Life and Labour* (P.S. King and Son, London, 1931), pp. 60–69.

Bowden, S., 'The new consumerism', in P. Johnson (ed.), *Twentieth Century Britain: Economic, Social and Cultural Change* (Longman, London, 1994), pp. 242–62.

Breazeale, K., 'In spite of women: *Esquire* magazine and the construction of the male consumer', *Signs*, vol. 20, no. 1 (1994), pp. 1–22.

Breward, C., 'The dandy laid bare: embodying practices an fashion for men', in S. Bruzzi and P. Church Gibson (eds), *Fashion Cultures: Theories, Explorations and Analysis* (Routledge, London, 2000), pp. 221–38.

Breward, C., 'Fashion and the man: from suburb to city street. The spaces of masculine consumption, 1870–1914', *New Formations*, no. 37 (1999), pp. 47–70.

Breward, C., 'Masculine pleasures: metropolitan identities and the commercial sites of dandyism, 1790–1840', *The London Journal*, vol. 28, no. 1 (2003), pp. 60–72.

Breward , C. (ed.), Special issue on masculinities, *Fashion Theory*, vol. 4, issue 4 (2000).

Breward, C., 'Style and subversion: postwar poses and the neo-Edwardian suit in mid-twentieth-century Britain', *Gender & History*, vol. 14, no. 3 (2002), pp. 560–83.

Buckley, C., '"De-humanised females and Amazonians": British wartime fashion and its representation in *Home Chat*, 1914–1918', *Gender & History*, vol. 14, no. 3 (2002), pp. 516–36.

Buettner, E., 'From somebodies to nobodies: Britons returning home from India', in M. Daunton and B. Rieger (eds), *Meanings of Modernity: Britain from the Late Victorian Era to World War II* (Berg, Oxford, 2001), pp. 221–40.

Burman, B., 'Better and bnrighter clothes: the Men's Dress Reform Party, 1929-1940', *Journal of Design History*, vol. 8, no. 4 (1995), pp. 275–90.

Burton, V., '"Whoring, drinking sailors": reflections on masculinity from the labour history of nineteenth-century British shipping', in M. Walsh (ed.), *Working Out Gender: Perspectives from Labour History* (Ashgate, Aldershot, 1999), pp. 84–101.

Callaway, H., 'Dressing for dinner in the bush: rituals of self-definition and British imperial authority', in R. Barnes and J.B. Eicher (eds), *Dress and Gender: Making and Meaning in Cultural Contexts* (Berg, Oxford, 1992), pp. 239–40.

Campbell, C., 'The sociology of consumption', in D. Miller (ed.), *Acknowledging Consumption: A Review of New Studies* (Routledge, London, 1995), pp. 96–126.

Campbell, C., 'When the meaning is not a message: a critique of the consumption as communication thesis', in M. Nava, A. Blake, I. MacRury and B. Richards (eds), *Buy This Book: Studies in Advertising and Consumption* (Routledge, London, 1997), pp. 103–19.

Chapman, M., '"Freezing the frame": dress and ethnicity in Brittany and Gaelic Scotland', in J.B. Eicher (ed.), *Dress and Ethnicity: Change Across Space and Time* (Berg, Oxford, 1995), pp. 7–28.

Chapman, S., 'The innovating entrepreneurs in the British ready-made clothing industry', *Textile History*, vol. 24, no. 1 (1993), pp. 5–25.

Chitham, F., 'Some problems of the tailoring trade', in A.S. Bridgland (ed.), *The Modern Tailor Outfitter and Clothier* (Caxton Publishing, London, n.d.), vol. 1, pp. 6–8.

Clarke, A., '"Mother swapping": the trafficking of nearly new children's wear', in P. Jackson, M. Lowe, D. Miller and F. Mort (eds), *Commercial Cultures: Economies, Practices, Spaces* (Berg, Oxford, 2000), pp. 85–100.

Colmore, G., 'Family budgets no. 3: eight hundred a year', *The Cornhill Magazine*, June 1901, pp. 790–801.

Cosgrove, S., 'The zoot suit and style warfare', in A. McRobbie (ed.), *Zoot Suits and Second-Hand Dresses: An Anthology of Fashion and Music* (Macmillan, Basingstoke, 1989), pp. 3–22.

Crossick, G., 'Past masters: in search of the artisan in European history', in G. Crossick (ed.), *The Artisan and the European Town, 1500–1900* (Scolar Press, Aldershot, 1997), pp. 1–40.

Cushman, J., '"The customer is always right": change and continuity in British and American department store salesmanship, 1945-1960', in J. Benson and L. Ugolini (eds), *Cultures of Selling: Perspectives on Consumption and Society Since 1700* (Ashgate, Aldershot, 2006), pp. 185–213.

de Grazia, V., 'Changing consumption regimes in Europe, 1930–1970: comparative perspectives on the distribution problem', in S. Strasser, C. McGovern and M. Judt (eds), *Getting and Spending: European and American Consumer Societies in the Twentieth Century* (Cambridge University Press, Cambridge, 1998), pp. 59–83.

Dewey, P., 'The new warfare and economic mobilisation', in J. Turner (ed.), *Britain and the First World War* (Unwin Hyman, London, 1988), pp. 70–84.

Dewey, P.E., 'Nutrition and living standards in wartime Britain', in R. Wall and J. Winter (eds), *The Upheaval of War: Family, Work and Welfare in Europe, 1914–1918* (Cambridge University Press, Cambridge, 1988), pp. 197–220.

Earle, Mrs, 'Family budgets no. 4: eighteen hundred a year', *The Cornhill Magazine*, July 1901, pp. 48–61.

Edwards, B., 'A man's world? Masculinity and metropolitan modernity at Simpson Piccadilly', in D. Gilbert, D. Matless and B. Short (eds), *Geographies of British Modernity: Space and Society in the Twentieth Century* (Blackwell Publishing, Oxford, 2003), pp. 151–67.

Finn, M.C., 'Men's things: masculine possessions in the consumer revolution', *Social History*, vol. 25, no. 2 (2000), pp. 133–55.

Finn, M.C., 'Scotch drapers and the politics of modernity: gender, class and national identity in the Victorian tally trade', in M. Daunton and M. Hilton (eds), *The Politics of Consumption: Material Culture and Citizenship in Europe and America* (Berg, Oxford, 2001), pp. 89–107.

Floud, R., 'Britain, 1860–1914: a survey', in R. Floud and D. McCloskey (eds), *The Economic History of Britain since 1700. Vol. 2: 1860–1939* (Cambridge University Press, Cambridge, second edition 1994; first published 1981), pp. 1–28.

French, D., 'The rise and fall of "business as usual"', in K. Burk (ed.), *War and the State: The Transformation of British Government, 1914–1919* (George Allen and Unwin, London, 1982), pp. 7–31.

Furlough, E., 'Selling the American way in interwar France: Prix Uniques and the salons des arts menagers', *Journal of Social History*, vol. 26, no. 3 (1993), pp. 491–519.

Gell, A., 'Newcomers to the world of goods: consumption among the Muria Gonds', in A. Appadurai (ed.), *The Social Life of Things: Commodities in Cultural Perspective* (Cambridge University Press, Cambridge, 1992; first published 1986), pp. 110–38.

Glennie, P. and Thrift, N., 'Consumption, shopping and gender', in N. Wrigley and M. Lowe (eds), *Retailing, Consumption and Capital: Towards the New Retail Geography* (Longman, Harlow, 1996), pp. 221–37.

Glennie, P.D. and Thrift, N.J., 'Modern consumption: theorising commodities *and* consumers', *Environment and Planning D: Society and Space*, vol. 11, no. 5 (1993), pp. 603–6.

Godley, A., 'The development of the UK clothing industry, 1850–1950: output and productivity growth', *Business History*, vol. 37, no. 4 (1995), pp. 46–63.

Godley, A., 'Singer in Britain: the diffusion of sewing machine technology and its impact on the clothing industry in the United Kingdom, 1860–1950', *Textile History*, vol. 27, no. 1 (1996), pp. 59–76.

Godley, A. (ed.), Special issue on the history of the ready-made clothing industry, *Textile History*, vol. 28, no. 1 (1997).

Goldfarb Marquis, A., 'Words as weapons: propaganda in Britain and Germany during the First World War', *Journal of Contemporary History*, vol. 13, no. 3 (1978), pp. 467–98.

Grant, J., 'A "real boy" and not a sissy: gender, childhood, and masculinity, 1890–1940', *Journal of Social History*, vol. 37, no. 4 (2004), pp. 329–51.

Grayzel, S.R., 'Nostalgia, gender and the countryside: placing the "Land Girl" in First World War Britain', *Rural History*, vol. 10, no. 2 (1999), pp. 155–70.

Greenfield, J., O'Connell, S. and Read, C., 'Gender, consumer culture and the middle-class male, 1918–39', in A. Kidd and D. Nicholls (eds), *Gender, Civic Culture and Consumerism: Middle-Class Identity in Britain, 1800–1940* (Manchester University Press, Manchester, 1999), pp. 183–97.

Gregory, A., 'Lost generations: the impact of military casualties on Paris, London and Berlin', in J. Winter and J.-L. Robert (eds), *Capital Cities at War: Paris, London, Berlin 1914–1919* (Cambridge University Press, Cambridge, 1999; first published 1997), pp. 57–103.

Gregson, N. and Crewe, L., 'Performance and possession: rethinking the act of purchase in the light of the car boot sale', *Journal of Material Culture*, vol. 2, no. 2 (1997), pp. 241–63.

Gregson, N., Brooks, K. and Crewe, L., 'Narratives of consumption and the body in the space of the charity / shop', in P. Jackson, M. Lowe, D. Miller and F. Mort (eds), *Commercial Cultures: Economies, Practices, Spaces* (Berg, Oxford, 2000), pp. 101–21.

Gullace, N.F., 'White feathers and wounded men: female patriotism and the memory of the Great War', *Journal of British Studies*, vol. 36, no. 2 (1997), pp. 178–206.

Hammerton, A.J., 'The English weakness? Gender, satire and "moral manliness" in the lower middle-class, 1870–1920', in A. Kidd and D. Nicholls (eds), *Gender, Civic Culture and Consumerism: Middle-Class Identity in Britain, 1800–1940* (Manchester University Press, Manchester, 1999), pp. 164–82.

Hatton, T., 'Unemployement and the labour market in inter-war Britain', in R. Floud and D. McCloskey (eds), *The Economic History of Britain since 1700. Vol. 2: 1860–1939* (Cambridge University Press, Cambridge, 1994; first published 1981), pp. 359–61.

Hilton, M., 'Advertising, the modernist aesthetic of the market place? The cultural relationship between the tobacco manufacturer and the "mass" of consumers in Britain, 1870–1940', in M. Daunton and B. Rieger (eds), *Meanings of Modernity: Britain from the Late Victorian Era to World War II* (Berg, Oxford, 2001), pp. 45–69.

Hilton, M., 'Retailing history as economic and cultural history: strategies of survival by specialist tobacconists in the mass market', *Business History*, vol. 40, no. 4 (1998), pp. 115–37.

Honeyman, K., 'Following suit: men, masculinity and gendered practices in the clothing trade in Leeds, England, 1890–1940', *Gender & History*, vol. 14, no. 3 (2002), pp. 426–46.

Honeyman, K., 'Style monotony and the business of fashion: the marketing of menswear in inter-war England', *Textile History*, vol. 34, no. 2 (2003), pp. 171–91.

Hosgood, C., 'Mrs Pooter's purchase: lower middle-class consumerism and the sales, 1870–1914', in A. Kidd and D. Nicholls (eds), *Gender, Civic Culture and Consumerism: Middle-class Identity in Britain, 1800–1940* (Manchester University Press, Manchester, 1999), pp. 146–63.

Hosgood, C.P., '"Doing the shops" at Christmas: women, men and the department store in England, c. 1880–1914', in G. Crossick and S. Jaumain (eds), *Cathedrals of Consumption: The European Department Store, 1850–1939* (Ashgate, Aldershot, 1999), pp. 97–115.

Hosgood, C.P., '"Mercantile monasteries": shops, shop assistants and shop life in late-Victorian and Edwardian Britain', *Journal of British Studies*, vol. 38, no. 3 (1999), pp. 322–52.

Hosgood, C.P., 'The "pigmies of commerce" and the working-class community: small shopkeepers in England, 1870–1914', *Journal of Social History*, vol. 22, no. 3 (1989), pp. 439–60.

Hughes, A., 'Representation and counter-representation of domestic violence on Clydeside between the two world wars', *Labour History Review*, vol. 62, no. 2 (2004), pp. 169–84.

Hulme, W.H., 'Tailoring as a vocation', in A.S. Bridgland (ed.), *The Modern Tailor Outfitter and Clothier* (Caxton Publishing, London, n.d.), vol. 1, pp. 9–15.

Johnston, R. and McIvor, A., 'Dangerous work, hard men and broken bodies: masculinity in the Clydeside heavy industries, c. 1930–1970s', *Labour History Review*, vol. 62, no. 2 (2004), pp. 135–41.

Kopytoff, I., 'The cultural biography of things: commoditization as process', in A. Appadurai (ed.), *The Social Life of Things: Commodities in Cultural Perspective* (Cambridge University Press, Cambridge, 1992; first published 1986), pp. 64–91.

Lawrence, J., 'Forging a peaceable kingdom: war, violence, and fear of brutalization in post-First World War Britain', *The Journal of Modern History*, vol. 75, no. 3 (2003), pp. 557–89.

Lawrence, J., 'Material pressures on the middle classes', in J. Winter and J.-L. Robert (eds), *Capital Cities at War: Paris, London, Berlin 1914–1919* (Cambridge University Press, Cambridge, 1999; first published 1997), pp. 229–54.

Lawrence, J., Dean, M. and Robert, J.-L., 'The outbreak of war and the urban economy: Paris, Berlin and London in 1914', *Economic History Review*, vol. 45, no. 3 (1992), pp. 564–93.

Layard, G.S.,'Family budgets no. 2: a lower-middle-class budget', *The Cornhill Magazine*, May 1901, pp. 655–66.

Lee, C., 'The service industries', in R. Floud and D. McCloskey (eds), *The Economic History of Britain since 1700. Vol. 2: 1860–1939* (Cambridge University Press, Cambridge, second edition 1994; first published 1981), pp. 117–44.

Levitt, S., 'Cheap mass produced men's clothing in the nineteenth and early twentieth centuries', *Textile History*, vol. 22, no. 2 (1991), pp. 179–92.

Llewellyn Smith, H. with Marsh, L.C. , 'Cost of living', in H. Llewellyn Smith (ed.), *The New Survey of London Life and Labour* (P.S. King and Son, London, 1931), pp. 87–90.

Lomax, S., 'The view from the shop: window display, the shopper and the formulation of theory', in J. Benson and L. Ugolini (eds), *Cultures of Selling: Perspectives on Consumption and Society Since 1700* (Ashgate, Aldershot, 2006), pp. 265–92.

Luck, K., 'Trouble in Eden, trouble with Eve: women, trousers and utopian socialism in nineteenth-century America', in J. Ash and E. Wilson (eds), *Chic Thrills: A Fashion Reader* (Pandora Press, London, 1992), pp. 200–212.

Lyon, P., Colquhoun, A. and Kinney, D., 'UK food shopping in the 1950s: the social context of customer loyalty', *International Journal of Consumer Studies*, vol. 28, no. 1 (2004), pp. 28–39.

Macdonald, J., 'Sweating in the tailoring trade', in R. Mudie Smith (ed.), *Sweated Industries: Being a Handbook of the Daily News Exhibition* (Bradbury, Agnew, London, 1906), pp. 65–7.

Maidment, B., '101 things to do with a fantail hat: dustmen, dirt and dandyism, 1820–1860', *Textile History*, vol. 33, no. 1 (2002), pp. 79–97.

Manning, J., 'Wages and purchasing power', in J. Winter and J.-L. Robert (eds), *Capital Cities at War: Paris, London, Berlin 1914–1919* (Cambridge University Press, Cambridge, 1999; first published 1997), pp. 255–85.

Matthews David, A., 'Decorated men: fashioning the French soldier, 1852–1914', *Fashion Theory*, vol. 7, issue 1 (2003), pp. 3–38.

McNeil, P., 'Macaroni masculinities', *Fashion Theory*, vol. 4, issue 4 (2000), pp. 373–403.

Morrison, A., 'Family budgets no. 1: a workman's budget', *The Cornhill Magazine*, April 1901, pp. 446–56.

Mort, F. and Thompson, P., 'Retailing, commercial culture and masculinity in 1950s Britain: the case for Montague Burton, tailor of taste', *History Workshop Journal*, issue 38 (1994), pp. 106–27.

Nicholson, R., 'From Ramsay's *Flora MacDonald* to Raeburn's *Mac Nab*: the use of tartan as a symbol of identity', *Textile History*, vol. 36, no. 2 (2005), pp. 146–67.

Nixon, S., 'Advertising executives as modern men: masculinity and the UK advertising industry in the 1980s', in M. Nava, A. Blake, I. MacRury and B. Richards (eds), *Buy this Book: Studies in Advertising and Consumption* (Routledge, London, 1997), pp. 103–19.

O'Connell, S. and Reid, C., 'Working-class consumer credit in the UK, 1925–60: the role of the check trader', *Economic History Review*, vol. lviii, no. 2 (2005), pp. 378–405.

Parkins, W., '"The epidemic of purple, white and green": fashion and the suffragette movement', in W. Parkins (ed.), *Fashioning the Body Politic: Dress, Gender, Citizenship* (Berg, Oxford, 2002), pp. 97–124.

Phillips, S. and Alexander, A., 'An efficient pursuit? Independent shopkeeping in 1930s Britain', *Enterprise and Society*, vol. 6, no. 2 (2005), pp. 278–304.

Potter, B., 'The tailoring trade', in C. Booth (ed.), *Life and Labour of the People in London* (Macmillan, London, 1893), vol. iv, pp. 37–68.

Proctor, T.M., 'Scouts, Guides, and the fashioning of empire, 1919–39', in W. Parkins (ed.), *Fashioning the Body Politic: Dress, Gender, Citizenship* (Berg, Oxford, 2002), pp. 125–44.

Purvis, M., 'Co-operative retailing in Britain', in J. Benson and G. Shaw (eds), *The Evolution of Retail Systems, c. 1800–1914* (Leicester University Press, Leicester, 1992), p. 107–34.

Reeves, N., 'Film propaganda and its audience: the example of Britain's official films during the First World War', *Journal of Contemporary History*, vol. 18, no. 3 (1983), pp. 463–94.

'Retail prices of clothing', *The Ministry of Labour Gazette*, vol. 29 (April 1921), pp. 178–9.

Ribeiro, A., 'Utopian dress', in J. Ash and E. Wilson (eds), *Chic Thrills: A Fashion Reader* (Pandora Press, London, 1992), p. 230.

Robert, J.-L., 'The image of the profiteer', in J. Winter and J.-L. Robert (eds), *Capital Cities at War: Paris, London, Berlin 1914–1919* (Cambridge University Press, Cambridge, 1999; first published 1997), pp. 104–32.

Roper, M., 'Between manliness and masculinity: the "war generation" and the psychology of fear in Britain, 1914–1950', *Journal of British Studies*, vol. 44, no. 2 (2005), pp. 343–62.

Roper, M., 'Maternal relations: moral manliness and emotional survival in letters home during the First World War', in S. Dudnik, K. Hagemann and J. Tosh (eds), *Masculinities in Politics and War: Gendering Modern History* (Manchester University Press, Manchester, 2004), pp. 295–315.

Rubin, G.R., 'From packmen, tallymen and "perambulating scotchmen" to Credit Drapers' Associations, c. 1840–1914', *Business History*, vol. 28, no. 2 (1986), pp. 206–25.

Rule, J., 'The property of skill in the period of manufacture', in P. Joyce (ed.), *The Historical Meanings of Work* (Cambridge University Press, Cambridge, 1987), pp. 99–118.

Scott, P., 'The twilight world of interwar British hire purchase', *Past & Present*, no. 177 (2002), pp. 195–225.

Seccombe, W., 'Patriarchy stabilized: the construction of the male breadwinner wage norm in nineteenth-century Britain', *Social History*, vol. 11, no. 1 (1986), pp. 53–76.

Sharpe, P., '"Cheapness and economy": manufacturing and retailing ready-made clothing in London and Essex 1830–50', *Textile History*, vol. 26, no. 2 (1995), pp. 203–13.

Shepard, A., 'Manhood, credit and patriarchy in early modern England, c. 1580–1640', *Past & Present*, no. 167 (2000), pp. 75–106.

Simmel, G., 'Fashion', *International Quarterly*, vol. 10, no. 1 (1904), pp. 130–55.

Sims, G.R., 'Sweated London', in G.R. Sims (ed.), *Living London: Its Work and its Play its Humours and its Pathos its Sights and its Scenes* (Cassell, London, 1902), vol. 1, pp. 53–4.

Springhall, J., 'Building character in the British boy: the attempt to extend Christian manliness to working-class adolescents, 1880 to 1914', in J.A. Mangan and J. Walvin (eds), *Manliness and Morality: Middle-Class Masculinity in Britain and America, 1800–1940* (Manchester University Press, Manchester, 1987), pp. 52–74.

Steele, V., 'Clothing and sexuality', in C. Brush Kidwell and V. Steele (eds), *Men and Women: Dressing the Part* (Smithsonian Institution Press, Washington, 1989), pp. 60–63.

Stevenson, N., Jackson, P. and Brooks, K., 'Ambivalence in men's lifestyle magazines', in P. Jackson, M. Lowe, D. Miller and F. Mort (eds), *Commercial Cultures: Economies, Practices, Spaces* (Berg, Oxford, 2000), pp. 189–212.

Styles, J., 'Clothing the North: The supply of non-elite clothing in the eighteenth-century North of England', *Textile History*, vol. 25, no. 2 (1994), pp. 139–66.

Styles, J., 'Product innovation in early modern London', *Past & Present*, vol. 168 (2000), pp. 124–69.

Taylor, A., '"Funny money", hidden charges and repossession: working-class experiences of consumption and credit in the inter-war years', in J. Benson and L. Ugolini (eds), *Cultures of Selling: Perspectives on Consumption and Society Since 1700* (Ashgate, Aldershot, 2006), pp. 153–82.

Tosh, J., 'Hegemonic masculinity and the history of gender', in S. Dudnik, K. Hagemann and J. Tosh (eds), *Masculinities in Politics and War: Gendering Modern History* (Manchester University Press, Manchester, 2004), pp. 41–58.

Tosh, J., 'Masculinities in an industrialising society: Britain, 1800–1914', *Journal of British Studies*, vol. 44, no. 2 (2005), pp. 330–42.

Tosh, J., 'What should historians do with masculinity? Reflections on nineteenth-century Britain', *History Workshop Journal*, issue 38 (1994), pp. 179–202.

Trentmann, F., 'Bread, milk and democracy: consumption and citizenship in Britain, c. 1903–51', in M. Daunton and M. Hilton (eds), *The Politics of Consumption: Material Culture and Citizenship in Europe and America* (Berg, Oxford, 2001), pp. 129–63.

Tuckwell, G., 'Preface', in R. Mudie Smith (ed.), *Sweated Industries: Being a Handbook of the Daily News Exhibition* (Bradbury, Agnew, London, 1906), p. 10–17.

Turbin, C., 'Collars and consumers: changing images of American manliness and business', in P. Scranton (ed.), *Beauty and Business: Commerce, Gender and Culture in Modern America* (Routledge, New York, 2001), pp. 87–108.

Ugolini, L., 'Clothes and the modern man in 1930s Oxford', *Fashion Theory*, vol. 4, issue 4 (2000), pp. 427–46.

Ugolini, L., 'Men, masculinities, and menswear advertising, c. 1890–1914', in J. Benson and L. Ugolini (eds), *A Nation of Shopkeepers: Five Centuries of British Retailing* (I.B. Tauris, London, 2003), pp. 80–104.

Ugolini, L., 'Ready-to-wear or made-to-measure? Consumer choice in the British menswear trade, 1900–1939', *Textile History*, vol. 34, no. 2 (2003), pp. 192–213.

Veitch, C., 'Play up! Play up! And win the war! Football, the nation and the First World War 1914–15', *Journal of Contemporary History*, vol. 20, no. 3 (1985), pp. 363–78.

Waites, B., 'The government of the Home Front and the "moral economy" of the working class', in P.H. Liddle (ed.) *Home Fires and Foreign Fields: British Social and Military Experience in the First World War* (Brassey's Defence Publishers, London, 1985), pp. 175–93.

Walker, P.J., '"I live but not yet I for Christ liveth in me": men and masculinity in the Salvation Army, 1865–90', in M. Roper and J. Tosh (eds), *Manful Assertions: Masculinities in Britain Since 1800* (Routledge, London, 1991), pp. 92–112.

White, S., '"Wearing 3 or 4 handkerchiefs around his collar and elsewhere about him": slaves' constructions of masculinity and ethnicity in French Colonial New Orleans', *Gender & History*, vol. 15, no. 3 (2003), pp. 528–49.

Winter, J., 'Paris, London, Berlin 1914–1919: capital cities at war', in J. Winter and J.-L. Robert (eds), *Capital Cities at War: Paris, London, Berlin 1914–1919* (Cambridge University Press, Cambridge, 1999; first published 1997), pp. 3–24.

Winter, J., 'Popular culture in wartime Britain', in A. Roshwald and R. Stites (eds), *European Culture in the Great War: The Arts, Entertainment and Propaganda, 1914–1918* (Cambridge University Press, Cambridge, 1999), pp. 330–48.

Woollacott, A., '"Khaki fever" and its control: gender, class, age and sexual morality on the British home front in the First World War', *Journal of Contemporary History*, vol. 29, no. 2 (1994), pp. 325–47.

Worth, R., '"Fashioning" the clothing product: technology and design at Marks and Spencer', *Textile History*, vol. 30, no. 2 (1999), pp. 234–50.

Worth, R., 'Rural working-class dress, 1850–1900: a peculiarly English tradition?', in C. Breward, B. Conekin and C. Cox (eds), *The Englishness of English Dress* (Berg, Oxford, 2002), pp. 97–112.

Zweiniger-Bargielowska, I., 'The culture of the abdomen: obesity and reducing in Britain, *circa* 1900–1939', *Journal of British Studies*, vol. 44, no. 2 (2005), pp. 239–73.

Published memoirs

Acton, H., *Memoirs of an Aesthete* (Hamish Hamilton, London, 1984; first published 1948).

Agate, J., *Ego* (Hamish Hamilton, London, 1935).

Aldin, C., *Time I Was Dead: Pages from my Autobiography* (Eyre and Spottiswoode, London, 1934).

Allingham, P., *Cheapjack* (William Heinemann, London, 1934).

Ambrose, E., *Melford Memories: Recollections of 94 Years* (Long Melford Historical and Archaeological Society, Long Melford, n.d. [c. 1972]).

Anon. [T. Carter], *Memoirs of a Working Man* (Charles Knight, London, 1845).

Anon., *The Private Papers of a Bankrupt Bookseller* (Oliver and Boyd, Edinburgh, 1931).

Anthony, F., *A Man's a Man* (Duckworth, London, 1932).

Armstrong, M., *Victorian Peep-Show* (Michael Joseph, London, 1938).

Ashby, M.K., *Joseph Ashby of Tysoe 1859–1919: A Study of English Village Life* (Cambridge University Press, Cambridge, 1961).

Ashley, J., *Journey into Silence* (The Bodley Head, London, 1973).

Ausden, K., *Up the Crossing* (BBC, London, 1981).

Baily, F.E., *Twenty-Nine Years' Hard Labour* (Hutchinson, London, n.d. [c. 1935]).

Bairnsfather, B., *Wide Canvas: An Autobiography* (John Lang, London, 1939).

Baldry, G., *The Rabbit Skin Cap* (The Boydell Press, Woodbridge, 1984; first published 1939).

Barke, J., *The Green Hills Far Away: A Chapter in Autobiography* (Collins, London, 1940).

Barker, E., *Father of the Man: Memories of Cheshire, Lancashire and Oxford, 1874–1898* (The National Council of Social Service, London, n.d. [c. 1948]).

Barnes, T., *My Dorset Days* (Dorset Publishing, Sherborne, 1980).

Barton, F., *We'll Go No More A-Roving: An Autobiography* (Joiner and Steele, London, 1937).

Bashford, H.H., *Lodgings for Twelve* (Constable, London, 1935).

Beales, H.L. and Lambert, R.S. (eds), *Memoirs of the Unemployed* (EP Publishing, Wakefield, 1973; first published 1934).

Beard, J., *My Shropshire Days on Common Ways* (Cornish Brothers, Birmingham, n.d. [c. 1948]).

Beckett, A., *Adventures of a Quiet Man* (Lambridges, Hove, 1933).

Bell, J.J., *I Remember* (The Porpoise Press, Edinburgh, 1932).

Bennett, A., *The Journals* (Penguin Books, Harmondsworth, 1984; first published in this edition 1971).

Bishop, R.W.S., *My Moorland Patients* (John Murray, London, 1922).

Blacker, H., *Just Like it Was: Memoirs of the Mittel East* (Vallentine, Mitchell, London, 1974).

Blake, J., *Memories of Old Poplar* (Stepney Books Publications, London, 1977).

Blatchford, R., *My 80 Years* (Cassell, London, 1931).

Blishen, E., *Sorry Dad* (Allison and Busby, London, 1984; first published 1978).

Blumenfeld, R.D., *All in a Lifetime* (Ernst Benn, London, 1931).

Bourne, G., *Change in the Village* (Gerald Duckworth, London, 1912).

Brenan, G., *A Life of One's Own: Childhood and Youth* (Hamish Hamilton, London, 1962).

Buckmaster H., *Buck's Book: Ventures, Adventures and Misadventures* (Grayson and Grayson, London, 1933).

Bullen, F.T., *Recollections* (Seeley, Service, London, 1915).

Bullock, J., *Bowers Row: Recollections of a Mining Village* (EP Publishing, Wakefield, 1976).

Burke, T., *Out and About: A Note-Book of London in War-Time* (George Allen and Unwin, London, 1919).

Cannell, B.G.A., *From Monk to Busman: An Autobiography* (Skeffington, London, 1935).

Cardus, N., *Autobiography* (Collins, London, 1947).

Carew, D., *The House is Gone: A Personal Retrospective* (Robert Hale, London, 1949).

Carrington, C., *Soldier from the Wars Returning* (Gregg Revivals and King's College London, Aldershot, 1991; first published 1965).

Carton, R., *The Gentle Adventure: A Victorian Prelude* (J.M. Dent, London, 1933).

Casson, S., *Steady Drummer* (G. Bell and Sons, London, 1935).

Charlton, L.E.O., *Charlton* (Faber and Faber, London, 1931).

Chatfield-Taylor, H.C., *Cities of Many Men: A Wanderer's Memories of London, Paris, New York and Chicago During Half a Century* (Stanley Paul, London, 1925).

Christie, A.V., *Brass Tacks and a Fiddle* (The Author, Kilmarnock, 1944; first published 1943).

Clark, A., *Echoes of the Great War: The Diary of the Reverend Andrew Clark 1914–1919* (Oxford University Press, Oxford, 1988).

Cloete, S., *A Victorian Son: An Autobiography 1897–1922* (Collins, London, 1972).

Clynes, J.R., *Memoirs 1869–1924* (Hutchinson, London, 1937).

Cohen, M., *I Was One of the Unemployed* (Victor Gollancz, London, 1945).

Collins, W.E.W., *Episodes of Rural Life* (William Blackwood and Sons, Edinburgh, 1902).

Connolly, C., *Enemies of Promise* (André Deutsch, London, 1988; first published 1938).

Cook, G.A., *A Hackney Memory Chest* (Centerprise Trust, London, 1983).

Coombes, B.L., *These Poor Hands: The Autobiography of a Miner Working in South Wales* (Victor Gollancz, London, 1939).

Coote, H., *While I Remember* (Spottiswoode, Ballantyne, London, 1937).

Coppard, A.E., *It's Me, O Lord!* (Methuen, London, 1957).

Coppard, G., *With a Machine Gun to Cambrai* (Papermac, London, 1986; first published 1980).

Copper, B., *Early to Rise: A Sussex Boyhood* (Heinemann, London, 1976).

Coward, N., *Autobiography* (Mandarin, London, 1992; first published in this edition 1986).

Crisp, Q., *The Naked Civil Servant* (Jonathan Cape, London, 1968).

Crowther, N., (ed.), *I Can Remember...* (Edward Arnold, London, 1976).

Cummins, J., *The Landlord Cometh* (Queenspark Books, Brighton, n.d. [c. 1982]).

Davies, C.S., *North Country Bred: A Working-Class Family Chronicle* (Routledge and Kegan Paul, London, 1963).

Davies, R., *Print of a Hare's Foot: An Autobiographical Beginning* (Seren, Bridgend, 1998; first published 1969).

Day, S., *London Born* (Fourth Estate, London, 2004).

Dickens, S., *Bending the Twig* (Arthur H. Stockwell, Ilfracombe, 1975).

Donnelly, P., *The Yellow Rock* (Eyre and Spottiswoode, London, 1950).

Douglas, R., *16 to 21* (A.M. Philpot, London, n.d., [c. 1925]).

Edwards, I., *No Gold on My Shovel* (The Porcupine Press, London, 1947).

Evans, G.E., *The Horse in the Furrow* (Faber and Faber, London, 1960).

Evans, G.E., *The Strength of the Hills: An Autobiography* (Faber and Faber, London, 1985; first published 1983).

Farshaw, H., *Stillage Makes his Way* (John Sherratt and Son, Attrincham, 1948).

Fish, W.F., *The Autobiography of a Counter-Jumper* (Lutterworths, London, 1929).

Fletcher, H., *A Life on the Humber: Keeling to Shipbuilding* (Faber and Faber, London, 1975).

Flint, E., *Hot Bread and Chips* (Museum Press, London, 1963).

Foakes, G., *Between High Walls: A London Childhood* (Athena Books, London, 1974).

Garratt, V.W., *A Man in the Street* (J.M. Dent and Sons, London, 1939).

Gibbons, J., *Roll on, Next War! The Common Man's Guide to Army Life* (Frederick Muller, London, 1935).

Gibbs, A., *In My Time* (Peter Davies, London, 1969).

Gibbs, P., *Realities of War* (Hutchinson, London, 1929; first published 1920).

Gillett, J.W., *Once Upon Hard Times: Life in the Village of Higher Cloughford* (Rowtenstall Civic Society, Rowtenstall, 1981).

Golding, L., *The World I Knew* (Hutchinson, London, n.d. [c. 1940]).

Goldman, W., *East End my Cradle* (Faber and Faber, London, 1940).

Goldring, D., *The Nineteen Twenties: A General Survey and Some Personal Memories* (Nicholson and Watson, London, 1945).

Gordon, H., *The Unreturning Army: A Field-Gunner in Flanders, 1917–18* (J.M. Dent and Sons, London, 1967).

Gormley, J., *Battered Cherub* (Hamish Hamilton, London, 1982).

Granger, A., *Life's a Gamble* (New Horizon, Bognor Regis, 1983).

Gray, J., *Gin and Bitters* (Jarrold Publishers, London, n.d. [c. 1938]).

Gray, N., *The Worst of Times: An Oral History of the Great Depression in Britain* (Wildwood House, London, 1985).

Green, A., *Growing Up in Attercliffe: Honey with a Ladle, Vinegar with a Teaspoon* (New City, Sheffield, 1981).

Green, H., *Pack My Bag: A Self-Portrait* (The Hogarth Press, London, 1992; first published 1940).

Greenwood, W., *There Was a Time* (Jonathan Cape, London, 1967).

Gresswell, F., *Bright Boots: An Autobiography* (David and Charles, Newton Abbot, 1982; first published 1956).

Griffith, W., *Up to Mametz* (Severn House, London, 1981; first published 1931).

Hales, H.K., *The Autobiography of 'The Card'* (Sampson Low, Marston, London, n.d [c. 1936]).

Halward, L., *Let Me Tell You* (Michael Joseph, London, 1938).

Hamilton Gibbs, A., *The Grey Wave* (Hutchinson and Gibbs, London, 1920).

Hancock, N., *An Innocent Grows Up* (J.M. Dent and Sons, London, 1947).

Hanson, L., *Shining Morning Face: The Childhood of Lance* (George Allen and Unwin, London, 1948).

Harman, N., *Loose End* (Arthur Barker, London, 1937).

Hartog, A., *Born to Sing* (Dennis Dobson, London, 1978).

Heaton, R., *Salford: My Home Town* (Neil Richardson, Manchester, 1982).

Herbert, G., *Shoemaker's Window: Recollections of a Midland Town Before the Railway Age* (B.H. Blackwell, Oxford, 1948).

Heren, L., *Growing Up Poor in London* (Phoenix, London, 2001; first published 1973).

Hesling, B., *Little and Orphan* (Constable, London, 1954).

Hillyer, R., *Country Boy* (Hodder and Stoughton, London, 1966).

Hilton, J., *Caliban Shrieks* (Cobden-Sanderson, London, 1935).

Hoggart, R., *A Local Habitation: Life and Times 1918–1940* (Chatto and Windus, London, 1988).

Holt, W., *I Haven't Unpacked: An Autobiography* (George G. Harrap, London, 1939).

Home M., *Autumn Fields* (Methuen, London, 1944).

Horrocks, B., *Reminiscences of Bolton* (Neil Richardson, Manchester, 1984).

Houseman, L., *The Unexpected Years* (Jonathan Cape, London, 1937).

Howarth, K., *Dark Days: Memories and Reminiscences of the Lancashire and Cheshire Coalmining Industry up to Nationalisation* (n.k., Manchester, 1978).

Hughes, M.V., *A London Family Between the Wars* (Oxford University Press, Oxford, 1979; first published 1940).

Hughes, M.V., *A London Home in the 1890s* (Oxford University Press, Oxford, 1979; first published 1946).

Jacobs, J., *Out of the Ghetto: My Youth in the East End. Communism and Fascism 1913–1939* (Janet Simon, London, 1978).

James, E., *Unforgettable Countryfolk: Midlands Reminiscences* (Cornish Brothers, Birmingham, n.d. [c. 1948]).

Jasper, A.S., *A Hoxton Childhood* (Barrie and Rockliff: The Cresset Press, London, 1969).

Jekyll, G., *Old West Surrey: Some Notes and Memories* (Longmans, Green, London, 1904).

Jobson A., *An Hour-Glass on the Run* (Michael Joseph, London, 1959).

Johnson, P., *The Vanished Landscape: A 1930s Childhood in the Potteries* (Weidenfeld and Nicolson, London, 2004).

Jones, J., *Unfinished Journey* (Hamish Hamilton, London, 1937).

Jones, T., *Rhymney Memories* (The Welsh Outlook Press, Newtown, 1938).

Keating, J., *My Struggle for Life* (Simpkin, Marshall, Hamilton, Kent, London, 1916).

Kenney, R., *Westering: An Autobiography of Rowland Kenney* (J.M. Dent and Sons, London, 1939).

Kerr, L., *The Eager Years: An Autobiography* (Collins, London, 1940).

Kessler, H., *The Diaries of a Cosmopolitan: 1918–1937* (Phoenix Press, London, 2001; first published in Great Britain 1971).

Kitchen, F., *Brother to the Ox: The Autobiography of a Farm Labourer* (Penguin, Harmondsworth, 1983; first published 1940).

Lakeman, M., *Early Tide: A Mevagissey Childhood* (Dyllanson Truran, Redruth, 1983; first published 1978).

Lamb, G.R., *Roman Road* (Sheed and Ward, London, 1950).

Lansbury, G., *My Life* (Constable, London, 1928).

Latymer, Lord, *Chances and Changes* (William Blackwood and Sons, Edinburgh, 1931).

Lax, W.H., *Lax his Book: The Autobiography of Lax of Poplar* (The Epworth Press, London, 1937).

Lee, R.L., *The Town that Died!* (R.L. Lee, London, 1930).

Levinson, M., *The Trouble with Yesterday* (Peter Davies, London, 1946).

Linton Andrews,W., *Haunting Years: The Commentaries of a War Territorial* (Hutchinson, London, n.d. [c. 1930]).

Llewelyn, M.G., *Sand in the Glass* (John Murray, London, 1943).

Lushington, F., *Portrait of a Young Man* (Faber and Faber, London, n.d. [c. 1940]).

MacDonagh, M., *In London During the Great War: The Diary of a Journalist* (Eyre and Spottiswoode, London, 1935).

Maclean, N., *The Former Days* (Hodder and Stoughton, London, 1945).

Macqueen-Pope, W., *Twenty Shillings in the Pound* (Hutchinson, London, n.d. [c. 1949]).

May, J.L., *The Path Through the Wood* (Geoffrey Bles, London, 1930).

McGeown, P., *Heat the Furnace Seven Times More* (Hutchinson, London, 1967).

McRobbie, A., *A Privileged Boyhood* (Richard Stenleke Publishing, Ochiltree, 1996).

Middleton, C.H., *Village Memories: A Collection of Short Stories and Reminiscences of Village Life* (Cassell, London, 1941).

Miles, H.E., *Untold Tales of War-Time London: A Personal Diary* (Cecil Palmer, London, 1930).

Millot Severn, J., *My Village: Owd Codnor, Derbyshire and the Village Folk When I Was a Boy* (The Author, Brighton, 1935).

Montague, C.E., *Disenchantment* (Chatto and Windus, London, 1922).

Morgan, R., *My Lamp Still Burns* (Gomer Press, Llandysul, 1981).

Mottram, R.H., *Another Window Seat or Life Observed: vol. 2 1919–1953* (Hutchinson, London, 1957).

Muir, E., *The Story and the Fable: An Autobiography* (George G. Harrap, London, 1940).

Neish, Lady, *A Scottish Husband: Making Cheerful Fun of One of Scotland's Best* (Robert Hall, London, 1940).

Nellist, G.W., *The Yorkshire Wolds of Yesteryear* (The Author, Driffield, n.d. [c. 1982]).

Nicholson, N., *Wednesday Early Closing* (Faber and Faber, London, 1975).

Noakes, F.E., *The Distant Drum: A Personal History of a Guardsman in the Great War* (The Author, Tunbridge Wells, n.d. [c. 1953]).

Norfolk Federation of Women's Institutes, *Norfolk Within Living Memory* (Countryside Books and Norfolk Federation of Women's Institutes, Newbury, 1995).

Okey, T., *A Basketful of Memories: An Autobiographical Sketch* (J.M. Dent and Sons, London, 1930).

Oman, C., *Memories of Victorian Oxford and of Some Early Years* (Methuen, London, 1941).

O'Mara, P., *The Autobiography of a Liverpool Slummy* (The Bluecoat Press, Liverpool, n.d., [c. 1934]).

Osborne, J.O., *A Better Class of Person: An Autobiography. Vol. I: 1929–1956* (Faber and Faber, London, 1981).

Palmer, H.E., *The Mistletoe Child: An Autobiography of Childhood* (J.M. Dent and Sons, London, 1935).

Paterson, A., *Across the Bridges or Life by the South London River-Side* (Edward Arnold, London, 1911).

Paton, J., *Proletarian Pilgrimage: An Autobiography* (George Routledge and Sons, London, 1935).

Pearson, A., *The Doings of a Country Solicitor* (The Author, Kendal, 1947).

Peel, C.S., *How We Lived Then 1914–1918: A Sketch of Social and Domestic Life in England During the War* (John Lane, The Bodley Head, London, 1929).

Playne, C.E., *Britain Holds On 1917, 1918* (George Allen and Unwin, London, 1933).

Playne, C.E., *Society at War 1914–1916* (George Allen and Unwin, London, 1931).

Pope, D., *Now I'm Sixteen: An Autobiography* (J.M. Dent and Sons, London, 1937).

Priestley, J.B., *Margin Released: A Writer's Reminiscences and Reflections* (Heinemann, London, 1962).

Redfern, P., *Journey to Understanding* (George Allen and Unwin, London, 1946).

Reilly, C.H., *Scaffolding in the Sky: A Semi-Architectural Autobiography* (George Routledge and Sons, London, 1938).

Renier, G.J., *He Came to England: A Self-portrait* (Peter Davies, London, 1933).

Roberts, R., *The Classic Slum: Salford Life in the First Quarter of the Century* (Penguin, Harmondsworth, 1974; first published 1971).

Rogerson, S., *Twelve Days* (Arthur Barker, London, n.d. [c. 1933]).

Rolph, C.H., *London Particulars* (Oxford University Press, Oxford, 1980).

Romilly, G. and Romilly, E., *Out of Bounds* (Hamish Hamilton, London, 1935).

Rose, W., *Good Neighbours* (Green Books, Bideford, 1988; first published 1942).

Rowse, A.L., *A Cornish Childhood: Autobiography of a Cornishman* (Jonathan Cape, London, 1974; first published 1942).

Samuel, R., *East End Underworld: Chapters in the Life of Arthur Harding* (Routledge and Kegan Paul, London, 1981).

Sassoon, S., *Memoirs of a Fox-Hunting Man* (Faber and Faber, London, 1989; first published 1928).

Sassoon, S., *Siegfried's Journey 1916–1920* (Faber and Faber, London, 1945).

Shaw, S., *Guttersnipe* (Sampson Low, Marston, London, 1946).

Sitwell, O., *The Scarlet Tree* (Macmillan, London, 1946).

Smithers, J., *The Early Life and Vicissitudes of Jack Smithers: An Autobiography* (Martin Secker, London, 1939).

Sparkes, J.H., *The Life and Times of a Grimsby Street Urchin* (Arthur H. Stockwell, Ilfracombe, 1981).

Synnott, E.F., *Five Years' Hell in a Country Parish* (Stanley Paul, London, 1920).

Thale, M. (ed.), *The Autobiography of Francis Place* (Cambridge University Press, Cambridge, 1972).

Thomas, G., *Autobiography 1891–1941* (Chapman and Hall, London, 1946).

Thomas, G., *A Tenement in Soho: Or Two Flights Up* (Jonathan Cape, London, 1931).

Tomlinson, G.A.W., *Coal-Miner* (Hutchinson, London, n.d. [c. 1937]).

Tregenza, L., *Harbour Village: Yesterday in Cornwall* (William Kimber, London, 1977).

Turner, B., *About Myself 1863–1930* (Humphrey Toulmin at the Cayme Press, London, 1930).

Tyndale-Biscoe, J., *Gunner Subaltern: Letters Written by a Young Man to his Father During the Great War* (Leo Cooper, London, 1971).

Vaughan, P., *Something in Linoleum: A Thirties Education* (Sinclair Stevenson, London, 1995; first published 1994).

Waugh, A., *Early Years* (Cassell, London, 1962).

Weir, M., *Shoes Were for Sunday* (Hutchinson, London, 1970).

Wells, H.G., *Experiment in Autobiography: Discoveries and Conclusions of a Very Ordinary Brain (since 1866)* (Faber and Faber, London, 1984; first published 1934).

Whittaker, J., *I, James Whittaker* (Rich and Cowan, London, 1934).

Williamson, H., *The Sun in the Sands* (Faber and Faber, London, n.d. [c. 1945]).

Willis, F., *101 Jubilee Road: A Book of London's Yesterdays* (Phoenix House, London, 1948).

Willis, F., *Peace and Dripping Toast* (Phoenix House, London, 1950).

Windsor, The Duke of, *A Family Album* (Cassell, London, 1960).

Wood, E.E., *Is this Theosophy?* (Rider, London, 1936).

Wollheim, R., *Germs: A Memoir of Childhood* (Black Swan, London, 2005; first published 2004).

Woodruff, W., *Beyond Nab End* (Abacus, London, 2003).

Woodruff, W., *The Road to Nab End: A Lancashire Childhood* (Eland, London, 2000; first published 1993).

Unpublished theses

Alexander, A., 'The Evolution of Multiple Retailing in Britain, 1870–1950: A Geographical Analysis', unpublished PhD, University of Exeter (1994).

Cullen, S.M., 'Gender and the Great War: British Combatants, Masculinity and Perceptions of Women, 1918–1939', unpublished DPhil, University of Oxford (1998).

Songs

Dacre, H. (author and composer), *The Mashah up to Datah!* (Francis, Day and Hunter, London, n.d. [c. 1891]).

Hall, A., Costling, H. and McCarthy, S. (authors and composers), *How Do We Go Now?* (Francis, Day and Hunter, London, n.d. [c. 1900]).

Hastings, W., Bateman, E. (authors) and Perry, A. (composer), *The Coat 'urts Me Underneath the Arm* (Francis, Day and Hunter, London, 1901).

Lauder, H., *Calligan – Call Again!* (Francis, Day and Hunter, London, n.d.).

Long, J.S. (author) and Royle, K. (composer), *She's Changed my Boots for a Set of Jugs* (Francis Brothers and Day, London, n.d. [c. 1888]).

Tarling, P. (author) and Lyle, K. (composer), *My Word, I'll Have Your Socks!* (Francis, Day and Hunter, London, n.d. [c. 1909]).

Weston, R.P., Barnes, F.J. and Bedford, H. (authors and composers), *It's Bound to Come in Fashion By and By* (Francis, Day and Hunter, London, 1910).

Archival and special collections

Bodleian Library Broadside Ballads, University of Oxford. Also available at www.bodley. ox.ac.uk/ballads. The *allegro* catalogue of ballads.

Bodleian Library, University of Oxford, John Johnson Collection of Printed Ephemera. Also available at www.bodley.ox.ac.uk/johnson.

British Library of Political and Economic Science Archives, London School of Economics (BLPES Archives), Papers of Charles Booth.

Imperial War Museum, Department of Art (IWM Art), Parliamentary Recruiting Committee Posters (PRC Posters), and First World War posters.

Imperial War Museum, Sound Archive.

National Social Policy and Social Change Archive, Albert Sloman Library, University of Essex (NSPSC Archive), The Edwardians: Family Life and Work Experience Before 1918, oral history collection (The Edwardians), QD1/FLWE.

Oxfordshire Record Office, Oxford, Diary and Notebooks of Henry Chandler of Grandpont, Oxford, 1872–c.1945, P408/J/I.

Oxfordshire Record Office, Oxford, Records of Castell and Son, Tailors and Robe Makers, Oxford, B22.

West Yorkshire Archive Service, Leeds, C.G. Southcott Co-partnership Ltd papers, Burton Archives; J. Hepworth and Sons Archives, William Blackburn Records,

Official publications

Census reports, 1881–1931.

Newspapers and Magazines

The Banbury Guardian and General Advertiser.
The Bystander.
Comic Cuts.
Financial Mail.
Fun.
The Gentleman's Magazine of Fashion.
Illustrated Chips.
John Bull.
Judy.
The London Tailor.
Man and his Clothes.
The Master Tailor and Cutter's Gazette.
Men's Wear.
News of the World.
The Outfitter.
The Oxford Times.
Progressive Advertising.
Punch.
Reading Mercury.
The Sartorial Gazette.
The Sketch.
The Tailor and Cutter.
The Tatler.
The Times.
Tit-Bits.
The Weekly Record of Fashion.
Woolwich Gazette and Plumstead News.
The Woolwich Herald.

Index